Office for National Statistics

Social Survey Division

Living in Britain

Results from the 1998 General Household Survey

An inter-departmental survey carried out by ONS
between April 1998 and March 1999

Ann Bridgwood

Robert Lilly

Margaret Thomas

Jo Bacon

Wendy Sykes

Stephen Morris

London: The Stationery Office

Cover: Library photographs

The Office for National Statistics works in partnership with others in the Government Statistical Service to provide Parliament, government and the wider community with the statistical information, analysis and advice needed to improve decision-making, stimulate research and inform debate. It also registers key life events. It aims to provide an authoritative and impartial picture of society and a window on the work and performance of government, allowing the impact of government policies and actions to be assessed.

Contents

Acknowledgements

12 Cross-topic analysis

Acknowledgements

We would like to thank everybody who contributed to the Survey and the production of this report. We were supported by our specialist colleagues in ONS who were responsible for sampling, fieldwork, coding and editing. Our thanks also go to colleagues who supported us with administrative duties. Particular thanks are due to the interviewers who worked on the 1998 survey, and to all those members of the public who gave their time and co-operation.

1 Introduction

Development and content of the survey

The General Household Survey (GHS) is a continuous survey which has been running since 1971[1] and is based each year on a sample of the general population resident in private (that is, non-institutional) households in Great Britain. Since the 1988 survey, the fieldwork has been conducted on a financial rather than calendar year basis, so for the 1998 survey interviews were carried out from April 1998 to March 1999. During this period, interviews were obtained with 15,853 people aged 16 and over, either in person or occasionally by proxy, in 8636 households throughout the country[2]. Since the 1994 survey, interviews have been conducted using computer-assisted personal interviewing (CAPI) on laptop computers and the BLAISE software. This has had the effect of reducing costs, the amount of missing data at individual questions, the amount of office-based coding and editing and the output timetables.

Since 1971, the GHS has included questions on population and fertility, family and household information, housing, health, employment and education. In so doing, it provides a unique opportunity to examine the inter-relationship between these important areas of social policy and to monitor changes in their associations over time. The survey is widely used by central government as a source of background information for decisions on resource allocation, and in making household and national population projections. It is also extensively used by a wide range of health professionals, and by researchers and secondary analysts with an interest in social policy and demographic issues.

The GHS provides valuable information about particular social groups, such as lone parents. For smaller groups, it may be necessary to aggregate data over a number of years in order to obtain large enough subsamples for analysis. The survey also helps to fill in some of the gaps in information about social changes between decennial population censuses. As an interview-based sample survey, the GHS can also examine more topics, in much greater depth, than the decennial census at national and regional level.

The GHS was designed as a 'modular' survey and, as a result, subjects other than those listed above are covered periodically and new topics are introduced from time to time. The 1998 survey repeated questions from earlier years on elderly people living in private households (the results of which are to be published in a separate report), smoking, drinking, contraception, hearing and childcare. A new section on tenure after marriage and cohabitation was also included.

The five-yearly review of the GHS

Since the establishment of the survey in 1971, and particularly during the 1990s, several specialist surveys have been established which cover some of the same topics as the GHS. These include the Health Survey for England, first carried out in 1991; the Family Resources Survey, which was established in 1992; and the Survey of English Housing, started in 1993. In addition, from March 1992, the Labour Force Survey began to produce data on a quarterly basis. Its large sample size, with interviews being carried out at 60,000 addresses per quarter, makes it the main source of data on employment and education.

In February 1998, following wide consultation inside and outside government, Socio-Economic Division of ONS issued GSS-wide guidelines for commissioning social surveys. One of the recommendations was that each continuous survey should be subject to a five-year review process which would cover, amongst other things, the future development of the survey. The GHS was the first government survey to be reviewed under this procedure. The review concluded that there was a continuing need for the GHS, but that the survey should be redesigned to ensure that it was being carried out in the most efficient and cost-effective way. These conclusions were endorsed by the Government Statistical Service Committee on Social Statistics, and by the ONS Board. GHS fieldwork was suspended for the 1999-2000 financial year while development work was carried out in preparation for the relaunch of the survey in April 2000.

The structure of the 2000/1 GHS

From April 2000, the survey will consist of two elements: the Continuous Survey and trailers. The Continuous Survey will remained unchanged for the five-year period April 2000-March 2005, apart from essential changes to take account of, for example, changes in benefits. It will consist of a household questionnaire, to be answered by the Household Reference Person or spouse (see below), and an individual questionnaire, to be completed by all adults aged 16 and over resident in the household. The household questionnaire will cover the following topics:

- demographic information about household members
- household accommodation
- housing tenure
- consumer durables
- migration.

The individual questionnaire will include sections on:

- employment
- pensions
- education
- health and use of health services
- smoking
- drinking in the last seven days
- family information
- income.

As in previous years, the GHS will retain its modular structure, which will allow a number of trailers to be included each year; some will appear only once during the five years; others will be included on a regular basis. The trailers which have been agreed for inclusion in 2000/1 are:

- usual alcohol consumption in the last 12 months
- informal carers
- social capital.

Development work for the 2000/1 GHS

A Task Force, consisting of representatives of the Socio-Economic Division, Social Survey Division (SSD), and Demography and Health Division of ONS, and of the Department of Environment, Transport and the Regions and the Department of Health was established to oversee and monitor the development work for the survey. The Task Force reported and made recommendations to the GHS Steering Group, which comprises representatives from all sponsoring Departments. All major decisions regarding the content and conduct of the survey were referred to the Steering Group for discussion and ratification. Wider consultation with data users has been undertaken by such means as public meetings at the Royal Statistical Society.

The rest of this chapter outlines the major development work under the broad headings of sample design, data collection, questionnaire content and data processing. The work has been documented in more detail in the January 2000 edition of SSD's *Survey Methodology Bulletin*[3].

The sample design

As outlined in Appendix B, the GHS uses a multi-stage stratified sample. In the 1998 survey, the Census-based stratifiers were Government Office Region (GOR), the proportion of households renting privately, the proportion of households renting from a local authority and the proportion of households headed by a member of socio-economic groups 1 to 5 or 13 (professionals). As part of

the preparation for 2000, Social Survey Division's Methodology Unit undertook a review of the sample design.

Stratification of a sample can lead to significant improvements in the precision of survey estimates. Precision is optimised if the stratifiers are those which correlate most highly with the survey variables. A set of 15 variables was agreed with GHS customers[4]. Analysis by the Social Survey Methodology Unit showed that precision would be increased for all 15 variables by using the following four stratifiers: Government Office Region with a metropolitan split and London divided into eight areas (four in inner and four in outer London); the proportion of households with no car; the proportion of households with a head of household in socio-economic groups 1-5 and 13; and the proportion of persons who are pensioners.

Alternative methods of data collection

The GHS requires that all adults aged 16 and over resident in sampled households are interviewed face-to-face. Interviewers try to gather all adults in a household together before they start interviewing, although this is not always possible in practice. As a last resort, interviewers can collect proxy information about a missing adult from another household member. The option of self-completion is available for some parts of the interview. Young people aged 16-17 are asked to fill in a paper questionnaire for the smoking and drinking questions, to minimise the possible effects of parental disapproval on reporting. In addition, all respondents aged 16-59, to whom the Family Information section is addressed, are offered a self-completion booklet where interviewers judge that there is a risk that lack of privacy might jeopardise accurate reporting.

During 1998 and 1999 SSD carried out several investigations and field trials to test the feasibility of using alternative methods of data collection. These included:

- exploring the feasibility of interviewing on first contact if the rules on getting household members together were relaxed;
- estimating the potential for reducing the number of interviewer visits by carrying out some interviews on the telephone, after at least one household member had been interviewed face-to-face;
- investigating whether proxy interviews could be converted to full personal interviews by contacting the people concerned by telephone;
- estimating whether any cost savings could be made by carrying out a proportion of interviews on the telephone, and

- exploring the feasibility of using computer-assisted self-completion (CASI) in place of paper questionnaires for sensitive sections of the GHS interview. As mentioned earlier, interviewers use computer-assisted personal interviewing (CAPI) for the GHS.

The results of these investigations and field trials are reported fully in the January 2000 volume of the *Survey Methodology Bulletin*. They showed that there was little scope for doing more interviewing on first contact or reducing the number of interviewer visits without increasing the number of proxy interviews. There was also little scope for cost savings by using alternative methods of data collection. Using CASI increased interview length and proved to be less confidential in some households than paper self-completion forms[5]. In contrast to these results, the telephone test was encouraging; during a two-month field trial, telephone interviewers managed to convert almost 40% of proxy interviews into full personal interviews.

On the basis of SSD's investigation, the Steering Group concluded that the GHS should use the following methods of data collection from April 2000. Interviewers will continue to try to gather all adults together before interviewing. Paper questionnaires will be used for the self-completion sections of the interview. If any household members have still not been contacted or agreed to take part once interviewing has started, interviewers will make as many additional visits as they can within the fieldwork period before taking proxy interviews. They will seek permission from respondents interviewed by proxy to be contacted by SSD's Telephone Interviewing Unit, who will then try to carry out a full interview.

Questionnaire content

Throughout 1998 and 1999, ONS has engaged in an ongoing consultation with GHS customers and data users about the questionnaire content. Several key principles informed this process of consultation:

- to ensure that the data being collected by the survey are those required by customers and thus to remove any redundant questions;
- to achieve an average interview length for the Continuous Survey of one hour per household;
- as far as possible, to maintain continuity with previous years of the GHS to allow time series to be continued; and
- to ensure that questions were harmonised with other major government surveys and with the 2001 Census.

In keeping with the last aim, the GHS will use the new Household Reference Person (HRP) definition instead of the current Head of Household definition from April 2000[6]. The survey will also include a new question on ethnicity which is harmonised with the Census. In common with other government surveys, the GHS will use the new National Statistics Socio-Economic Classification (NS-SEC) from April 2001[7].

Only minor changes have been made to most sections of the GHS questionnaire. For example, the questions on second jobs have been removed as the Labour Force Survey (LFS) is the main source of data on this topic. Questions on Personal Equity Plans (PEPs) were deleted as PEPs are no longer available. New questions have been added asking about access to the Internet and visits to practice nurses in GP surgeries.

More substantial changes have been made to the education questions, and SSD has carried out a programme of cognitive and other testing to develop new questions on cohabitation histories and social capital. It has worked with the Department of Health to streamline the trailer on informal carers.

Education questions

Educational data are used primarily as analysis variables by the GHS; because of its larger sample size, the LFS is the main source of estimates on education. The educational measures needed by GHS customers are: respondents' highest educational qualification, the age at which they finished their full-time education, and whether or not they are currently a full-time student[8]. It is also desirable to be able to derive the International Standard Classification of Educational Definitions (ISCED).

Hitherto, the GHS has asked respondents for details of all their qualifications, and used the resulting information to calculate their highest qualification. A different approach will be used in 2000, aimed at producing the same output, but by asking fewer questions. Respondents will first be asked if they have any qualifications. Those who do will be shown a card with a list of qualifications and asked to name all the qualifications they have. They will then be asked the minimum number of questions needed to establish their highest qualification. Thus, for example, a respondent who says he or she has a degree will be asked whether they have a higher degree and, if they do, whether it is a doctorate, a masters or some other higher degree. For both GHS and ISCED purposes, this respondent needs to be asked no further questions about their qualifications, as they will be coded as 'Degree or equivalent' for the GHS and at Level 5 or Level 6 for ISCED purposes. Interviewers will need to ask slightly more questions of respondents who have a range of vocational qualifications, as these can be at a variety of levels. Thus, for example, a respondent who has both a BTEC and an RSA qualification will need to be asked about both in order to establish which is at the higher level.

Social capital

As part of a much wider programme of work on social capital, the Health Development Agency (HDA, formerly the Health Education Authority) has commissioned SSD in partnership with the University of Surrey (UniS) to develop a module of questions on social capital, that is, the collective resources to which the family, neighbourhood and community has access, for inclusion in the 2000/1 GHS. UniS carried out a programme of cognitive interviewing in August 1999 to explore respondents' understanding of some of the key concepts underlying the dimensions of social capital and to test a set of questions drawn up jointly by the HDA, SSD and UniS. These were piloted in September 1999 and again in the GHS dress rehearsal in November 1999. The module will be included as one of three trailers in the 2000/1 survey.

The module, which takes 10-15 minutes to administer, will be addressed to one randomly selected adult aged 16 and over in each responding household. It includes questions designed to measure several dimensions of social capital, including respondents' views of their neighbourhood, reciprocity and trust, civic engagement, attitudes towards institutions, social networks and social support.

Informal carers

The GHS periodically includes questions addressed to informal carers, most recently in 1995. As noted earlier, this will be one of three trailers included in the 2000 survey. The module has been streamlined and new questions asking about the effect of caring on respondents' health and social life have been added. The 2001 Census will include a question on informal carers for the first time, and the relevant GHS questions have been harmonised with the Census to allow comparisons to be made between the two sets of data.

Data processing

As noted earlier, until 1994, the GHS was carried out using paper questionnaires; in that year, the switch to CAPI was made. The data processing systems are, to some extent, still based on the paper-and-pencil model, with some case-by-case editing carried out in the office. Part of the preparation for the relaunch in 2000 has been to review the data processing systems, with the aim of developing a more streamlined system which will maintain the same level of quality. It is planned to speed up the timetable for the release of data, to have simpler databases, to reduce the number of derived variables from the current 750 or so to a core of 250, and to improve the documentation for data users.

The report

This report on the 1998 survey is the twenty-seventh annual report of results from the GHS. In addition to the latest information available on a wide range of topics, the report provides data on a number of trends and changes measured by the GHS since it began. The main analysis presented in Chapters 2-12 is followed, as usual, by a number of appendices. These include a glossary of definitions and terms used throughout the report and useful notes on how these have changed over time (Appendix A); information about the sample design and response (B); the household and individual questionnaires used in 1998, excluding self-completion forms and prompt cards (C) and a list of the main topics covered by the survey since 1971 (D).

The availability of unpublished data

Unpublished GHS data can be made available to researchers, for a charge, if resources are available, and provided that confidentiality of informants is preserved. Any work based on the GHS data is the responsibility of the individuals concerned, but ONS should be given the opportunity to comment in advance on any report or paper using GHS data, whether prepared for publication or for a lecture, conference or seminar.

In addition, copies of GHS datasets are available for specific research projects, subject to similar conditions, through the Data Archive at the University of Essex[9].

Notes and references

1. A list of published reports from the survey, including details of the report of preliminary findings from the 1998 survey published in December 1999, is given at the end of this report.
2. See Appendix B 'Sample design and response' for full details of the sample design and size since 1971.
3. The January 2000 edition of SSD's Survey Methodology Bulletin includes papers giving an overview of the preparation and development work for the 2000 survey, on sample design, on testing different methods of data collection, on the development of new questions to collect information on cohabitation histories,

and on the development of a trailer to measure social capital.

4. The variables were: the proportion of adults who are heavy drinkers; the proportion of households with an elderly person/people; the proportion of respondents who have consulted a GP in the last 2 weeks; households with a divorced Head Of Household; households with an ethnic minority; households that are owner-occupied; respondents who were an inpatient in the last year; respondents who have a limiting longstanding illness; households that are single person households; employed with a pension scheme; adults who are current smokers; families with dependent children that are headed by a single parent; children that are stepchildren; households below bedroom standard; and adults who cohabit.

5. CASI has been shown to be more confidential than paper questionnaires for sensitive information, and is widely used by SSD for surveys on which only one person in the household is interviewed. On these surveys, it is no more time-consuming. The requirement to interview all adults in households sampled for the GHS means that each respondent has to complete the questionnaire in turn, thus increasing the total interviewing time.

6. Martin J et al. A new definition for the Household Reference Person in *Survey Methodology Bulletin* No 43, July 1998, pp. 1-8.

7. Martin J. A new social classification for Government statistics in *Survey Methodology Bulletin* No 44, January 1999, pp. 37-38.

8. This information is needed to establish whether or not 16-18 year-olds are dependent children, which in turn is used to derive family type variables.

9. For further information, contact:
    Data Archive
    University of Essex
    Wivenhoe Park
    Colchester
    Essex
    CO4 3SQ
    Tel: 01206 872 001
    Fax: 01206 872 003
    e-mail: archive@essex.ac.uk
    website: www.data-archive.ac.uk

Notes to Tables

1. **Harmonised outputs:** where appropriate, tables including marital status, living arrangements, ethnic groups, tenure, economic activity, accommodation type, length of residence and general health have adopted the harmonised output categories described in the publication '*Harmonised Concepts and Questions for Government Social Surveys*' London: ONS (1996). However, where data from the 1998 survey has been combined with data from earlier years to provide sufficient sample size for analysis and where long established time series are shown, harmonised outputs have not generally been used.

2. **Classification variables:** variables such as age and income, are not presented in a standard form throughout the report partly because the groupings of interest depend on the subject matter of the chapter, and partly because many of the trend series were started when the results used in the report had to be extracted from tabulations prepared to meet different departmental requirements.

3. **Non-response and missing information:** the information from a household which co-operates in the survey may be incomplete, either because of a partial refusal (eg to income), or because information was collected by proxy and certain questions omitted because considered inappropriate for proxy interviews (eg marriage and income data), or because a particular item was missed because of lack of understanding or an error.

Household and individuals who did not co-operate at all are omitted from all the analyses; those who omitted whole sections (eg marriages) because they were partial refusals or interviewed by proxy are omitted from the analyses of that section. In 1998 the 'no answers' arising from omission of particular items have been excluded from the base numbers shown in the tables and from the bases used in percentaging. The number of 'no answers' is generally less than 0.5% of the total and at the level of precision used on GHS the percentages for valid answers are not materially affected by the treatment of 'no answers'.

Socio-economic group and income variables are the most common variables which have too many missing answers to ignore.

4. **Base numbers:** Very small bases have been avoided wherever possible because of the relatively high sampling errors that attach to small numbers. Often where the numbers are not large enough to justify the use of all categories, classifications have been condensed; however, an item within a classification is occasionally shown separately, even though the base is small, because to combine it with another large category would detract from the value of the larger category. In general, percentage distributions are shown if the base is 50 or more. Where the base is 20-49, the percentages are shown in square brackets.

For some analysis several years data have been combined to increase the sample size to enable appropriate analysis.

5. **Percentages:** A percentage may be quoted in the text for a single category that is identifiable in the tables only by summing two or more component percentages. In order to avoid rounding errors, the percentage has been recalculated for the single category and therefore may differ by one percentage point from the sum of the percentages derived from the tables.

The row or column percentages may add to 99% or 101% because of rounding.

6. **Conventions:** The following conventions have been used within tables:

.. data not available
- category not applicable
0 less than 0.5% or no observations
[ ] the numbers in square brackets are percentages on a base of 20-49. See note 4.

7. **Statistical significance:** Unless otherwise stated, changes and differences mentioned in the text have been found to be statistically significant at the 95% confidence level.

8. **Mean:** Throughout the report the arithmetic term 'mean' is used rather than 'average'. The mean is a measure of the central tendency for continuous variables, calculated as the sum of all scores in a distribution, divided by the total number of scores.

families headed by never-married mothers has risen markedly from 1% in 1971 to 9% in 1998. The likelihood of families being headed by a divorced or separated mother more than tripled during the same period, from 4% to 13%.

People

Since its inception, the GHS sample has mirrored the ageing of the population, with the proportion of people aged 75 and over almost doubling from 4% in 1971 to 7% in 1991, since when it has remained largely unchanged.

The increase in the proportion of people living alone is particularly marked among the 25-44 age group; whereas 2% of this age group lived alone in 1971, 8% did so in 1993 and 10% in 1998.   **Chapter 3**

Marriage and cohabitation

Information about the marital status of household members has been collected since 1971. Women aged 18-49 were first asked questions on cohabitation in 1979, and from 1986 these questions were asked of all adults aged 16-59. The longest time series for detailed information on marriage and cohabitation is therefore for women aged 18-49 from 1979. Between 1979 and 1998, there was a marked change in the proportion of women aged 18-49 in different legal marital statuses. The proportion who were married declined from 74% to 53%. In contrast, the proportion of never-married women in this age group has almost doubled from 18% in 1979 to 30% in 1998. The percentage of divorced women almost tripled during the same period, from 4% to 11%. There has been an increase in the proportion of non-married women aged 18-49 who were cohabiting at the time of interview, from 11% in 1979 to 29% in 1998.   **Chapter 5**

Housing and consumer durables

Information about household accommodation and tenure has been collected since 1971.

Housing tenure

There has been a marked increased in home ownership. About half of all households were owner occupiers in 1971. This increased to about two thirds in the 1980s, since when the increase has levelled off. There was a corresponding decline in the 1980s in the proportion of households living in social housing, from about a third to about a quarter of all households. The proportion living in council housing continued to decline during the 1990s. In 1998, it was 16%. The likelihood of renting from a housing association has more than doubled since 1989 from 2% of households to 5% in 1998.

Cars and consumer durables

There has been an increase in the proportion of households with access to a car from 52% in 1972 to 67% in 1989 rising to 72% in 1998. The proportion of households with two or more cars has more than trebled, from 9% in 1972 to 28% in 1998.

The GHS has collected information on the household availability of consumer durables since 1972. New items are added from time to time to reflect the emergence of new goods. The goods asked about in the survey fall into two broad groups; household goods and entertainment items.

The availability of some consumer goods, such as televisions, has always been high, and is now almost universal. Others started at relatively high levels in 1972, and quickly became even more widespread; for example, 73% of households had a refrigerator in 1972, a proportion which had risen to 92% by the end of the 1970s. Other household amenities and items were available to only a minority of households when the GHS first asked about them, but are now widespread. For example, whereas 37% of households had central heating and 42% a telephone in 1972, the proportions had risen to 90% and 96% respectively by 1998. The proportion of households with access to more recently introduced items, such as microwave ovens, tumble driers and dishwashers is still growing.

Household access to some entertainment items has been particularly rapid; 18% of households had a video recorder in 1983, a proportion which had risen to 85% in 1998. The household availability of CD players rose from 15% in 1989 to 68% in 1998. The increase in the proportion of households with a home computer has been much slower; 19% of households reported having one in 1989, and 34% in 1998.   **Chapter 4**

Pensions

The GHS has included questions on pensions from time to time since 1971. A change in July 1988 in the rules governing personal pension arrangements means, however, that a strictly comparable time series on occupational pensions can only be presented from 1988.

Trends in membership of occupational schemes have varied since 1988 for male and female, full- and part-time employees. Whereas the proportion of full-time male employees belonging to their employer's scheme has declined from 64% to 57% during this period, among full-time women workers, there has been no clear pattern over time, with the proportions belonging to a scheme ranging from 53% to 56%. Among women working part time, however, the likelihood of participating in their employer's scheme has more than doubled from 12% in 1988 to 27% in 1998. This increase, which was particularly marked after 1994, reflects an increase in the proportion of women joining a scheme provided by their employer, rather than an increase in the proportion of employers providing such a scheme. **Chapter 6**

Health

Since 1972 the GHS has asked respondents whether they have a longstanding illness, disability or infirmity. Those who report such a chronic illness are asked whether it limits their activities in any way. The prevalence of longstanding illness has increased over the lifetime of the GHS. Whereas 21% of respondents reported a chronic condition in 1972, the corresponding proportion in 1998 was 33%. The likelihood of reporting such a condition increased steadily during the 1970s, and has since ranged from 29% to 35%, with no clear pattern over time. The increase in the prevalence of limiting longstanding conditions is less marked; whereas the increase in all chronic conditions was nine percentage points, from 24% to 33%, between 1975 and 1998, the prevalence of limiting conditions increased by only five percentage points, from 15% to 20%, during the same period. It should be noted that reports of chronic sickness are based on respondents' own assessments; increases in prevalence may reflect increased expectations which people have about their health as well as changes in the actual prevalence of sickness.

The proportions reporting an acute sickness in the 14 days before interview increased in the 1970s, from 8% of adults and children in 1972 to 13% in 1979. Prevalence was 12-13% in the 1980s, with some evidence of an increase in the 1990s. In 1998, the prevalence of acute sickness was 15%.

There has also been an increase in the reported use of some health services. The proportion of people seeing a GP in the 14 days prior to interview has risen in each decade since the 1970s, from 12% in 1972 to 16% in 1995. The likelihood of doing so was lower, at 14%, in 1998 than in most other years of the 1990s, which may indicate that the proportion consulting a GP is levelling off. An upward trend, from 10% in 1972 to 16% in 1998, has been ob-served in the proportion of people visiting an outpatient or casualty department at least once in the three months prior to interview. The likelihood of attending a hospital as a day patient in the last year has increased since this question was first asked in 1992 from 4% to 6% among males and from 4% to 7% among females. The proportion reporting an inpatient stay in the 12 months prior to

interview has changed very little since 1982[3], remaining at 9%-10%. **Chapter 7**

Smoking

The GHS first included questions on smoking in 1972, when they were addressed to all adults aged 18 and over. The questions were extended to 16-17 year-olds in 1974, so a time series exists for all adults aged 16 and over from that date. There has been a substantial reduction in the proportion of current cigarette smokers, from 51% of men and 41% of women in 1974 to 28% and 26% respectively in 1998. However, while prevalence declined steadily throughout the 1970s and 1980s, it levelled out during the 1990s.

The reduction in prevalence among men is due more to men not having started smoking than to a rise in the proportion of ex-smokers, whereas the reverse is true among women. Among men, the proportion of respond-ents who had never smoked rose from 25% in 1974 to 41% in 1998, compared with an increase in the proportion of ex-smokers from 23% to 31% during the same period. A different pattern is evident among women. Throughout the period, about half of women have reported that they had never smoked, with the likelihood of never smoking increasing by only four percentage points, from 49% to 53% between 1974 and 1998. The proportion of women who said they had given up smoking increased from 11% to 21% during the same period. **Chapter 8**

Drinking

As outlined in Chapter 9, the Department of Health's current advice on sensible drinking is based on daily benchmarks, and the GHS included questions designed to measure daily alcohol consumption for the first time in 1998. The survey has, however, collected information on usual weekly alcohol consumption since 1972 from respondents aged 18 and over. These questions were extended to 16 and 17 year-olds in 1988. Since 1988, there has been very little change in the proportion of men whose usual alcohol consumption exceeded the sensible drinking level of 21 units a week; it has been at 26-27% throughout the period. The proportion of women whose usual weekly consumption exceeded 14 units has increased from 10% in 1988 to 15% in 1998. **Chapter 9**

Contraception

The GHS first included questions on contraception in 1983 when they were addressed to women aged 18-49, and to women aged 16-17 who were or who had been married.

Since 1986, they have been asked of all women aged 16-49, so a time series exists for that age group covering a period of 12 years. Between 1986 and 1998 the proportion of women aged 16-49 using some form of contraception has ranged from 69% to 73%. Although differences between individual years are statistically significant, changes have been small and no very clear trend emerges from the data. The contraceptive pill, surgical sterilisation of the woman or her partner, and the male condom have remained the three most commonly used methods of contraception. The prevalence of sterilisation, of the woman or her partner, as a method of contraception has changed little since 1986, with levels of usage remaining at or around a quarter of women aged 16-49. Between 1989 and 1993, the percentage of women using the pill increased from 22% to 25%, since when it has remained at roughly the same level. The proportion of women whose partners used the condom increased from 13% in 1986 to 18% in 1995, since when it has remained unchanged. **Chapter 10**

Notes and references

1. *The General Household Survey: Introductory Report.* (1973) (London: HMSO).

2. Each of the subsequent sections of this chapter cites the relevant chapter where more detailed discussion of the topic in question can be found. The data quoted can be found in the tables which follow Chapters 3-10.

3. GHS respondents were first asked about any hospital inpatient stays in the 12 months before interview in 1982. Between 1971 and 1976, respondents were asked about inpatient stays in the last three months.

3 Households, families and people

The GHS collects demographic information about all household members. This chapter describes some of the characteristics of households, families and people.

Household size and composition

Trends over time

- The average (mean) household size in 1998 was 2.36, continuing the downward trend that the GHS has recorded since it began in 1971, when the average household size was 2.91.

Underpinning this trend are a number of factors. First, the number of single person households has been steadily increasing: in 1998, one person households accounted for 29% of all households, compared with 17% in 1971. During the 1970s, this increase was driven by the growing proportion of households with one adult aged 60 or over, which increased from 12% in 1971 to 16% in 1983 and has remained stable ever since. During the 1980s and 1990s, it has been the proportion of households consisting of one adult aged 16-59 that has seen the most significant increase. These households accounted for 13% of the total in 1998, compared with 7% in 1981.

Second, the proportion of households consisting of married or cohabiting couples with dependent children has declined - down from 31% in 1979 to 23% in 1998 - and the proportion of married or cohabiting couples with no dependent children has increased from 27% to 30%.

Third, there has been an increase in the number of households consisting of a lone parent with dependent children. In 1979, 4% of households were of this type. By 1993, this figure had increased to 7% and has since remained stable.   **Tables 3.1-3.3 Figures 3A-3B**

Families with dependent children

Trends over time
Since 1971, the profile of families with dependent children has changed.

- In 1971, 92% of families with dependent children were married or cohabiting couple families, with the remaining 8% headed by a lone parent. In 1998, these figures were 75% and 25% respectively. An overwhelming majority of lone parents are women.

At the same time, the proportion of children living in families headed by a lone-parent has increased from about 8% in 1972 to 23% in 1998.   **Tables 3.4-3.5, Figure 3C**

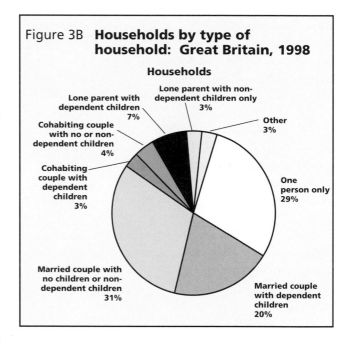

Figure 3B **Households by type of household: Great Britain, 1998**

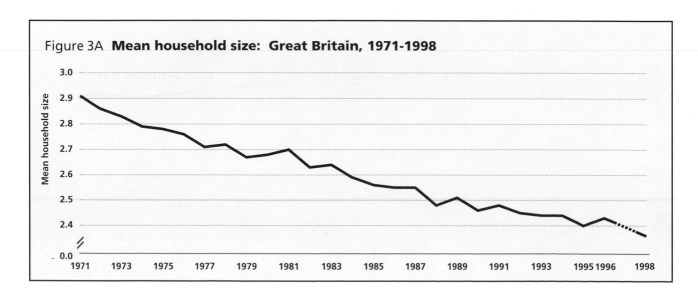

Figure 3A **Mean household size: Great Britain, 1971-1998**

Number of dependent children

- Among families with dependent children, the average number of dependent children per family declined between 1971 (2.0) and 1981 (1.8), and has remained stable since.

Since 1971, the average number of dependent children per lone parent family has been consistently lower than for couple families, and in 1998 the figures were 1.7 and 1.9 respectively.

The numbers of dependent children for married and cohabiting couples have been separately analysed since 1996. In 1996 and 1998, the average number of children per family with dependent children was lower - at 1.7 - in cohabiting couple families than in married couple families, where it was 1.9.   **Table 3.6**

Age of youngest dependent child

In 1998, the proportion of families whose youngest child was aged under five was similar in families headed by a couple or by a lone mother; this was the case in 42% and 40% respectively of these families. Lone fathers were more likely to have older children: while the youngest child was under five in 13% of lone-father families, in 51% of such families, the youngest dependent child was aged between 10 and 15.   **Table 3.7**

Income

There was a disparity in income between different types of families with dependent children. Married couple families had the highest usual gross weekly household income, followed by cohabiting couples with dependent children and then lone-parent families.

- In 1998, 57% of married couple families with dependent children had a gross weekly household income of over £500. This compares with 37% of cohabiting couples with dependent children and 8% of lone-parent families.

While couple families were concentrated in the top band in terms of usual gross weekly household income, lone-mother families were concentrated in the lowest two bands. Among families headed by lone mothers, 27% had a usual gross weekly household income of £100 or less and a further 24% an income of between £100.01 and £150, compared with 5% or fewer of couple families.

Although the numbers of lone fathers were relatively small (60), there was a marked difference between the pattern of their income distribution and that of lone mothers.

- While 28% of families headed by lone fathers had a usual gross weekly income of £100 or less - similar to the figure for lone-mother families - 20% of lone-father families had a usual gross weekly income in excess of £500, compared with 6% of lone-mother families.   **Table 3.8**

Step families

The GHS asks respondents aged 16-59 whether they have any stepchildren living with them. In 1998, among stepfamilies in which there was at least one dependent child from a previous marriage or relationship of one or both of the partners:

- 87% consisted of a couple with at least one child from a previous relationship of the woman;

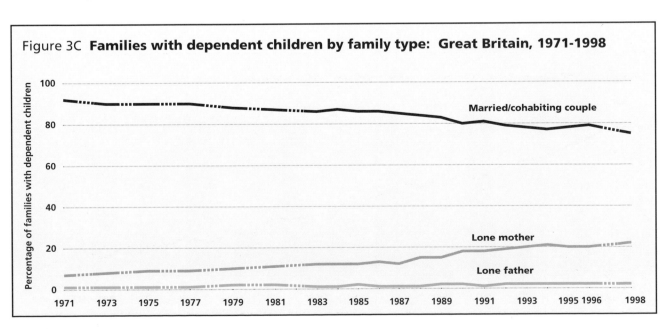

Figure 3C **Families with dependent children by family type: Great Britain, 1971-1998**

- 5% consisted of a couple with at least one child from a previous relationship of the man;
- in 7% of stepfamilies there was a couple and children from both partners' previous relationships.   **Table 3.9**

People

Changes in the age profile of the GHS sample since 1971 have reflected the gradual ageing of the population. Between 1971 and 1998 the proportion of people in the 75 and over age group increased from 4% to 7%. In 1998, 61% of this age group were women.   **Tables 3.10-3.11**

People aged 65 and over

Among people aged 65 and over, the proportion of those aged 75 and over increased from 36% in 1980 to 42% in 1998. Throughout that period, the proportion of women aged 75 and over was greater than the proportion of men, although the gap between the sexes lessened, reflecting increased longevity. In 1998, among those aged 65 and over 46% of women were in the 75 and over age group, compared with 38% of men. In 1980, the proportions of those in the 75 and over age group were approximately two in five women and roughly three in ten men.

Table 3.12

In 1998, the GHS included a module of questions which were asked of people aged 65 and over. The results are to be published in a separate report.

Living alone

The steady increase in one person households between 1971 and 1998 has already been highlighted. This trend is also shown in the growth in the proportion of people living alone, which increased from 9% in 1973 to 14% in 1991 and since then has remained largely unchanged. Sixteen per cent of people lived alone in 1998. The increase has mainly occurred within two age groups:

- people aged 25 to 44, the group showing the largest increase, 2% of whom lived alone in 1973 and 10% in 1998;
- people aged 75 and over, the group of people with the largest proportion who live alone. Forty per cent of this age group lived alone in 1973; this had increased to 50% in 1987 and has remained at about this level since.   **Table 3.13**

Ethnic group

The majority (93%) of respondents described themselves as White in 1998; 96% of this group were born in the UK.

Among the other ethnic groups the distribution of those born in the UK differed by age, reflecting the time-patterns of immigration. Based on aggregated data for 1995, 1996 and 1998:

- of those describing themselves as Indian, 91% of the under-25s and 13% of those aged 25 and over were born in the UK;
- among those describing themselves as Pakistani or Bangladeshi, 80% of the under-25s and 10% of those aged 25 and over were born in the UK;
- and for those describing themselves as Black, the figures were 82% and 32% respectively.

Tables 3.18-3.19, Figure 3D

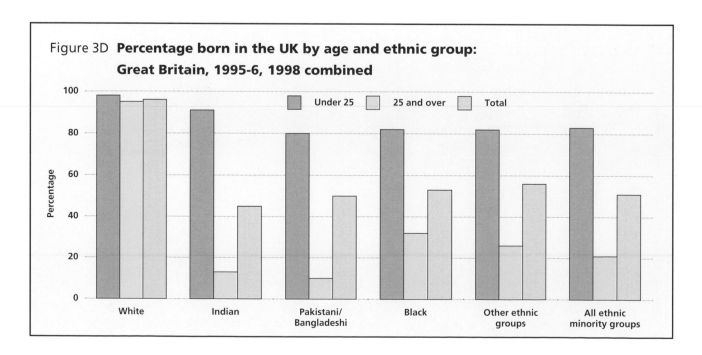

Figure 3D **Percentage born in the UK by age and ethnic group: Great Britain, 1995-6, 1998 combined**

Based on combined data for 1995, 1996 and 1998, the average (mean) household size for Pakistani and Bangladeshi households was the highest, at 4.4 persons. Indian households averaged 3.5 persons, Black 2.6 and White 2.4.

Table 3.20

Among the Pakistani and Bangladeshi population, there was a high proportion (41%) of children aged under 16. This compared with 31% of the Black, 30% of the Indian and 21% of the White populations.

Conversely, the proportion of people aged 65 and over was higher (16%) in the White population than in any of the other groups; 6% of Black, 5% of Indian and 3% of Pakistani/Bangladeshi populations were in this age group.

Table 3.21

Table 3.1 **Household size: 1971 to 1998**

(a) Households and (b) Persons　　　　　　　　　　　　　　　　　　　　　　　　　　　　*Great Britain*

Number of persons in household (all ages)	1971	1975	1981	1983	1985	1989	1991	1993	1995	1996	1998
					Percentage of households of each size						
(a) Households	%	%	%	%	%	%	%	%	%	%	%
1	17	20	22	23	24	25	26	27	28	27	29
2	31	32	31	32	33	34	34	35	35	34	36
3	19	18	17	17	17	17	17	16	16	16	15
4	18	17	18	18	17	16	16	15	15	15	14
5	8	8	7	7	6	6	6	5	5	5	5
6 or more	6	5	4	3	2	2	2	2	2	2	2
Base = 100%	*11988*	*12097*	*12006*	*10068*	*9993*	*10085*	*9955*	*9852*	*9758*	*9158*	*8636*
Average (mean) household size	2.91	2.78	2.70	2.64	2.56	2.51	2.48	2.44	2.40	2.43	2.36
					Percentage of persons in households of each size						
(b) Persons	%	%	%	%	%	%	%	%	%	%	%
1	6	7	8	9	10	10	11	11	12	11	12
2	22	23	23	24	26	27	27	28	29	28	30
3	20	19	19	19	20	21	20	19	20	20	19
4	25	25	27	27	27	26	25	25	24	25	24
5	15	14	14	13	12	11	11	10	10	10	10
6 or more	13	11	9	7	6	5	5	6	5	6	5
Base = 100%	*34849*	*33579*	*32410*	*26587*	*25555*	*25269*	*24657*	*24079*	*23385*	*22274*	*20396*

Table 3.2 **Household type: 1971 to 1998**

(a) Households and (b) Persons　　　　　　　　　　　　　　　　　　　　　　　　　　　　*Great Britain*

Household type	1971	1975	1981	1983	1985	1989	1991	1993	1995	1996	1998
					Percentage of households of each type						
(a) Households	%	%	%	%	%	%	%	%	%	%	%
1 adult aged 16-59	5	6	7	7	8	9	10	10	12	11	13
2 adults aged 16-59	14	14	13	13	15	16	16	16	17	15	16
Youngest person aged 0-4	18	15	13	14	13	13	14	14	13	13	13
Youngest person aged 5-15	21	22	22	19	18	17	16	16	16	17	16
3 or more adults	13	11	13	13	12	13	12	11	10	11	9
2 adults, 1 or both aged 60 or over	17	17	17	18	17	16	16	17	16	16	17
1 adult aged 60 or over	12	15	15	16	16	16	16	17	15	16	16
Base = 100%	*11934*	*12090*	*12006*	*10068*	*9993*	*10085*	*9955*	*9852*	*9758*	*9158*	*8636*
					Percentage of persons in each type of household						
(b) Persons	%	%	%	%	%	%	%	%	%	%	%
1 adult aged 16-59	2	2	3	3	3	4	4	4	5	5	5
2 adults aged 16-59	10	10	10	10	12	13	13	13	14	13	14
Youngest person aged 0-4	27	23	21	21	21	21	22	22	20	21	21
Youngest person aged 5-15	31	34	33	30	28	26	25	25	26	27	25
3 or more adults	15	13	16	17	17	17	16	15	15	15	13
2 adults, 1 or both aged 60 or over	11	12	12	13	13	13	13	14	14	13	14
1 adult aged 60 or over	4	5	6	6	6	7	7	7	6	7	7
Base = 100%	*34720*	*33561*	*32410*	*26587*	*25555*	*25269*	*24657*	*24079*	*23385*	*22274*	*20396*

Table 3.3 **Type of household: 1979 to 1998**

(a) Households and (b) Persons   *Great Britain*

Household type	1979	1983	1985	1989	1991	1993	1995	1996	1998
				Percentage of households of each type					
(a) Households	%	%	%	%	%	%	%	%	%
1 person only	23	23	24	25	26	27	28	27	29
2 or more unrelated adults	3	3	4	3	3	3	2	3	2
Married/cohabiting couple									
with dependent children	31	30	28	26	25	24	24	25	23
with non-dependent children only	7	8	8	9	8	7	6	6	6
no children	27	27	27	27	28	28	29	28	30
Married couple									
with dependent children	..	..	..	..	..	..	..	23	20
with non-dependent children	..	..	..	..	..	..	..	6	5
no children	..	..	..	..	..	..	..	25	26
Cohabiting couple									
with dependent children	..	..	..	..	..	..	..	3	3
with non-dependent children	..	..	..	..	..	..	..	0	0
no children	..	..	..	..	..	..	..	4	4
Lone parent									
with dependent children	4	5	4	5	6	7	7	7	7
with non-dependent children only	4	4	4	4	4	3	3	3	3
Two or more families	1	1	1	1	1	1	1	1	1
Base = 100%	*11454*	*10031*	*9993*	*10085*	*9955*	*9852*	*9738*	*9138*	*8617*
				Percentage of persons in each type of household					
(b) Persons	%	%	%	%	%	%	%	%	%
1 person only	9	9	10	10	11	11	12	11	12
2 or more unrelated adults	2	3	3	3	2	3	2	3	2
Married/cohabiting couple									
with dependent children	49	47	45	42	41	41	40	42	39
with non-dependent children only	9	11	11	12	11	9	9	9	8
no children	20	21	21	22	23	23	25	24	26
Married couple									
with dependent children	..	..	..	..	..	..	..	37	34
with non-dependent children	..	..	..	..	..	..	..	9	8
no children	..	..	..	..	..	..	..	21	22
Cohabiting couple									
with dependent children	..	..	..	..	..	..	..	4	5
with non-dependent children	..	..	..	..	..	..	..	0	0
no children	..	..	..	..	..	..	..	3	4
Lone parent									
with dependent children	5	5	5	6	7	8	8	8	9
with non-dependent children only	3	3	4	3	3	3	3	3	3
Two or more families	2	2	1	2	2	2	1	1	2
Base = 100%	*30546*	*26425*	*25454*	*25269*	*24657*	*24079*	*23325*	*22190*	*20350*

See Appendix A for the definition of a household.

Table 3.4 **Family type, and marital status of lone mothers: 1971 to 1998**

*Families with dependent children**   *Great Britain*

Family type	1971	1975	1981	1983	1985	1989	1991	1993	1995	1996	1998
	%	%	%	%	%	%	%	%	%	%	%
Married/cohabiting couple†	92	90	87	86	86	83	81	78	78	79	75
Lone mother	7	9	11	12	12	15	18	20	20	20	22
single	1	1	2	3	3	5	6	8	8	7	9
widowed	2	2	2	2	1	1	1	1	1	1	1
divorced	2	3	4	5	5	6	6	7	7	6	8
separated	2	2	2	2	3	3	4	4	5	5	5
Lone father	1	1	2	1	2	2	1	2	2	2	2
All lone parents	8	10	13	14	14	17	19	22	22	21	25
Base = 100%	*4864*	*4776*	*4445*	*3538*	*3348*	*3223*	*3143*	*3145*	*3022*	*2975*	*2659*

* Dependent children are persons under 16, or aged 16-18 and in full-time education, in the family unit, and living in the household.
† Including married women whose husbands were not defined as resident in the household.

Table 3.5 **Family type and number of dependent children: 1972 to 1998**

*Dependent children**   *Great Britain*

	Percentage of all dependent children in each family type										
	1972	1975	1981	1983	1985	1989	1991	1993	1995	1996	1998
	%	%	%	%	%	%	%	%	%	%	%
Married/cohabiting couple with											
1 dependent child	16	17	18	18	19	18	17	15	16	17	15
2 or more dependent children	76	74	70	69	69	67	66	65	64	63	62
Lone mother with											
1 dependent child	2	3	3	3	4	4	5	6	5	5	6
2 or more dependent children	5	6	7	8	7	9	12	12	14	13	15
Lone father with											
1 dependent child	0	0	1	0	1	1	0	1	1	0	1
2 or more dependent children	1	1	1	1	1	1	1	1	1	1	1
Base = 100%	*9474*	*9293*	*8216*	*6522*	*5966*	*5827*	*5799*	*5794*	*5559*	*5431*	*4897*

* Dependent children are persons under 16, or aged 16-18 and in full-time education, in the family unit, and living in the household.

Table 3.6 Average (mean) number of dependent children by family type: 1971 to 1998

Families with dependent children*   *Great Britain*

Family type	Average (mean) number of children										
	1971	1975	1981	1983	1985	1989	1991	1993	1995	1996	1998
Married/cohabiting couple†	2.0	2.0	1.9	1.9	1.8	1.8	1.9	1.9	1.9	1.9	1.9
Married couple	..	..	..	..	..	..	..	..	..	1.9	1.9
Cohabiting couple	..	..	..	..	..	..	..	..	..	1.7	1.7
Lone parent	1.8	1.7	1.6	1.7	1.6	1.6	1.7	1.7	1.7	1.7	1.7
Total: all families with dependent children	2.0	1.9	1.8	1.8	1.8	1.8	1.8	1.8	1.8	1.8	1.8
Bases											
Married/cohabiting couple	*4482*	*4299*	*3887*	*3047*	*2890*	*2680*	*2541*	*2453*	*2358*	*2329*	*2004*
Married couple	*..*	*..*	*..*	*..*	*..*	*..*	*..*	*..*	*..*	*2086*	*1753*
Cohabiting couple	*..*	*..*	*..*	*..*	*..*	*..*	*..*	*..*	*..*	*243*	*251*
Lone parent	*382*	*477*	*558*	*491*	*458*	*543*	*595*	*682*	*658*	*635*	*652*
Total	*4864*	*4776*	*4445*	*3538*	*3348*	*3223*	*3136*	*3135*	*3016*	*2964*	*2656*

* Dependent children are persons aged under 16, or aged 16-18 and in full-time education, in the family unit, and living in the household.
† Including married women whose husbands were not defined as resident in the household.

Table 3.7 Age of youngest dependent child by family type

Families with dependent children*   *Great Britain: 1996 and 1998 combined*

Family type		Age of youngest dependent child					
		0-4	5-9	10-15	16 and over	Base = 100%	Total
							%
Married/cohabiting couple†	%	42	26	26	7	4094	76
Lone mother	%	40	29	25	6	1170	22
Lone father	%	13	25	51	10	119	2
All lone parents	%	37	29	28	6	1289	24
Total	%	41	26	27	7	5383	100

* Dependent children are persons aged under 16, or aged 16-18 and in full-time education, in the family unit, and living in the household.
† Including married women whose husbands were not defined as resident in the household.

Table 3.8 Usual gross weekly household income by family type

Families with dependent children*   *Great Britain: 1998*

Family type		Usual gross weekly household income										
		£0.01-£100.00	£100.01-£150.00	£150.01-£200.00	£200.01-£250.00	£250.01-£300.00	£300.01-£350.00	£350.01-£400.00	£400.01-£450.00	£450.01-£500.00	£500.01 and over	Base = 100%†
Married couple	%	2	2	3	3	4	6	6	8	8	57	1571
Cohabiting couple	%	4	5	6	5	9	7	8	9	9	37	224
Lone mother	%	27	24	13	8	7	6	4	2	3	6	542
Single	%	41	23	11	6	3	3	5	1	2	4	205
Widowed	%	[9]	[9]	[18]	[0]	[14]	[9]	[5]	[0]	[5]	[32]	22
Divorced	%	17	28	14	10	8	7	4	4	4	5	195
Separated	%	21	23	13	11	11	7	5	1	2	7	120
Lone father	%	28	15	8	13	0	2	3	7	3	20	60
All lone parents	%	27	23	12	9	6	5	4	2	3	8	602

* Dependent children are persons aged under 16, or aged 16-18 and in full-time education, in the family unit, and living in the household.
† Bases exclude cases where income is not known.

Table 3.9 **Stepfamilies by family type**

Stepfamilies with dependent children*
(Family head aged 16-59)   *Great Britain: 1998*

Type of stepfamily	
	%
Couple with child(ren) from the woman's previous marriage/ cohabitation	87
Couple with child(ren) from the man's previous marriage/ cohabitation	5
Couple with child(ren) from both partners' previous marriage/ cohabitation	7
Base = 100%†	*165*

* Dependent children are persons under 16, or aged 16-18 and in full-time
  education, in the family unit, and living in the household.

† Base includes a small number of lone parents with stepchildren.

Table 3.10 **Age by sex: 1971 to 1998**

All persons   *Great Britain*

Age	1971	1975	1981	1983	1985	1989	1991	1993	1995	1996	1998
	%	%	%	%	%	%	%	%	%	%	%
Males											
0- 4	9	8	7	7	7	7	8	8	7	7	8
5-15*	19	18	18	18	16	15	15	16	16	16	16
16-44*	39	40	41	41	42	42	41	40	39	39	38
45-64	24	23	22	22	22	23	22	23	24	23	24
65-74	7	8	8	8	9	8	8	9	9	8	9
75 and over	3	3	4	4	4	5	5	5	5	6	5
Base = 100%	*16908*	*16242*	*15735*	*12860*	*12551*	*12157*	*11913*	*11514*	*11376*	*10781*	*9831*
	%	%	%	%	%	%	%	%	%	%	%
Females											
0- 4	8	6	6	7	6	7	7	7	6	7	7
5-15*	16	17	16	15	15	14	14	14	14	15	14
16-44*	37	38	39	39	41	41	39	38	39	39	38
45-64	24	24	22	22	21	21	22	22	24	23	24
65-74	9	10	10	10	10	9	10	10	9	9	9
75 and over	5	6	7	7	8	8	8	8	8	7	8
Base = 100%	*17871*	*17328*	*16675*	*13727*	*13522*	*13112*	*12744*	*12565*	*12009*	*11493*	*10564*
	%	%	%	%	%	%	%	%	%	%	%
Total											
0- 4	8	7	6	7	6	7	7	7	7	7	7
5-15*	17	17	17	16	15	15	15	15	15	15	15
16-44*	38	39	40	40	42	41	40	39	39	39	38
45-64	24	23	22	22	21	22	22	22	24	23	24
65-74	8	9	9	9	9	9	9	10	9	9	9
75 and over	4	4	5	6	6	6	7	7	6	7	7
Base = 100%	*34779*	*33570*	*32410*	*26587*	*26073*	*25269*	*24657*	*24079*	*23385*	*22274*	*20395*

* 5-14 and 15-44 in 1971 and 1975.

Table 3.11 Sex by age

All persons   *Great Britain: 1998*

Age		Males	Females	Base = 100%
0- 4	%	51	49	1446
5-15	%	51	49	3075
16-19	%	51	49	928
20-24	%	48	52	957
25-29	%	46	54	1411
30-34	%	48	52	1542
35-39	%	47	53	1584
40-44	%	50	50	1324
45-49	%	50	50	1365
50-54	%	48	52	1398
55-59	%	48	52	1091
60-64	%	50	50	1038
65-69	%	48	52	984
70-74	%	46	54	878
75 and over	%	39	61	1374
Total	%	48	52	20395

Table 3.12 Age of the population aged 65 and over: 1980-1998

Persons aged 65 and over   *Great Britain*

Age	1980	1985	1991	1994	1996	1998
	%	%	%	%	%	%
Men						
65-69	41	36	35	33	32	33
70-74	30	30	26	32	27	28
75-79	17	22	21	16	23	21
80-84	9	9	12	12	12	10
85 and over	3	4	6	6	6	7
Women						
65-69	34	27	31	27	28	28
70-74	27	28	24	30	27	26
75-79	21	23	22	18	21	24
80-84	11	12	14	14	14	12
85 and over	8	9	9	11	9	10
All elderly people						
65-69	37	31	33	30	30	30
70-74	28	29	25	31	27	27
75-79	20	22	22	18	22	23
80-84	10	11	13	13	13	11
85 and over	6	7	8	9	8	8
Base = 100%						
Men	1842	1498	1580	1458	1447	1412
Women	2674	2193	2205	2043	1840	1824
All elderly people	4516	3691	3785	3501	3287	3236

Table 3.13 Percentage living alone, by age: 1973 to 1998

All persons aged 16 and over   *Great Britain*

	Percentage who lived alone									
	1973	1983	1985	1987	1989	1991	1993	1995	1996	1998
16-24	2	2	4	3	4	3	4	5	4	4
25-44	2	4	5	6	6	7	8	9	8	10
45-64	8	9	11	10	11	11	11	12	11	14
65-74	26	28	29	28	27	29	28	27	31	27
75 and over	40	47	47	50	48	50	50	51	47	48
All aged 16 and over	9	11	12	12	13	14	14	15	14	16
Bases = 100%										
16-24	3811	3498	3367	3558	3137	2819	2574	2318	2233	1885
25-44	8169	7017	7234	7418	7324	7118	6875	6761	6489	5861
45-64	7949	5947	5644	5802	5557	5493	5360	5615	5114	4892
65-74	2847	2494	2210	2389	2231	2196	2303	2129	1943	1862
75 and over	1432	1490	1498	1596	1619	1603	1581	1451	1485	1374
All aged 16 and over	24208	20446	19953	20763	19868	19229	18693	18274	17264	15874

Table 3.14 **Percentage living alone, by age and sex**

All persons aged 16 and over   *Great Britain: 1998*

	Percentage who lived alone		
	Men	Women	Total
16-24	5	3	4
25-44	13	6	10
45-64	13	15	14
65-74	19	34	27
75 and over	29	59	48
All aged 16 and over	14	17	16
All persons*	11	14	12
Bases = 100%			
16-24	*938*	*947*	*1885*
25-44	*2788*	*3073*	*5861*
45-64	*2393*	*2499*	*4892*
65-74	*873*	*989*	*1862*
75 and over	*539*	*835*	*1374*
All aged 16 and over	*7531*	*8343*	*15874*
*All persons**	*9831*	*10564*	*20395*

* Including children.

Table 3.15 **Socio-economic group based on own current or last job by sex: 1975 to 1998**

All persons aged 16 and over   *Great Britain*

Socio-economic group*	1975	1979	1981	1983	1985	1989	1991	1993	1995	1996	1998
	%	%	%	%	%	%	%	%	%	%	%
Men											
Professional	5	6	4	5	6	7	7	7	7	6	9
Employers and managers	15	15	15	17	19	20	19	20	21	22	21
Intermediate and junior non-manual	17	17	17	15	17	16	17	17	17	17	19
Skilled manual and own account non-professional	41	40	41	39	37	38	38	37	35	35	32
Semi-skilled manual and personal service	17	17	18	18	16	15	14	14	15	15	14
Unskilled manual	5	5	5	5	5	5	5	4	4	5	5
Base = 100%	*10902*	*10280*	*10880*	*8886*	*8787*	*8815*	*8596*	*8089*	*8004*	*7573*	*6983*
	%	%	%	%	%	%	%	%	%	%	%
Women											
Professional	1	1	1	1	1	1	1	2	2	2	2
Employers and managers	4	5	5	6	7	9	9	10	10	9	11
Intermediate and junior non-manual	46	45	46	46	48	47	48	49	49	50	50
Skilled manual and own account non-professional	9	9	9	9	9	9	9	8	8	9	8
Semi-skilled manual and personal service	31	30	29	30	27	25	22	22	22	23	22
Unskilled manual	9	10	10	9	7	8	11	10	8	8	8
Base = 100%	*11799*	*11102*	*11743*	*9754*	*9439*	*9600*	*9254*	*9009*	*8720*	*8137*	*7543*
	%	%	%	%	%	%	%	%	%	%	%
Total											
Professional	3	3	2	3	3	4	4	4	4	4	5
Employers and managers	9	10	9	11	13	14	14	15	15	15	16
Intermediate and junior non-manual	32	32	32	31	33	32	33	34	34	34	35
Skilled manual and own account non-professional	24	24	24	24	23	23	23	22	21	21	19
Semi-skilled manual and personal service	24	24	24	24	22	20	18	18	19	19	18
Unskilled manual	7	8	8	7	6	7	8	7	6	6	6
Base = 100%	*22701*	*21382*	*22623*	*18640*	*18226*	*18415*	*17850*	*17098*	*16724*	*15710*	*14526*

* The socio-economic group shown is based on the informant's own job (or last job if not in employment). Excluding those in the Armed Forces and any who have never worked.

Table 3.16 **Socio-economic group by sex: 1971 to 1998**

All persons   *Great Britain*

Socio-economic group*	1971†	1975	1979	1983	1985	1989	1991	1993	1995	1996	1998
	%	%	%	%	%	%	%	%	%	%	%
Males											
Professional	5	5	6	5	6	7	8	7	7	6	9
Employers and managers	15	15	15	17	19	20	19	20	21	21	23
Intermediate and junior non-manual	18	17	17	16	17	17	18	19	19	19	19
Skilled manual and own account non-professional	40	41	40	39	37	36	36	35	33	33	31
Semi-skilled manual and personal service	17	18	17	18	16	15	14	15	15	16	14
Unskilled manual	5	4	5	6	5	5	5	5	5	5	4
Base = 100%	*14320*	*15664*	*14068*	*12081*	*11728*	*11689*	*11535*	*11076*	*10877*	*10296*	*9448*
	%	%	%	%	%	%	%	%	%	%	%
Females											
Professional	4	4	5	4	5	6	6	6	6	5	8
Employers and managers	14	13	14	15	17	19	18	18	20	20	20
Intermediate and junior non-manual	24	23	23	23	25	24	25	27	26	25	25
Skilled manual and own account non-professional	33	34	32	31	29	28	28	27	26	27	26
Semi-skilled manual and personal service	20	21	20	21	19	18	17	16	17	17	16
Unskilled manual	6	5	6	6	5	5	6	6	5	5	6
Base = 100%	*14932*	*16452*	*15075*	*12841*	*12221*	*12572*	*12279*	*12049*	*11510*	*10961*	*10037*

* Socio-economic group corresponds to the present job of those currently working and to the last job of those not currently working. Married women whose husbands were in the household are classified according to their husband's occupation; children under 16 are classified according to their father's occupation. No answers, members of the Armed Forces, full-time students and those who have never worked are excluded.
† England and Wales in 1971.

Table 3.17 (a) Socio-economic group by sex and age
(b) Age and sex by socio-economic group

All persons   *Great Britain: 1998*

| | Socio-economic group* | | | | | | |
	Professional	Employers and managers	Intermediate and junior non-manual	Skilled manual and own account non-professional	Semi-skilled manual and personal service	Unskilled manual	Total
(a)	%	%	%	%	%	%	%
Males							
0 - 4	7	8	8	6	9	6	7
5 - 15	15	16	17	14	17	17	16
16 - 44	38	35	40	37	37	36	37
45 - 64	29	27	21	27	21	26	25
65 - 74	7	8	9	11	9	10	9
75 and over	3	6	5	6	7	6	6
Base = 100%	*851*	*2152*	*1787*	*2912*	*1327*	*419*	*9448*
	%	%	%	%	%	%	%
Females							
0 - 4	6	6	6	7	8	5	6
5 - 15	19	15	12	15	15	15	14
16 - 44	41	39	38	38	35	27	37
45 - 64	27	27	22	26	21	24	24
65 - 74	5	8	10	9	11	13	10
75 and over	2	5	11	5	10	17	8
Base = 100%	*768*	*2015*	*2501*	*2580*	*1616*	*557*	*10037*
(b)							*Base = 100%*
Males							
0 - 4	%	9	25	21	24	17	4	*698*
5 - 15	%	9	23	21	27	15	5	*1471*
16 - 44	%	9	21	20	31	14	4	*3509*
45 - 64	%	11	24	16	33	12	5	*2366*
65 - 74	%	7	21	18	35	15	5	*868*
75 and over	%	5	24	17	32	17	5	*536*
Total	%	9	23	19	31	14	4	*9448*
Females							
0 - 4	%	7	18	24	27	19	5	*641*
5 - 15	%	10	20	21	26	16	6	*1443*
16 - 44	%	8	21	26	26	15	4	*3758*
45 - 64	%	8	22	23	27	14	5	*2456*
65 - 74	%	4	17	27	26	19	8	*958*
75 and over	%	2	13	34	17	22	12	*781*
Total	%	8	20	25	26	16	6	*10037*

* See the first footnote to Table 3.16.

Table 3.18 **Ethnic group: 1983 to 1998**

All persons   *Great Britain*

Ethnic group	1983	1987	1989	1991	1993	1995	1996	1998
	%	%	%	%	%	%	%	%
White	95	95	95	94	92	94	94	93
Indian	2	1	1	2	2	2	2	2
Pakistani/Bangladeshi	1	1	1	1	1	1	1	2
Black Caribbean*	1	1	1	1	1	1	1	1
Remaining groups	1	2	2	2	2	2	2	3
No answers	1	1	0	0	1	0	0	0
Base = 100%	*26587*	*26418*	*25269*	*24657*	*24079*	*23385*	*22274*	*20396*

* West Indian/Guyanese in 1983, 1987 and 1989.

Table 3.19 **Percentage born in the UK by age and ethnic group**

All persons   *Great Britain: 1995-6, 1998 combined*

Ethnic group	Percentage born in the United Kingdom			Base = 100%		
	Age			Age		
	Under 25	25 and over	Total	Under 25	25 and over	Total
White	98	95	96	*19045*	*42770*	*61815*
Indian	91	13	45	*420*	*616*	*1036*
Pakistani/Bangladeshi	80	10	50	*508*	*375*	*883*
Black	82	32	53	*448*	*638*	*1086*
Remaining groups	82	26	56	*628*	*540*	*1168*
All ethnic minority groups	83	21	51	*2004*	*2169*	*4173*
Total	96	92	93	*21049*	*44939*	*65988*

Table 3.20 **Average household size by ethnic group of head of household**

Households   *Great Britain: 1995-6, 1998 combined*

Ethnic group	Average (mean) household size	Base = numbers of households
White	2.4	*26230*
Indian	3.5	*319*
Pakistani/Bangladeshi	4.4	*211*
Black	2.6	*448*
Remaining groups	2.7	*330*
All ethnic minority groups	3.1	*1308*
Total	2.4	*27538*

Table 3.21 **Age by ethnic group**

All persons   *Great Britain: 1995-6, 1998 combined*

Age	Ethnic group						All
	White	Indian	Pakistani/ Bangladeshi	Black	Remaining groups	All ethnic minority groups	
	%	%	%	%	%	%	%
0- 15	21	30	41	31	42	36	22
16 - 24	10	11	16	11	12	12	10
25 - 44	29	36	28	36	31	33	29
45 - 64	24	18	11	16	12	15	24
65 and over	16	5	3	6	3	4	16
Base = 100%	*61831*	*1040*	*885*	*1086*	*1168*	*4179*	*66010*

Table 3.22 **Sex by ethnic group**

All persons   *Great Britain: 1995-6, 1998 combined*

Ethnic group		Male	Female	*Base = 100%*
White	%	48	52	*61831*
Indian	%	49	51	*1040*
Pakistani/Bangladeshi	%	50	50	*886*
Black	%	48	52	*1086*
Remaining groups	%	49	51	*1168*
All ethnic minority groups	%	49	51	*4180*
Total	%	48	52	*66011*

Table 3.23 **Government Office Region by ethnic group**

All persons   *Great Britain: 1995-6, 1998 combined*

Government Office Region	Ethnic group						Total
	White	Indian	Pakistani/ Bangladeshi	Black	Remaining groups	All ethnic minority groups	
	%	%	%	%	%	%	%
England							
North East	6	0	1	1	2	1	5
North West and Merseyside	12	6	15	4	11	9	12
Yorkshire and the Humber	9	8	14	4	3	7	9
East Midlands	7	14	4	5	4	7	7
West Midlands	9	24	23	11	8	16	9
Eastern	10	4	3	4	7	5	9
London	8	32	29	63	45	43	11
South East	14	7	7	4	10	7	14
South West	9	2	1	2	4	3	9
Wales	6	1	1	1	3	1	5
Scotland	10	2	2	1	4	2	9
Base = 100%	*61831*	*1040*	*886*	*1086*	*1168*	*4180*	*66011*

4 Housing and consumer durables

The General Household Survey has included questions since 1971 on housing and the availability of consumer durables. This chapter looks at trends up to 1998. The effect of the breakdown of marriage and cohabitation on housing tenure is also examined.

Tenure

Trends over time

In 1998, 69% of households owned their own home compared with 54% in 1981. Most of the increase in owner occupation occurred during the 1980s. By 1989, two-thirds of households were owner occupiers and the proportion remained at about that level until 1996. In 1998, there was an increase in the percentage of outright owners, bringing the total for all owners to 69%.

Over the same period (1981-1998):

- the proportion renting council housing declined from 34% in 1981 to 24% in 1989 and 16% in 1998;
- the proportion of households renting from a housing association was static at 2% throughout the 1980s, followed by a slow but steady increase to 5% in 1996 and has remained at that level in 1998;
- the proportion of private renters declined during the 1980s (from 10% in 1981 to 7% in 1991). This was followed by an increase in the early 1990s to 9% in 1996 and 1998. In 1998, 7% rented unfurnished and 2% rented furnished accommodation.

Tables 4.1 and 4.3, Figure 4A

Type of accommodation

The type of accommodation varies considerably with tenure. In 1998:

- nearly all (92%) owner occupiers lived in a house, just over two-thirds were living in a detached or semi-detached house. In comparison, 63% of private renters and 56% of social sector tenants lived in a house;
- a higher proportion (41%) of social renters lived in a purpose built flat or maisonette than other groups (18% of private renters and 6% of owners);
- private renters were the most likely to be living in a converted flat (19% compared with 7% of housing association tenants, 2% of council tenants and 2% of owners).

Table 4.3

Age of building

In 1998, about one in five households lived in housing built before 1919 and about one in ten lived in housing built since 1985. The age of the building in which a household lived varied considerably by tenure.

- Households renting privately were the most likely to live in pre-1919 housing (40% compared with 23% of owner occupiers, 14% of housing association tenants and 3% of council tenants.
- Council tenants were the most likely (43%) to live in accommodation built between 1945 and 1964.
- Housing association tenants were the most likely to live in recently built accommodation. Thirty per cent lived in accommodation built since 1985 compared with 12% of owner occupiers, 8% of private renters and 5% of council tenants.
- Owners buying with a mortgage tend to have newer accommodation on the whole than those who own outright. The distribution for owner occupiers is however far more even than for other tenures.

Table 4.5

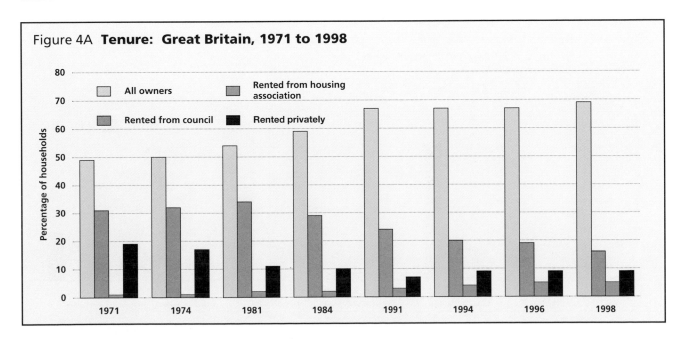

Figure 4A **Tenure: Great Britain, 1971 to 1998**

Household characteristics

Household tenure varied according to the number and ages of people in the household, their income and the ethnicity of the head of household.

Household composition

*   Households consisting of two adults (either both aged under 60 or at least one aged 60 or over) or large adult households were the most likely to be living in owner occupied accommodation (78% - 80% did so).
*   Nearly two-thirds of family households lived in owner occupied accommodation. A further 24% of small family[1] households and 29% of large family[1] households lived in social sector housing.
*   Households consisting of single adults aged 60 or over were the most likely (36%) to be social sector tenants - 28% rented from the council and 8% rented from a housing association.
*   Households consisting of single adults aged under 60 were the most likely (18%) to be private renters.
*   Lone-parent families were more likely than other families to live in social sector housing (53% compared with 14% of other families).   **Tables 4.6-4.7**

Income

*   Households buying with a mortgage had on average the highest household income (£557 gross per week).
*   Those with the lowest income were households living in social sector housing (housing association tenants - £184 gross per week; council tenants - £174 gross per week).
*   Private renters had on average a household income of £306 per week.   **Table 4.16**

Ethnic group

For the years 1995, 1996 and 1998 combined:

*   79% of Indian households were either buying their home with a mortgage or owned their home outright compared with 69% of White households, 57% of Pakistani or Bangladeshi households and 43% of Black households.
*   White households were the most likely (27%) to own their home outright.
*   Indian households were the most likely (57%) to be buying their accommodation with a mortgage.
*   Households headed by a Black person were more likely than others to be renting from a local authority or housing association (44% compared with 31% of Pakistani or Bangladeshi, 22% of White and 9% of Indian households).   **Table 4.17, Figure 4B**

Divorce, separation and housing tenure

The 1998 GHS looked at the effect of divorce and separation on housing tenure among people who were previously married or cohabiting. Similar questions were asked in 1991-1993 but the emphasis then was only on the effect of divorce.

At the time of the 1998 interview, respondents who were divorced or separated were asked about the tenure of their accommodation when they were last married or living with someone as a couple:

*   38% were previously owner occupiers;
*   37% were previously renters;
*   and a further 25% were not householders in their own right.

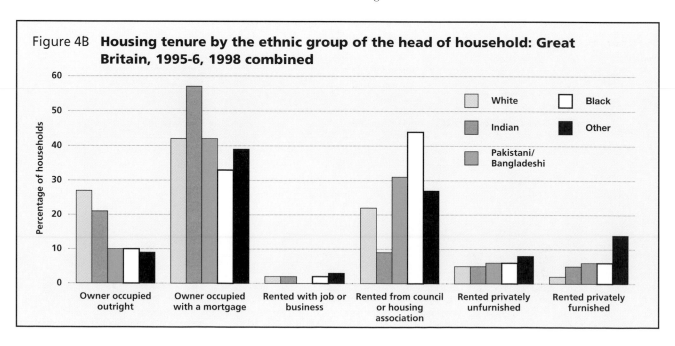

Figure 4B **Housing tenure by the ethnic group of the head of household: Great Britain, 1995-6, 1998 combined**

At the time of the interview:

- nearly eight out of ten (78%) of those who were previously owner occupiers still lived in owner occupied accommodation. The proportion was similar amongst both men and women;
- the proportion of those who previously rented their accommodation and continued to do so was also 78%;
- women who were previously renters were more likely than men to continue as renters if they lived in local authority or housing association accommodation (65% compared with 34%) but less likely if they lived in other rented accommodation (19% compared with 32%);
- of those who were not previously a householder, men were more likely than women to continue as a non-householder (28% compared with 15%);
- twelve months after divorce, separation or death of a partner, a smaller proportion of men than women were living in their former home (37% compared with 48%). **Tables 4.18-4.19**

Of those who had moved from their home within the twelve months following their divorce or separation or the death of their partner:

- 43% who were previously owner occupiers remained owner occupiers, 35% of owners had become renters and about a fifth were no longer a householder in their own right;
- about two-thirds who were previously renters continued to rent, 7% of renters had become owner occupiers and about a quarter were no longer a householder;
- women were less likely than men to have changed their tenure when they moved (of those who were previously owner occupiers, 49% of women compared with 37% of men remained owner occupiers; of those who previously rented, 74% of women compared with 57% of men remained renters). **Table 4.20**

Cars and vans

Trends over time

In 1998, 72% of households had access to a car or van, compared with 70% in 1996 and 68% in 1991. This continues the trend of a lower rate of increase in car ownership in the 1990s than in the 1980s.

- Most of the increase in car ownership between 1996 and 1998 was due to an increase in the proportion of households with access to two or more cars (from 24% in 1996 to 28% in 1998).
- The proportion of households with two cars increased steadily from 12% in 1981 to 19% in 1991 and 23% in 1998.
- Throughout the 1990s, the proportion of households with three or more cars remained constant at 4% until the increase to 6% in 1998.
- Car ownership was highest amongst professional, employer and managerial households. In 1998, over nine out of ten (96%) households in these groups had access to a car compared with about six out of ten (62%) unskilled manual workers, the group with the least access.
- Almost three-fifths (59%) of all professional, employer and managerial households had access to two or more cars compared with less than a fifth (18%) of semi-skilled and unskilled manual workers.

Tables 4.21-4.23, Figure 4C

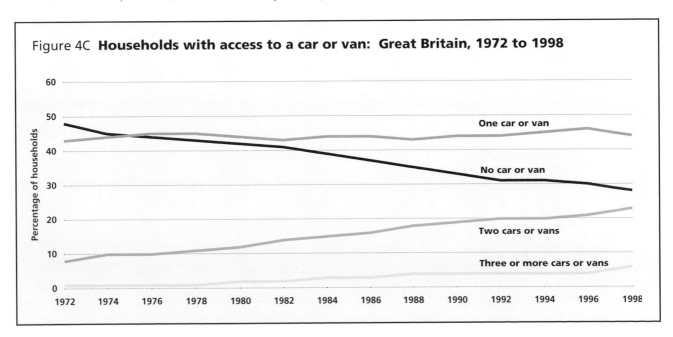

Figure 4C **Households with access to a car or van: Great Britain, 1972 to 1998**

41

Consumer durables

Trends over time

The steady increase in the ownership of consumer durables which has been evident since the 1970s continued throughout the 1990s for all consumer durables except colour and black and white televisions which are now available to nearly all households. Between 1996 and 1998, the greatest increase occurred in the proportion of households with:

- satellite receiver (from 18% with a satellite receiver in 1996 to 29% with a satellite or cable receiver in 1998);
- CD players (from 58% to 68%);
- home computers (from 27% to 34%);
- microwave ovens (from 74% to 79%).

Table 4.23, Figure 4D

Socio-economic group

Households headed by semi or unskilled manual workers were the least likely to have any of the consumer durables listed with the exception of televisions and satellite TV. The most notable differences were in the availability of:

- home computers - professional, employer and managerial households were the most likely to have a home computer (74% and 61% respectively) compared with the least likely, semi-skilled and unskilled manual households (27% and 18% respectively);
- dishwashers - also most likely to be available in professional, employer and managerial households (53% and 50% respectively) compared with 9% of unskilled manual households. **Table 4.24**

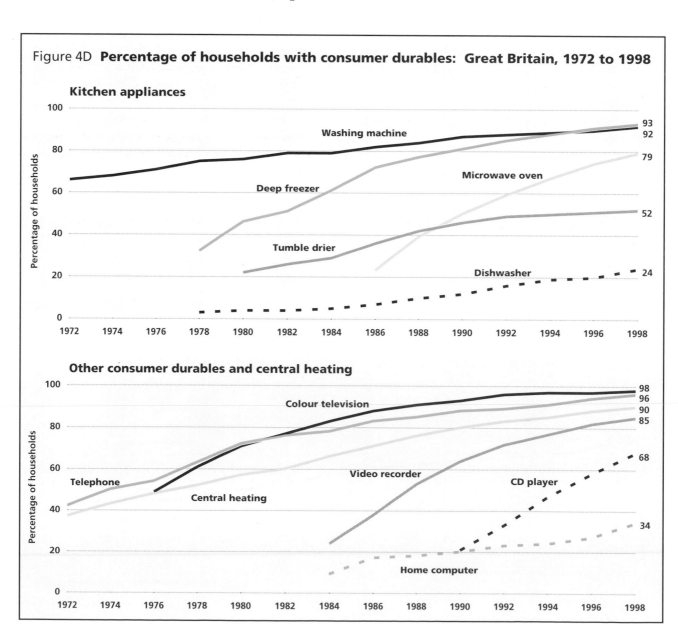

Figure 4D **Percentage of households with consumer durables: Great Britain, 1972 to 1998**

Gross weekly income

The higher the income, the more likely a household was to have consumer durables. In 1998, households with a gross weekly income of over £500 were far more likely than households with an income of £50 or less to have a:

- dishwasher (46% compared with 10%);
- home computer (60% compared with 25%);
- CD player (92% compared with 60%);
- video recorder (97% compared with 67%);
- tumble drier (67% compared with 39%).   **Table 4.25**

Household type

Large adult households and family households were the most likely to have 'entertainment items'. Those least likely to do so were older households and households consisting of a single person aged under 60. In 1998, for example:

- 47% of large adult households, 43% of large and 40% of small family households had satellite TV compared with 23% of single person households aged under 60, 19% of older two person and 9% of older single person households;
- 55% of large adult households, 53% of large and 48% of small family households had a home computer compared with 28% of single person households aged under 60, 18% of older two person and 4% of older single person households;
- nearly all types of household (95%-97%) had a video recorder, with the exception of single person house-

holds aged under 60 (80%), older two person households (85%) and older single person households (53%);
- older households aged 60 or over were the least likely to have a CD player (48% of older two person, 23% of older single person households compared with over 70% of other households).

Single person households, particularly where the householder was aged 60 or over were less likely to have domestic appliances than other households. In 1998:

- 82% of single person households had a deep freeze compared with 95%-98% of other households;
- 82% of single person households aged under 60 and 76% of older single person households had a washing machine compared with nearly all (95%-99%) other households;
- 39% of single person households aged under 60 and 30% of older single person households had a tumble drier compared with at least half of other households;
- 58% of older single person households owned a microwave oven compared with at least 70% of other households;
- 86%-87% of single person households of all ages had central heating compared with 91-93% of all other households.   **Table 4.26**

Notes

1   For a definition of small and large families see Appendix A.

Table 4.1 **Tenure: 1971 to 1998**

Households   *Great Britain*

Tenure	1971	1975	1979	1981	1983	1985	1989	1991	1993	1995	1996	1998
	%	%	%	%	%	%	%	%	%	%	%	%
Owner occupied, owned outright	22	22	22	23	24	24	24	25	26	25	26	28
Owner occupied, with mortgage	27	28	30	31	33	37	42	42	41	42	41	41
Rented from council*	31	33	34	34	32	28	24	24	22	18	19	16
Rented from housing association	1	1	1	2	2	2	2	3	3	4	5	5
Rented with job or business	5	3	3	2	2	2	2	1	1	2	**	**
Rented privately, unfurnished†	12	10	8	6	5	5	4	4	4	5	7	7
Rented privately, furnished	3	3	2	2	2	2	2	2	3	3	3	2
Base = 100%	11936	11970	11432	11939	9995	9933	10085	9922	9823	9723	9155	8631

* Council includes local authorities, New Towns and Scottish Homes from 1996.
† Unfurnished includes the answer 'partly furnished'.
** From 1996 all tenants whose accommodation goes with the job of someone in the household have been allocated to 'rented privately'. Squatters are also included in the
   privately rented category.

Table 4.2 **Type of accommodation: 1971 to 1998**

Households   *Great Britain*

Type of accommodation*	1971	1975	1979	1981	1983	1985	1989	1991	1993	1995	1996	1998
	%	%	%	%	%	%	%	%	%	%	%	%
Detached house	16	15	17	16	18	19	20	19	19	22	21	23
Semi-detached house	33	34	32	32	32	31	31	32	31	31	32	33
Terraced house	30	28	29	31	31	29	29	29	29	28	27	26
Purpose-built flat or maisonette	13	14	15	15	14	15	14	14	15	15	15	15
Converted flat or maisonette/rooms	6	8	6	5	4	5	4	4	5	4	5	4
With business premises/other	2	1	1	1	1	1	1	1	1	1	0	0
Base = 100%	11846	12041	11375	11978	10003	9890	10049	9917	9830	9730	9128	8615

* Tables for type of accommodation exclude households living in caravans.

Table 4.3 (a) Type of accommodation by tenure
(b) Tenure by type of accommodation

Households   *Great Britain: 1998*

Tenure		Type of accommodation*							Base = 100%
		Detached house	Semi-detached house	Terraced house	All houses	Purpose-built flat or maisonette	Converted flat or maisonette/rooms	All flats/rooms	
(a)									
Owner occupied, owned outright	%	36	37	20	93	6	1	7	2403
Owner occupied, with mortgage	%	27	36	29	92	6	2	8	3552
All owners	%	31	36	25	92	6	2	8	5955
Rented from council†	%	1	29	28	58	40	2	42	1410
Rented from housing association	%	1	19	27	47	46	7	53	444
Social sector tenants	%	1	27	28	56	41	3	44	1854
Rented privately, unfurnished**	%	17	23	30	69	16	15	31	575
Rented privately, furnished	%	8	12	27	47	23	30	53	213
Private renters††	%	15	20	29	63	18	19	37	790
Total	%	23	33	26	82	15	4	18	8599
(b)									
		%	%	%	%	%	%	%	%
Owner occupied, owned outright		44	31	21	32	11	10	11	28
Owner occupied, with mortgage		49	45	45	46	18	24	19	41
All owners		93	77	67	78	29	34	30	69
Rented from council†		1	15	18	12	44	9	37	16
Rented from housing association		0	3	5	3	16	10	15	5
Social sector tenants		1	18	23	15	60	19	52	22
Rented privately, unfurnished**		5	5	8	6	7	27	11	7
Rented privately, furnished		1	1	3	1	4	20	7	2
Private renters††		6	6	10	7	11	47	18	9
Base = 100%		*1967*	*2807*	*2237*	*7011*	*1267*	*321*	*1588*	*8599*

*   Tables for type of accommodation exclude households living in caravans.
†   Council includes local authorities, New Towns and Scottish Homes from 1996.
** Unfurnished includes the answer 'partly furnished'.
†† From 1996 all tenants whose accommodation goes with the job of someone in the household have been allocated to 'rented privately'. Squatters are also included in the
    privately rented category.

Table 4.4 **Type of accommodation occupied by households renting from a council compared with other households: 1981 to 1998**

Households   *Great Britain*

Type of accommodation	1981	1987	1989	1991	1993	1995	1996	1998
	%	%	%	%	%	%	%	%
Renting from council								
Detached house	1	1	1	1	1	0	1	1
Semi-detached house	30	28	26	28	26	28	28	29
Terraced house	34	35	34	34	33	33	31	28
Purpose-built flat or maisonette	33	34	36	35	37	38	38	40
Converted flat or maisonette	2	2	3	3	3	1	2	2
Base = 100%	*4007*	*2600*	*2451*	*2339*	*2121*	*1770*	*1748*	*1410*
	%	%	%	%	%	%	%	%
Other households								
Detached house	24	25	26	25	24	26	25	27
Semi-detached house	33	33	33	33	33	32	33	33
Terraced house	29	28	28	28	28	27	27	26
Purpose-built flat or maisonette	6	7	7	8	9	10	9	10
Converted flat or maisonette	7	5	5	5	6	4	5	4
Base = 100%	*7904*	*7511*	*7573*	*7578*	*7699*	*7953*	*7379*	*7189*
	%	%	%	%	%	%	%	%
All households								
Detached house	16	18	20	19	19	22	21	23
Semi-detached house	32	32	31	32	31	31	32	33
Terraced house	31	30	29	29	29	28	27	26
Purpose-built flat or maisonette	15	14	14	14	15	15	15	15
Converted flat or maisonette	5	5	4	4	5	4	5	4
Base = 100%	*11911*	*10111*	*10024*	*9917*	*9820*	*9723*	*9127*	*8599*

Table 4.5 **Age of building by tenure**

Households   *Great Britain: 1998*

Age of building* containing household's accommodation	Tenure									
	Owners			Social sector tenants			Private renters			Total
	Owned outright	With mortgage	All owners	Council†	Housing association	Social sector tenants	Unfurnished private**	Furnished private	Private Renters††	
(a)	%	%	%	%	%	%	%	%	%	%
Before 1919	22	23	23	3	14	6	39	45	40	21
1919-1944	21	19	20	18	11	16	20	24	21	19
1945-1964	25	17	20	43	17	36	16	8	14	23
1965-1984	25	26	26	31	28	30	17	15	17	26
1985 or later	7	15	12	5	30	11	8	8	8	11
Base = 100%	*2393*	*3538*	*5931*	*1345*	*427*	*1772*	*555*	*201*	*757*	*8460*

*   For an assessment of the reliability of age of building estimates, see Birch F, Age of buildings (OPCS Social Survey Division, GHS Series No.7, 1974).
†
**   See the footnotes to Table 4.3.
††

Table 4.6 **(a) Household type by tenure**
         (b) Tenure by household type

Households   *Great Britain: 1998*

Tenure		1 adult aged 16-59	2 adults aged 16-59	Small family	Large family	Large adult household	2 adults, 1 or both aged 60 or over	1 adult aged 60 or over	Base = 100%
(a)									
Owner occupied, owned outright	%	6	9	4	1	11	39	30	2419
Owner occupied, with mortgage	%	14	25	29	8	17	6	2	3555
All owners	%	11	18	19	5	14	19	13	5974
Rented from council*	%	14	8	22	8	8	14	26	1418
Rented from housing association	%	18	7	26	9	7	10	24	445
Social sector tenants	%	15	8	23	8	8	13	26	1863
Rented privately, unfurnished†	%	21	18	26	5	7	10	14	578
Rented privately, furnished	%	38	25	12	4	15	3	3	214
Private renters**	%	25	20	22	5	10	8	11	794
Total	%	13	16	20	6	13	17	16	8631
(b)									Total
		%	%	%	%	%	%	%	%
Owner occupied, owned outright		13	16	5	6	25	65	53	28
Owner occupied, with mortgage		44	62	60	58	55	14	5	41
All owners		57	78	65	64	80	79	58	69
Rented from council*		18	8	18	21	10	14	28	16
Rented from housing association		7	2	7	8	3	3	8	5
Social sector tenants		25	10	24	29	13	17	36	22
Rented privately, unfurnished†		11	7	9	5	4	4	6	7
Rented privately, furnished		7	4	1	2	3	0	0	2
Private renters**		18	11	10	7	7	4	6	9
Base = 100%		1110	1400	1720	511	1079	1454	1357	8631

```
*
†   See the footnotes to Table 4.1.
**
```

Table 4.7 **Housing profile by family type: lone-parent families compared with other families**

Families with dependent children*   *Great Britain: 1996 and 1998 combined*

	Lone-parent families	Other families
Tenure	%	%
Owner occupied, owned outright	7	6
Owner occupied, with mortgage	27	73
Rented with job or business	0	2
Rented from council or from housing association	53	14
Rented privately unfurnished	11	3
Rented privately furnished	2	1
Central heating	%	%
Yes	88	93
No	12	7
Type of accommodation	%	%
Detached house	8	28
Semi-detached house	31	37
Terraced house	38	28
Purpose-built flat or maisonette	19	5
Converted flat or maisonette/rooms	4	1
With business premises/other	0	0
Bedroom standard	%	%
2 or more below standard	1	1
1 below standard	9	4
Equals standard	55	34
1 above standard	32	45
2 or more above standard	4	16
Persons per room	%	%
Under 0.5	19	7
0.5-0.99	73	76
1.0-1.49	8	16
1.5 or above	0	1
Base = 100%	1287	4089

* Dependent children are persons aged under 16, or aged 16-18 and in full-time education, in the family unit, and living in the household.

Table 4.8 **Type of accommodation by household type**

Households   *Great Britain: 1998*

Household type		Type of accommodation*							Base = 100%
		Detached house	Semi-detached house	Terraced house	All houses	Purpose-built flat or maisonette	Converted flat or maisonette/ rooms	All flats/ rooms	
One adult aged 16-59	%	10	21	26	57	30	13	43	1107
Two adults aged 16-59	%	27	32	25	84	12	4	16	1400
Small family	%	21	35	30	87	11	2	13	1716
Large family	%	22	40	31	92	7	1	8	511
Large adult household	%	28	37	28	94	5	1	6	1078
Two adults, one or both aged 60 or over	%	32	37	21	90	9	2	10	1447
One adult aged 60 or over	%	18	29	24	70	27	3	30	1345
Total	%	23	33	26	82	15	4	18	8604

* See the first footnote to Table 4.3.

Table 4.9 Persons per room: 1971 to 1998

Households *Great Britain*

Persons per room	1971	1975	1979	1981	1985	1989	1991	1993	1995	1996	1998
	%	%	%	%	%	%	%	%	%	%	%
Under 0.5	37	39	41	42	45	48	50	51	52	51	55
0.5 to 0.65	25	25	26	25	26	26	24	24	25	24	23
0.66 to 0.99	24	23	23	23	21	20	19	19	18	19	18
1	9	8	7	7	6	5	5	5	5	5	4
Over 1 to 1.5	4	3	2	2	1	1	1	1	1	1	1
Over 1.5	1	0	0	0	0	0	0	0	0	0	0
Base = 100%	11990	12096	11484	12002	9982	10085	9646	9663	9754	9154	8636
Mean persons per room	..	0.57	0.57	0.56	0.52	0.50	0.50	0.49	0.48	0.49	0.47

Table 4.10 Persons per room and mean household size by tenure

Households *Great Britain: 1998*

Persons per room*	Tenure									Total
	Owners			Social sector tenants			Private renters			
	Owned outright	With mortgage	All owners	Council†	Housing association	Social sector tenants	Unfur-nished private**	Furnished private	Private renters††	
	%	%	%	%	%	%	%	%	%	%
Under 0.5	78	44	58	50	44	49	51	41	48	55
0.5 to 0.65	17	26	22	24	24	24	25	24	25	23
0.66 to 0.99	5	25	17	18	23	19	19	20	19	18
1	0	4	2	6	7	6	3	14	6	4
Over 1	0	1	1	2	2	2	2	1	2	1
Base =100%	2419	3555	5974	1418	445	1863	578	214	794	8631
Mean persons per room	0.35	0.51	0.45	0.50	0.53	0.51	0.48	0.55	0.50	0.47
Mean household size	1.89	2.83	2.45	2.17	2.19	2.17	2.20	2.10	2.18	2.36

* Boxed figures indicate median density of occupation.

†
** See the footnotes to Table 4.3.
††

Table 4.11 Closeness of fit relative to the bedroom standard by tenure

Households *Great Britain: 1998*

Difference from bedroom standard (bedrooms)	Tenure									Total
	Owners			Social sector tenants			Private renters			
	Owned outright	With mortgage	All owners	Council*	Housing association	Social sector tenants	Unfur-nished private†	Furnished private	Private renters**	
	%	%	%	%	%	%	%	%	%	%
1 or more below standard	0	2	1	4	3	4	2	5	3	2
Equals standard	9	21	16	51	64	54	35	50	39	27
1 above standard	37	42	40	32	27	31	40	29	37	37
2 or more above standard	54	36	43	14	5	12	22	17	21	34
Base =100%	2419	3555	5974	1418	445	1863	578	214	794	8631

* Council includes local authorities, New Towns and Scottish Homes from 1996.

† Unfurnished includes the answer 'partly furnished'.

** From 1996 all tenants whose accommodation goes with the job of someone in the household have been allocated to 'rented privately'. Squatters are also included in the privately rented category.

Table 4.12 (a) Age of head of household by tenure
(b) Tenure by age of head of household

Heads of household   *Great Britain: 1998*

Tenure		Age of head of household*								Base = 100%
		Under 25	25-29	30-44	45-59	60-64	65-69	70-79	80 and over	
(a)										
Owner occupied, owned outright	%	0	0	5	22	14	17	30	12	*2419*
Owner occupied, with mortgage	%	2	10	46	34	5	2	2	0	*3555*
All owners	%	1	6	29	29	8	8	13	5	*5974*
Rented from council†	%	6	8	24	21	7	7	18	9	*1418*
Rented from housing association	%	7	10	30	16	6	5	15	10	*445*
Social sector tenants	%	6	8	25	20	7	7	17	10	*1863*
Rented privately, unfurnished**	%	10	15	33	19	4	4	8	7	*578*
Rented privately, furnished	%	22	26	36	10	2	2	1	0	*214*
Private renters††	%	13	18	34	16	4	4	6	5	*794*
Total	%	3	8	29	26	8	7	14	6	*8631*
(b)										Total
		%	%	%	%	%	%	%	%	%
Owner occupied, owned outright		2	2	5	24	51	64	62	56	28
Owner occupied, with mortgage		20	54	65	54	25	11	6	2	41
All owners		21	56	70	78	76	75	68	58	69
Rented from council†		30	16	14	13	15	16	22	26	16
Rented from housing association		11	7	5	3	4	4	6	9	5
Social sector tenants		41	23	19	16	20	20	28	35	22
Rented privately, unfurnished**		20	13	8	5	4	4	4	8	7
Rented privately, furnished		17	8	3	1	1	1	0	0	2
Private renters††		37	21	11	6	4	5	4	8	9
Base = 100%		*281*	*669*	*2475*	*2237*	*651*	*638*	*1168*	*512*	*8631*

* Boxed figures indicate median age-groups.

†
** See the footnotes to Table 4.3.
††

Table 4.13 Tenure by sex and marital status of head of household

Heads of household   *Great Britain: 1998*

Tenure	Males						Females						Total
	Married	Cohabiting	Single	Widowed	Divorced/ separated	All males	Married	Cohabiting	Single	Widowed	Divorced/ separated	All females	
	%	%	%	%	%	%	%	%	%	%	%	%	%
Owner occupied, owned outright	31	5	15	53	16	27	††	††	16	54	14	32	28
Owner occupied, with mortgage	52	61	37	9	37	49	††	††	26	6	34	20	41
All owners	83	65	52	62	53	75	††	††	42	60	48	52	69
Rented from council*	9	16	17	26	25	12	††	††	27	27	32	29	16
Rented from housing association	3	5	6	7	6	4	††	††	12	7	10	9	5
Social sector tenants	11	22	23	33	31	16	††	††	39	34	42	38	22
Rented privately, unfurnished†	5	9	11	4	13	6	††	††	12	5	7	8	7
Rented privately, furnished	1	4	14	0	3	3	††	††	6	0	2	2	2
Private renters	6	13	25	5	17	9	††	††	18	5	9	10	9
Base = 100%	*4450*	*622*	*605*	*301*	*378*	*6356*	*6*	*13*	*568*	*949*	*739*	*2275*	*8631*

*

† See the footnotes to Table 4.1.

**

†† Base too small to enable reliable analysis to be made.

Table 4.14 **(a) Socio-economic group and economic activity status of head of household by tenure**
(b) Tenure by socio-economic group and economic activity status of head of household

Heads of households   *Great Britain: 1998*

Socio-economic group and economic activity status of head of household*	Tenure									Total
	Owners			Social sector tenants			Private renters			
	Owned outright	With mortgage	All owners	Council†	Housing association	Social sector tenants	Unfurnished private**	Furnished private	Private Renters††	
(a)	%	%	%	%	%	%	%	%	%	%
Economically active heads:										
Professional	3	10	8	0	0	0	4	12	6	6
Employers and managers	7	25	17	2	3	3	10	10	10	13
Intermediate non-manual	4	13	9	2	3	2	11	15	12	8
Junior non-manual	3	9	7	5	6	5	7	9	7	6
Skilled manual and own account non-professional	8	24	17	12	12	12	16	12	15	16
Semi-skilled manual and personal service	4	8	6	11	11	11	12	10	11	8
Unskilled manual	1	2	2	4	5	4	2	1	2	2
Economically inactive heads	70	10	34	64	61	63	38	32	36	41
Base = 100%	*2414*	*3518*	*5932*	*1395*	*439*	*1834*	*542*	*196*	*740*	*8506*
(b)										*Base = 100%*
Economically active heads:										
Professional	%	16	74	90	1	0	1	5	5	9	*500*
Employers and managers	%	14	76	90	3	1	4	5	2	6	*1142*
Intermediate non-manual	%	15	66	80	5	2	6	9	4	13	*681*
Junior non-manual	%	14	59	73	12	5	17	7	3	10	*529*
Skilled manual and own account non-professional	%	14	62	76	12	4	16	6	2	8	*1357*
Semi-skilled manual and personal service	%	14	41	55	24	8	32	10	3	13	*647*
Unskilled manual	%	16	36	52	30	11	41	6	1	7	*186*
Economically inactive heads	%	49	10	59	26	8	33	6	2	8	*3464*
Total	%	28	42	70	16	5	22	6	2	9	*8506*

*   Excluding members of the Armed Forces, and economically active full-time students and those who were unemployed and had never worked.

†
**   See the footnotes to Table 4.3.
††

Table 4.15 (a) Length of residence of head of household by tenure
(b) Tenure by length of residence of head of household

Heads of household   *Great Britain: 1998*

Length of residence* (years)		Tenure									Total
		Owners			Social sector tenants			Private renters			
		Owned outright	With mortgage	All owners	Council†	Housing association	Social sector tenants	Unfurn-ished** private	Furnished private	Private Renters††	
(a)		%	%	%	%	%	%	%	%	%	%
Less than 12 months		3	9	7	11	17	13	30	45	35	10
12 months but less than 2 years		3	9	6	9	9	9	13	[17]	14	8
2 years but less than 3 years		2	9	6	7	11	8	[11]	14	[11]	7
3 years but less than 5 years		5	13	10	13	[18]	14	12	14	12	11
5 years but less than 10 years		9	[22]	17	[18]	20	[18]	10	6	9	[17]
10 years or more		[78]	38	[54]	42	25	38	24	5	19	47
Base = 100%		*2419*	*3555*	*5974*	*1418*	*445*	*1863*	*577*	*214*	*793*	*8630*
(b)										.	*Base = 100%*
Less than 12 months	%	9	35	44	17	9	26	19	11	30	*905*
12 months but less than 2 years	%	10	47	57	20	6	26	11	5	17	*659*
2 years but less than 3 years	%	8	52	60	17	8	25	10	5	15	*610*
3 years but less than 5 years	%	13	49	62	19	8	28	7	3	10	*936*
5 years but less than 10 years	%	16	56	71	18	6	24	4	1	5	*1433*
10 years or more	%	46	33	79	15	3	17	3	0	4	*4087*
Total	%	28	41	69	16	5	22	7	2	9	*8630*

*   Boxed figures indicate median length of residence.

†
** See the footnotes to Table 4.3.
††

Table 4.16 Usual gross weekly income by tenure

Households   *Great Britain: 1998*

Usual gross weekly income (£)	Tenure									Total
	Owners			Social sector tenants			Private renters			
	Owned outright	With mortgage	All owners	Council*	Housing association	Social sector tenants	Unfurnished private†	Furnished private	Private renters**	
Income of head of household										
Mean	220	401	328	130	142	133	231	250	236	277
Lower quartile	78	209	116	73	72	73	73	51	70	88
Median	152	346	266	104	106	104	162	144	154	202
Upper quartile	282	498	434	166	179	169	317	301	314	375
Base	*2419*	*3555*	*5974*	*1418*	*445*	*1863*	*578*	*214*	*794*	*8631*
Income of head of household and partner										
Mean	220	401	328	131	142	134	232	250	236	277
Lower quartile	78	209	117	73	72	73	73	51	70	88
Median	152	346	266	104	106	104	162	144	154	202
Upper quartile	282	500	434	167	179	171	322	301	317	375
Base	*2419*	*3555*	*5974*	*1418*	*445*	*1863*	*578*	*214*	*794*	*8631*
Total household income										
Mean	293	557	450	174	184	177	297	331	306	378
Lower quartile	92	288	152	77	77	77	83	78	81	106
Median	204	500	373	126	133	128	215	234	224	275
Upper quartile	385	713	612	230	250	235	416	394	405	532
Base	*2419*	*3555*	*5974*	*1418*	*445*	*1863*	*578*	*214*	*794*	*8631*

*
† See the footnotes to Table 4.1.
**

Table 4.17 Housing tenure by ethnic group of head of household

Households   *Great Britain: 1995-96, 1998 combined*

Tenure	White	Indian	Pakistani/ Bangladeshi	Black*	Remaining groups	All ethnic minority groups	Total
	%	%	%	%	%	%	%
Owner occupied, owned outright	27	21	14	10	9	13	26
Owner occupied, with mortgage	42	57	42	33	39	42	42
Rented with job or business	2	2	0	2	3	2	2
Rented from council or from housing association	22	9	31	44	27	29	23
Rented privately unfurnished	5	5	6	6	8	6	5
Rented privately furnished	2	5	6	6	14	8	3
Base = 100%	*26139*	*319*	*210*	*447*	*330*	*1306*	*27445*

* Black includes Black Caribbean, Black African and other Black groups.

Table 4.18 **Current tenure by tenure of former home by sex**

Divorced, separated or widowed persons, aged 20-59, formerly married or cohabiting   *Great Britain: 1998*

Current tenure	Tenure when married/cohabiting			
	Owner occupied	Rented	Not a householder	Total
	%	%	%	%
Men				
Owner occupied, owned outright	16	1	4	7
Owner occupied, with mortgage	63	17	18	36
Rented from council or housing association	4	34	29	21
Other rented	11	32	20	21
Not a householder	7	16	28	16
Base = 100%	*171*	*149*	*109*	*429*
	%	%	%	%
Women				
Owner occupied, owned outright	23	2	10	12
Owner occupied, with mortgage	54	8	14	26
Rented from council or housing association	10	65	41	39
Other rented	6	19	20	15
Not a householder	7	5	15	8
Base = 100%	*221*	*242*	*152*	*615*
	%	%	%	%
Total				
Owner occupied, owned outright	20	2	7	10
Owner occupied, with mortgage	58	11	16	30
Rented from council or housing association	7	53	36	32
Other rented	8	24	20	17
Not a householder	7	9	21	11
Base = 100%	*392*	*391*	*261*	*1044*
				Base = 100%
Tenure when married/cohabiting (% of total) %	38	37	25	*1044*

Table 4.19 **Tenure of former home by sex by whether living in the previously shared home 12 months after divorce, separation or death of partner**

Divorced, separated or widowed persons, aged 20-59, formerly married or cohabiting   *Great Britain: 1998*

Tenure of home when married/cohabiting	Whether living in previously shared home 12 months after divorce, separation, or death of partner					
	Men		Women		Total	
	Yes	No	Yes	No	Yes	No
	%	%	%	%	%	%
Owner occupied, owned outright	11	2	7	2	9	2
Owner occupied, with mortgage	51	23	41	23	45	23
Rented from council or housing association	21	12	32	19	29	16
Other rented	9	26	9	16	9	21
Not a householder	7	37	10	39	9	38
Base = 100%	*149*	*257*	*271*	*299*	*420*	*555*
% living in former home	37	63	48	52	43	57

Table 4.20 **Tenure 12 months after divorce, separation or death of partner if moved by tenure when married or cohabiting by sex**

Divorced, separated or widowed persons, aged 20-59, formerly married or cohabiting   *Great Britain: 1998*

Tenure 12 months after divorce/ separation if moved	Tenure when married/cohabiting			
	Owner occupied	Rented	Not a householder	Total
	%	%	%	%
Men				
Owner occupied, owned outright	8	1	3	4
Owner occupied, with mortgage	29	10	10	15
Rented from council or housing association	3	14	18	13
Other rented	35	43	26	35
Not a householder	24	31	43	34
Base = 100%	*62*	*97*	*96*	*255*
	%	%	%	%
Women				
Owner occupied, owned outright	14	0	3	5
Owner occupied, with mortgage	35	5	9	14
Rented from council or housing association	11	40	27	28
Other rented	22	34	24	27
Not a householder	19	21	36	26
Base = 100%	*74*	*105*	*117*	*296*
	%	%	%	%
Total				
Owner occupied, owned outright	11	0	3	4
Owner occupied, with mortgage	32	7	10	15
Rented from council or housing association	7	28	23	21
Other rented	28	39	25	31
Not a householder	21	26	39	30
Base = 100%	*136*	*202*	*213*	*551*

Table 4.21 **Cars or vans: 1972 to 1998**

Households   *Great Britain*

Cars or vans	1972	1975	1979	1981	1983	1985	1989	1991	1993	1995	1996	1998
	%	%	%	%	%	%	%	%	%	%	%	%
Households with:												
no car or van	48	44	43	41	41	38	33	32	32	29	30	28
one car or van	43	45	44	44	43	45	43	44	45	45	46	44
two cars or vans	8	10	12	12	14	14	19	19	20	22	21	23
three or more cars or vans	1	1	2	2	3	3	4	4	4	4	4	6
Base = 100%	*11624*	*11929*	*11459*	*11989*	*10053*	*9963*	*10085*	*9910*	*9851*	*9758*	*9158*	*8636*

Table 4.22 Availability of a car or van by socio-economic group of head of household

Households   *Great Britain: 1998*

Number of cars or vans available to household	Socio-economic group of head of household*							Economically inactive heads	Total
	Economically active heads								
	Professional	Employers and managers	Intermediate non-manual	Junior non-manual	Skilled manual and own account non-professional	Semi-skilled manual and personal service	Unskilled manual		
	%	%	%	%	%	%	%	%	%
None	4	4	14	21	11	30	38	48	28
1	35	39	52	49	46	52	45	42	44
2 or more	61	58	34	30	43	18	18	9	28
Base = 100%	500	1142	683	530	1357	648	186	3465	8511

* Excluding members of the Armed Forces, and economically active full-time students and those who were unemployed and had never worked.

Table 4.23 Consumer durables, central heating and cars: 1972 to 1998

Households   *Great Britain*

Percentage of households with:	1972	1975	1979	1981	1983	1985	1989	1991	1993	1995	1996	1998
Television												
colour	93	96	66	74	81	86	93	95	95	97	97	98
black and white only			31	23	17	11	5	4	3	2	2	1
(combined)			97	97	98	98	98	98	98	98	99	98
satellite TV	..	..	..	..	..	..	..	..	..	..	18	29
Video recorder	..	..	..	..	18	31	60	68	73	79	82	85
CD player	..	..	..	..	..	..	15	27	39	52	58	68
Home computer	..	..	..	..	..	13	19	21	24	25	27	34
Microwave oven	..	..	..	..	..	..	47	55	62	70	74	79
Refrigerator*	73	88	92	93	94	95	..	..	..	..	..	..
Deep freezer*	..	..	40	49	57	66	79	83	86	89	91	93
Washing machine	66	71	74	78	80	81	86	87	88	90	90	92
Tumble drier	..	..	19	23	28	33	45	48	49	51	51	52
Dishwasher	..	..	3	4	5	6	12	14	16	20	20	24
Telephone	42	54	67	75	77	81	87	88	90	93	94	96
Central heating	37	43	55	59	64	69	78	82	83	86	88	90
A car or van	43	45	44	44	43	45	43	44	45	45	46	44
- more than 1	9	11	11	14	17	17	23	23	23	26	24	28
(combined)	52	56	57	59	59	62	67	67	68	71	70	72
Base = 100%	11663	11929	11490	11718	10068	9993	10085	9955	9850	9757	9156	8636

* Fridge freezers are attributed to both 'refrigerator' and 'deep freezer' from 1979 on.

Table 4.24 Consumer durables, central heating and cars by socio-economic group of head of household

Heads of household   *Great Britain: 1998*

Consumer durables	Socio-economic group of head of household*								Economically inactive heads
	Economically active heads								
	Professional	Employers and managers	Intermediate non-manual	Junior non-manual	Skilled manual and own account non-professional	Semi-skilled manual and personal service	Unskilled manual	Total	
Percentage of households with:									
Television									
colour	99	99	97	98	98	97	99	98	97
black and white	0	0	1	0	1	0	1	0	1
satellite TV	31	40	30	32	42	36	31	36	18
Video recorder	95	95	93	92	95	90	90	94	72
CD player	89	90	87	84	85	78	73	85	43
Home computer	74	61	54	37	34	27	18	45	15
Microwave oven	84	87	84	86	88	82	78	86	68
Deep freezer/fridge freezer	96	97	92	94	96	92	91	95	89
Washing machine	99	98	94	94	96	92	89	96	87
Tumble drier	67	67	56	57	59	54	48	60	41
Dishwasher	53	50	29	23	24	12	9	31	13
Telephone	100	99	99	98	97	93	88	97	94
Central heating	97	95	92	93	90	87	83	92	88
Car or van - more than one	61	58	34	30	43	18	18	42	9
Base = 100%	*500*	*1142*	*683*	*530*	*1357*	*648*	*186*	*5046*	*3465*

* Excluding members of the Armed Forces, and economically active full-time students and those who were unemployed and had never worked.

Table 4.25 Consumer durables, central heating and cars by usual gross weekly household income

Households   *Great Britain: 1998*

Consumer durables	Usual gross weekly household income (£)											
	0.01-50.00	50.01-100.00	100.01-150.00	150.01-200.00	200.01-250.00	250.01-300.00	300.01-350.00	350.01-400.00	400.01-450.00	450.01-500.00	500.01 or more	Total*
Percentage of households with:												
Television												
colour	89	93	97	97	99	98	98	99	99	99	99	98
black and white only	2	4	2	1	1	0	1	1	0	0	0	1
satellite TV	23	15	18	22	24	27	25	35	37	40	39	29
Video recorder	67	57	70	80	84	89	88	93	94	95	97	85
CD player	60	34	41	50	58	68	72	79	83	88	92	68
Home computer	25	8	13	15	18	24	30	36	36	42	60	34
Microwave oven	65	56	67	74	74	80	80	83	87	85	88	79
Deep freezer/fridge freezer	79	81	87	91	92	94	93	95	97	96	97	93
Washing machine	77	73	85	89	93	94	93	95	98	98	99	92
Tumble drier	39	28	37	44	49	50	52	53	59	63	67	53
Dishwasher	10	4	6	9	11	14	18	19	26	31	46	24
Telephone	81	86	93	94	96	98	96	99	99	100	100	96
Central heating	85	83	87	87	88	88	87	91	93	93	96	90
Car or van - more than 1	18	3	4	6	9	12	22	22	31	37	59	29
Base = 100%	*126*	*837*	*816*	*668*	*565*	*475*	*468*	*408*	*403*	*380*	*2403*	*8537*

* Total includes no answers to income.

Table 4.26 **Consumer durables, central heating and cars by household type**

Households   *Great Britain: 1998*

Consumer durables	Household type							
	1 adult aged 16-59	2 adults aged 16-59	Small family	Large family	Large adult household	2 adults, 1 or both aged 60 or over	1 adult aged 60 or over	Total
Percentage of households with:								
Television								
colour	93	99	99	98	99	99	95	98
black and white only	2	0	0	1	0	1	2	1
satellite TV	23	33	40	43	47	19	9	29
Video recorder	80	95	96	95	97	85	53	85
CD player	71	86	87	85	90	48	23	68
Home computer	28	42	48	53	55	18	4	34
Microwave oven	70	85	87	88	89	76	58	79
Deep freezer/fridge freezer	82	95	97	97	98	96	82	93
Washing machine	82	97	98	98	99	95	76	92
Tumble drier	39	56	63	73	66	49	30	52
Dishwasher	10	31	30	39	34	23	7	24
Telephone	90	98	96	96	99	98	94	96
Central heating	86	92	92	91	93	91	87	90
Car or van - more than 1	7	46	37	38	57	18	1	28
Base = 100%	*1111*	*1401*	*1720*	*511*	*1081*	*1454*	*1358*	*8636*

5 Marriage and cohabitation

The GHS collects information from the person answering the household questionnaire (usually the head of house-hold or their spouse) about the marital status of all adults aged 16 or over. Each household member aged 16-59 is asked detailed questions about their marriage and cohabitation history later in the interview, making the GHS a key source of information on these topics. Where interviewers judge that lack of privacy may affect reporting, they can offer respondents a self-completion questionnaire to fill in. In 1998, 8% of respondents chose this option.

For the first time in 1998, respondents aged 16-59 were asked whether they had ever lived as a couple with some-one of the opposite sex, whom they did not subsequently marry. Those who said they had were asked how many such relationships they had had. This chapter reports on responses to these new questions and to other questions on marital status and cohabitation.

Marital status

In 1998, the de facto[1] marital status of adults aged 16 and over was as follows:

- 59% of men and 54% of women were married;
- 8% of both men and women were cohabiting;
- 22% of men and 17% of women were single;
- 4% of men and 12% of women were widowed; and
- 6% of men were either divorced or separated, compared with 9% of women.   **Table 5.1**

Separation and remarriage

The proportion of marriages which ended in separation within the first five years was higher among marriages which began between 1985 and 1989 than among those contracted between 1965 and 1969. Among those married for the first time before the age of 30:

- 3% of men and 2% of women who married between 1965 and 1969 were separated within three years, compared with 8% and 9% respectively of those married between 1985 and 1989;
- the proportion of men and women separating within five years of marriage rose from 7% of those married in 1965-1969 to 13% of men and 16% of women married between 1985 and 1989;
- about a quarter of men (25%) and women (26%) married between 1965 and 1969 had separated within 20 years of being married.   **Table 5.3**

Women who first married before the age of 20 were more likely than women who married in their twenties to have separated within five years of marriage. Among women aged 20-59 and first married before the age of 30:

- for marriages which began in 1965-1969, 11% of women who were under 20 at marriage had separated within five years, compared with 6% and 3% respectively of women who were 20-24 and 25-29 when they married;
- for marriages which took place between 1985 and 1989, nearly a quarter (24%) of women who married before the age of 20 had separated within five years, compared with 16% and 8% respectively of women who married at the age of 20-24 and 25-29;
- about seven in ten men and about six in ten women who were separated before the age of 35 had remarried within 10 years.   **Tables 5.4-5.6**

Cohabitation

Questions on cohabitation have been addressed to women aged 18-49 since 1979. Since 1986, they have been asked of both men and women aged 16-59. In 1998:

- 12% of men and 11% of women aged 16-59 were cohabiting[2];
- among non-married respondents, including separated respondents, approximately a quarter of men (26%) and women (25%) in the same age group were cohabiting;
- respondents in their twenties and early thirties were most likely to cohabit; over one in five of those aged 20-34 were doing so, compared with about one in 25 of the 50-59 age group.   **Table 5.7, Figure 5A**

Data from 1996 and 1998 were combined to provide a sufficiently large sample to analyse cohabitation by age and legal marital status. Divorced men and women were cohabiting in the largest proportions; 38% of divorced men and 29% of divorced women were doing so, compared with 25% or fewer of other men and women.

Table 5.8

The longest time series on cohabitation exists for women aged 18-49. Among this group:

- there has been a marked increase in the proportion of non-married women who were cohabiting, from 11% in 1979 to 29% in 1998;
- the proportion of single women cohabiting has almost quadrupled, from less than one in ten (8%) in 1979 to almost one in three (31%) by 1998;
- the proportion of divorced women who were cohabiting rose from one in five (20%) in 1979 to nearly a third (30%) by 1989, and has since remained at roughly that level.   **Table 5.11, Figure 5B**

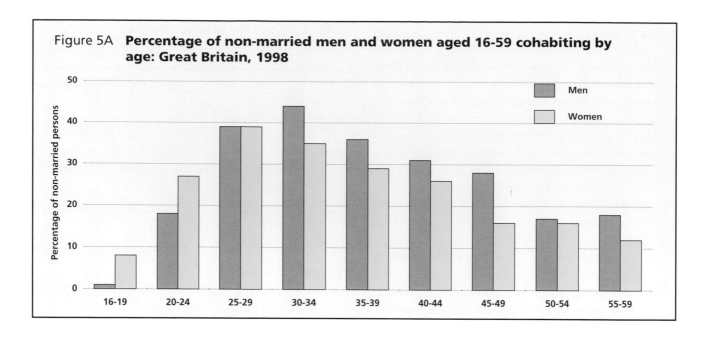

Figure 5A **Percentage of non-married men and women aged 16-59 cohabiting by age: Great Britain, 1998**

Cohabitation among women and the presence of children

Non-married women aged 16-59 with dependent children were more likely than those without dependent children to be cohabiting. In 1998:

- 30% of non-married women with dependent children were cohabiting, compared with 22% of non-married women without dependent children;
- two in five (40%) single women with dependent children were cohabiting, compared with slightly over one in five (21%) single women without dependent children. **Table 5.12**

Periods of cohabitation not leading to marriage

Since 1979, the GHS has asked women who are or have been married whether they cohabited prior to their current or most recent marriage; from 1989 these questions have been asked of men and women about each of their marriages. In 1998, for the first time, men and women aged 16-59 were asked whether they had ever lived as a couple with someone of the opposite sex, whom they had not subsequently married. These periods of completed cohabitation did not include the current relationship of respondents who were living as a couple at the time of interview. With the exception of those who chose the self-completion option, the majority of married and cohabiting respondents were interviewed in the presence of their partner; it is therefore possible that there was some under-reporting of previous cohabitations.

Figure 5B **Percentage of single, divorced and separated women* aged 18-49 cohabiting by legal marital status: Great Britain, 1979 to 1998**

* Widows have not been included because their numbers are so small

Among adults aged 16-59:

- 14% reported at least one cohabiting union that did not lead to marriage;
- 9% had only one such relationship, 3% two, and 2% three or more;
- a higher proportion of men than of women reported at least one cohabitation not leading to marriage; 15% and 13% respectively did so;
- the highest proportions reporting at least one such relationship were found among men and women aged between 25-34;
- almost a quarter of adults aged 25-29 reported a previous cohabiting union, compared with about one in 20 adults in the 50-59 age group.

During 1999, Social Survey Division carried out a programme of cognitive testing to explore the feasibility of extending the questions on cohabiting unions to collect information on the duration of such relationships. As a result of this work, which is reported on in full in the *Survey Methodology Bulletin*[3], new questions on duration will be included in the 2000/1 GHS.   **Table 5.13**

Previous cohabiting unions by marital status

The proportion of respondents reporting cohabiting unions that did not end in marriage varied by marital status for both men and women. Married respondents were less likely than others to report such relationships. Among those aged 16-59:

- 9% of married men reported at least one cohabitation not leading to marriage, compared with 28% of separated, 27% of divorced, 19% of single and 15% of cohabiting men;
- among women, 7% of married women said they had lived as a couple with a man whom they did not subsequently marry, compared with 26% of single, 23% of divorced and 20% of cohabiting women;
- 4% of divorced, cohabiting and single men reported three or more completed cohabiting relationships, compared with only 1% of married men.   **Table 5.14**

Notes and references

1. Respondents who were single, widowed, divorced or separated but who were cohabiting are here classified as cohabiting, rather than by their legal marital status.
2. 'Cohabiting' includes same sex cohabitees.
3. Lilly R. Developing questions on cohabitation histories. *Survey Methodology Bulletin*. No. 46. January 2000.

Table 5.1 **Sex by marital status**

All persons aged 16 and over   *Great Britain: 1998*

Marital status*	Men		Women	
	%		%	
Married	59		54	
Cohabiting	8		8	
Single	22		17	
Widowed	4		12	
Divorced	4 ⎤	6	7 ⎤	9
Separated	2 ⎦		3 ⎦	
Base = 100%	7531		8343	

* Marital status as recorded at the beginning of the interview.

Table 5.2 (a) Age by sex by marital status
(b) Marital status by sex by age

Persons aged 16 and over   *Great Britain: 1998*

Age	Marital status*						
	Married	Cohabiting	Single	Widowed	Divorced	Separated	Total
(a)	%	%	%	%	%	%	%
Men							
16-24	1	12	50	0	0	3	12
25-34	14	47	25	0	8	14	18
35-44	22	21	11	3	22	21	19
45-54	23	13	6	6	33	36	18
55-64	19	4	4	12	19	13	14
65-74	14	2	4	29	16	9	12
75 and over	8	0	1	51	3	3	7
Base = 100%	*4476*	*634*	*1665*	*316*	*306*	*116*	*7513*
	%	%	%	%	%	%	%
Women							
16-24	2	21	52	0	1	5	11
25-34	18	43	26	0	12	27	19
35-44	23	21	9	1	27	29	18
45-54	23	9	3	5	30	22	17
55-64	17	4	3	12	17	9	13
65-74	13	1	3	32	7	5	12
75 and over	5	0	4	50	6	4	10
Base = 100%	*4482*	*636*	*1408*	*1020*	*544*	*239*	*8329*
	%	%	%	%	%	%	%
Total							
16-24	1	17	51	0	0	4	12
25-34	16	45	25	0	10	23	19
35-44	22	21	10	1	25	26	18
45-54	23	11	4	5	32	26	17
55-64	18	4	4	12	18	10	13
65-74	14	1	3	31	10	6	12
75 and over	6	0	2	50	4	4	9
Base = 100%	*8958*	*1270*	*3073*	*1336*	*850*	*355*	*15842*

Age		Married	Cohabiting	Single	Widowed	Divorced	Separated	Base = 100%
(b)								
Men								
16-24	%	3	8	89	0	0	0	*937*
25-34	%	45	22	30	0	2	1	*1378*
35-44	%	70	10	13	1	5	2	*1394*
45-54	%	75	6	7	1	8	3	*1351*
55-64	%	80	3	7	4	5	1	*1041*
65-74	%	74	1	7	10	6	1	*873*
75 and over	%	65	1	3	30	1	1	*539*
Total	%	60	8	22	4	4	2	*7513*
Women								
16-24	%	7	14	77	0	0	1	*945*
25-34	%	51	17	23	0	4	4	*1559*
35-44	%	68	9	8	1	10	5	*1506*
45-54	%	74	4	3	4	12	4	*1409*
55-64	%	71	2	4	11	9	2	*1087*
65-74	%	57	1	4	33	4	1	*988*
75 and over	%	28	0	7	60	4	1	*835*
Total	%	54	8	17	12	7	3	*8329*
Total								
16-24	%	5	11	83	0	0	1	*1882*
25-34	%	48	19	27	0	3	3	*2937*
35-44	%	69	9	11	1	7	3	*2900*
45-54	%	74	5	5	2	10	3	*2760*
55-64	%	76	3	5	7	7	2	*2128*
65-74	%	65	1	6	22	5	1	*1861*
75 and over	%	42	0	5	48	3	1	*1374*
Total	%	57	8	19	8	5	2	*15842*

* Marital status as recorded at the beginning of the interview.

Table 5.3 **Cumulative percentages of men and women separated within a given period by year of marriage**

Persons born 1940-78 and first married aged under 30   *Great Britain: 1998*

| Year of marriage | Percentage of first marriages ending in separation within: | | | | Base = 100% |
	3 years	5 years	10 years	20 years	
Men					
1965-69	3	7	14*	25*	418
1970-74	6	10	19	29*	480
1975-79	7*	14	23*		365
1980-84	6	10*	20		331
1985-89	8	13*			362
Women					
1965-69	2	7	14*	26*	541
1970-74	5*	10	19*	32*	597
1975-79	7	13*	25		484
1980-84	7	14	26		480
1985-89	9	16			513

* Analysis was done using life table technique so that account could be taken of people who were widowed. The asterisked cells are those affected.

Table 5.4 **Cumulative percentages of women separated within a given period by age at, and year of, marriage**

Women born 1940-78 and first married aged under 30   *Great Britain: 1998*

| Age at marriage / Year of marriage | Percentage of first marriages ending in separation within: | | | | Base = 100% |
	3 years	5 years	10 years	20 years	
Less than 20					
1965-69	4	11	22	36*	171
1970-74	7*	13	26*	47*	201
1975-79	11	18*	32		142
1980-84	9	14	28		105
1985-89	10	24			91
20-24					
1965-69	2	6	10*	21*	340
1970-74	4	9	17	26*	323
1975-79	5	10	20		257
1980-84	6	13	26		288
1985-89	10	16			288
25-29					
1965-69	3	3	7	20*	30
1970-74	4	7	14	22*	73
1975-79	7	14	26		85
1980-84	7	16	26		87
1985-89	5	8			134

* See the footnote to Table 5.3.

Table 5.5 **Cumulative percentages of men remarried within a given period following separation, by year of separation**

Men aged 16-59 who were under 35 when
their first marriage ended in separation   *Great Britain: 1996 and 1998 combined*

Year of separation*		Percentages remarried within:							Base = 100%
		1 year	2 years	3 years	4 years	6 years	8 years	10 years	
1967-70	%	1	7	21	31	58	67	75	72
1969-72	%	1	14	28	38	62	71	75	118
1971-74	%	0	10	23	36	60	69	72	137
1973-76	%	1	8	23	33	52	62	66	143
1975-78	%	1	11	26	39	52	61	65	163
1977-80	%	3	10	24	38	54	64	67	182
1979-82	%	3	12	25	34	52	64	69	174
1981-84	%	1	12	27	34	54	62	68	157
1983-86	%	2	9	22	29	46	53		147
1985-88	%	2	8	20	28	42			160
1987-90	%	1	6	17	25				174
1989-92	%	0	3	12					151

* The groupings overlap in order to extend the trend series.

Table 5.6 **Cumulative percentages of women remarried within a given period following separation, by year of separation**

Women aged 16-59 who were under 35 when
their first marriage ended in separation   *Great Britain: 1996 and 1998 combined*

Year of separation*		Percentages remarried within:							Base = 100%
		1 year	2 years	3 years	4 years	6 years	8 years	10 years	
1967-70	%	1	9	20	29	49	55	64	87
1969-72	%	1	9	20	36	53	62	67	134
1971-74	%	1	9	21	34	52	63	70	199
1973-76	%	3	12	23	33	51	61	68	239
1975-78	%	4	15	22	31	48	57	62	231
1977-80	%	4	13	20	26	40	48	54	228
1979-82	%	3	10	19	26	39	47	53	214
1981-84	%	3	7	19	25	38	48	54	253
1983-86	%	1	7	16	25	36	44		297
1985-88	%	1	7	17	25	36			269
1987-90	%	1	6	16	22				284
1989-92	%	1	5	14					295

* See the footnote to Table 5.5.

Table 5.7 Percentage cohabiting by sex and age

Men and women aged 16-59   *Great Britain: 1998*

Age	Percentage cohabiting		Base = 100%	
	All	Non-married*	All	Non-married*
Men				
16-19	1	1	368	368
20-24	17	18	338	316
25-29	28	39	556	390
30-34	19	44	635	275
35-39	12	36	643	208
40-44	9	31	566	169
45-49	9	28	589	190
50-54	4	17	583	134
55-59	4	18	484	96
Total	12	26	4762	2146
Women				
16-19	8	8	377	372
20-24	23	27	431	373
25-29	23	39	698	410
30-34	14	35	773	310
35-39	10	29	805	266
40-44	9	26	632	216
45-49	5	16	651	183
50-54	4	16	672	177
55-59	3	12	536	148
Total	11	25	5575	2455

* Men and women describing themselves as 'separated' were, strictly speaking, legally married. However, because the separated can cohabit, they have been included in the 'non-married' category.

Table 5.8 Percentage cohabiting by legal marital status and age

Men and women aged 16-59   *Great Britain: 1996 and 1998 combined*

Legal marital status*	Percentage cohabiting					Bases = 100%				
	16-24	25-34	35-49	50-59	Total	16-24	25-34	35-49	50-59	Total
Men										
Married	-	-	-	-	-	53	1159	2683	1715	5610
Non-married										
Single	9	39	25	8	22	1536	1188	517	132	3373
Widowed	0	†	[14]	[6]	9	0	1	28	47	76
Divorced	†	54	39	27	38	1	106	383	208	698
Separated	†	27	27	22	25	6	55	134	55	250
(all non-married)	9	40	30	19	24					
Total	9	21	8	4	11	1596	2509	3745	2157	10007
Women										
Married	-	-	-	-	-	150	1645	3122	1793	6710
Non-married										
Single	18	37	24	7	25	1602	1068	358	109	3137
Widowed	0	†	5	4	5	0	7	73	149	229
Divorced	†	36	30	22	29	8	218	638	285	1149
Separated	[4]	12	9	10	10	26	145	215	73	459
(all non-married)	18	34	23	14	24					
Total	17	16	7	4	10	1786	3083	4406	2409	11684

* Men and women describing themselves as 'separated' were, strictly speaking, legally married. However, because the separated can cohabit they have been included in the 'non-married' category.

† Base too small to enable reliable analysis to be made.

67

Table 5.9 Cohabiters: age by sex

Cohabiting persons aged 16-59   *Great Britain: 1998*

Age	Men	Women
	%	%
16-19	1	5
20-24	10	16
25-29	28	26
30-34	22	18
35-39	13	13
40-44	9	9
45-49	10	5
50-54	4	5
55-59	3	3
Base = 100%	*556*	*607*

Table 5.10 Legal marital status of women aged 18-49: 1979 to 1998

Women aged 18-49   *Great Britain*

Legal marital status*	1979	1981	1983	1985	1989	1991	1993	1995	1996	1998
	%	%	%	%	%	%	%	%	%	%
Married	74	72	70	68	63	61	59	58	57	53
Non-married										
Single	18	20	21	22	26	26	28	28	29	30
Widowed	1	1	1	1	1	1	1	1	1	1
Divorced	4	5	6	6	7	8	9	9	9	11
Separated	3	3	2	3	3	3	4	4	4	5
Base = 100%	*6006*	*6524*	*5285*	*5364*	*5483*	*5359*	*5171*	*4953*	*4695*	*4181*

* See the first footnote to Table 5.8.

Table 5.11 Percentage of women aged 18-49 cohabiting by legal marital status: 1979 to 1998

Women aged 18-49   *Great Britain*

Legal marital status*	1979	1981	1985	1989	1991	1993	1995	1996	1998
				Percentage cohabiting					
Married	-	-	-	-	-	-	-	-	-
Non-married									
Single	8	9	14	19	23	23	26	28	31
Widowed	0	6	5	9	2	[8]	[8]	[5]	[8]
Divorced	20	20	21	30	30	25	27	31	31
Separated	17	19	20	17	13	11	11	7	12
(Non-married total)	*11*	*12*	*16*	*21*	*23*	*22*	*25*	*26*	*29*
Total	3	3	5	8	9	9	10	11	13
Bases = 100%									
Married	*4461*	*4674*	*3653*	*3457*	*3265*	*3053*	*2864*	*2683*	*2234*
Non-married									
Single	*1061*	*1303*	*1175*	*1433*	*1416*	*1431*	*1405*	*1361*	*1268*
Widowed	*61*	*66*	*55*	*55*	*55*	*49*	*40*	*44*	*36*
Divorced	*256*	*314*	*338*	*387*	*448*	*453*	*437*	*421*	*443*
Separated	*167*	*167*	*143*	*151*	*175*	*185*	*206*	*186*	*200*
Total	*6006*	*6524*	*5364*	*5483*	*5359*	*5171*	*4952*	*4695*	*4181*

* See the first footnote to Table 5.8.

† Base too small to enable reliable analysis to be made.

Table 5.12 **Women aged 16-59: percentage cohabiting by legal marital status and whether has dependent children in the household**

Women aged 16-59   *Great Britain: 1998*

Legal marital status	Percentage cohabiting			Bases = 100%		
	Has dependent children	No dependent children	Total	Has dependent children	No dependent children	Total*
Married	-	-	-	1657	1458	3117
Non-married						
Single	40	21	26	373	1120	1503
Widowed	[13]	2	5	23	82	105
Divorced	28	30	29	279	319	601
Separated	10	13	11	157	89	246
	30	22	24			
Total	10	11	11	2489	3068	5572

* Totals with dependent children and without dependent children do not sum to the total because the dependency of some children could not be established.

† Base too small to enable reliable analysis to be made.

Table 5.13 **Number of periods of cohabitation not leading to marriage by sex and age**

Men and women aged 16-59   *Great Britain: 1998*

Age		Number of periods of cohabitation					Base = 100%
		None	One	Two	Three or more	Total at least one	
Men							
16-19	%	99	1	0	0	1	368
20-24	%	86	9	3	2	14	338
25-29	%	77	17	5	2	23	555
30-34	%	77	13	6	4	23	631
35-39	%	80	13	4	4	20	643
40-44	%	85	9	4	2	15	565
45-49	%	87	8	4	2	13	588
50-54	%	93	5	0	1	7	583
55-59	%	93	4	2	1	7	483
Total	%	85	9	3	2	15	4754
Women							
16-19	%	95	4	1	0	5	377
20-24	%	82	13	3	2	18	428
25-29	%	77	17	4	2	23	698
30-34	%	78	16	4	2	22	772
35-39	%	83	13	3	1	17	803
40-44	%	88	7	3	1	12	631
45-49	%	91	6	2	1	9	649
50-54	%	95	4	1	0	5	670
55-59	%	97	2	0	1	3	535
Total	%	87	10	3	1	13	5563
All							
16-19	%	97	3	0	0	3	745
20-24	%	84	11	3	2	16	766
25-29	%	77	17	4	2	23	1253
30-34	%	78	15	5	3	22	1403
35-39	%	82	13	3	2	18	1446
40-44	%	87	8	3	2	13	1196
45-49	%	89	7	3	1	11	1237
50-54	%	94	4	1	1	6	1253
55-59	%	95	3	1	1	5	1018
Total	%	86	9	3	2	14	10317

Table 5.14 **Number of periods of cohabitation not leading to marriage by marital status and sex**

Men and women aged 16-59   *Great Britain: 1998*

Number of cohabitations	Marital status						
	Married	Non-married					
		Cohabiting	Single	Widowed	Divorced	Separated	Total
Men							
None	91	75	81	[87]	73	72	85
One	6	15	11	[13]	17	13	9
Two	1	5	5	[0]	7	8	3
Three or more	1	4	4	[0]	4	7	2
Total at least one	9	15	19	[13]	27	28	15
Base = 100%	*2623*	*534*	*1242*	*38*	*212*	*89*	*4754*
Women							
None	93	80	74	95	77	87	87
One	5	15	18	5	16	11	10
Two	1	4	6	0	5	1	3
Three or more	0	2	2	0	2	0	1
Total at least one	7	20	26	5	23	13	13
Base = 100%	*3136*	*586*	*1099*	*104*	*420*	*206*	*5563*

* Total includes a small number of same sex cohabitees.

6 Occupational and personal pension schemes

Over the 20 years between 1976 and 1996, the latest year for which figures are available, life expectancy at birth in the United Kingdom increased from 69.6 to 74.3 for males and from 75.2 to 79.5 for females[1]. During the same period, the proportion of people aged 50 and over in employment has been steadily falling. In 1975, among men, 93% of the 50-59 age group and 81% of those aged 60-64 were working. By 1996, this had fallen to 76% and 39% respectively. There has been very little change for women; 59% of the 50-59 age group and 29% of those aged 60-64 were working in 1975, while the corresponding proportions in 1996 were 58% and 22%[2]. The combination of these two trends means that people, on average, have a longer period of retirement than formerly; assuming a retirement age of 55-60, men will spend an average of 15-20 years, and women an average of 20-25 years in retirement.

Against this background, ensuring that people have made financial provision for their retirement assumes increasing importance. The Government has outlined plans in a recent Green Paper[3] to replace SERPS (State Earnings Related Pension Scheme) with the new Second State Pension from April 2002 for those with low to moderate earnings up to £20,000 a year. All contributing employees earning less than £9,000 a year (but, as now, above the National Insurance Lower Earnings Limit) would be treated in the new Second State Pension as if they had earnings at that level. This will mean a rise in pension entitlement for this group of employees. Carers and long-term disabled people who are off work will receive 'credits' towards the Second State Pension. The Government also proposes to introduce Stakeholder Pension Schemes from April 2001 aimed at people earning about £9,000-£20,000 a year. For employees, these will be a means of contracting out of SERPS or the new Second State Pension.

The GHS has collected information on occupational pensions since 1971, although the questions have not been asked every year. Questions on personal pensions were introduced in 1987. This chapter presents information on occupational and personal pensions for employees and for the self-employed.

Pension scheme membership[4] among employees

All employees, in addition to paying National Insurance contributions towards a basic state pension, must currently contribute to a second-tier pension, SERPS, unless they opt out and make alternative provision. This can either be through an occupational scheme or a personal pension

arrangement. In 1998, among employees, 72% of men and 64% of women working full time and 15%[5] of men and 34% of women working part time were members of an occupational scheme or had personal pension arrangements at the time of interview. Some had both types of pension. Looked at another way, this means that more than a quarter of the men and over a third of the women who were employed full time, and over four-fifths of the men and almost two-thirds of the women employed part time were making no pension provision beyond the basic state pension or SERPS. It should be noted that the questions asked about respondents' current employer; some respondents who were not currently members of a scheme may have held entitlements in schemes to which they formerly contributed.   **Table 6.1**

Membership of current employer's pension scheme

The likelihood of belonging to an employer's pension scheme varied with sex, age, and employment circumstances. Working full time, in a professional occupation, in a large organisation, being with the same employer for five or more years and having a high income all increased the likelihood of belonging to a pension scheme.

- Among those working full time, 57% of men and 56% of women said they belonged to the scheme run by their current employer. This compares with only 9% of male and 27% of women part-time employees who belonged to their employer's scheme.
- The likelihood of belonging to an occupational scheme was lowest among those aged under 25. For example, among the 18-24 age group, 20% of men and 25% of women working full time and 5% of women working part time belonged to their employer's scheme.
- Men and women aged 35-54 were most likely to belong to their employer's scheme; about two-thirds of those working full time and about a third of women working part time did so.
- Part-time employees were more likely than full-time workers to work for an employer who did not have a pension scheme. They were also more likely not to belong to a scheme when one did exist. Among women, for example, whereas 45% of part-time employees said their employer did not have a pension scheme, the corresponding proportion among full-time women workers was 26%. Similarly, 26% of part-time, but only 17% of full-time women employees did not belong to the occupational scheme run by their employer   **Table 6.2, Figure 6A**

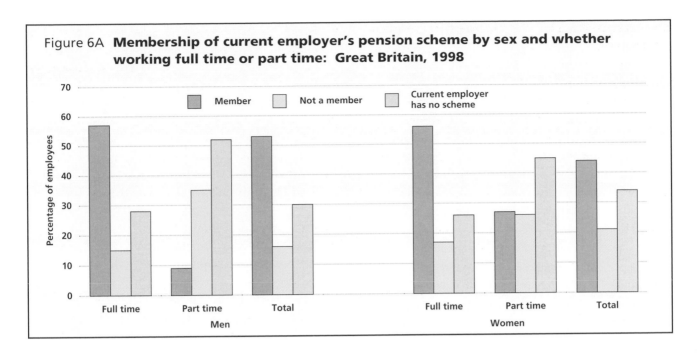

Figure 6A **Membership of current employer's pension scheme by sex and whether working full time or part time: Great Britain, 1998**

Trends in membership of occupational pension schemes

Personal pension arrangements were introduced in July 1988 to replace retirement annuities. They are available to employees and the self-employed. Employees can opt out of an employer's occupational scheme and contribute to a personal pension. Previously those not in an occupational scheme could arrange to pay for a personal pension plan but they could not leave SERPS. Furthermore, members of occupational schemes which are not contracted out of SERPS can now contract out of the state scheme individually. Personal pension arrangements for those who have contracted out of SERPS receive contributions from the DSS which represent the difference between the full National Insurance rate and the lower contracted-out rate. As a result of these changes to the rules, the time series shown in Table 6.3 is not strictly comparable from 1988 with previous years.

Trends in membership of occupational schemes have varied since 1988 for male and female, full- and part-time employees.

- Whereas the proportion of full-time male employees belonging to their employer's scheme has declined from 64% to 57% during this period, among full-time women workers, there is no reliable statistical evidence of a change over time, with the proportions belonging to a scheme ranging from 53% to 56%.

- Among women working part time, however, the likelihood of participating in their employer's scheme has more than doubled from 12% in 1988 to 27% in 1998. Table 6.4 shows that this increase, which has been particularly marked after 1994, reflects an increase in the proportion of women joining a scheme provided by their employer, rather than an increase in the proportion of employers providing such a scheme, which has remained at just over half for most of the period. **Tables 6.3-6.4**

Personal pension arrangements among employees

In 1998, about one in four full-time male employees, one in six full-time female employees and one in ten women working part time was making personal pension arrangements. As with occupational pensions, the likelihood of making such arrangements varied with age, with the pattern of association resembling an inverted U-shaped curve. **Table 6.1**

- The youngest and oldest age groups were least likely to report making personal pension arrangements. For example, among those employed full time, about one in three men and about one in five women aged 25-44 had personal pension arrangements. This compares with one in ten men and one in 20 women in the 18-24 age group and about one in five men and one in 12 women aged 55 and over.

Characteristics of employees in pension schemes

Socio-economic group

There were marked differences in the proportions of respondents from different socio-economic groups who currently either belonged to their employer's occupational scheme or had personal pension arrangements. In order to provide sufficient data for analysis, information for three years[6] has been analysed by socio-economic group. In 1995-1998 combined, a higher proportion of non-manual workers than of manual workers had either occupational or personal pension arrangements; the proportion being lower in the junior non-manual group than among other non-manual workers. Full-time professional employees were approximately twice as likely as those in the unskilled manual group to be covered by a pension scheme at the time of interview. Among women working part time, professional employees were almost four times as likely as those in the unskilled manual group to be members of a scheme.

- Among full-time male employees, 75% of the professional group, but only 37% of the unskilled manual group, were members of their employer's pension scheme. The corresponding proportions for those making personal pension arrangements were 28% and 18% respectively.
- 69% of full-time women workers in professional occupations, compared with 29% in unskilled manual occupations belonged to an occupational scheme.

Twenty two per cent and 16% respectively were contributing to a personal pension.

Table 6.5, Figure 6B

Earnings

The likelihood of belonging to a pension scheme increased with respondents' usual gross weekly earnings. Sixty nine per cent[7] of those earning £200 a week or less, which includes the group which stand to benefit most under the State Second Pension proposals, were neither members of an occupational pension scheme nor contributing to a personal pension at the time of interview. This figure was almost exactly reversed among respondents earning between £200 and £400 a week, which includes most of those at whom the Stakeholder Pensions are currently aimed; among this group, 72% either belonged to an occupational scheme or were making personal pension arrangements. Among those earning more than £400 per week, 90% either belonged to an occupational scheme or were making personal pension arrangements.

- Among those employed full time, whereas only 20% of men and 28% of women earning between £100 and £200 a week belonged to their employer's pension scheme, over 75% and over 80% respectively of those earning more than £400 a week did so.
- Lower earners were also less likely to be making personal pension arrangements; just over one in eight of those earning £100-£200 a week were, compared with approximately three in ten men and two in ten women with weekly earnings of more than £400.

Table 6.6

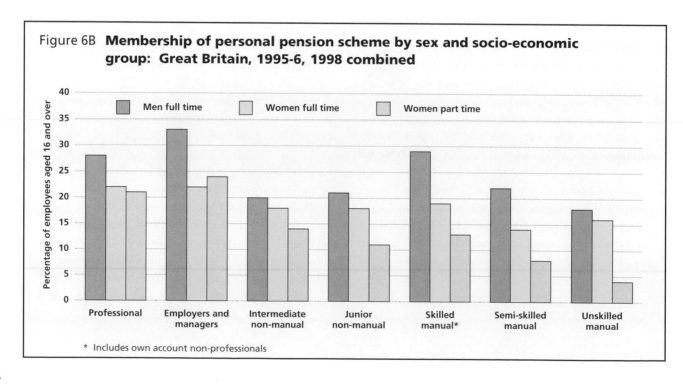

Figure 6B **Membership of personal pension scheme by sex and socio-economic group: Great Britain, 1995-6, 1998 combined**

Percentage of employees aged 16 and over

Men full time Women full time Women part time

Professional | Employers and managers | Intermediate non-manual | Junior non-manual | Skilled manual* | Semi-skilled manual | Unskilled manual

* Includes own account non-professionals

Length of time with current employer

Respondents who had worked for their current employer for five years or more were two to three times as likely as those who had been with the same employer for less than two years to belong to the employer's pension scheme. For example:

- among those working full time, three-quarters of men and women who had been with their current employer for five years or more were members of an occupational pension scheme, compared with nearly a third of those who had worked for their present employer for less than two years;

- 41% of part-time women employees with more than five years service with their present employer, but only 12% of those who had been with the employer for less than two years, belonged to the employer's scheme.

There was no association between the length of time spent with the current employer and the likelihood of making personal pension arrangements. **Table 6.7**

Size of establishment

The likelihood of belonging to an occupational pension scheme increased with the size of the establishment at which respondents were employed.

- Among men working full time, the proportion belonging to their employer's scheme increased from 34% of those working in establishments with 3-24 employees to 85% of those in firms of 1,000 or more.

- The corresponding proportions for women were 38% and 77% respectively.

Only among men working full time was making personal pension arrangements associated with size of establishment, with those working in small firms most likely to report being members. For example, one in three men in firms with less than 25 employees were making such arrangements, compared with one in seven of those in establishments of 1,000 or more. **Table 6.8**

Industry group

As with socio-economic group, three years data have been combined to provide sufficient numbers for analysis by industry group. Sample sizes in some groups, such as mining (excluding coal), manufacture of metals, minerals and chemicals, are still small and the results should therefore be treated with caution[8].

The highest proportion of respondents belonging to an occupational pension scheme was among those working in public and other personal services[9]; 81% of men and 68% of women working full time and 34% of women working part time in this sector were members of their employer's scheme.

Apart from agriculture, forestry and fishing, which had very small sample sizes, the distribution, hotels, catering and repairs sector had the lowest proportion belonging to an employer's scheme. Thirty seven per cent of men and 34% of women working full time, and 13% of women employed part time, were members of such a scheme. **Table 6.9**

Personal pension arrangements among the self-employed

Self-employed people, like employees, must pay National Insurance contributions towards a basic state pension. Unlike employees, however, they cannot contribute to SERPS; the only second pension choice for them is a personal pension, although many self-employed people make some provision for their retirement through other savings vehicles and investments[10]. As among employees, the likelihood of making personal pension arrangements was greater among self-employed respondents working full time than among those working part time.

- 65% of male and 53% of female self-employed respondents who were working full time were making personal pension arrangements, compared with 22% and 17% respectively of those working part time.

- Almost half of men and almost three-quarters of women who were working part time had never belonged to a personal pension scheme.

It is possible, although data are not available to confirm this, that some of the self-employed had previously worked as employees and belonged to an occupational scheme.

The likelihood of having personal pension arrangements was also associated with the length of time spent in self-employment. A higher proportion of men who had been self-employed for five years or more than of other men were contributing to a personal pension; in the three years 1995-6 and 1998, 71% of men in this group who were working full-time were, compared with less than half of those who had been self-employed for less than five years.

75

Self-employed full-time women were almost twice as likely to be making arrangements for a personal pension if they had been self-employed for five or more years than women who had been self-employed for less than two years.

Tables 6.10-6.11

Notes and references

1. Table 5.1 Expectation of life (in years) at birth and selected ages. *Population Trends*, 97 Autumn 1999. Figures are not available for Great Britain, the coverage area of the GHS. The figures for England and Wales rose from 69.9 for males and 76.0 for females in 1976 to 74.6 and 79.7 respectively in 1996. In Scotland, life expectancy at birth increased from 68.2 for males and 72.2 for females in 1976 to 74.4 and 77.8 respectively in 1996. The figures for 1996 are provisional.

2. See Table 5.10 in Thomas M et al. *Living in Britain: results from the 1996 General Household Survey*. The Stationery Office London 1998. It should be noted that the Labour Force Survey is the main source of data on employment. GHS figures have been cited to allow changes over time to be commented on.

3. Department of Social Security. *A new contract for welfare: partnership in pensions*. Cm 4179 London The Stationery Office 1998.

4. The figures shown in Table 6.1 for current pension scheme membership in 1996 and 1998 are lower than in previous years because, prior to 1996, the proportion of employees who were members of an occupational pension and the proportion with a personal pension were added together, not taking into account individuals who may have been contributing to both.

5. Figures for part-time male employees are not shown on Table 6.1, as the bases are too small to analyse by age.

6. There was no fieldwork for the GHS in 1997/8. Data for 1995, 1996 and 1998 have been combined to produce Table 6.5.

7. The proportion rises to 71% if men working part time are included in the total.

8. For example, the 95% confidence interval for the proportion (46%) of men employed full time in this group is 35-57%.

9. This group includes public administration, education, health and welfare, and personal services.

10. *Welfare Reform and Pensions Bill - Factsheet 2.*

Table 6.1 **Current pension scheme membership by age and sex**

Employees aged 16 and over excluding YT and ET   *Great Britain: 1998*

Pension scheme members	Age						Total
	16-17	18-24	25-34	35-44	45-54	55 and over	
				Percentages			
Men full time							
Occupational pension*	4	20	54	67	69	55	57
Personal pension	0	10	31	29	24	19	25
Any pension	4	28	73	84	81	67	72
Women full time							
Occupational pension*	8	25	58	67	64	59	56
Personal pension	0	5	20	18	14	8	15
Any pension	8	28	69	76	72	62	64
Women part time							
Occupational pension*	1	5	29	35	31	20	27
Personal pension	0	1	16	10	8	8	9
Any pension	1	6	42	43	36	25	34
Bases=100%							
Men full time	*54*	*368*	*991*	*1013*	*859*	*412*	*3697*
Women full time	*25*	*314*	*641*	*558*	*536*	*170*	*2244*
Women part time	*79*	*117*	*372*	*460*	*381*	*265*	*1674*

* Including a few people who were not sure if they were in a scheme but thought it possible.

Table 6.2 **Membership of current employer's pension scheme by sex and whether working full time or part time**

Employees aged 16 and over excluding YT and ET   *Great Britain: 1998*

Pension scheme coverage	Men			Women		
	Working full time	Working part time	Total*	Working full time	Working part time	Total*
	%	%	%	%	%	%
Present employer has a pension scheme						
Member†	57	9	53	56	27	44
Not a member	15 | 72	35 | 44	16 | 69	17 | 73	26 | 53	21 | 65
Does not know if a member	0	0	0	0	0	0
Present employer does not have a pension scheme	28	52	30	26	45	34
Does not know if present employer has a pension scheme - not a member	1	4	1	0	2	1
Base = 100%	*3697*	*342*	*4050*	*2244*	*1674*	*3922*

* Including a few people whose hours of work were not known.
† Including a few people who were not sure if they were in a scheme but thought it possible.

Table 6.3 **Membership of current employer's pension scheme by sex: 1975 to 1998**

Employees aged 16 and over excluding YT and ET*　　　　　　　　　　　　　　　　　　　　　　　　　　　　*Great Britain*

Pension scheme members†	1975	1979	1983	1987	1988	1989	1991	1992	1993	1994	1995	1996	1998
						Percentages							
Full-time													
Men	63	68	66	63	64	64	61	62	60	60	58	58	57
Women	47	55	55	52	54	55	55	54	54	53	55	53	56
Total	59	65	61	59	61	61	59	59	58	58	57	56	57
Women part-time employees	..	..	13	11	12	15	17	19	19	19	24	26	27
Bases = 100%													
Full-time													
Men	*7321*	*6887*	*5087*	*5129*	*4941*	*4906*	*4563*	*4313*	*3976*	*4006*	*4062*	*3937*	*3697*
Women	*2772*	*2324*	*2256*	*2562*	*2595*	*2602*	*2484*	*2396*	*2239*	*2345*	*2331*	*2143*	*2244*
Total	*10093*	*9211*	*7343*	*7691*	*7536*	*7508*	*7047*	*6709*	*6215*	*6351*	*6393*	*6080*	*5941*
Women part-time employees	*..*	*..*	*1638*	*2126*	*2015*	*2102*	*1977*	*2067*	*1938*	*1930*	*2038*	*1908*	*1674*

* Prior to 1985 full-time students are excluded. Figures for 1987-1993 include full-time students who were working but exclude those on Government schemes. This represents a re-classification from that used in the GHS 1987 and 1988 reports. Figures for 1987 and 1988 have been re-calculated accordingly and may therefore differ from previously published data.

† Including a few people who were not sure if they were in a scheme but thought it possible.

Table 6.4 **Membership of current employer's pension scheme by sex: 1983 to 1998**

Employees aged 16 and over excluding YT and ET*   *Great Britain*

Pension scheme coverage	1983	1987	1988	1989	1991	1992	1993	1994	1995	1996	1998
	%	%	%	%	%	%	%	%	%	%	%
Men full time											
Present employer has a pension scheme											
Member†	66	63	64	64	61	62	60	60	58	58	57
Not a member	10 |77	12 |74	13 |78	14 |79	16 |77	15 |77	16 |76	15 |75	16 |74	16 |74	15 |72
Does not know if a member	1	0	0	0	1	0	0	0	0	0	0
Present employer does not have a pension scheme	22	22	19	19	21	21	22	24	25	25	28
Does not know if present employer has a pension scheme - not a member	2	3	3	2	2	2	2	1	1	1	1
Base = 100%	*5087*	*5129*	*4941*	*4906*	*4563*	*4313*	*3976*	*4006*	*4062*	*3937*	*3697*
	%	%	%	%	%	%	%	%	%	%	%
Women full time											
Present employer has a pension scheme											
Member†	55	52	54	55	55	54	54	53	55	53	56
Not a member	17 |72	16 |68	19 |74	21 |76	21 |77	22 |77	22 |77	19 |73	20 |76	20 |73	17 |73
Does not know if a member	0	1	0	0	0	0	0	0	0	0	0
Present employer does not have a pension scheme	24	28	23	21	20	21	22	27	24	26	26
Does not know if present employer has a pension scheme - not a member	4	4	3	3	3	2	2	1	1	1	0
Base = 100%	*2256*	*2562*	*2595*	*2602*	*2484*	*2396*	*2239*	*2345*	*2331*	*2143*	*2244*
	%	%	%	%	%	%	%	%	%	%	%
Women part time											
Present employer has a pension scheme											
Member†	13	11	12	15	17	19	19	19	24	26	27
Not a member	39 |53	34 |46	35 |48	37 |52	34 |52	34 |54	35 |55	33 |52	32 |55	28 |53	26 |53
Does not know if a member	0	0	0	0	1	0	0	0	0	0	0
Present employer does not have a pension scheme	40	44	42	40	39	39	38	45	42	44	45
Does not know if present employer has a pension scheme - not a member	7	10	9	7	8	7	7	3	3	2	2
Base = 100%	*1638*	*2126*	*2015*	*2102*	*1977*	*2067*	*1938*	*1930*	*2038*	*1908*	*1674*

* See the footnotes to Table 6.3.
†

Table 6.5 **Current pension scheme membership by sex and socio-economic group**

Employees aged 16 and over excluding YT and ET   *Great Britain: 1995-6, 1998 combined*

Pension scheme members	Socio-economic group†							
	Professional	Employers and managers	Intermediate non-manual	Junior non-manual	Skilled manual and own account non-professional	Semi-skilled manual and personal service	Unskilled manual	Total
	Percentages							
Men full time								
Occupational pension*	75	67	71	61	47	45	37	58
Personal pension	28	33	20	21	29	22	18	27
Any pension	91	86	83	74	69	61	49	75
Women full time								
Occupational pension*	69	64	70	51	40	31	29	55
Personal pension	22	22	18	18	19	14	16	18
Any pension	79	76	79	63	54	43	40	66
Women part time								
Occupational pension*	52	39	46	27	19	20	13	25
Personal pension	21	24	14	11	13	8	4	10
Any pension	66	56	56	36	30	26	17	33
Bases=100%								
Men full time	991	2728	1325	1045	3263	1722	399	11696
Women full time	242	1223	1697	2000	301	1064	80	6718
Women part time	56	211	841	2002	149	1253	666	5620

* Including a few people who were not sure if they were in a scheme but thought it possible.

† Members of the Armed Forces, full-time students and those who have never worked are not shown as separate categories but are included in the figures for all persons.

Table 6.6 **Current pension scheme membership by sex and usual gross weekly earnings: all employees**

Employees aged 16 and over excluding YT and ET   *Great Britain: 1998*

Pension scheme members	Usual gross weekly earnings (£)							
	0.01-100.00	100.01-200.00	200.01-300.00	300.01-400.00	400.01-500.00	500.01-600.00	600.01 or more	Total†
	Percentages							
Men full time								
Occupational pension*	[22]	20	44	62	74	76	80	57
Personal pension	[7]	13	24	28	29	23	32	25
Any pension	[24]	28	62	80	90	89	93	72
Women full time								
Occupational pension*	22	28	58	76	84	81	88	56
Personal pension	5	11	17	16	18	14	29	15
Any pension	24	38	69	83	90	88	93	64
Women part time								
Occupational pension*	15	43	73	[67]	**	**	**	27
Personal pension	6	14	15	[12]	**	**	**	9
Any pension	20	52	80	[75]	**	**	**	34
Bases=100%								
Men full time	45	342	747	635	470	314	398	3697
Women full time	74	531	597	356	216	90	90	2244
Women part time	956	400	91	24	6	5	4	1674

* Including a few people who were not sure if they were in a scheme but thought it possible.

† Totals include no answers to income.

** Base too small to enable reliable analysis to be made.

Table 6.7 **Current pension scheme membership by sex and length of time with current employer**

Employees aged 16 and over excluding YT and ET   *Great Britain: 1998*

Pension scheme members	Length of time with current employer			
	Less than 2 years	2 years, but less than 5 years	5 years or more	Total†
	Percentages			
Men full time				
Occupational pension*	28	47	75	57
Personal pension	23	28	25	25
Any pension	45	66	88	72
Women full time				
Occupational pension*	32	49	74	56
Personal pension	12	15	17	15
Any pension	41	58	81	64
Women part time				
Occupational pension*	12	26	41	27
Personal pension	8	12	9	9
Any pension	19	35	47	34
Bases=100%				
Men full time	*1022*	*660*	*1987*	*3697*
Women full time	*668*	*429*	*1132*	*2244*
Women part time	*640*	*306*	*720*	*1674*

* Including a few people who were not sure if they were in a scheme but thought it possible.

† Including a few where length of time in job was not known.

Table 6.8 **Current pension scheme membership by sex and number of employees in the establishment**

Employees aged 16 and over excluding YT and ET   *Great Britain: 1998*

Pension scheme members	Number of employees at establishment					
	1-2	3-24	25-99	100-999	1000 or more	Total†
	Percentages					
Men full time						
Occupational pension*	40	34	52	70	85	57
Personal pension	35	31	27	22	14	25
Any pension	61	59	68	80	88	72
Women full time						
Occupational pension*	26	38	59	66	77	56
Personal pension	15	16	15	15	12	15
Any pension	38	50	66	72	81	64
Women part time						
Occupational pension*	6	17	28	42	60	27
Personal pension	12	10	8	10	11	9
Any pension	17	26	34	47	64	34
Bases=100%						
Men full time	*102*	*913*	*991*	*1248*	*384*	*3697*
Women full time	*68*	*600*	*622*	*686*	*248*	*2244*
Women part time	*95*	*669*	*443*	*357*	*85*	*1674*

* Including a few people who were not sure if they were in a scheme but thought it possible.

† Includes a few people for whom the number of employees at establishment was not known.

Table 6.9 Current pension scheme membership by sex and industry group

Employees aged 16 and over excluding YT and ET   *Great Britain: 1995-6, 98 combined*

Pension scheme members	Industry group†										
	Agriculture, forestry, fishing	Coal mining, energy and water supply	Mining (excl coal), manufact-ure of metals, minerals and chemicals	Metal goods, engineer-ing and vehicle	Other manufact-uring	Construc-tion	Distribu-tion, hotels, catering repairs	Transport and commun-ications	Banking, finance, insurance business services	Public and other personal services	Total
					Percentages						
Men full time											
Occupational pension*	24	70	46	58	54	44	37	61	58	81	58
Personal pension	43	25	34	28	27	34	31	23	32	14	27
Any pension	59	83	72	77	72	69	60	75	77	87	75
Women full time											
Occupational pension*	[26]	67	**	48	44	51	34	55	52	68	55
Personal pension	[21]	18	**	21	19	22	21	14	24	15	18
Any pension	[45]	77	**	61	57	65	49	64	66	76	66
Women part time											
Occupational pension*	12	**	**	21	23	18	13	35	28	34	25
Personal pension	10	**	**	16	11	15	8	8	15	10	10
Any pension	22	**	**	34	32	33	20	40	40	41	33
Bases = 100%											
Men full time	203	263	103	1859	1891	948	1613	1031	1518	2245	11674
Women full time	47	66	16	397	863	104	980	250	1151	2835	6709
Women part time	50	14	7	125	432	72	1770	155	575	2412	5612

*   Including a few people who were not sure if they were in a scheme but thought it possible.

†   Standard Industrial Classification, 1992.

** Base too small for reliable analysis to be made.

Table 6.10 Membership of personal pension scheme by sex and whether working full time or part time: self-employed persons

Self-employed persons aged 16 and over   *Great Britain: 1998*

Pension scheme coverage	Men			Women		
	Working full time	Working part time	Total*	Working full time	Working part time	Total*
	%	%	%	%	%	%
Informant belongs to a personal pension scheme	65	22	59	53	17	34
Informant no longer has a personal pension scheme	10	31	13	6	9	8
Informant has never had a personal pension scheme	26	46	29	40	74	58
Base = 100%	683	108	796	141	157	302

* Including a few people whose hours of work were not known.

Table 6.11 **Membership of personal pension scheme by sex and length of time in self-employment**

Self-employed persons aged 16 and over   *Great Britain: 1995-6, 1998 combined*

	Length of time in self-employment			
	Less than 2 years	2 years, but less than 5 years	5 years or more	Total
	Percentage of self-employed who belong to a personal pension scheme			
Men full time	36	51	71	63
Women full time	28	44	52	45
Women part time	11	17	31	22
Bases = 100%				
Men full time	*300*	*362*	*1584*	*2246*
Women full time	*98*	*88*	*272*	*458*
Women part time	*135*	*133*	*275*	*543*

7 General health, use of health services and hearing

The GHS has included a series of questions about health and about the use of health services since its inception in 1971. Although periodic changes have been made to the content of the health section, it is possible to monitor changes in health over a period of almost 30 years. This chapter presents information on self-reported health, the use of health services and hearing.

Self-reported sickness

The GHS includes two measures of self-reported sickness:

- chronic sickness - respondents aged 16 and over are asked whether they have any longstanding illness or disability which has troubled them for some time. This question has been included in the GHS in its present form since 1972. Information about children is collected from a responsible adult, usually the mother. Those who report a longstanding condition, either on their own behalf or that of their children, are asked whether it limits their activities in any way. This question has been asked since 1975;

- acute sickness - respondents are asked whether they had to cut down on their normal activities in the two weeks prior to interview as a result of illness or injury. Information from these questions is used to estimate the average number of days of restricted activity in the last year.

Chronic sickness

In 1998, 33% of males and 34% of females reported a longstanding condition, while 19% of males and 21% of females said they had a condition which limited their activities in some way.   **Table 7.1, Figure 7A**

Not surprisingly, the likelihood of reporting a chronic condition, whether limiting or not, increased with age.

- The prevalence of longstanding illnesses, disabilities or infirmities increased from 15% of the 0-4 age group to 66% of those aged 75 and over;
- the proportion reporting a limiting condition increased from only 4% of children aged under 5 to 50% of adults in the 75 and over age group;
- the increase in prevalence was particularly marked after the age of 44. Whereas about one in five respondents aged under 45 reported a longstanding illness, over one in two of those aged 45 and over did so. Roughly one in ten respondents aged 0-44 reported a limiting longstanding illness, compared with about a third of older respondents.

Further strengthening this clear association with age, evidence from other surveys suggests that older people are likely to under-report chronic conditions. Among those aged 65 and over, a proportion of those who are assessed as having a disability[1] or who report difficulties with activities of daily living[2,3], nevertheless say they have no chronic illness or disability. It appears that elderly people regard limitations in their daily activities as a normal part of growing old, not as evidence of illness or disability. Among people aged 65 and over in the 1998 GHS sample, a small proportion of those not reporting a longstanding illness said they could not manage at least one locomotion activity unaided (table not shown).

The prevalence of longstanding illness has increased over the lifetime of the GHS. Whereas 21% of respondents reported a chronic condition in 1972, the corresponding

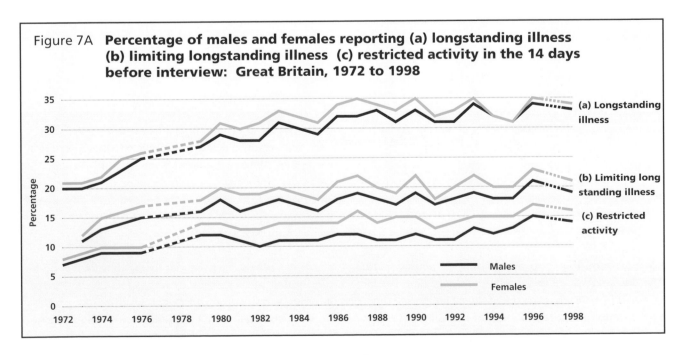

Figure 7A   **Percentage of males and females reporting (a) longstanding illness (b) limiting longstanding illness (c) restricted activity in the 14 days before interview: Great Britain, 1972 to 1998**

proportion in 1998 was 33%. The likelihood of reporting such a condition increased steadily during the 1970s, and has since ranged from 29% to 35%, with no clear pattern over time. The increase in the prevalence of limiting conditions is less marked; whereas the increase in all chronic conditions was nine percentage points, from 24% to 33%, between 1975 and 1998, the prevalence of limiting conditions increased by only five percentage points, from 15% to 20%, during the same period.

It should be noted that reports of chronic sickness are based on respondents' own assessments; increases in prevalence may reflect increased expectations which people have about their health as well as changes in the actual prevalence of sickness. It should also be remembered that some people are more troubled by a certain kind of symptom than others, and that the need to limit activities will depend on what people usually do.

The 1996 GHS included a set of questions measuring self-reported functional ability, known as the EuroQol questionnaire. The prevalence of longstanding illness was higher in 1996 than in 1995; it was argued in the 1996 report that the inclusion of these questions may have affected the reporting of chronic conditions[4]. The 1998 data appear to support this hypothesis. Prevalence was lower in 1998 than in 1996, and appears more in line with previous trends. Furthermore, the increase in 1996 was only apparent among adults, to whom the EuroQol questions were addressed. Children under 16, about whom the questions were not asked, did not show the same increase in prevalence in 1996.

Acute sickness
In 1998, 14% of males and 16% of females reported an acute sickness during the two weeks prior to interview. As with chronic conditions, an age gradient was evident, but it was not so steep. About a tenth of those aged under 16 had an acute sickness which restricted their activities during the reference period, increasing to about a quarter of the 75 and over age group. Again, the increase in prevalence was most marked among those aged 45 and over.

The proportions reporting acute sickness increased in the 1970s, from 8% in 1972 to 13% in 1979. Prevalence was 12-13% in the 1980s, with some evidence of an increase in the 1990s.   **Tables 7.1-7.2**

Socio-economic group and economic activity status
The Independent Inquiry into Health Inequalities, which reported in 1998, concluded that 'inequalities in health exist, whether measured in terms of mortality, life expect-

ancy or health status, whether categorised by socio-economic measures or by ethnic group or gender'[5]. *Our Healthier Nation*[6] argued that people's health is affected by their circumstances, including socio-economic factors such as poverty, employment and social exclusion. It is therefore interesting to examine socio-economic differences in reported ill health.

Tables 7.3-7.5 show that the prevalence of chronic and acute conditions varied between members of households in different socio-economic groups. Respondents living in households in the manual group were more likely than those in non-manual households to report a longstanding illness (of any kind), a limiting longstanding illness and an acute sickness, but the difference was not statistically significant for all age groups. Thus, for example:

- 38% of males and 37% of females in manual households reported a longstanding condition, compared with 30% and 31% respectively in non-manual households;
- the difference between people in manual and in non-manual households was statistically significant for all males and for women aged 16-44;
- 23% of males and 24% of females in manual households reported a limiting longstanding illness, compared with 15% and 19% respectively of those in non-manual households. Again, the difference between people in manual and in non-manual households was statistically significant for all males and for women aged 16-44;
- 12% of males and 15% of females from non-manual households reported an acute condition in the 14 days before interview, compared with 15% of males and 17% of females in manual households. The difference was significant for men aged 45 and over and for women aged 45-64.   **Tables 7.3-7.5**

It is possible that there is some under-reporting of longstanding illnesses by the manual groups. In an analysis of the 1984-5 Health and Lifestyles Survey data, Blaxter found that those belonging to a non-manual social class were more ready to declare a chronic condition, even if it was not functionally troublesome or accompanied by symptoms[7]. Informants in manual social classes, particularly men, were likely to say they had a named disease only if it was actually troublesome; this was particularly true for mental disorders.

Our Healthier Nation argued that 'being in work is good for your health' and stated that joblessness had been clearly linked to poor physical and mental health. Among GHS respondents, unemployed respondents were more likely than those in work to report a longstanding illness, disability or infirmity, but the difference was only statistically significant for limiting conditions. This may, in part, be due to the small sample sizes in the unemployed group.

- 18% of unemployed respondents reported a limiting longstanding condition, compared with 12% of those who were working at the time of interview.

The prevalence of both chronic and acute sickness was highest among economically inactive respondents. The difference was most marked for limiting longstanding conditions; 46% of men and 39% of women in the economically inactive group reported a limiting illness, compared with 12% of working adults and 18% of the unemployed. The difference between economically inactive and working respondents was significant for all age groups. **Tables 7.6-7.8**

Regional variations

Whereas previous GHS reports have presented data for Standard Statistical Regions, in 1998 the GHS, in common with other government surveys, has analysed regional data by Government Office Region[8]. Data for health regions are also presented differently from previous years. Regional Health Authorities were reorganised into National Health Service Regional Offices in April 1996; information is therefore presented for the Regional Offices rather than for Regional Health Authorities, as in the past.

For both Government Office Region and NHS Regional Office, the prevalence of chronic conditions, whether limiting or not, was highest in Wales.

- 41% of respondents in Wales, 33% in England and 32% in Scotland reported a chronic condition;
- the proportions reporting a limiting longstanding illness were 27% in Wales, 20% in England and 19% in Scotland.
- Within England, the prevalence of chronic illness, whether limiting or not, was lowest in the London and South East Government Office Regions;
- a similar pattern was evident among NHS Regional Offices, with Anglia and Oxford, North Thames and South Thames having the lowest proportions reporting a longstanding illness. **Tables 7.9-7.12**

Details of longstanding conditions

Respondents aged 16 and over who reported a longstanding illness or condition were asked 'What is the matter with you?' Details of the illness were recorded by the interviewer and coded during the interview using a computer-assisted coding frame[9]. The broad categories into which respondents' replies were coded were later collapsed into even broader groups which approximate to the chapter headings of the International Classification of Diseases (ICD). Studies of the validity of self-reported data have shown that there is a high level of agreement both between prevalence based on self-reporting and on medical examinations[10], and between self-reporting and doctor diagnosis of specific conditions[11]. The level of agreement is highest for those conditions which require ongoing treatment, have commonly recognised names and are salient to respondents because they cause discomfort or worry[12].

As in previous years of the GHS, the most common conditions reported by respondents were musculoskeletal problems and conditions of the heart and circulatory system.

- 154 men and 173 women per 1000 reported a musculoskeletal condition;
- the rate for conditions of the heart and circulatory system was 113 per 1000 for men and 99 per 1000 for women. **Table 7.13**

With the exception of skin conditions and infectious diseases, the rate for all conditions increased with age, although the increase was more marked for some complaints than others.

- Whereas 94 men and 64 women per 1000 in the 16-44 age group reported a musculoskeletal condition, the corresponding rates among the 75 and over age group were 260 and 383.
- Only 19 men and 13 women per 1000 aged 16-44 said they had a condition of the heart and circulatory system, compared with 310 men and 299 women aged 75 and over.

A more detailed breakdown of individual conditions shows that the higher rate of musculoskeletal conditions among women than among men in the oldest age group was largely accounted for by the high proportion of women reporting arthritis and rheumatism; 254 women out of 1000 aged 75 and over reported these conditions, compared with 145 men in the same age group.

This more detailed analysis also shows that there was little age difference in the proportions reporting asthma; 3-5% of men and 5-6% of women of all ages reported this condition. **Tables 7.14-7.18**

Use of health services

GHS respondents are asked about their use of a number of health services:

- whether they have seen a GP in the two weeks before interview;
- whether they have attended an outpatient or casualty department in the three months before interview;
- whether they have been a day patient in the last 12 months; and
- whether they have been an inpatient in the last 12 months.

With some exceptions, women and girls were more likely than men and boys to have made use of any of these services. Use was also highest among the youngest and the oldest age groups.

GP consultations

In 1998, 17% of females and 12% of males consulted a GP during the 14 days prior to interview. The difference between men and women was particularly marked in the 16-44 age group, among whom 9% and 17% respectively had seen a GP. It is likely that some of the consultations by women of this age were related to birth control or pregnancy, which would account for at least some of the difference. The likelihood of having seen a GP was highest among children aged under 5 and adults aged 65 and over. The average number of consultations per year was 4 for males and 5 for females.

The proportion of respondents seeing a GP has risen in each decade since the 1970s. The likelihood of doing so was lower in 1998 than in most other years of the 1990s, which may indicate that the proportion consulting their GP is levelling off. **Tables 7.19-7.20, Figure 7B**

In 1998, 84% of consultations took place at the GP's surgery, a proportion which has remained largely unchanged in the 1990s. Six per cent of consultations took place at the respondent's home, while the remaining 10% were on the telephone.

The proportion of consultations taking place in respondents' homes has decreased from 22% in 1971 to 6% in 1998, while the likelihood of consulting a GP on the telephone increased from 4% to 10% over the same period. The oldest age group was most likely to have been seen by their GP at home; 25% of those aged 75 and over reported a home consultation, compared with 2% of the 16-44 age group. **Tables 7.21-7.23**

Respondents living in households in the manual socio-economic groups were more likely than those in the non-manual groups to have seen a GP in the reference period; 13% of males and 18% of females had done so, compared with 11% of males and 15% of females in non-manual households. The difference was not statistically significant for all age groups.

Economically inactive men were twice as likely as men who were working, and one and a half times as likely as unemployed men to have a seen a GP in the last fortnight. The proportion of economically inactive women who had consulted a GP was higher than among women who were working or unemployed, but the differences were less marked than among men.

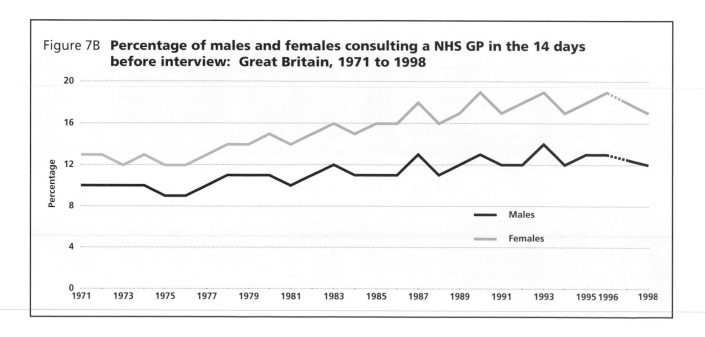

Figure 7B **Percentage of males and females consulting a NHS GP in the 14 days before interview: Great Britain, 1971 to 1998**

As in previous years, all but a small percentage of GP consultations were with NHS doctors: 97% of all consultations. **Tables 7.24-7.27**

Hospital visits

Outpatient visits

Sixteen per cent of respondents had visited an outpatient or casualty department at least once in the three months prior to interview, an increase of one percentage point since 1996. An upward trend has been observed in the GHS since 1972, when 10% of respondents reported such visits.

- Older respondents were most likely to have attended an outpatient department: 25% of men and 21% of women aged 65-74 and 29% of men and 26% of women aged 75 and over had done so, compared with 18% or fewer of other respondents;

- the proportion of respondents attending an outpatient or casualty department has also increased more among elderly respondents than among others. Among the 75 and over age group, for example, the proportion doing so increased from 10% to 29% among men and from 13% to 26% among women between 1972 and 1998. **Table 7.28**

Day patients

In 1998, 6% of men and 7% of women attended hospital as a day patient. As in previous years, there was no clear association with age among adults. Although the propor-

tion of men aged 75 and over who were day patients in 1998 was higher than among other men, this may be a function of the small sample size in this group. Previous years did not show such a clear difference between this age group and younger men. The proportion of respondents attending hospitals as day patients has increased since this question was first asked in 1992 from 4% to 6% among males and from 4% to 7% among females. Women who were admitted as a day patient to have a baby are included in the 7%. However, as this group of women accounted for only 2% of all women who made day patient visits, their inclusion does not account for the changes over time. As with outpatient attendances, the increase in attendance as a day patient was greatest among older respondents. **Tables 7.29-7.30**

Inpatients

The likelihood of reporting an inpatient stay in the 12 months prior to interview has changed very little since 1982[13]; remaining at 9%-10%. In 1998, 8% of males and 10% of females said they had had at least one inpatient stay.

Those aged 75 and over were most likely to report an inpatient stay; 21% of men and 15% of women in this age group did so. This age group is also an exception to the general trend over time; the likelihood of being an inpatient rose from 14% of men and 12% of women in 1982. **Tables 7.31-7.33, Figure 7C**

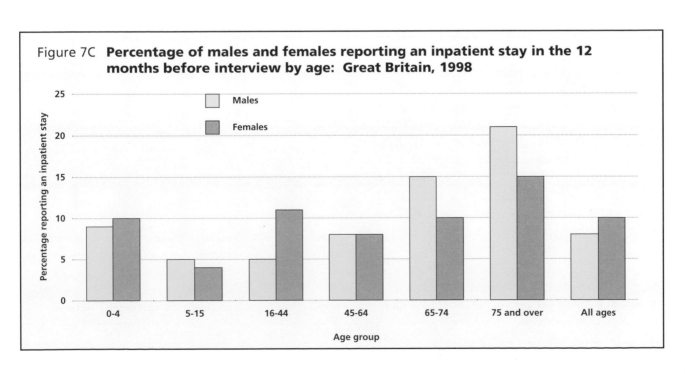

Figure 7C **Percentage of males and females reporting an inpatient stay in the 12 months before interview by age: Great Britain, 1998**

Hearing

Adults aged 16 and over were asked if they experienced any difficulties with hearing; those who did were asked whether they used a hearing aid and a further set of questions about any aids they did have.

Hearing difficulties increased markedly with age, and men were more likely than women, at all ages, to report difficulties with their hearing. For example:

- whereas 8% of men and 5% of women aged 16-44 said they had any hearing difficulties, the corresponding proportions among the 75 and over age group were 53% and 41%;
- there has been an increase in the proportion of men aged 45 and over reporting hearing difficulties since 1979;
- there has been little change in the prevalence of hearing difficulties among women and younger men since 1979;
- the proportion of men aged 45-64 who reported a hearing difficulty, but did not use an aid rose from 17% in 1979 to 22% in 1998. Most of this increase occurred between 1992 and 1995;
- among men aged 75 and over, the likelihood of wearing a hearing aid increased from 12% in 1979 to 23% in 1998.

Using a hearing aid did not necessarily overcome all hearing problems; among the 3% of respondents using an aid, 59% said they still had hearing difficulties even when wearing an aid.

- In 1998, 166 respondents (1%) said they had an aid, but did not use it. Of this group, 43% said the aid did not help their hearing, while 27% found it awkward, uncomfortable or badly fitting;
- just over one in five aids were purchased privately. Among the 99 respondents who had bought an aid privately, 65% said this was because there was a better choice, 28% said it was not available on the NHS, and 15% could obtain the aid more quickly.

Tables 7.34-7.37

Notes and references

1. Martin J et al. *The prevalence of disability among adults: OPCS surveys of disability in Great Britain; Report 1.* HMSO (London 1988).
2. Hunt A. *The elderly at home.* HMSO (London 1976).
3. Heady P et al. *1991 Census Validation Survey: quality report.* The Stationery Office (London 1996).
4. Thomas M et al. *Living in Britain: results from the 1996 General Household Survey.* The Stationery Office (London 1998).
5. *Independent Inquiry into Inequalities in Health.* The Stationery Office (London 1998).
6. Department of Health. *Our healthier nation.* The Stationery Office (London 1998).
7. Blaxter M. *Health and Lifestyles.* Routledge (London 1990).
8. Government Office Region was used as the regional stratifier for the 1998 GHS sample. See Appendix B for details.
9. The interviewers checked whether respondents had more than one complaint. They recorded details of, and coded up to six complaints.
10. Blaxter M. Self-reported health in *The Health and Lifestyles Survey.* Health Promotion Research Trust (London: 1987).
11. Bennett N et al. *Health Survey for England 1993: Appendix D.* HMSO (London 1995).
12. Discrepancies do not necessarily indicate that data from self-reported sources are inaccurate. Respondents may not have brought a condition to the attention of a doctor, medical records could be inaccurate, doctors may not have informed patients of their diagnosis, and lay descriptions may be different from those given by a doctor (see Blaxter and Bennett).
13. GHS respondents were first asked about any hospital inpatient stays in the 12 months before interview in 1982. Between 1971 and 1976, respondents were asked about inpatient stays in the last three months.

Table 7.1 **Trends in self-reported sickness by sex and age, 1972 to 1998: percentage of persons who reported**
(a) longstanding illness
(b) limiting longstanding illness
(c) restricted activity in the 14 days before interview

All persons   *Great Britain*

	1972	1975	1979	1981	1983	1985	1989	1991	1993	1995	1996	1998	*Base (1998)* = 100%*
						(a) Longstanding illness							
Percentage who reported:													
Males													
0- 4	5	8	8	12	11	11	14	13	15	14	14	15	*743*
5-15†	9	11	14	17	17	18	20	17	21	20	19	21	*1552*
16-44†	14	17	21	22	23	21	24	23	26	23	27	24	*3715*
45-64	29	35	39	40	44	42	42	42	45	43	46	44	*2388*
65-74	48	50	50	51	58	55	58	61	62	55	61	59	*873*
75 and over	54	63	56	60	67	58	61	63	64	56	64	68	*539*
Total	20	23	27	28	31	29	31	31	34	31	34	33	*9810*
Females													
0- 4	3	6	6	7	9	9	10	10	12	11	13	15	*701*
5-15†	6	9	10	13	13	13	16	15	16	17	16	19	*1511*
16-44†	13	16	20	21	23	22	24	23	26	22	27	23	*4003*
45-64	31	33	38	41	45	43	43	41	45	39	47	43	*2492*
65-74	48	54	52	58	63	56	57	55	59	54	58	59	*988*
75 and over	65	61	64	70	70	65	70	65	69	66	68	65	*834*
Total	21	25	28	30	33	31	33	32	35	31	35	34	*10529*
All persons													
0- 4	4	7	7	10	10	10	12	12	13	13	13	15	*1444*
5-15†	8	10	12	15	15	16	18	16	19	19	18	20	*3063*
16-44†	13	16	20	21	23	22	24	23	26	23	27	24	*7718*
45-64	30	34	38	41	44	43	43	41	45	41	47	44	*4880*
65-74	48	52	51	55	61	56	58	58	60	55	59	59	*1861*
75 and over	62	62	61	67	69	63	66	65	67	63	66	66	*1373*
Total	21	24	27	29	32	30	32	31	34	31	35	33	*20339*
						(b) Limiting longstanding illness							
Percentage who reported:													
Males													
0- 4	..	3	2	3	3	4	6	4	5	5	4	4	*742*
5-15†	..	6	7	8	8	8	8	7	9	8	8	8	*1552*
16-44†	..	9	10	10	11	10	10	10	13	12	14	12	*3715*
45-64	..	24	26	26	27	27	26	25	28	28	31	28	*2388*
65-74	..	36	37	35	40	38	37	40	41	37	42	36	*872*
75 and over	..	46	45	44	53	43	44	46	45	41	50	48	*539*
Total	..	14	16	16	18	16	17	17	19	18	21	19	*9808*
Females													
0- 4	..	2	2	3	2	3	2	3	3	3	4	5	*701*
5-15†	..	4	5	6	6	6	7	5	8	8	8	8	*1511*
16-44†	..	9	10	11	12	11	12	11	15	13	16	13	*4003*
45-64	..	22	24	26	28	26	25	25	29	26	32	29	*2490*
65-74	..	39	38	41	45	38	36	34	39	37	40	39	*988*
75 and over	..	49	54	56	54	51	53	51	52	52	53	51	*834*
Total	..	16	18	19	20	18	19	18	22	20	23	21	*10527*
All persons													
0- 4	..	2	2	3	3	3	4	4	4	4	4	4	*1443*
5-15†	..	5	6	7	7	7	7	6	9	8	8	8	*3063*
16-44†	..	9	10	11	12	10	11	10	14	12	15	13	*7718*
45-64	..	23	25	26	27	26	25	25	29	27	32	28	*4878*
65-74	..	38	37	38	43	38	37	37	40	37	41	38	*1860*
75 and over	..	48	51	52	54	48	50	49	50	48	52	50	*1373*
Total	..	15	17	17	19	17	18	18	20	19	22	20	*20335*

* Bases for earlier years are of a similar size and can be found in GHS reports for each year.
† These age-groups were 5-14 and 15-44 in 1972 to 1978.

Table 7.1 - *continued*

All persons   *Great Britain*

	1972	1975	1979	1981	1983	1985	1989	1991	1993	1995	1996	1998	Base (1998)* = 100%
						(c) Restricted activity							
Percentage who reported:													
Males													
0- 4	5	10	12	13	15	13	12	11	13	11	12	10	743
5-15†	6	9	11	12	12	11	12	11	11	10	10	9	1552
16-44†	7	7	10	8	8	9	9	9	11	10	13	11	3714
45-64	9	10	14	12	11	11	12	12	15	15	18	18	2389
65-74	10	8	12	11	12	13	13	14	16	17	19	18	872
75 and over	10	12	17	15	17	17	19	18	17	20	23	24	538
Total	7	9	12	11	11	11	11	11	13	13	15	14	9808
Females													
0- 4	6	8	10	12	14	13	12	10	10	11	9	8	701
5-15†	5	7	11	11	11	12	13	9	11	10	9	11	1510
16-44†	8	10	13	11	13	13	13	12	13	13	15	13	4005
45-64	9	10	14	13	15	14	15	13	17	17	22	20	2495
65-74	10	12	16	17	19	18	19	16	19	20	21	23	988
75 and over	14	13	22	21	20	23	26	21	23	26	25	27	833
Total	8	10	14	13	14	14	15	13	15	15	17	16	10532
All persons													
0- 4	6	9	11	13	15	13	12	11	11	11	10	9	1444
5-15†	6	8	11	12	12	11	12	10	11	10	10	10	3062
16-44†	8	9	11	10	11	11	11	10	12	12	14	12	7719
45-64	9	10	14	12	13	12	14	13	16	16	20	19	4884
65-74	10	11	14	14	16	16	17	15	18	19	20	21	1860
75 and over	13	13	20	19	19	21	23	20	21	24	24	26	1371
Total	8	9	13	12	13	12	13	12	14	14	16	15	20340

* Bases for earlier years are of a similar size and can be found in GHS Reports for each year.
† These age-groups were 5-14 and 15-44 in 1972 to 1978.

Table 7.2 **Acute sickness: average number of restricted activity days per person per year, by sex and age**

All persons *Great Britain: 1998*

	Number of days			Bases = 100%		
	Males	Females	Total	*Males*	*Females*	*Total*
Age						
0- 4	15	14	14	*743*	*701*	*1444*
5-15	12	13	13	*1552*	*1510*	*3062*
16-44	20	23	21	*3714*	*4005*	*7719*
45-64	42	44	43	*2385*	*2493*	*4878*
65-74	47	59	53	*872*	*987*	*1859*
75 and over	72	80	77	*536*	*832*	*1368*
Total	29	34	31	*9802*	*10528*	*20330*

Table 7.3 **Chronic sickness: prevalence of reported longstanding illness by sex, age and socio-economic group of head of household**

All persons *Great Britain: 1998*

Socio-economic group of head of household*	Males					Females				
	Age					Age				
	0-15	16-44	45-64	65 and over	Total	0-15	16-44	45-64	65 and over	Total
	Percentage who reported longstanding illness									
Professional	15	22	31	57	27	14	19	35	59	25
Employers and managers	18 _18_	22 _23_	37 _38_	57 _57_	30 _30_	16 _17_	19 _22_	35 _38_	57 _61_	28 _31_
Intermediate non-manual	22	23	39	59	32	17	21	38	67	32
Junior non-manual	19	24	47	57	31	20	29	46	60	38
Skilled manual and own account										
non-professional	19	25	49	66	37	19	23	46	62	34
Semi-skilled manual and personal service	21 _20_	30 _27_	50 _50_	67 _66_	38 _38_	19 _19_	30 _26_	52 _49_	64 _63_	39 _37_
Unskilled manual	26	28	58	64	40	20	27	56	65	43
All persons	19	24	44	62	33	18	23	43	62	34
Bases = 100%										
Professional	*189*	*329*	*251*	*90*	*859*	*195*	*315*	*206*	*63*	*779*
Employers and managers	*519*	*751*	*571*	*310*	*2151*	*411*	*794*	*549*	*276*	*2030*
Intermediate non-manual	*222*	*400*	*228*	*142*	*992*	*222*	*493*	*294*	*213*	*1222*
Junior non-manual	*235*	*315*	*146*	*109*	*805*	*244*	*466*	*257*	*305*	*1272*
Skilled manual and own account										
non-professional	*574*	*1081*	*783*	*473*	*2911*	*547*	*1004*	*671*	*394*	*2616*
Semi-skilled manual and personal service	*335*	*477*	*282*	*218*	*1312*	*352*	*550*	*344*	*344*	*1590*
Unskilled manual	*96*	*156*	*104*	*61*	*417*	*111*	*147*	*130*	*155*	*543*
All persons	*2295*	*3715*	*2388*	*1412*	*9810*	*2212*	*4003*	*2492*	*1822*	*10529*

* Members of the Armed Forces, persons in inadequately described occupations and all persons who have never worked are not shown as separate categories, but are included in the figure for all persons (see Appendix A for details).

Table 7.4 Chronic sickness: prevalence of reported limiting longstanding illness by sex, age and socio-economic group of head of household

All persons   *Great Britain: 1998*

Socio-economic group of head of household*	Males					Females				
	Age					Age				
	0-15	16-44	45-64	65 and over	Total	0-15	16-44	45-64	65 and over	Total
	Percentage who reported limiting longstanding illness									
Professional	8	9	12	37	12	6	9	16	46	13
Employers and managers	4	10	22	34	15	8	9	22	41	17
Intermediate non-manual	9	11	22	37	17	6	13	27	44	20
Junior non-manual	3	12	29	28	15	7	16	31	42	23
(subtotal)	5	10	21	34	15	7	11	24	42	19
Skilled manual and own account non-professional	7	12	33	47	22	7	14	32	46	22
Semi-skilled manual and personal service	7	16	36	44	23	10	19	36	48	27
Unskilled manual	12	16	43	51	27	7	16	39	47	29
(subtotal)	8	14	35	46	23	8	15	34	47	24
All persons	6	12	28	41	19	7	13	29	45	21
Bases = 100%										
Professional	189	329	251	90	859	195	315	206	63	779
Employers and managers	519	751	571	310	2151	411	794	548	276	2029
Intermediate non-manual	222	400	228	142	992	222	493	294	213	1222
Junior non-manual	235	315	146	109	805	244	466	257	305	1272
Skilled manual and own account non-professional	573	1081	783	473	2910	547	1004	671	394	2616
Semi-skilled manual and personal service	335	477	282	218	1312	352	550	344	344	1590
Unskilled manual	96	156	104	61	417	111	147	130	155	543
All persons	2294	3715	2388	1411	9808	2212	4003	2490	1822	10527

* See the footnote to Table 7.3.

Table 7.5 **Acute sickness**
(a) Prevalence of reported restricted activity in the 14 days before interview, by sex, age, and socio-economic group of head of household
(b) Average number of restricted activity days per person per year, by sex, age, and socio-economic group of head of household

All persons   *Great Britain: 1998*

Socio-economic group of head of household*	Males					Females				
	Age					Age				
	0-15	16-44	45-64	65 and over	Total	0-15	16-44	45-64	65 and over	Total
(a) Percentage who reported restricted activity in the 14 days before interview										
Professional	8	8	12	21	10	13	12	12	24	13
Employers and managers	9	11	16	16	12	10	11	14	25	14
Intermediate non-manual	8	13	14	19	13	11	14	19	26	17
Junior non-manual	10	10	17	15	12	8	15	23	25	17
(subtotal)	9	11	15	17	12	10	13	17	25	15
Skilled manual and own account non-professional	9	10	20	21	14	9	12	22	24	15
Semi-skilled manual and personal service	12	11	21	28	16	11	16	24	27	19
Unskilled manual	16	17	27	20	20	11	12	26	25	19
(subtotal)	10	11	21	23	15	10	13	23	25	17
All persons	10	11	18	20	14	10	13	20	25	16
(b) Average number of restricted activity days per person per year										
Professional	12	11	25	53	20	14	23	26	61	25
Employers and managers	9	18	33	47	24	12	17	29	64	26
Intermediate non-manual	12	23	28	57	27	18	26	47	76	38
Junior non-manual	14	21	49	42	27	15	24	41	67	36
(subtotal)	11	18	32	49	24	14	22	35	68	31
Skilled manual and own account non-professional	9	20	49	55	31	12	20	49	65	33
Semi-skilled manual and personal service	20	21	50	80	37	16	29	54	74	41
Unskilled manual	24	32	72	57	44	14	25	61	70	44
(subtotal)	14	21	51	62	34	13	24	52	69	37
All persons	12	20	42	56	29	14	23	43	69	34
Bases = 100%										
Professional	189	329	251	90	859	195	315	206	63	779
Employers and managers	519	751	571	310	2151	411	795	550	276	2032
Intermediate non-manual	222	401	229	142	994	222	492	295	213	1222
Junior non-manual	235	315	146	109	805	244	466	257	305	1272
Skilled manual and own account non-professional	574	1081	783	473	2911	546	1005	672	394	2617
Semi-skilled manual and personal service	335	476	282	217	1310	352	550	344	343	1589
Unskilled manual	96	156	104	61	417	111	148	130	155	544
All persons	2295	3714	2389	1410	9808	2211	4005	2495	1821	10532

* See the footnote to Table 7.3.

Table 7.6 **Chronic sickness: prevalence of reported longstanding illness by sex, age, and economic activity status**

Persons aged 16 and over   *Great Britain: 1998*

Economic activity status	Men				Women			
	Age				Age			
	16-44	45-64	65 and over	Total	16-44	45-64	65 and over	Total
	Percentage who reported longstanding illness							
Working	22	34	47	27	20	32	40	24
Unemployed	26	47	*	31	29	[37]	0	31
Economically inactive	43	72	64	62	32	59	63	53
All aged 16 and over	24	44	62	38	23	43	62	38
Bases = 100%								
Working	*3060*	*1720*	*111*	*4891*	*2773*	*1421*	*72*	*4266*
Unemployed	*235*	*70*	*2*	*307*	*149*	*46*	*0*	*195*
Economically inactive	*419*	*597*	*1299*	*2315*	*1078*	*1025*	*1750*	*3853*
All aged 16 and over	*3714*	*2387*	*1412*	*7513*	*4000*	*2492*	*1822*	*8314*

* Base too small for analysis.

Table 7.7 **Chronic sickness: prevalence of reported limiting longstanding illness by sex, age, and economic activity status**

Persons aged 16 and over   *Great Britain: 1998*

Economic activity status	Men				Women			
	Age				Age			
	16-44	45-64	65 and over	Total	16-44	45-64	65 and over	Total
	Percentage who reported limiting longstanding illness							
Working	9	16	19	12	10	16	18	12
Unemployed	14	30	*	18	15	[28]	0	18
Economically inactive	34	61	43	46	22	46	46	39
All aged 16 and over	12	28	41	22	13	29	45	25
Bases = 100%								
Working	*3060*	*1720*	*111*	*4891*	*2773*	*1420*	*72*	*4265*
Unemployed	*235*	*70*	*2*	*307*	*149*	*46*	*0*	*195*
Economically inactive	*419*	*597*	*1298*	*2314*	*1078*	*1024*	*1750*	*3852*
All aged 16 and over	*3714*	*2387*	*1411*	*7512*	*4000*	*2490*	*1822*	*8312*

* Base too small for analysis.

Table 7.8 **Acute sickness**
(a) Prevalence of reported restricted activity in the 14 days before interview, by sex, age and economic activity status
(b) Average number of restricted activity days per person per year, by sex, age, and economic activity status

Persons aged 16 and over   *Great Britain: 1998*

Economic activity status	Men				Women			
	Age				Age			
	16-44	45-64	65 and over	Total	16-44	45-64	65 and over	Total
(a) Percentage who reported restricted activity in the 14 days before interview								
Working	10	12	10	10	11	14	12	12
Unemployed	10	16	*	11	11	[13]	0	11
Economically inactive	21	36	21	25	17	28	26	24
All aged 16 and over	11	18	20	15	13	20	25	18
(b) Average number of restricted activity days per person per year								
Working	15	24	24	19	18	26	26	21
Unemployed	24	36	*	27	24	24	0	24
Economically inactive	50	95	59	67	35	69	70	60
All aged 16 and over	20	42	56	34	23	44	69	39
Bases = 100%								
Working	3061	1720	111	4892	2774	1422	72	4268
Unemployed	234	70	2	306	149	46	0	195
Economically inactive	418	598	1297	2313	1079	1027	1749	3855
All aged 16 and over	3713	2388	1410	7511	4002	2495	1821	8318

* Base too small for analysis.

Table 7.9 **Self-reported sickness by sex and Government Office Region: percentage of persons who reported**
(a) longstanding illness
(b) limiting longstanding illness
(c) restricted activity in the 14 days before interview

All persons   *Great Britain: 1998*

Government Office Region*	(a) Longstanding illness	(b) Limiting longstanding illness	(c) Restricted activity	Base = 100%
Males				
England				
North East	37	22	18	542
North West	36	21	14	906
Merseyside	38	26	13	209
Yorkshire and the Humber	34	18	13	875
East Midlands	34	21	14	682
West Midlands	36	19	12	944
Eastern	31	17	12	961
London	27	16	13	1016
South East	30	16	12	1358
South West	36	19	13	897
All England	33	19	13	8390
Wales	39	24	21	527
Scotland	31	17	14	892
Great Britain	33	19	14	9809
Females				
England				
North East	39	25	18	549
North West	35	22	16	959
Merseyside	32	21	14	259
Yorkshire and the Humber	37	25	16	961
East Midlands	33	20	16	768
West Midlands	33	22	15	981
Eastern	32	20	17	990
London	30	18	14	1145
South East	30	17	15	1436
South West	33	19	15	956
All England	33	21	16	9004
Wales	43	30	21	552
Scotland	33	21	17	971
Great Britain	34	21	16	10527
All persons				
England				
North East	38	23	18	1091
North West	36	22	15	1865
Merseyside	35	23	14	468
Yorkshire and the Humber	35	22	14	1836
East Midlands	33	21	15	1450
West Midlands	34	20	14	1925
Eastern	32	18	14	1951
London	29	17	14	2161
South East	30	17	13	2794
South West	35	19	14	1853
All England	33	20	14	17394
Wales	41	27	21	1079
Scotland	32	19	16	1863
Great Britain	33	20	15	20336

* The data have not been standardised to take account of age or socio-economic group.

Table 7.10 **Prevalence of longstanding illness by sex and NHS Regional Office area**

All persons *Great Britain: 1998*

NHS Regional Office area	Males	Females	All persons
Northern and Yorkshire	35	38	36
Trent	34	34	34
Anglia and Oxford	29	29	29
North Thames	28	31	30
South Thames	30	31	30
South and West	35	33	34
West Midlands	36	33	35
North West	37	35	36
England	33	33	33
Wales	39	43	41
Scotland	31	33	32
Great Britain	33	34	33
Bases = 100%			
Northern and Yorkshire	*1262*	*1323*	*2585*
Trent	*860*	*974*	*1834*
Anglia and Oxford	*782*	*835*	*1617*
North Thames	*1146*	*1197*	*2343*
South Thames	*1030*	*1139*	*2169*
South and West	*1320*	*1412*	*2732*
West Midlands	*947*	*985*	*1932*
North West	*1049*	*1147*	*2196*
England	*8396*	*9012*	*17408*
Wales	*521*	*546*	*1067*
Scotland	*893*	*971*	*1864*
Great Britain	*9810*	*10529*	*20339*

Table 7.11 **Prevalence of limiting longstanding illness by sex and NHS Regional Office area**

All persons *Great Britain: 1998*

NHS Regional Office area	Males	Females	All persons
Northern and Yorkshire	19	24	22
Trent	21	21	21
Anglia and Oxford	15	16	16
North Thames	16	20	18
South Thames	17	18	18
South and West	19	19	19
West Midlands	19	22	20
North West	22	23	23
England	19	21	20
Wales	24	30	27
Scotland	17	21	19
Great Britain	19	21	20
Bases = 100%			
Northern and Yorkshire	*1262*	*1323*	*2585*
Trent	*860*	*974*	*1834*
Anglia and Oxford	*782*	*835*	*1617*
North Thames	*1146*	*1197*	*2343*
South Thames	*1030*	*1138*	*2168*
South and West	*1319*	*1412*	*2731*
West Midlands	*947*	*985*	*1932*
North West	*1049*	*1146*	*2195*
England	*8395*	*9010*	*17405*
Wales	*521*	*546*	*1067*
Scotland	*892*	*971*	*1863*
Great Britain	*9808*	*10527*	*20335*

Table 7.12 **Prevalence of reported restricted activity in the 14 days before interview, by sex and NHS Regional Office area**

All persons   *Great Britain: 1998*

NHS Regional Office area	Males	Females	All persons
Northern and Yorkshire	15	16	15
Trent	15	16	15
Anglia and Oxford	10	15	13
North Thames	12	16	14
South Thames	12	15	13
South and West	14	16	15
West Midlands	13	15	14
North West	14	15	15
England	13	16	14
Wales	21	21	21
Scotland	14	17	16
Great Britain	14	16	15
Bases = 100%			
Northern and Yorkshire	1261	1324	2585
Trent	860	974	1834
Anglia and Oxford	782	835	1617
North Thames	1146	1198	2344
South Thames	1029	1139	2168
South and West	1319	1414	2733
West Midlands	949	985	1934
North West	1049	1146	2195
England	8395	9015	17410
Wales	521	546	1067
Scotland	892	971	1863
Great Britain	9808	10532	20340

Table 7.13   **Chronic sickness: rate per 1000 reporting longstanding condition groups, by sex**

Persons aged 16 and over   *Great Britain: 1998*

Condition group	Men	Women	Total
XIII Musculoskeletal system	154	173	164
VII Heart and circulatory system	113	99	106
VIII Respiratory system	72	76	74
III Endocrine and metabolic	39	50	45
IX Digestive system	34	39	37
VI Nervous system	31	35	33
V Mental disorders	25	32	29
VI Eye complaints	18	19	19
VI Ear complaints	19	16	17
X Genito-urinary system	12	15	14
II Neoplasms and benign growths	10	14	12
XII Skin complaints	8	10	9
IV Blood and related organs	2	5	4
Other complaints*	6	6	6
I Infectious diseases	2	3	3
Average number of conditions reported by those with a longstanding illness	1.5	1.6	1.5
Bases = 100% (all persons 16 and over)	*7531*	*8343*	*15874*

* Including general complaints such as insomnia, fainting, generally run down, old age and general infirmity and non-specific conditions such as war wounds or road accident injuries where no further details were given.

Table 7.14 **Chronic sickness: rate per 1000 reporting longstanding condition groups, by age**

Persons aged 16 and over   *Great Britain: 1998*

Condition group	16-44	45-64	65-74	75 and over
XIII Musculoskeletal system	78	205	286	335
VII Heart and circulatory system	16	130	274	303
VIII Respiratory system	68	70	91	96
III Endocrine and metabolic	15	59	99	84
IX Digestive system	19	46	58	74
VI Nervous system	28	38	35	41
V Mental disorders	28	37	16	25
VI Eye complaints	7	12	35	86
VI Ear complaints	7	24	24	42
X Genito-urinary system	7	14	26	33
II Neoplasms and benign growths	3	15	24	35
XII Skin complaints	11	7	9	3
IV Blood and related organs	3	3	5	9
Other complaints*	6	5	8	6
I Infectious diseases	3	3	1	1
Average number of conditions reported by those with a longstanding illness	1.3	1.5	1.7	1.8
Bases = 100% (all persons 16 and over)	*7746*	*4892*	*1862*	*1374*

* Including general complaints such as insomnia, fainting, generally run down, old age and general infirmity and non-specific conditions such as war wounds or road accident injuries where no further details were given.

Table 7.15 **Chronic sickness: rate per 1000 reporting selected longstanding condition groups, by age and sex**

Persons aged 16 and over   *Great Britain: 1998*

Condition group		16-44	45-64	65-74	75 and over	All ages
XIII Musculoskeletal system	Men	94	197	226	260	154
	Women	64	213	340	383	173
VII Heart and circulatory system	Men	19	155	281	310	113
	Women	13	106	268	299	99
VIII Respiratory system	Men	66	62	100	115	72
	Women	70	78	83	84	76
III Endocrine and metabolic	Men	13	53	81	82	39
	Women	18	65	114	86	50
IX Digestive system	Men	20	46	52	59	34
	Women	18	46	64	84	39
VI Nervous system	Men	26	34	38	41	31
	Women	30	42	33	42	35
Bases = 100%	*Men*	*3726*	*2393*	*873*	*539*	*7531*
	Women	*4020*	*2499*	*989*	*835*	*8343*

Table 7.16   **Chronic sickness: rate per 1000 reporting selected longstanding conditions, by age and sex**

Persons aged 16 and over   *Great Britain: 1998*

Condition	Men					Women				
	16-44	45-64	65-74	75 and over	All ages	16-44	45-64	65-74	75 and over	All ages
Musculoskeletal (XIII)										
Arthritis and rheumatism	16	81	142	145	61	18	123	218	254	97
Back problems	40	66	40	26	47	30	55	48	29	39
Other bone and joint problems	38	49	44	89	46	16	35	74	101	37
Heart and circulatory (VII)										
Hypertension	6	48	63	59	30	5	53	103	73	38
Heart attack	3	40	89	111	32	0	18	65	86	22
Stroke	1	8	26	30	8	1	5	15	41	8
Other heart complaints	6	41	73	85	30	5	21	53	63	21
Other blood vessel/embolic disorders	2	16	25	19	10	2	8	24	29	9
Respiratory (VIII)										
Asthma	48	33	40	43	42	58	54	57	50	56
Bronchitis and emphysema	2	15	39	35	13	1	10	17	12	7
Hay fever	9	4	2	2	6	7	3	2	1	5
Other respiratory complaints	7	9	18	35	11	4	12	7	20	8
Bases = 100% (all persons 16 and over)	*3726*	*2393*	*873*	*539*	*7531*	*4020*	*2499*	*989*	*835*	*8343*

Table 7.17   **Chronic sickness: rate per 1000 reporting selected longstanding condition groups, by socio-economic group of head of household**

Persons aged 16 and over   *Great Britain: 1998*

Condition group		Professional	Employers and managers	Inter-mediate and junior non-manual	Skilled manual and own account non-pro-professional	Semi-skilled manual and personal service	Unskilled manual	Total*
XIII	Musculoskeletal system	95	125	161	175	219	259	164
VII	Heart and circulatory system	60	83	102	123	130	168	106
VIII	Respiratory system	52	56	69	84	87	115	74
III	Endocrine and metabolic	39	44	39	48	51	56	45
IX	Digestive system	30	32	31	41	50	45	37
VI	Nervous system	24	26	35	32	46	42	33
Average number of condition groups reported by those with a longstanding illness		1.33	1.40	1.46	1.55	1.64	1.79	1.51
Bases = 100% (all persons aged 16 and over)		*1258*	*3260*	*3377*	*4414*	*2216*	*756*	*15869*

* Persons whose head of household was in the Armed Forces or a full-time student are not shown as separate categories but are included in the totals.

Table 7.18 **Chronic sickness: rate per 1000 reporting selected longstanding condition groups, by age and sex and whether non-manual or manual socio-economic group of head of household**

Persons aged 16 and over   *Great Britain: 1998*

Condition group		Men 16-44	Men 45-64	Men 65 and over	Men Total	Women 16-44	Women 45-64	Women 65 and over	Women Total	All aged 16 and over 16-44	All aged 16 and over 45-64	All aged 16 and over 65 and over	All aged 16 and over Total
XIII Musculoskeletal system	Non-manual	83	141	175	118	55	172	349	151	68	157	274	136
	Manual	108	249	295	192	75	259	372	202	92	254	337	197
VII Heart and circulatory system	Non-manual	13	119	253	91	10	80	275	85	11	99	266	88
	Manual	26	193	323	141	17	132	296	119	22	163	308	130
VIII Respiratory system	Non-manual	60	48	75	59	61	55	79	63	61	52	77	61
	Manual	72	75	133	86	81	105	87	90	77	90	108	88
III Endocrine and metabolic	Non-manual	14	54	72	38	20	56	85	44	17	55	79	41
	Manual	13	53	89	41	15	73	121	58	14	63	106	50
IX Digestive system	Non-manual	19	37	45	30	18	34	65	33	19	36	56	31
	Manual	21	56	64	41	21	59	82	47	21	57	74	44
VI Nervous system	Non-manual	22	28	41	27	26	37	36	32	24	33	38	30
	Manual	32	39	37	35	35	45	39	39	33	42	38	37
Base = 100%	*Non-manual*	*1804*	*1197*	*651*	*3652*	*2074*	*1310*	*859*	*4243*	*3878*	*2507*	*1510*	*7895*
	Manual	*1716*	*1171*	*752*	*3639*	*1706*	*1148*	*893*	*3747*	*3422*	*2319*	*1645*	*7386*

Table 7.19 **Trends in consultations with an NHS GP in the 14 days before interview: 1972 to 1998**

All persons   *Great Britain*

	1972	1979	1981	1983	1985	1989	1991	1993	1995	1996	1998	Base (1998)* = 100%
					Percentage consulting GP							
Males												
0- 4	13	19	21	21	22	24	23	23	22	23	18	*743*
5-15†	7	8	8	10	9	10	10	11	9	9	8	*1552*
16-44†	8	9	7	8	7	8	9	11	10	10	9	*3713*
45-64	11	14	12	12	12	12	11	15	14	15	14	*2389*
65-74	12	15	13	18	15	16	17	21	17	19	17	*873*
75 and over	19	16	17	20	19	19	21	22	22	21	21	*537*
Total	10	11	10	12	11	12	12	14	13	13	12	*9807*
Females												
0- 4	15	15	17	20	21	21	21	22	21	20	18	*701*
5-15†	6	8	9	9	11	11	11	10	13	9	10	*1510*
16-44†	15	15	15	17	17	18	17	20	18	20	17	*4004*
45-64	12	13	13	15	15	17	17	19	17	19	18	*2495*
65-74	15	17	16	18	17	19	19	20	23	21	19	*989*
75 and over	20	23	20	21	20	22	19	23	23	23	20	*834*
Total	13	14	14	16	16	17	17	19	18	19	17	*10533*
All persons												
0- 4	14	17	19	20	21	23	22	22	21	22	18	*1444*
5-15†	7	8	9	10	10	10	10	11	11	9	9	*3062*
16-44†	12	12	11	12	12	13	13	16	14	15	13	*7717*
45-64	12	14	12	14	14	15	14	17	16	17	16	*4884*
65-74	14	16	15	18	16	18	18	21	20	20	18	*1862*
75 and over	20	21	19	21	20	21	19	22	23	22	21	*1371*
Total	12	13	12	14	14	15	14	17	16	16	14	*20340*

* See the footnotes to Table 7.1.
†

104

Table 7.20 **Average number of NHS GP consultations per person per year: 1972 to 1998**

All persons*   *Great Britain*

	1972†	1979	1981	1983	1985	1989	1991	1993	1995	1996	1998
Males											
0- 4	4	6	7	7	7	9	7	8	7	8	6
5-15**	2	2	2	3	3	3	3	3	3	3	2
16-44**	3	3	2	2	2	2	3	4	3	3	3
45-64	4	4	4	4	4	4	4	5	4	5	4
65-74	4	5	4	5	5	5	5	6	5	6	5
75 and over	7	5	6	7	6	6	7	7	8	7	7
Total	3	3	3	4	3	4	4	5	4	4	4
Females											
0- 4	5	5	5	6	7	7	7	7	7	6	6
5-15**	2	3	3	3	3	3	3	3	4	3	3
16-44**	5	5	5	5	5	6	5	6	6	7	5
45-64	4	4	4	5	5	5	5	6	5	6	6
65-74	5	5	5	6	5	6	6	6	7	7	6
75 and over	7	8	6	7	7	7	6	7	7	7	6
Total	4	5	4	5	5	6	5	6	6	6	5
All persons											
0- 4	4	5	6	7	7	8	7	8	7	7	6
5-15**	2	2	3	3	3	3	3	3	3	3	3
16-44**	4	4	4	4	4	4	4	5	4	5	4
45-64	4	4	4	4	4	5	4	5	5	5	5
65-74	4	5	4	6	5	6	6	6	6	6	6
75 and over	7	7	6	7	6	7	6	7	7	7	6
Total	4	4	4	4	4	5	5	5	5	5	4

*   Bases for 1998 are shown in Table 7.1. Bases for earlier years are of a similar size and can be found in GHS reports for each year.
†   1972 figures relate to England and Wales.
** These age-groups were 5-14 and 15-44 in 1972 to 1978.

Table 7.21 **(NHS) GP consultations: trends in site of consultation: 1971 to 1998**

Consultations in the 14 days before interview   *Great Britain*

Site of consultation	1971	1979	1981	1983	1985	1989	1991	1993	1995	1996	1998
	%	%	%	%	%	%	%	%	%	%	%
Surgery*	73	76	79	79	79	78	81	84	84	84	84
Home	22	16	14	15	14	14	11	9	9	8	6
Telephone	4	7	7	6	7	8	8	7	7	8	10
Base = 100%	*5031*	*4678*	*4704*	*4287*	*4123*	*4520*	*4228*	*4873*	*4385*	*4341*	*3504*

* Includes consultations with a GP at a health centre and those who had answered 'elsewhere'.

Table 7.22 **(NHS) GP consultations: consultations with doctors in the 14 days before interview, by sex and age of person consulting, and by site of consultation**

Consultations in the 14 days before interview   *Great Britain: 1998*

Site of consultation	Males						Females						All persons					
	Age						Age						Age					
	0-4	5-15	16-44	45-64	65-74	75 and over	0-4	5-15	16-44	45-64	65-74	75 and over	0-4	5-15	16-44	45-64	65-74	75 and over
	%	%	%	%	%	%	%	%	%	%	%	%	%	%	%	%	%	%
Surgery*	82	87	91	84	83	66	89	87	85	85	77	68	85	87	87	85	79	67
Home	7	4	1	6	8	28	1	5	2	5	13	23	4	5	2	5	11	25
Telephone	11	9	8	10	9	6	10	8	12	10	10	9	11	8	11	10	10	8
Base = 100%	*166*	*138*	*377*	*376*	*175*	*140*	*150*	*175*	*829*	*555*	*220*	*203*	*316*	*313*	*1206*	*931*	*395*	*343*

* Includes consultations with a GP at a health centre and those who had answered 'elsewhere'.

Table 7.23 **(NHS) GP consultations: percentage of persons consulting a doctor in the 14 days before interview, by sex and by site of consultation, and by age and by site of consultation**

Persons who consulted in the 14 days before interview   *Great Britain: 1998*

Site of consultation	Total	Males	Females	Age					
				0-4	5-15	16-44	45-64	65-74	75 and over
	%	%	%	%	%	%	%	%	%
Surgery	87	87	86	88	88	90	88	84	71
At home	6	7	6	4	4	2	5	10	26
Telephone	11	10	11	13	9	11	11	9	10
Base (all persons consulting) = 100%*	*2905*	*1151*	*1754*	*258*	*270*	*993*	*770*	*332*	*282*

* Percentages add to more than 100 because some people consulted at more than one site during the reference period.

Table 7.24   **(NHS) GP consultations**
(a) Percentage of persons who consulted a doctor in the 14 days before interview, by sex, age, and socio-economic group of head of household
(b) Average number of consultations per person per year, by sex, age, and socio-economic group of head of household

All persons   *Great Britain: 1998*

Socio-economic group of head of household*	Males						Females					
	Age						Age					
	0-4	5-15	16-44	45-64	65 and over	Total	0-4	5-15	16-44	45-64	65 and over	Total
(a) Percentage who consulted a doctor in the 14 days before interview												
Professional	16	4	5	9	22	9	[8]	8	16	16	14	14
Employers and managers	18	6	7	13	17	11	23	5	15	13	19	14
Intermediate non-manual	20	7	8	14	17	11	19	17	15	20	15	17
Junior non-manual	14	6	10	14	16	11	15	9	17	22	18	17
(subtotal)	17	6	8	13	18		18	9	16	17	17	15
Skilled manual and own account non-professional	17	10	9	15	21	13	20	10	18	17	20	17
Semi-skilled manual and personal service	21	8	10	13	18	13	20	12	19	20	21	19
Unskilled manual	[19]	7	12	12	11	12	[10]	16	22	24	23	21
(subtotal)	18	9	10	14	19		19	12	18	19	21	18
All persons	18	8	9	14	18	12	18	10	17	18	19	17
(b) Average number of consultations per person per year												
Professional	5	1	1	3	8	3	3	3	6	5	4	3
Employers and managers	6	2	3	4	5	4	6	1	4	4	6	4
Intermediate non-manual	7	2	3	4	5	4	7	5	5	6	5	5
Junior non-manual	4	2	3	4	5	3	5	3	6	7	6	5
(subtotal)	6	2	2	4	6		6	3	5	5	5	5
Skilled manual and own account non-professional	5	3	3	5	7	4	6	3	6	5	6	5
Semi-skilled manual and personal service	8	3	3	4	6	4	6	4	6	7	6	6
Unskilled manual	6	2	4	4	3	4	5	5	7	7	8	7
(subtotal)	6	3	3	4	6		6	4	6	6	7	6
All persons	6	2	3	4	6	4	6	3	5	6	6	5
Bases = 100%												
Professional	62	127	329	251	90	859	49	146	315	206	63	779
Employers and managers	176	343	751	571	310	2151	117	294	796	549	277	2033
Intermediate non-manual	75	147	399	229	142	992	73	149	493	295	213	1223
Junior non-manual	71	164	315	145	109	804	80	164	466	257	306	1273
Skilled manual and own account non-professional	175	399	1080	784	472	2910	174	372	1005	672	394	2617
Semi-skilled manual and personal service	115	220	477	282	217	1311	120	232	549	344	343	1588
Unskilled manual	27	69	156	104	61	417	31	80	148	131	155	545
All persons	743	1552	3713	2389	1410	9807	701	1510	4004	2495	1823	10533

* See the footnote to Table 7.3.

Table 7.25 **(NHS) GP consultations**
(a) Percentage of persons who consulted a doctor in the 14 days before interview, by sex, age, and economic activity status
(b) Average number of consultations per person per year, by sex, age, and economic activity status

All persons aged 16 and over   *Great Britain: 1998*

Economic activity status	Men				Women			
	Age				Age			
	16-44	45-64	65 and over	Total	16-44	45-64	65 and over	Total
(a) Percentage who consulted a doctor in the 14 days before interview								
Working	8	10	11	9	16	15	17	15
Unemployed	12	11	*	12	17	20	0	18
Economically inactive	14	23	19	19	19	22	20	20
All aged 16 and over	9	14	18	12	17	18	19	18
(b) Average number of consultations per person per year								
Working	2	3	3	3	5	5	4	5
Unemployed	3	3	*	3	6	7	0	7
Economically inactive	4	7	6	6	6	7	6	6
All aged 16 and over	3	4	6	4	5	6	6	6
Bases = 100%								
Working	*3055*	*1718*	*111*	*4884*	*2771*	*1420*	*72*	*4263*
Unemployed	*235*	*70*	*2*	*307*	*149*	*46*	*0*	*195*
Economically inactive	*419*	*598*	*1297*	*2314*	*1077*	*1028*	*1751*	*3856*
All aged 16 and over	*3709*	*2386*	*1410*	*7505*	*3997*	*2494*	*1823*	*8314*

* Base too small for analysis.

Table 7.26 **(NHS) GP consultations: percentage of persons consulting a doctor in the 14 days before interview who obtained a prescription from the doctor, by sex, age and non-manual/manual socio-economic group of head of household**

Persons who consulted in the 14 days before interview   *Great Britain: 1998*

Socio-economic group of head of household*	Males					Females				
	Age					Age				
	0-15	16-44	45-64	65 and over	Total	0-15	16-44	45-64	65 and over	Total
Percentage consulting who obtained a prescription										
Non-manual	63	59	73	69	66	55	59	67	69	62
Manual	71	66	72	73	70	77	70	74	80	74
All persons consulting	68	63	72	71	69	67	64	70	75	68
Bases = 100%										
Non-manual	*113*	*138*	*150*	*115*	*516*	*125*	*326*	*219*	*148*	*818*
Manual	*121*	*169*	*168*	*143*	*601*	*141*	*312*	*213*	*188*	*854*
All persons consulting	*250*	*320*	*323*	*260*	*1153*	*278*	*673*	*448*	*354*	*1753*

* See the footnote to Table 7.3.

Table 7.27 **GP consultations: consultations with doctors in the 14 days before interview by whether consultation was NHS or private**

Consultations in the 14 days before interview   *Great Britain: 1998*

Type of consultation	Males	Females	All persons
	%	%	%
NHS	96	97	97
Private	4	3	3
Base (all consultations) =100%	*1586*	*2371*	*3957*

Table 7.28 **Trends in percentages of persons who reported attending an outpatient or casualty department in a 3 month reference period: 1972 to 1998**

All persons*   *Great Britain*

	1972†	1975	1979	1981	1983	1985	1989	1991	1993	1995	1996	1998
						Percentages						
Males												
0- 4	8	9	13	12	10	13	11	14	14	12	13	16
5-15**	9	8	10	11	10	12	12	11	12	11	12	12
16-44**	11	9	11	11	12	12	12	11	12	12	13	13
45-64	11	10	13	12	13	16	15	15	15	16	16	17
65-74	10	11	15	14	15	16	18	18	20	21	20	25
75 and over	10	12	13	14	19	15	16	22	24	26	25	29
Total	10	10	12	11	12	13	13	13	14	14	15	16
Females												
0- 4	6	8	10	9	9	11	10	11	10	12	9	13
5-15**	6	6	8	8	9	9	9	8	10	9	10	11
16-44**	9	9	12	11	11	12	13	12	12	12	13	13
45-64	11	10	13	13	15	15	17	16	17	17	18	18
65-74	12	12	16	16	18	17	19	18	18	21	22	21
75 and over	13	10	16	16	16	17	20	20	22	22	24	26
Total	10	9	12	12	12	13	14	14	14	14	15	16
All persons												
0- 4	7	9	11	10	10	12	10	13	12	12	11	14
5-15**	8	7	9	10	10	10	11	10	11	10	11	11
16-44**	10	9	11	11	11	12	13	12	12	12	13	13
45-64	11	10	13	13	14	15	16	16	16	16	17	18
65-74	11	11	15	15	17	17	18	18	19	21	21	23
75 and over	12	10	15	15	17	16	18	21	22	24	24	27
Total	10	9	12	12	12	13	14	13	14	14	15	16

*   Bases for 1998 are shown in Table 7.1. Bases for earlier years are of a similar size and can be found in GHS Reports for each year.
†   1972 figures relate to England and Wales.
** These age-groups were 5-14 and 15-44 from 1972 to 1978.

Table 7.29 **Trends in day-patient treatment in the 12 months before interview, 1992 to 1998**

All persons   *Great Britain*

	1992	1993	1994	1995	1996	1998	Base (1998)* = 100%
			Percentage receiving day-patient treatment				
Males							
0- 4	4	4	4	4	5	6	743
5-15	2	3	3	3	3	4	1552
16-44	4	5	5	6	5	6	3716
45-64	4	4	5	7	6	7	2388
65-74	5	5	6	6	7	6	872
75 and over	4	3	5	5	6	12	537
Total	4	4	5	5	5	6	9808
Females							
0- 4	2	3	3	3	3	5	701
5-15	2	3	3	2	4	4	1509
16-44	5	6	7	6	7	8	4005
45-64	5	5	5	7	8	8	2495
65-74	4	5	5	5	6	6	989
75 and over	3	5	5	5	7	8	835
Total	4	5	5	5	6	7	10534
All persons							
0- 4	3	3	3	3	4	5	1444
5-15	2	3	3	3	3	4	3061
16-44	4	6	6	6	6	7	7721
45-64	5	5	5	7	7	8	4883
65-74	4	5	5	6	7	6	1861
75 and over	3	4	5	5	6	9	1372
Total	4	5	5	5	6	7	20342

* See the first footnote to Table 7.1.

Table 7.30 **Average number of separate days spent in hospital as a day-patient during the last 12 months**

All day-patients   *Great Britain: 1998*

Age	Male	Female	Total	Male	Female	Total
		Average number of days			Base (all day-patients)	
0-4	2	2	2	43	33	76
5-15	1	2	2	65	58	123
16-44	2	2	2	235	311	546
45-64	2	2	2	175	194	369
65-74	2	5	3	52	59	111
75 and over	2	3	3	62	67	129
All persons	2	2	2	632	722	1354

Table 7.31 **Trends in inpatient stays in the 12 months before interview, 1982 to 1998**

All persons   *Great Britain*

	1982	1985	1987	1989	1991	1993	1995	1996	1998	Base (1998)* = 100%
					Percentage with inpatient stay					
Males										
0- 4	14	12	10	12	10	10	9	9	9	743
5-15	6	8	6	7	6	6	5	5	5	1552
16-44	5	6	6	6	6	6	5	5	5	3716
45-64	8	8	9	8	8	9	9	8	8	2389
65-74	12	13	12	12	13	14	15	13	15	872
75 and over	14	17	20	17	20	21	21	18	21	538
Total	7	8	8	8	8	8	8	7	8	9810
Females										
0- 4	12	8	8	9	8	7	8	7	10	701
5-15	4	5	5	5	4	5	4	4	4	1510
16-44	15	16	16	15	15	13	12	12	11	4005
45-64	8	8	9	9	9	9	8	10	8	2495
65-74	8	18	11	11	11	10	11	12	10	989
75 and over	12	13	14	17	16	16	20	16	15	835
Total	11	11	12	12	11	11	10	10	10	10535
All persons										
0- 4	13	10	9	10	9	9	9	8	9	1444
5-15	5	6	6	6	5	5	4	4	5	3062
16-44	10	11	11	11	10	9	8	9	8	7721
45-64	8	8	9	9	8	9	8	9	8	4884
65-74	10	10	12	11	12	12	13	12	12	1861
75 and over	13	15	16	17	18	18	20	17	17	1373
Total	9	10	10	10	10	9	9	9	9	20345

* See the first footnote to Table 7.1.

Table 7.32 **Inpatient stays and outpatient attendances**
(a) Average number of inpatient stays per 100 persons in a 12 month reference period, by sex and age
(b) Average number of outpatient attendances per 100 persons per year, by sex and age

All persons   *Great Britain: 1998*

Age	(a) Average number of inpatient stays per 100 persons in a 12 month reference period			(b) Average number of outpatient attendances per 100 persons per year			Bases = 100%		
	Males	Females	Total	Males	Females	Total	Males	Females	Total
0- 4	12	13	12	92	74	83	743	701	1444
5-15	7	5	6	81	81	81	1552	1510	3062
16-44	6	8	7	108	118	113	3716	4005	7721
45-64	13	11	12	151	152	151	2389	2495	4884
65-74	21	12	16	246	186	214	872	989	1861
75 and over	28	20	23	240	206	219	538	835	1373
Total	11	10	10	133	131	132	9810	10535	20345

Table 7.33 **Average number of nights spent in hospital as an inpatient during the last 12 months**

All inpatients   *Great Britain: 1998*

Age	Male	Female	Total	Male	Female	Total
	Average number of nights			Base (all inpatients)		
0-4	6	7	6	70	67	137
5-15	6	6	6	82	57	139
16-44	5	4	4	170	453	623
45-64	9	7	8	190	200	390
65-74	12	10	11	122	91	213
75 and over	12	13	12	105	123	228
All persons	9	6	7	739	991	1730

Table 7.34 Difficulty with hearing, by sex and age: 1979, 1992, 1995 and 1998

Persons aged 16 and over   *Great Britain*

Age	1979					1992			
		Wears an aid	Hearing difficulty, and no aid	No hearing difficulty	Base = 100%		Wears an aid	Hearing difficulty, and no aid	No hearing difficulty	Base = 100%
Men										
16-44	%	0	6	93	5370	%	0	6	94	4209
45-64	%	2	17	82	3139	%	3	17	80	2598
65-74	%	7	24	69	1192	%	11	25	64	1024
75 and over	%	12	30	58	509	%	20	25	55	580
All aged 16 and over	%	2	13	85	10210	%	4	13	83	8411
Women										
16-44	%	0	5	94	5738	%	0	4	96	4775
45-64	%	2	10	88	3519	%	2	9	90	2829
65-74	%	6	18	77	1574	%	6	15	79	1227
75 and over	%	12	27	61	971	%	17	24	59	932
All aged 16 and over	%	2	10	87	11802	%	3	9	88	9763
Total										
16-44	%	0	5	94	11108	%	0	5	95	8984
45-64	%	2	13	84	6658	%	2	13	85	5427
65-74	%	6	21	74	2766	%	8	19	72	2251
75 and over	%	12	28	60	1480	%	18	25	57	1512
All aged 16 and over	%	2	11	86	22012	%	3	11	86	18174

Age	1995					1998			
		Wears an aid	Hearing difficulty, and no aid	No hearing difficulty	Base = 100%		Wears an aid	Hearing difficulty, and no aid	No hearing difficulty	Base = 100%
Men										
16-44	%	0	7	93	3763	%	0	7	92	3108
45-64	%	2	21	77	2453	%	2	22	76	2136
65-74	%	9	30	61	950	%	8	26	66	832
75 and over	%	21	27	51	513	%	23	30	47	502
All aged 16 and over	%	3	15	81	7679	%	4	16	80	6578
Women										
16-44	%	0	5	94	4327	%	0	5	95	3726
45-64	%	2	11	88	2755	%	2	11	87	2364
65-74	%	6	14	80	1104	%	5	16	79	956
75 and over	%	16	25	59	871	%	15	25	59	789
All aged 16 and over	%	3	10	87	9057	%	3	10	87	7835
Total										
16-44	%	0	6	94	8090	%	0	6	94	6834
45-64	%	2	16	83	5208	%	2	16	82	4500
65-74	%	7	21	71	2054	%	6	21	73	1788
75 and over	%	18	26	56	1384	%	18	27	55	1291
All aged 16 and over	%	3	12	84	16736	%	3	13	84	14413

Table 7.35 **Whether hearing problems continue when wearing hearing aid by age**

Persons aged 16 and over who wear a hearing aid   *Great Britain: 1998*

Age	Proportions who continue to have hearing problems when wearing aid	Base = 100%
16-44	*	17
45-64	63%	84
65-74	61%	116
75 and over	57%	235
All	59%	452

* Base too small for analysis.

Table 7.36 **Reasons for not wearing a hearing aid**

Persons aged 16 and over who no longer wear a working aid they possess   *Great Britain: 1998*

Reasons for not wearing aid*	
Doesn't help hearing	43%
Awkward/uncomfortable/badly fitting	27%
Appearance	11%
Hearing has improved	4%
Other	43%
Base = 100%	166

* The reasons given total more than 100%, because respondents could give more than one reason.

Table 7.37 **Reasons for buying a private hearing aid**

Persons aged 16 and over who have bought a private hearing aid   *Great Britain: 1998*

Reasons for buying private hearing aid*	
Better choice	65%
Not available on NHS	28%
Obtain aid more quickly	15%
Other	37%
Base = 100%	99

* The reasons given total more than 100%, because respondents could give more than one reason.

8 Smoking

Questions about smoking behaviour have been asked of all GHS respondents aged 16 and over in alternate years since 1974.

Data from the survey have demonstrated a decline in the prevalence of cigarette smoking since the mid-1970s. In 1992, these trends were used to help inform The Health of the Nation targets aimed at reducing cigarette smoking in England[1].

In the 1996 Living In Britain report, it was argued that the downward trend in the prevalence of cigarette smoking appeared to have 'levelled out during the 1990s'[2]. In December 1998 *Smoking Kills - a White Paper on tobacco* was released[3]. The White Paper expressed concern that increases in smoking prevalence reported in the 1996 GHS report may have represented 'a new upward trend in smoking'. It included revised targets for reducing the prevalence of cigarette smoking among adults from 28% to 24% by 2010 (with an interim target of 26% by 2005). Although these targets apply to all social classes, the White Paper states that 'smoking is disproportionately higher among the more disadvantaged' and argues that 'if we are to reduce smoking overall and reduce health inequalities we must start with the groups who smoke the most'.

This chapter presents data on trends in cigarette smoking, and focuses particularly on gender, age and socio-economic differences. In light of the observations concerning a possible levelling out or reversal of the downward trend in smoking prevalence, findings relating to the 1990s are discussed as well as overall trends since 1974. Other topics covered in the chapter include cigarette smoking and economic activity status; regional variations; consumption patterns; and types of cigarette smoked. The chapter concludes with a discussion of the age at which people start smoking and perceived dependency on cigarettes.

As noted in previous GHS reports, it is likely that the GHS underestimates consumption, and possibly prevalence. First, although young people aged 16 or 17 are given a self-completion questionnaire for this section of the survey, this may not completely eliminate the under-reporting of smoking behaviour due to the potential effect of parental disapproval. Second, it has been suggested that when respondents are asked to state the number of cigarettes that they smoke there may be a tendency for them to round down to the nearest multiple of ten[4]. Third, under-reporting of smoking behaviour among all adults may have increased in more recent years because of a general increase in negative attitudes towards smoking.

Trends in the prevalence of cigarette smoking

In 1998, 28% of men and 26% of women were current cigarette smokers. This represents a substantial reduction in the proportion of smokers since 1974, from 51% and 41% respectively. However, while prevalence declined steadily throughout the 1970s and 1980s, as mentioned earlier, it levelled out during the 1990s.

In 1998, prevalence for both men and women was the same as that in 1994. However, between 1996 and 1998, the prevalence of smoking fell by two percentage points for women and one percentage point for men, although the latter was not statistically significant. This suggests that the hypothesis of a possible upturn in smoking among

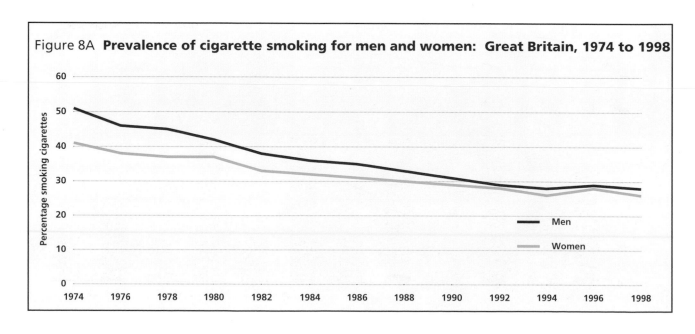

Figure 8A **Prevalence of cigarette smoking for men and women: Great Britain, 1974 to 1998**

women, expressed in the 1996 GHS report, may have been overly pessimistic.

Prevalence varied among different age groups. In 1998, cigarette smoking was:

- highest among those aged 20-24 years old (42% for men and 39% for women);
- lowest among men and women aged 60 and over (16% for both sexes).

Between 1996 and 1998, the only group reporting a significant change in smoking prevalence was women aged 60 and over; among this group prevalence declined from 19% to 16%. Smoking among younger respondents is a key area of interest. It should be noted that whilst prevalence increased by four percentage points, to 30%, among men aged 16-19 and decreased for women in this age group by one percentage point, to 31%, neither of these changes was statistically significant.

The proportion of ex-regular cigarette smokers in 1998 was 31% among men and 21% among women. These proportions have remained largely unchanged for men since 1986 and for women since 1992. Among older age groups, there was a marked difference between the sexes in the proportion of ex-regular smokers. For example, 54% of men aged 60 and over were ex-regular smokers in 1998 compared to 29% of women in this age group.

Between 1974 and 1998 there has been a large increase, from 25% to 41%, in the proportion of men who have never been regular smokers. Table 8.1 shows that since 1974, smoking has been more common among men than

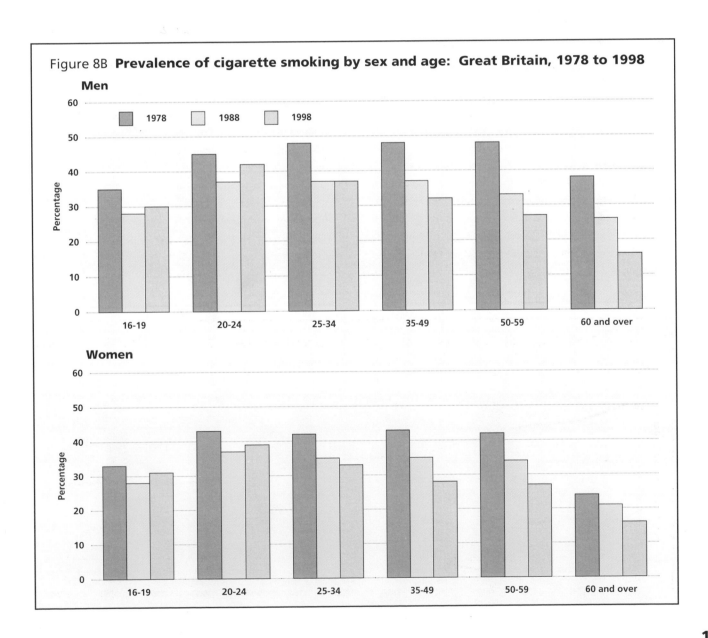

Figure 8B **Prevalence of cigarette smoking by sex and age: Great Britain, 1978 to 1998**

women. This helps to explain why the change in the proportion of women who have never been regular smokers is less marked than it is among men; since 1974, about half of women have been in this category.

In 1998, the only group which experienced a decrease in the proportion who had never smoked regularly was women aged 60 and over; 63% in 1974 and 55% in 1998 had never smoked.

The difference in smoking trends between men and women can be explained by two main factors. First, there is a cohort effect which results from the fact that smoking was more common among men several years before it became so with women. Second, men who smoked cigarettes were more likely than women to have given up. However, it should be noted that it is more common for

men who give up smoking cigarettes, compared with women, to begin smoking cigars or pipes.

Tables 8.1- 8.3, Figures 8A,8B

The data presented so far have been for Great Britain, the area covered by the GHS. However GHS data can be analysed to provide figures for England. Table 8.31 shows that in 1998 overall prevalence in England, at 28% for men and 26% for women, is the same as that for Great Britain. The Health Survey for England is a household survey commissioned by the Department of Health from the National Centre for Social Research (formerly SCPR) which includes information about smoking. The two surveys give broadly similar results for England, as confirmed by a report from the National Centre[5]. Since the two surveys cover different ranges of subject areas, the context of the questions on smoking in the two surveys also differs, which may affect responses.   **Tables 8.4-8.5**

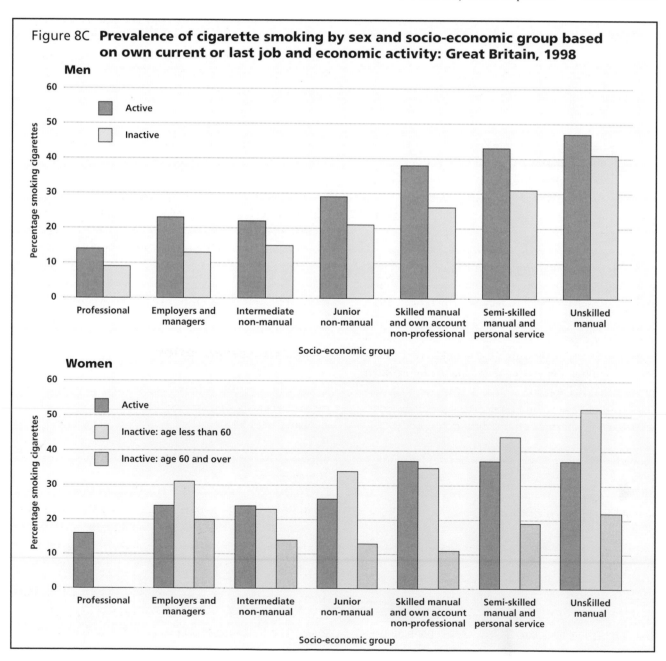

Figure 8C **Prevalence of cigarette smoking by sex and socio-economic group based on own current or last job and economic activity: Great Britain, 1998**

Cigarette smoking and socio-economic group

This section discusses smoking prevalence among different socio-economic groups.

Prior to 1992, the method for assigning socio-economic group to GHS respondents involved classifying married or cohabiting women according to their partner's present (or last) job (other adults in the household were classified according to their own current or previous job). In 1992, for the first time, the chapter on smoking behaviour included a table that classified all household members by the socio-economic group of the head of household. The former definition has been retained to permit analysis of change over time, as in, for example Tables 8.7 and 8.13. Otherwise, either the head of household's socio-economic group (Tables 8.6 and 8.21) or the respondent's own socio-economic group (Table 8.8) is used where appropriate.

- In 1998, 35% of men living in households in the manual group smoked cigarettes compared to 21% of those from non-manual households. The corresponding proportions for women were 31% and 21%.

Men who lived in households in the unskilled manual group were nearly three times as likely as those who lived in professional households to smoke; 44% did so, compared to 15%. **Table 8.6**

As stated in the introduction, it had been hypothesised that the general decline in prevalence may have levelled out during the 1990s. Among women from both manual and non-manual households, between 1990 and 1998, there was some evidence of a downward trend in smoking. During this period, prevalence decreased significantly among women living in manual households from 34% to 31% and among women from non-manual households it fell four percentage points to 21%. There was no statistically significant change in prevalence among men from manual and non-manual groups during this period.

Among both men and women there has not been any noticeable change in the differences in prevalence between respondents from manual compared with non-manual socio-economic groups. **Table 8.7**

Analysis by economic activity status indicates that men who were economically active were more likely than men who were economically inactive to smoke; 31% and 23% respectively did so. This finding holds true for all socio-economic groups. Lower smoking prevalence among economically inactive men can be partly explained by the lower prevalence of smoking among men aged 60 and over; this age group forms the majority of economically inactive men.

Among women, prevalence was highest among those aged 16-59 and who were economically inactive (34%) and least likely among those aged 60 and over who were economically inactive (15%). However, this varied among different socio-economic groups.

Between 1996 and 1998, the prevalence of cigarette smoking among all economically inactive women fell, from 26% to 23%. This reduction was partly due to a four percentage point fall in smoking, from 19% to 15%, among economically inactive women aged 60 and over (table not shown). **Table 8.8, Figure 8C**

Regional variation in cigarette smoking

In 1998, as in previous years, prevalence was higher in Scotland (30%) than in England (27%) or Wales (27%). During the 1990s, the proportion of smokers has ranged from 30% to 34% in Scotland and from 27% to 29% in England. In Wales, prevalence has been 27% since 1994. In all three countries, the decline in prevalence has been slower in the 1990s than in the previous two decades.

Within the standard regions of England, prevalence was highest in the North West and lowest in East Anglia; 31% compared with 22% respectively. Among men the highest proportion of current cigarette smokers was in Greater London (33%) and the lowest was in East Anglia (23%). Among women, smoking prevalence was highest in the North West (32%) and lowest in East Anglia (21%). **Table 8.10**

Cigarette consumption

In 1998, as in previous years, male smokers smoked more cigarettes per week on average than female smokers; 109 compared with 93.

Cigarette consumption varied by age. For both men and women smokers:

- those aged 16-19 tended to smoke the fewest cigarettes per week (72 for men and 70 for women);
- those aged 50-59 tended, on average, to smoke most cigarettes per week (125 for men and 105 for women).

Among women aged less than 35, there has been a decline in the average number of cigarettes smoked per week since 1974; for example women aged 25-34 smoked 108 cigarettes in 1974 and 87 in 1998. However, despite some variations over time, there is some evidence of an increase in the average number of cigarettes smoked per week by women in the older age groups; for example in 1974 women aged 60 and over smoked an average of 68 cigarettes a week compared with 84 in 1998. Among men, the average number of cigarettes men smoked per week decreased from 125 to 109 between 1974 and 1998. This downward trend was particularly evident among men aged under 50.

Consumption levels were higher among male and female smokers from manual socio-economic groups than those from non-manual groups. For example, in 1998:

- men from the unskilled manual group smoked on average 120 cigarettes a week, while those from the professional group smoked an average of 91;
- among women, those in the semi-skilled manual group smoked 102 cigarettes per week on average compared to those in the professional group who smoked 65 a week. **Tables 8.12-8.13**

In 1998, 19% of women were light smokers (fewer than 20 cigarettes a day), while 7% were heavy smokers (20 or more a day). The equivalent proportions for men were 18% and 10% respectively. The GHS shows that, since 1974, female cigarette smokers have tended to be light rather than heavy smokers, for example in 1974 28% were light and 13% were heavy smokers. However, among male cigarette smokers, the shift towards lighter smoking did not emerge until the early 1980s; for example, in 1974 26% of men were heavy and 25% were light smokers compared with 10% and 18%, respectively, in 1998.

Table 8.14

Lighter cigarette smoking is more common than heavier smoking across all age groups. However, it is particularly pronounced among the younger age groups. For example, in 1998 27% of men and 28% of women aged 16-19 were light smokers and 3% were heavy smokers, while the equivalent proportions for men aged 50-59 years old were 14% and 13% and for women 17% and 10%.

Table 8.15

Cigarette type and tar level

Filter cigarettes continue to be the most widely smoked, especially among women; in 1998 92% of female smokers smoked this type of cigarette compared to 74% of male smokers. There were small increases in the proportion smoking mainly hand-rolled cigarettes, 25% of men and

7% of women smoked this type of cigarette in 1998 (compared with 23% and 6% respectively in 1996). While these increases were not statistically significant, they represent a continuation of the steady increase in the use of hand-rolled cigarettes that has been evident since 1974.

Table 8.18

Tables 8.20 and 8.21 show the proportions smoking cigarettes yielding different levels of tar; information which is only available for manufactured cigarettes.[6] The same groupings have been used as in previous GHS reports. However, this year the actual tar yields are shown.

In 1998, brands with a tar yield of between 12 but less than 15 milligrams were most commonly smoked; 47% of men and 41% of women smoked brands yielding this level of tar. Such brands were particularly likely to be smoked by younger smokers; around half of smokers aged under 25 smoked such brands.

Brands with a tar yield of 12 but less than 15 milligrams were more likely to be smoked by men (52%) and women (47%) smokers from the manual socio-economic groups than by those from the non-manual groups, among whom 42% of men and 34% of women smoked these brands.

Among smokers, men from the non-manual groups were more likely than men from the manual groups to smoke cigarettes with a tar yield of less than 8 milligrams; 30% did so, compared with 10%. The equivalent figures for women present a similar pattern of smoking; 28% of women smokers from the non-manual and 16% from the manual groups smoked these brands. **Tables 8.20-8.21**

Cigar and pipe smoking

A decline in the prevalence of pipe and cigar smoking among men has been evident since the survey began, with most of the reduction occurring in the 1970s and 1980s. In 1974, 34% of men smoked cigars compared with 6% in 1998. Only a small number of women smoked cigars in 1974, and by 1998, the percentages were scarcely measurable on the GHS. **Table 8.22**

Age started smoking

Smoking Kills stated that people who start smoking earlier are more likely to smoke for a longer period of time and are more likely to die prematurely from a smoking-related disease. Data from the GHS indicate that there are sex and socio-economic differences in the age at which people start smoking.

- Nearly two-thirds of people who had smoked regularly, started before they were 18, and well over a third started before they reached the age of 16.

Among people who had ever smoked regularly, men were more likely than women to have begun smoking before they were 16; 43% and 31% respectively did so. Over a fifth of women (22%) did not start smoking until they were in their twenties or over, compared with 15% of men.

In 1998, those from manual socio-economic groups were more likely than those from non-manual groups to have started smoking at a younger age. For example, among those who had ever smoked regularly:

- 59% of men and 40% of women from the unskilled manual socio-economic group started smoking before the age of 16;
- 30% of men and 20% of women from the professional group started smoking before 16. **Table 8.24**

Dependence on cigarette smoking

Since 1992, the GHS has asked questions concerning the level of dependency among cigarette smokers. They cover three main areas:

- how difficult or easy it would be not to smoke for a whole day;

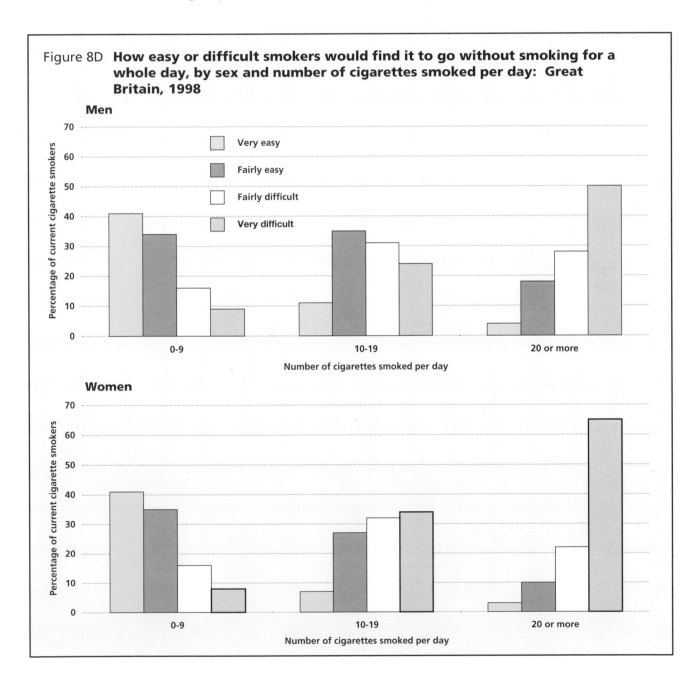

Figure 8D **How easy or difficult smokers would find it to go without smoking for a whole day, by sex and number of cigarettes smoked per day: Great Britain, 1998**

- whether respondents would like to stop smoking;
- the time between waking and smoking the first cigarette.

In 1998, 58% of smokers felt that it would be either very or fairly difficult to go without smoking for a whole day. Not surprisingly, those who smoked more cigarettes per day were more likely to say this was the case. For example, 82% of those smoking 20 or more a day said that not smoking for a day would be difficult. The equivalent proportion for those smoking 10-19 cigarettes a day was 61% and for those smoking fewer than 10 a day it was 24%. Among those who smoked 10 or more cigarettes a day, women were more likely than men to say that they would find it difficult to go a whole day without a cigarette.   **Table 8.25, Figure 8D**

The proportions of men and women who would like to give up smoking were very similar; 69% and 70% said they would. Analysis by the number of cigarettes smoked per day indicates that, for both sexes, those who smoke between 10 and 19 a day were more likely to say they would like to give up; 73% of men and 75% of women in this group did so. Those smoking fewer than 10 cigarettes a day were least likely to say they wanted to give up; 62% of men and 65% of women smoking this amount wanted to quit.   **Table 8.27**

Between 69% and 73% of those aged 16-59 wanted to quit. This compares with 60% of those aged 60 and over.
                                Table 8.28

In 1998, 15% of smokers had their first cigarette within five minutes of waking up. The likelihood of doing so was associated with the number smoked per day; for example, those smoking 20 or more cigarettes a day were more likely than those using less than 10 a day to smoke a cigarette within five minutes of waking; 31% of the former and 2% of the latter did so.   **Table 8.30**

The shorter the time between waking and smoking the first cigarette, the greater the likelihood that smokers would say they would find it difficult not to smoke for a whole day. This was particularly true for women.   Among those who smoked their first cigarette within five minutes of waking, for example, 85% said they would find it difficult not to smoke for a day, while the equivalent figure for those who waited at least two hours before smoking was only 19%.   **Table 8.32**

Notes and references

1. Department of Health. *The Health of the Nation: a strategy for health in England*, London: HMSO 1992.

2. Thomas M et al, *Living in Britain. Results from the 1996 General Household Survey*, London: The Stationery Office 1998.

3. *Smoking kills - a White Paper on tobacco*, The Stationery Office (1998).

4. Bennett N et al, *Living in Britain. Results from the 1994 General Household Survey*, London: HMSO 1996.

5. Evaluating the Health Survey for England (HSE) as a Vehicle for Monitoring Trends in Smoking, published in July 1999.

6. Information on tar yields is only collected for manufactured cigarettes. Tar yields are provided by the laboratory of the Government Chemist.

Table 8.1 Prevalence of cigarette smoking by sex and age: 1974 to 1998

Persons aged 16 and over *Great Britain*

Age	1974	1976	1978	1980	1982	1984	1986	1988	1990	1992	1994	1996	1998	Base (1998)* =100%
						Percentage smoking cigarettes								
Men														
16-19	42	39	35	32	31	29	30	28	28	29	28	26	30	364
20-24	52	47	45	44	41	40	41	37	38	39	40	43	42	340
25-34	56	48	48	47	40	40	37	37	36	34	34	38	37	1192
35-49	55	50	48	45	40	39	37	37	34	32	31	30	32	1802
50-59	53	49	48	47	42	39	35	33	28	28	27	28	27	1068
60 and over	44	40	38	36	33	30	29	26	24	21	18	18	16	1813
All aged 16 and over	51	46	45	42	38	36	35	33	31	29	28	29	28	6579
Women														
16-19	38	34	33	32	30	32	30	28	32	25	27	32	31	373
20-24	44	45	43	40	40	36	38	37	39	37	38	36	39	434
25-34	46	43	42	44	37	36	35	35	34	34	30	34	33	1474
35-49	49	45	43	43	38	36	34	35	33	30	28	30	28	2091
50-59	48	46	42	44	40	39	35	34	29	29	26	26	27	1211
60 and over	26	24	24	24	23	23	22	21	20	19	17	19	16	2247
All aged 16 and over	41	38	37	37	33	32	31	30	29	28	26	28	26	7830
Total														
16-19	40	36	34	32	30	31	30	28	30	27	27	29	31	737
20-24	48	46	44	42	40	38	39	37	38	38	39	39	40	774
25-34	51	45	45	46	38	38	36	36	35	34	32	36	35	2666
35-49	52	48	45	44	39	37	36	36	34	31	30	30	30	3893
50-59	51	47	45	45	41	39	35	33	29	29	27	27	27	2279
60 and over	34	31	30	29	27	26	25	23	21	20	17	18	16	4060
All aged 16 and over	45	42	40	39	35	34	33	32	30	28	27	28	27	14409

* Bases for earlier years are of a similar size and can be found in GHS Reports for each year.

Table 8.2 Ex-regular cigarette smokers by sex and age: 1974 to 1998

Persons aged 16 and over *Great Britain*

Age	1974	1976	1978	1980	1982	1984	1986	1988	1990	1992	1994	1996	1998	Base (1998)* = 100%
						Percentage of ex-regular cigarette smokers								
Men														
16-19	3	5	4	5	4	5	5	4	4	5	5	5	5	364
20-24	9	11	9	8	9	8	11	10	8	8	7	10	8	340
25-34	18	20	18	18	20	20	20	17	16	16	16	13	13	1192
35-49	21	27	26	27	32	31	33	31	32	29	27	27	22	1802
50-59	30	33	35	35	38	37	38	41	42	41	40	41	41	1068
60 and over	37	43	43	45	47	48	52	53	52	55	55	55	54	1813
All 16 and over	23	27	27	28	30	30	32	32	32	32	31	32	31	6579
Women														
16-19	4	5	5	4	6	6	7	5	6	5	6	5	7	373
20-24	9	10	8	9	9	9	9	8	8	9	10	11	8	434
25-34	12	13	14	13	15	16	16	16	14	15	14	13	14	1474
35-49	10	12	13	13	15	17	20	21	20	22	21	18	19	2091
50-59	13	15	18	17	19	18	18	19	20	22	22	25	25	1211
60 and over	11	14	16	19	20	22	23	25	27	29	29	28	29	2247
All 16 and over	11	12	14	14	16	17	18	19	19	21	21	20	21	7830

* See the footnote to Table 8.1.

Table 8.3 **Percentage who have never smoked cigarettes regularly by sex and age: 1974 to 1998**

Persons aged 16 and over   *Great Britain*

Age	1974	1976	1978	1980	1982	1984	1986	1988	1990	1992	1994	1996	1998	Base (1998)* = 100%
						Percentage who have never smoked regularly								
Men														
16-19	56	56	61	62	65	66	65	69	68	67	67	69	64	364
20-24	38	42	46	48	50	52	47	53	54	52	53	47	49	340
25-34	26	32	33	34	39	39	43	46	48	50	50	49	50	1192
35-49	24	23	26	27	28	30	30	32	34	39	42	43	46	1802
50-59	16	18	17	18	20	24	26	26	31	31	33	31	32	1068
60 and over	18	18	18	19	20	22	19	22	24	24	27	28	30	1813
All 16 and over	25	27	29	30	32	34	34	35	37	38	40	40	41	6579
Women														
16-19	58	61	62	63	64	62	62	67	62	70	67	63	62	373
20-24	47	45	49	51	51	55	54	55	53	54	52	54	53	434
25-34	42	45	44	43	48	48	48	50	52	51	55	53	53	1474
35-49	41	43	44	44	47	47	46	44	48	49	51	52	52	2091
50-59	38	39	39	39	41	43	47	48	51	49	52	49	48	1211
60 and over	63	62	60	57	57	55	55	54	54	52	54	53	55	2247
All 16 and over	49	50	49	49	51	51	51	51	52	52	54	53	53	7830

* See the footnote to Table 8.1.

Table 8.4   **Cigarette-smoking status by age and sex: 1998 General Household Survey**

Persons aged 16 and over   *England: 1998*

Cigarette-smoking status*	Age							Total
	16-24	25-34	35-44	45-54	55-64	65-74	75 and over	
	%	%	%	%	%	%	%	%
Men								
Current smokers:								
Less than 10	12	10	7	5	4	3	4	7
10, less than 20	16	16	12	11	8	6	2	11
20 or more	8	10	13	14	10	6	2	10
Total current cigarette smokers†	36	37	32	30	23	16	8	28
Ex-regular smokers	7	14	21	33	46	56	61	31
Never or only occasionally smoked cigarettes	57	49	48	36	31	28	30	41
Base = 100%	*604*	*1035*	*1033*	*1000*	*815*	*714*	*430*	*5631*
Women								
Current smokers:								
Less than 10	16	11	7	7	6	6	5	8
10, less than 20	16	15	11	11	10	5	4	11
20 or more	5	7	10	10	7	4	2	7
Total current cigarette smokers†	36	33	27	28	23	16	12	26
Ex-regular smokers	8	14	19	24	23	34	26	21
Never or only occasionally smoked cigarettes	56	53	54	48	54	50	62	53
Base = 100%	*675*	*1258*	*1221*	*1117*	*891*	*824*	*680*	*6666*

* Current smokers of cigars and pipes only are classified according to their cigarette-smoking status ie. 'never regularly smoked' or 'ex-regular smoker'.

† Includes those for whom number of cigarettes was not known.

Table 8.5   **Cigarette-smoking status by age and sex: 1998 Health Survey**

Persons aged 16 and over   *England: 1998*

Cigarette-smoking status*	Age							Total
	16-24	25-34	35-44	45-54	55-64	65-74	75 and over	
	%	%	%	%	%	%	%	%
Men								
Current smokers:								
Less than 10	13	11	5	5	4	4	4	7
10, less than 20	18	15	12	9	9	8	3	11
20 or more	9	10	13	14	11	6	2	10
All current smokers†	40	36	31	28	23	18	9	28
Ex-regular smokers	6	13	23	35	47	54	62	31
Never regularly smoked	54	50	46	37	29	28	28	40
Base = 100%	*857*	*1335*	*1304*	*1285*	*985*	*836*	*561*	*7163*
Women								
Current smokers:								
Less than 10	16	10	8	5	6	6	5	8
10, less than 20	15	14	12	11	11	9	3	11
20 or more	6	9	10	10	8	4	2	8
All current smokers†	38	34	30	26	25	19	10	27
Ex-regular smokers	8	14	18	24	25	33	33	21
Never regularly smoked	54	53	52	50	50	48	57	52
Base = 100%	*991*	*1629*	*1571*	*1483*	*1147*	*967*	*906*	*8694*

* Current smokers of cigars and pipes only are classified according to their cigarette-smoking status ie. 'never regularly smoked' or 'ex-regular smoker'.

† Includes those for whom number of cigarettes was not known.

Table 8.6 **Cigarette-smoking status by sex and socio-economic group of head of household**

Persons aged 16 and over   *Great Britain: 1998*

Socio-economic group of head of household		Current cigarette smokers			Current non-smokers of cigarettes		Base = 100%
		Light (under 20 per day)	Heavy (20 or more per day)	All current smokers	Ex-regular cigarette smokers	Never or only occasionally smoked cigarettes	
Men							
Professional	%	11	4	15	29	56	*578*
Employers and managers	%	13	8	21	34	45	*1431*
Intermediate and junior non-manual	%	16	8	24	29	47	*1219*
Skilled manual and own account non-professional	%	20	13	33	32	36	*2009*
Semi-skilled manual & personal service	%	23	15	38	32	30	*857*
Unskilled manual	%	27	16	44	25	32	*276*
Total non-manual	%	14	7	21	31	48	*3228*
Total manual	%	21	14	35	31	34	*3142*
All aged 16 and over*	%	18	10	28	31	41	*6579*
Women							
Professional	%	12	2	14	21	65	*545*
Employers and managers	%	15	5	20	21	59	*1521*
Intermediate and junior non-manual	%	18	6	24	21	54	*1907*
Skilled manual and own account non-professional	%	20	10	30	21	49	*1957*
Semi-skilled manual & personal service	%	22	11	33	20	48	*1174*
Unskilled manual	%	22	10	32	22	46	*409*
Total non-manual	%	16	5	21	21	57	*3973*
Total manual	%	21	10	31	21	48	*3540*
All aged 16 and over*	%	19	7	26	21	53	*7830*

* Persons whose head of household was in the Armed Forces or a full-time student are not shown as separate categories but are included in the total.

Table 8.7 Prevalence of cigarette smoking by sex and socio-economic group: 1974 to 1998

Persons aged 16 and over   *Great Britain*

Socio-economic group*	1974	1976	1978	1980	1982	1984	1986	1988	1990	1992	1994	1996	1998	Base (1998)† =100%
							Percentage smoking cigarettes							
Men														
Professional	29	25	25	21	20	17	18	16	16	14	16	12	15	569
Employers and managers	46	38	37	35	29	29	28	26	24	23	20	20	21	1437
Intermediate and junior non-manual	45	40	38	35	30	30	28	25	25	25	24	24	23	1209
Skilled manual and own account non-professional	56	51	49	48	42	40	40	39	36	34	33	32	33	2004
Semi-skilled manual and personal service	56	53	53	49	47	45	43	40	39	39	38	41	38	869
Unskilled manual	61	58	60	57	49	49	43	43	48	42	40	41	45	278
Total non-manual	45	37	36	33	28	28	26	24	23	22	21	21	21	3215
Total manual	56	52	51	49	44	43	40	40	38	36	35	35	36	3151
All aged 16 and over*	51	46	45	42	38	36	35	33	31	29	28	29	28	6579
Women														
Professional	25	28	23	21	21	15	19	17	16	13	12	11	14	536
Employers and managers	38	35	33	33	29	29	27	26	23	21	20	18	20	1511
Intermediate and junior non-manual	38	36	33	34	30	28	27	27	27	27	23	28	24	1916
Skilled manual and own account non-professional	46	42	42	43	39	37	36	35	32	31	29	30	30	1926
Semi-skilled manual and personal service	43	41	41	39	36	37	35	37	36	35	32	36	33	1185
Unskilled manual	43	38	41	41	41	36	33	39	36	35	34	36	33	417
Total non-manual	38	35	32	32	29	27	26	25	25	23	21	22	21	3963
Total manual	45	41	41	41	38	37	36	36	34	33	31	33	31	3528
All aged 16 and over*	41	38	37	37	33	32	31	30	29	28	26	28	26	7830

* Socio-economic group corresponds to the present job of those currently working and to the last job of those not currently working. Married women whose husbands were in the household are classified according to their husband's occupation. Members of the Armed Forces, persons in inadequately described occupations and all persons who have never worked have not been shown as separate categories but are included in the figures shown as totals.

† See the footnote to Table 8.1.

Table 8.8 **Prevalence of cigarette smoking by sex and socio-economic group based on own current or last job, whether economically active or inactive, and, for economically inactive women, age**

Persons aged 16 and over   *Great Britain: 1998*

Socio-economic group*	Men			Women				
	Active	Inactive	Total	Active	Inactive 16-59	Inactive 60 and over	Total inactive	Total
				Percentage smoking cigarettes				
Professional	14	9	13	16	†	†	[7]	14
Employers and managers	23	13	20	24	31	20	25	24
Intermediate non-manual	22	15	20	24	23	14	18	22
Junior non-manual	29	21	27	26	34	13	21	24
Skilled manual and own account non-professional	38	26	34	37	35	11	19	28
Semi-skilled manual and personal service	43	31	39	37	44	19	30	33
Unskilled manual	47	41	44	37	52	22	30	33
Total	31	23	28	28	34	15	23	26
Bases=100%								
Professional	*434*	*108*	*542*	*125*	*14*	*13*	*27*	*152*
Employers and managers	*927*	*411*	*1338*	*551*	*100*	*140*	*240*	*791*
Intermediate non-manual	*498*	*170*	*668*	*900*	*176*	*282*	*458*	*1358*
Junior non-manual	*360*	*147*	*508*	*1187*	*379*	*641*	*1020*	*2209*
Skilled manual and own account non-professional	*1268*	*674*	*1942*	*268*	*100*	*185*	*285*	*553*
Semi-skilled manual and personal service	*572*	*305*	*878*	*748*	*358*	*452*	*810*	*1559*
Unskilled manual	*168*	*113*	*281*	*222*	*93*	*241*	*334*	*556*
Total	*4439*	*2138*	*6577*	*4175*	*1583*	*2069*	*3652*	*7827*

* Full-time students, members of the Armed Forces, and those who have never worked are not shown as separate categories but are included in the totals.
† Base too small to enable reliable analysis to be made.

Table 8.9 **Cigarette-smoking status by sex and marital status**

Persons aged 16 and over   *Great Britain: 1998*

Marital status		Current cigarette smokers			Current non-smokers of cigarettes		Base = 100%
		Light (under 20 per day)	Heavy (20 or more per day)	Total	Ex-regular cigarette smokers	Never or only occasionally smoked cigarettes	
Men							
Single	%	26	9	35	11	54	*1355*
Married/cohabiting	%	15	10	25	35	39	*4506*
Married couple	%	13	9	23	38	40	*3944*
Cohabiting couple	%	31	15	46	17	37	*562*
Widowed/divorced/separated	%	17	15	32	39	29	*702*
All aged 16 and over	%	18	10	28	31	41	*6563*
Women							
Single	%	27	5	32	10	58	*1223*
Married/cohabiting	%	17	7	24	22	54	*4848*
Married couple	%	15	6	21	23	55	*4242*
Cohabiting couple	%	30	12	41	16	43	*606*
Widowed/divorced/separated	%	19	9	28	24	48	*1745*
All aged 16 and over	%	19	7	26	21	53	*7816*

Table 8.10 Prevalence of cigarette smoking by sex and standard region: 1976 to 1998

Persons aged 16 and over   *Great Britain*

Percentage smoking cigarettes

Standard region*	1976	1978	1980	1982	1984	1986	1988	1990	1992	1994	1996	1998	Base† (1998) =100%
Men													
England													
North	49	43	44	43	36	38	37	33	28	29	28	25	431
Yorkshire and Humberside	45	43	44	39	41	35	32	29	28	29	30	29	550
North West	50	46	45	37	36	34	32	34	29	26	30	29	660
East Midlands	46	43	44	35	33	33	34	29	27	28	25	26	462
West Midlands	47	44	40	39	35	38	29	31	28	25	28	31	638
East Anglia	45	44	40	35	27	36	30	28	30	27	24	23	245
Greater London	46	48	44	38	42	36	38	32	32	32	32	33	674
Outer Metropolitan Area	41	40	38	35	33	32	30	31	26	26	24 ⌉	26	1338
Outer South East	45	44	43	37	32	32	32	29	30	28	29 ⌋		
South West	43	43	36	35	30	31	29	29	28	27	28	25	632
All England	45	44	42	37	35	34	32	31	29	28	28	28	5630
Wales	46	44	45	36	42	33	35	30	32	28	28	28	357
Scotland	50	48	46	45	43	37	36	33	34	31	33	33	592
Great Britain	46	45	42	38	36	35	33	31	29	28	29	28	6579
Women													
England													
North	42	39	39	38	35	33	35	31	32	27	32	29	504
Yorkshire and Humberside	35	36	38	32	38	32	31	29	28	28	25	28	715
North West	42	41	41	35	35	35	34	33	30	28	30	32	789
East Midlands	37	36	35	31	30	29	31	28	23	24	27	25	585
West Midlands	39	34	35	32	31	31	29	28	25	23	28	25	690
East Anglia	33	33	32	25	20	28	28	24	25	21	25	21	285
Greater London	38	37	36	34	33	31	31	29	26	26	27	27	815
Outer Metropolitan Area	35	34	33	29	28	29	28	27	27	24	25 ⌉	22	1535
Outer South East	32	31	35	30	30	29	25	27	26	25	26 ⌋		
South West	37	37	32	33	29	27	26	25	23	22	26	24	747
All England	37	36	36	32	32	31	30	28	27	25	27	26	6665
Wales	37	37	39	34	32	30	28	31	33	27	27	26	422
Scotland	43	42	42	39	35	35	37	35	34	29	31	29	743
Great Britain	38	37	37	33	32	31	30	29	28	26	28	26	7830
All persons													
England													
North	45	41	41	41	36	35	36	32	31	28	31	27	935
Yorkshire and Humberside	40	39	40	35	39	34	32	29	28	28	28	28	1265
North West	46	43	43	36	35	35	33	33	30	27	30	31	1449
East Midlands	41	39	39	33	31	31	32	28	25	26	26	26	1047
West Midlands	43	39	37	35	33	34	29	29	26	24	28	28	1328
East Anglia	39	38	36	30	24	31	29	26	27	24	25	22	530
Greater London			40	36	37	33	34	31	29	29	29	30	1489
Outer Metropolitan Area	39	39	35	32	30	31	29	29	26	25	25 ⌉	24	2873
Outer South East			39	33	31	30	28	28	28	27	28 ⌋		
South West	40	39	34	34	30	29	28	27	25	24	27	24	1379
All England	41	40	39	35	33	32	31	29	28	26	28	27	12295
Wales	41	40	42	35	37	31	31	31	32	27	27	27	779
Scotland	46	45	44	42	39	36	37	34	34	30	32	30	1335
Great Britain	42	40	39	35	34	33	32	30	28	27	28	27	14409

* The data have not been standardised to take account of age or socio-economic group.
† Bases for earlier years are of a similar size and can be found in GHS Reports for each year.

Table 8.11 **Prevalence of cigarette smoking by sex and NHS Regional Office area in England**

Persons aged 16 and over   England: 1998

NHS Regional Office area	Men	Women	Total
		Percentage smoking cigarettes	
Northern and Yorkshire	27	29	28
Trent	28	25	26
Anglia and Oxford	24	19	21
North Thames	30	27	28
South Thames	30	23	26
South and West	25	24	24
West Midlands	31	25	28
North West	29	32	31
All England	28	26	27
Bases = 100%			
Northern and Yorkshire	822	990	1812
Trent	553	726	1279
Anglia and Oxford	538	623	1161
North Thames	724	856	1580
South Thames	725	848	1573
South and West	938	1100	2038
West Midlands	642	693	1335
North West	694	834	1528
All England*	5636	6670	12306

* Addresses are classified to health regions according to their full postcode, but to standard regions according to postcode sector only.

Table 8.12 **Average weekly cigarette consumption per smoker by sex and age: 1974 to 1998**

Current cigarette smokers aged 16 and over   Great Britain

Age	1974	1976	1978	1980	1982	1984	1986	1988	1990	1992	1994	1996	1998	Standard deviation (1998)	Base (1998)* = 100%
						Mean number of cigarettes per week									
Men															
16-19	110	106	98	99	87	87	86	84	89	81	71	82	72	43.6	111
20-24	132	135	122	113	114	107	108	109	110	92	94	101	96	56.4	144
25-34	136	138	134	135	121	114	110	120	115	100	107	102	92	50.9	443
35-49	138	141	138	140	137	130	133	136	135	130	126	126	121	76.6	575
50-59	127	130	137	130	129	126	120	132	121	129	142	119	125	76.4	291
60 and over	100	108	104	102	109	103	103	102	106	102	99	107	112	66.5	293
All aged 16 and over	125	129	127	124	121	115	115	120	118	112	114	111	109	68.2	1857
Women															
16-19	86	89	90	84	76	80	77	79	80	70	70	68	70	39.6	115
20-24	99	110	101	102	100	91	85	95	92	88	90	79	83	57.1	169
25-34	108	109	113	111	109	105	101	103	103	97	97	92	87	55.6	487
35-49	104	112	109	115	108	107	112	113	106	111	104	109	103	60.6	593
50-59	91	103	101	105	101	98	99	102	107	105	106	109	105	54.1	329
60 and over	68	75	79	73	77	80	84	81	81	81	89	89	84	49.8	352
All aged 16 and over	94	101	101	102	98	96	97	99	97	97	97	96	93	56.2	2045

* See the footnote to Table 8.1.

Table 8.13 Average weekly cigarette consumption per smoker by sex and socio-economic group: 1974 to 1998

Current cigarette smokers aged 16 and over* *Great Britain*

Socio-economic group*	1974	1976	1978	1980	1982	1984	1986	1988	1990	1992	1994	1996	1998	Standard deviation (1998)	Base (1998)† = 100%
							Mean number of cigarettes per week								
Men															
Professional	107	103	100	98	108	108	85	109	101	99	103	90	91	61.9	85
Employers and managers	134	132	128	125	139	121	130	132	126	123	122	121	104	72.3	295
Intermediate and junior non-manual	118	124	120	120	109	108	103	113	104	100	103	99	98	63.8	284
Skilled manual and own account non-professional	130	133	131	130	126	121	118	122	122	114	119	115	115	66.4	661
Semi-skilled manual and personal service	120	128	126	122	118	108	114	117	117	111	107	110	112	62.8	334
Unskilled manual	117	118	120	118	120	114	110	111	120	109	118	117	120	82.2	124
All aged 16 and over*	125	129	127	124	121	115	115	120	118	112	114	111	109	68.4	1857
Women															
Professional	82	81	72	86	73	78	82	90	94	74	93	82	65	49.8	75
Employers and managers	97	101	94	96	97	93	101	101	96	95	94	99	85	54.2	305
Intermediate and junior non-manual	89	98	97	95	92	93	91	88	90	86	83	87	89	56.9	461
Skilled manual and own account non-professional	100	107	107	110	106	101	99	104	100	106	106	102	97	54.0	569
Semi-skilled manual and personal service	92	102	103	103	98	99	101	102	102	98	100	101	102	56.1	391
Unskilled manual	91	96	102	97	93	96	92	104	99	103	106	99	100	60.8	136
All aged 16 and over*	94	101	101	102	98	96	97	99	97	97	97	96	93	56.2	2045

* See the first footnote to Table 8.7.
† See the footnote to Table 8.1.

Table 8.14 Cigarette-smoking status by sex: 1974 to 1998

Persons aged 16 and over *Great Britain*

	1974	1976	1978	1980	1982	1984	1986	1988	1990	1992	1994	1996	1998
							Percentages						
Men													
Current cigarette smokers													
Light (under 20 per day)	25	22	22	21	20	20	20	18	17	17	17	17	18
Heavy (20 or more per day)	26	24	23	21	18	16	15	15	14	12	12	11	10
Total current cigarette smokers	51	46	45	42	38	36	35	33	31	29	28	29	28
Ex-regular cigarette smokers	23	27	27	28	30	30	32	32	32	32	31	32	31
Never or only occasionally smoked cigarettes	25	27	29	30	32	34	34	35	37	38	40	40	41
Base = 100%	9852	10888	10480	10454	9199	8417	8874	8673	8106	8417	7642	7172	6579
Women													
Current cigarette smokers													
Light (under 20 per day)	28	24	23	23	22	22	21	20	20	19	18	19	19
Heavy (20 or more per day)	13	14	13	13	11	10	10	10	9	9	8	8	7
Total current cigarette smokers	41	38	37	37	33	32	31	30	29	28	26	28	26
Ex-regular cigarette smokers	11	12	14	14	16	17	18	19	19	21	21	20	21
Never or only occasionally smoked cigarettes	49	50	49	49	51	51	51	51	52	52	54	53	53
Base = 100%	11480	12554	12156	12100	10641	9788	10304	10122	9445	9764	9108	8501	7830

Table 8.15 Cigarette-smoking status by sex and age

Persons aged 16 and over   *Great Britain: 1998*

Age		Current cigarette smokers			Current non-smokers of cigarettes		Base =100%
		Light (under 20 per day)	Heavy (20 or more per day)	All current smokers	Ex-regular cigarette smokers	Never or only occasionally smoked cigarettes	
Men							
16-19	%	27	3	30	5	64	*364*
20-24	%	30	12	42	8	49	*340*
25-34	%	26	11	37	13	50	*1192*
35-49	%	18	14	32	22	46	*1802*
50-59	%	14	13	27	41	32	*1068*
60 and over	%	9	7	16	54	30	*1813*
All aged 16 and over	%	18	10	28	31	41	*6579*
Women							
16-19	%	28	3	31	7	62	*373*
20-24	%	32	7	39	8	53	*434*
25-34	%	26	7	33	14	53	*1474*
35-49	%	18	10	28	19	52	*2091*
50-59	%	17	10	27	25	48	*1211*
60 and over	%	12	4	16	29	55	*2247*
All aged 16 and over	%	19	7	26	21	53	*7830*

Table 8.16 Number of cigarettes smoked per day by sex: 1974 to 1998

Current cigarette smokers aged 16 and over   *Great Britain*

No. of cigarettes smoked per day	1974	1976	1978	1980	1982	1984	1986	1988	1990	1992	1994	1996	1998
	%	%	%	%	%	%	%	%	%	%	%	%	%
Men													
Under 10	18	18	18	19	15	20	21	19	19	24	23	22	23
10-19	31	30	31	31	35	36	36	35	36	35	36	39	40
20-29	36	36	36	36	37	35	32	34	34	31	31	29	28
30 or more	15	16	15	14	13	10	11	12	11	10	10	10	9
Base = 100%	*4968*	*4986*	*4618*	*4394*	*3323*	*3045*	*3057*	*2849*	*2487*	*2469*	*2142*	*2044*	*1850*
Women													
Under 10	31	28	29	27	23	28	28	27	26	27	27	28	31
10-19	36	35	35	37	41	40	40	40	42	42	43	41	42
20-29	27	29	28	29	30	27	27	28	27	27	26	26	24
30 or more	6	8	8	7	6	5	5	5	4	4	4	4	4
Base = 100%	*4627*	*4728*	*4426*	*4416*	*3274*	*3127*	*3171*	*3076*	*2734*	*2693*	*2332*	*2338*	*2043*

Table 8.17 Number of cigarettes smoked per day by sex and age

Current cigarette smokers aged 16 and over *Great Britain: 1998*

Age		Men				Base = 100%	Women				Base = 100%
		No. of cigarettes smoked per day					No. of cigarettes smoked per day				
		Under 10	10-19	20-29	30 or more		Under 10	10-19	20-29	30 or more	
16-19	%	44	46	9	1	110	50	40	10	0	115
20-24	%	26	45	26	3	144	36	46	16	2	169
25-29	%	30	47	22	1	219	36	45	16	3	233
30-34	%	25	41	31	3	223	32	43	21	4	254
35-49	%	20	37	28	15	574	24	41	28	7	592
50-59	%	18	34	32	15	290	22	40	33	5	329
60 and over	%	20	38	33	8	290	36	39	23	2	351
All aged 16 and over	%	23	40	28	9	1850	31	42	24	4	2043

Table 8.18 Type of cigarette smoked by sex: 1974 to 1998

Current cigarette smokers aged 16 and over *Great Britain*

Type of cigarette smoked	1974	1976	1978	1980	1982	1984	1986	1988	1990	1992	1994	1996	1998
	%	%	%	%	%	%	%	%	%	%	%	%	%
Men													
Mainly filter	69	71	75	77	72	77	78	79	80	80	78	75	74
Mainly plain	18	15	11	8	7	6	4	3	2	2	2	1	1
Mainly hand-rolled	13	14	14	15	21	17	18	18	18	18	21	23	25
Base = 100%	*4993*	*4989*	*4646*	*4422*	*3469*	*3062*	*3072*	*2849*	*2510*	*2473*	*2150*	*2052*	*1857*
Women													
Mainly filter	91	93	95	95	94	95	96	96	97	97	96	93	92
Mainly plain	8	6	4	3	3	2	1	1	1	1	1	1	1
Mainly hand-rolled	1	1	1	1	3	3	2	2	2	2	4	6	7
Base = 100%	*4600*	*4697*	*4421*	*4441*	*3522*	*3144*	*3192*	*3076*	*2748*	*2698*	*2336*	*2341*	*2044*

Table 8.19 Type of cigarette smoked by age and sex

Current cigarette smokers aged 16 and over *Great Britain: 1998*

Type of cigarette smoked	Age					
	16-24	25-34	35-49	50-59	60 and over	All aged 16 and over
	%	%	%	%	%	%
Men						
Mainly filter	87	79	71	66	69	74
Mainly plain	2	0	0	1	4	1
Mainly hand-rolled	11	20	29	33	27	25
Base=100%	*255*	*443*	*575*	*291*	*293*	*1857*
Women						
Mainly filter	92	90	91	92	95	92
Mainly plain	3	0	0	0	1	1
Mainly hand-rolled	5	10	8	8	4	7
Base=100%	*284*	*487*	*593*	*329*	*351*	*2044*

133

Table 8.20 Tar yields* by sex and age

Current smokers of manufactured† cigarettes aged 16 and over

Great Britain: 1998

		Tar yield						No regular brand	2 brands smoked/ don't know tar yield	Base = 100%
		Less than 4mg	4<8mg	8<10mg	10<12mg	12<15mg	15+mg			
Men										
16-19	%	0	10	0	14	57	0	1	18	104
20-24	%	2	21	2	8	57	0	0	10	122
25-34	%	3	23	7	9	47	0	1	9	353
35-49	%	4	16	6	13	44	0	2	14	407
50-59	%	4	14	5	19	39	0	3	16	194
60 and over	%	2	7	15	13	50	0	2	11	215
Total	%	3	16	7	12	47	0	2	13	1395
Women										
16-19	%	1	16	2	10	54	0	0	18	114
20-24	%	4	31	1	6	48	0	1	9	157
25-34	%	4	21	12	9	42	0	1	11	438
35-49	%	5	14	13	14	41	0	1	12	543
50-59	%	8	13	17	10	38	0	1	14	303
60 and over	%	7	12	18	14	36	0	1	11	338
Total	%	5	17	13	11	41	0	1	12	1893
Total										
16-19	%	0	13	1	12	55	0	0	18	218
20-24	%	3	27	2	7	52	0	0	9	279
25-34	%	4	22	9	9	45	0	1	10	791
35-49	%	4	15	10	13	42	0	2	13	950
50-59	%	6	13	12	14	38	0	1	15	497
60 and over	%	5	10	17	13	42	0	1	11	553
Total	%	4	16	10	12	44	0	1	12	3288

* Tar levels have been grouped by actual tar yield in 1998.

† Twenty five per cent of male smokers and 7 per cent of female smokers said they mainly smoked hand-rolled cigarettes and have been excluded from this analysis.

Table 8.21 Tar yields* by socio-economic group of head of household

Current smokers of manufactured† cigarettes aged 16 and over Great Britain: 1998

Socio-economic group of head of household		Tar yields						No regular brand	2 brands smoked/ don't know tar yield	Base = 100%
		Less than 4mg	4<8mg	8<10mg	10<12mg	12<15mg	15+mg			
Men										
Professional	%	1	28	3	8	42	0	5	14	79
Employers and managers	%	6	24	6	10	40	0	3	10	249
Intermediate and junior non-manual	%	4	26	10	6	42	0	0	11	233
Skilled manual and own account non-professional	%	3	7	7	16	52	0	1	14	463
Semi-skilled manual and personal service	%	1	9	6	15	52	0	2	14	236
Unskilled manual	%	3	4	5	19	45	0	1	22	73
Total non-manual	%	4	25	7	8	42	0	2	11	561
Total manual	%	2	8	7	16	52	0	1	14	772
All aged 16 and over**	%	3	16	7	12	47	0	2	13	1395
Women										
Professional	%	16	35	12	7	21	0	3	7	75
Employers and managers	%	5	20	15	11	34	0	1	13	300
Intermediate and junior non-manual	%	7	18	12	10	37	0	0	15	434
Skilled manual and own account non-professional	%	4	15	13	13	42	0	1	12	530
Semi-skilled manual and personal service	%	5	10	10	13	52	0	1	10	344
Unskilled manual	%	2	4	18	12	54	0	0	10	118
Total non-manual	%	7	21	13	10	34	0	1	14	809
Total manual	%	4	12	12	13	47	0	1	11	992
All aged 16 and over**	%	5	17	13	11	41	0	1	12	1893

* ⎤
† ⎦ See the footnotes to Table 8.20.

** See the footnote to Table 8.6.

Table 8.22 Prevalence of smoking by sex and type of product smoked: 1974 to 1998

Persons aged 16 and over Great Britain

	1974	1976	1978	1980	1982	1984	1986	1988	1990	1992	1994	1996	1998
						Percentage smoking							
Men													
Cigarettes*	51	46	45	43	38	37	35	33	31	29	28	29	28
Pipe	12	11	10	..	..	..	6	4	4	4	3	2	2
Cigars†	34	31	16	14	12	10	10	9	8	7	6	6	6
All smokers**	64	60	55	50††	45††	43††	44	40	38	36	33	33	33
Base = 100%	9862	10894	10439	10433	9171	8377	8884	8673	8119	8427	7662	7186	6579
Women													
Cigarettes*	41	38	37	37	33	32	31	30	29	28	26	28	26
Cigars†	3	3	1	0	0	0	1	0	0	0	0	0	0
All smokers**	41	39	37	37	34	33	31	31	29	28	26	28	26
Base = 100%	11419	12515	12079	12067	10559	9681	10312	10122	9455	9772	9137	8512	7830

* Figures for cigarettes include all smokers of manufactured and hand-rolled cigarettes.
† For 1974 and 1976 the figures include occasional cigar smokers, that is, those who smoked less than one cigar a month.
** The percentages for cigarettes, pipes and cigars add to more than the percentage for all smokers because some people smoked more than one type of product.
†† In 1980, 1982 and 1984 men were not asked about pipe smoking, and therefore the figures for all smokers exclude those who smoked only a pipe.

135

Table 8.23 **Prevalence of smoking by type of product smoked by sex and age**

Persons aged 16 and over   *Great Britain: 1998*

Age	Men					Women			
	Cigarettes*	Pipe†	Cigars†	All smokers**	Base = 100%	Cigarettes*	Cigars†	All smokers	Base = 100%
	Percentage smoking					Percentage smoking			
16-19	30	0	4	32	*364*	31	1	31	*373*
20-24	42	0	6	44	*340*	39	0	39	*434*
25-29	39	1	5	40	*555*	33	0	33	*699*
30-34	35	0	6	38	*637*	33	0	33	*775*
35-49	32	1	7	36	*1802*	28	0	28	*2091*
50-59	27	4	8	35	*1068*	27	0	27	*1211*
60 and over	16	2	4	21	*1813*	16	0	16	*2247*
All aged 16 and over	28	2	6	33	*6579*	26	0	26	*7830*

*   Figures for cigarettes include all smokers of both manufactured and hand-rolled cigarettes.
†   Young people aged 16-17 were not asked about cigar or pipe-smoking.
** See the third footnote to Table 8.22.

Table 8.24 **Age started smoking regularly by socio-economic group of head of household and sex**

Persons aged 16 and over who had ever smoked regularly   *Great Britain: 1998*

Age started smoking regularly	Socio-economic group of head of household							
	Professional	Employers and managers	Intermediate non-manual	Junior non-manual	Skilled manual and own account non-professional	Semi-skilled manual and personal service	Unskilled manual	All persons
	%	%	%	%	%	%	%	%
Men								
Under 16	30	38	31	39	48	47	59	43
16-17	24	26	25	33	24	28	19	26
18-19	25	22	24	17	14	13	12	17
20-24	18	10	16	8	10	8	7	10
25 and over	3	4	4	2	4	5	4	4
Base = 100%	*250*	*780*	*369*	*278*	*1292*	*593*	*188*	*3750*
Women								
Under 16	20	25	21	29	38	37	40	31
16-17	27	29	26	30	30	29	22	29
18-19	26	23	24	17	14	13	15	18
20-24	22	16	20	15	11	11	10	14
25 and over	5	8	8	9	6	9	13	8
Base = 100%	*189*	*627*	*396*	*470*	*986*	*613*	*218*	*3499*
All persons								
Under 16	26	32	25	33	44	42	49	37
16-17	25	27	26	31	27	29	20	27
18-19	26	22	24	17	14	13	13	18
20-24	20	13	18	12	10	10	9	12
25 and over	4	6	6	7	5	7	9	6
Base = 100%	*439*	*1407*	*765*	*748*	*2278*	*1206*	*406*	*7249*

Table 8.25 **How easy or difficult smokers would find it to go without smoking for a whole day, by sex and number of cigarettes smoked per day**

Current cigarette smokers aged 16 and over   *Great Britain: 1998*

Ease or difficulty of not smoking for a day	Number of cigarettes per day			
	20 or more	10-19	0-9	Total*
	%	%	%	%
Men				
Very easy	4	11	41	16
Fairly easy	18	35	34	28
Fairly difficult	28	31	16	26
Very difficult	50	24	9	30
Base=100%	679	729	431	1845
	%	%	%	%
Women				
Very easy	3	7	41	16
Fairly easy	10	27	35	25
Fairly difficult	22	32	16	24
Very difficult	65	34	8	35
Base=100%	567	844	625	2038
	%	%	%	%
All smokers				
Very easy	4	9	41	16
Fairly easy	14	30	35	26
Fairly difficult	25	31	16	25
Very difficult	57	29	8	33
Base=100%	1246	1573	1056	3883

* Includes a few smokers who did not say how many cigarettes a day they smoked.

Table 8.26 **Proportion of smokers who would find it difficult to go without smoking for a whole day, by sex, age and number of cigarettes smoked per day**

Current cigarette smokers aged 16 and over   *Great Britain: 1998*

Number of cigarettes smoked per day	Age					
	16-24	25-34	35-49	50-59	60 and over	Total
			Percentages			
Men						
20 or more	65	77	80	85	75	78
10 - 19	45	51	60	55	59	54
0 - 9	15	21	24	29	43	25
All smokers*	39	50	61	65	63	56
Women						
20 or more	79	90	89	83	86	87
10 - 19	55	67	69	69	67	66
0 - 9	19	21	27	19	33	24
All smokers*	43	57	66	63	59	59
Total						
20 or more	71	83	84	84	80	82
10 - 19	50	60	64	63	63	61
0 - 9	18	21	26	23	36	24
All smokers*	41	54	64	64	61	58
Bases=100%						
Men						
20 or more	*52*	*128*	*244*	*137*	*118*	*679*
10 - 19	*116*	*191*	*214*	*98*	*110*	*729*
0 - 9	*86*	*121*	*116*	*52*	*56*	*431*
*All smokers**	*255*	*441*	*575*	*288*	*286*	*1845*
Women						
20 or more	*42*	*109*	*206*	*123*	*87*	*567*
10 - 19	*122*	*212*	*242*	*133*	*135*	*844*
0 - 9	*119*	*165*	*142*	*72*	*127*	*625*
*All smokers**	*283*	*486*	*591*	*328*	*350*	*2038*
Total						
20 or more	*94*	*237*	*450*	*260*	*205*	*1246*
10 - 19	*238*	*403*	*456*	*231*	*245*	*1573*
0 - 9	*205*	*286*	*258*	*124*	*183*	*1056*
*All smokers**	*538*	*927*	*1166*	*616*	*636*	*3883*

* Includes a few smokers who did not say how many cigarettes a day they smoked.

Table 8.27 **Whether would like to give up smoking altogether, by sex and number of cigarettes smoked per day**

Current cigarette smokers aged 16 and over   *Great Britain: 1998*

Whether would like to give up altogether	Number of cigarettes per day			
	20 or more	10-19	0-9	Total*
	%	%	%	%
Men				
Yes	69	73	62	69
No	31	27	38	31
Base=100%	*677*	*723*	*423*	*1829*
	%	%	%	%
Women				
Yes	68	75	65	70
No	32	25	35	30
Base=100%	*564*	*834*	*610*	*2010*
	%	%	%	%
All smokers				
Yes	69	74	64	69
No	31	26	36	31
Base=100%	*1241*	*1557*	*1033*	*3839*

* Includes a few smokers who did not say how many cigarettes a day they smoked.

Table 8.28 **Proportion of smokers who would like to give up smoking altogether, by sex, age and number of cigarettes smoked per day**

Current cigarette smokers aged 16 and over   *Great Britain: 1998*

Number of cigarettes smoked per day	Age					
	16-24	25-34	35-49	50-59	60 and over	Total
			Percentages			
Men						
20 or more	64	79	71	67	58	69
10 - 19	75	71	75	72	71	73
0 - 9	63	67	61	61	53	62
All smokers*	69	72	70	68	61	69
Women						
20 or more	63	81	70	69	49	68
10 - 19	82	75	76	72	72	75
0 - 9	71	66	71	67	52	65
All smokers*	74	73	73	70	59	70
Total						
20 or more	64	80	71	68	54	69
10 - 19	79	73	75	72	71	74
0 - 9	68	66	67	64	52	64
All smokers*	72	73	72	69	60	69
Bases=100%						
Men						
20 or more	*50*	*128*	*241*	*138*	*120*	*677*
10 - 19	*114*	*189*	*213*	*97*	*110*	*723*
0 - 9	*79*	*120*	*116*	*51*	*57*	*423*
*All smokers**	*243*	*438*	*571*	*287*	*290*	*1829*
Women						
20 or more	*41*	*109*	*206*	*122*	*86*	*564*
10 - 19	*115*	*212*	*241*	*131*	*135*	*834*
0 - 9	*106*	*163*	*141*	*72*	*128*	*610*
*All smokers**	*262*	*484*	*589*	*325*	*350*	*2010*
Total						
20 or more	*91*	*237*	*447*	*260*	*206*	*1241*
10 - 19	*229*	*401*	*454*	*228*	*245*	*1557*
0 - 9	*185*	*283*	*257*	*123*	*185*	*1033*
*All smokers**	*505*	*922*	*1160*	*612*	*640*	*3839*

* Includes a few smokers who did not say how many cigarettes a day they smoked.

Table 8.29 **Proportion of smokers who would like to stop smoking altogether, by sex and whether they would find it easy or difficult to go without smoking for a whole day**

Current cigarette smokers aged 16 and over   *Great Britain: 1998*

| | Ease or difficulty of not smoking for a day | | | | |
	Very easy	Fairly easy	Fairly difficult	Very difficult	Total
	Percentage who would like to stop altogether				
Men	59	67	76	70	69
Women	60	69	75	72	70
All smokers	59	68	75	71	70
Bases=100%					
Men	*277*	*512*	*476*	*554*	*1819*
Women	*330*	*491*	*483*	*701*	*2005*
All smokers	*607*	*1003*	*959*	*1255*	*3824*

Table 8.30 **Time between waking and the first cigarette, by sex and number of cigarettes smoked per day**

Current cigarette smokers aged 16 and over   *Great Britain: 1998*

| Time between waking and the first cigarette | Number of cigarettes per day | | | |
	20 or more	10-19	0-9	Total*
Men	%	%	%	%
Less than 5 minutes	31	11	2	16
5 - 14 minutes	27	16	3	17
15 - 29 minutes	17	16	5	14
30 minutes but less than 1 hour	17	24	11	18
1 hour but less than 2 hours	6	20	17	14
2 hours or more	3	13	62	21
Base=100%	*683*	*733*	*431*	*1854*
Women	%	%	%	%
Less than 5 minutes	31	12	1	14
5 - 14 minutes	29	16	3	15
15 - 29 minutes	21	18	7	15
30 minutes but less than 1 hour	11	22	13	17
1 hour but less than 2 hours	5	15	13	12
2 hours or more	2	16	63	26
Base=100%	*568*	*848*	*624*	*2042*
All smokers	%	%	%	%
Less than 5 minutes	31	12	2	15
5 - 14 minutes	28	16	3	16
15 - 29 minutes	19	17	6	15
30 minutes but less than 1 hour	14	23	12	17
1 hour but less than 2 hours	6	18	15	13
2 hours or more	2	15	63	24
Base=100%	*1251*	*1581*	*1055*	*3896*

* Includes a few smokers who did not say how many cigarettes a day they smoked.

Table 8.31 **Proportion of smokers who have their first cigarette within five minutes of waking, by sex, age and number of cigarettes smoked per day**

Current cigarette smokers aged 16 and over   *Great Britain: 1998*

Number of cigarettes smoked per day	Age					
	16-24	25-34	35-49	50-59	60 and over	Total
			Percentages			
Men						
20 or more	21	25	38	30	30	31
10 - 19	12	11	9	12	9	11
0 - 9	2	2	3	2	2	2
All smokers*	11	13	20	19	16	16
Women						
20 or more	[38]	35	31	24	31	31
10 - 19	10	12	14	16	9	12
0 - 9	1	1	2	0	2	1
All smokers*	10	14	17	16	12	14
Total						
20 or more	29	30	35	27	30	31
10 - 19	11	12	12	14	9	12
0 - 9	1	2	2	1	2	2
All smokers*	10	13	19	17	14	15
Bases=100%						
Men						
20 or more	*52*	*128*	*244*	*138*	*121*	*683*
10 - 19	*116*	*193*	*214*	*99*	*111*	*733*
0 - 9	*86*	*120*	*116*	*52*	*57*	*431*
*All smokers**	*255*	*442*	*575*	*290*	*292*	*1854*
Women						
20 or more	*42*	*109*	*206*	*124*	*87*	*568*
10 - 19	*123*	*213*	*243*	*133*	*136*	*848*
0 - 9	*118*	*165*	*142*	*72*	*127*	*624*
*All smokers**	*283*	*487*	*592*	*329*	*351*	*2042*
Total						
20 or more	*94*	*237*	*450*	*262*	*208*	*1251*
10 - 19	*239*	*406*	*457*	*232*	*247*	*1581*
0 - 9	*204*	*285*	*258*	*124*	*184*	*1055*
*All smokers**	*538*	*929*	*1167*	*619*	*643*	*3896*

* Includes a few smokers who did not say how many cigarettes a day they smoked.

Table 8.32 **How easy or difficult smokers would find it to go without smoking for a whole day, by sex and time between waking and the first cigarette**

Current cigarette smokers aged 16 and over   *Great Britain: 1998*

Ease or difficulty of not smoking for a day	Time between waking and the first cigarette						Total
	Less than 5 minutes	5 - 14 minutes	15 - 29 minutes	30 minutes but less than 1 hour	1 hour but less than 2 hours	2 hours or more	
	%	%	%	%	%	%	%
Men							
Very easy	3	3	9	7	17	46	15
Fairly easy	14	21	20	34	43	35	28
Fairly difficult	23	31	34	34	25	14	26
Very difficult	60	45	37	25	16	5	30
Base=100%	*302*	*310*	*253*	*336*	*260*	*382*	*1843*
	%	%	%	%	%	%	%
Women							
Very easy	2	3	5	7	13	46	16
Fairly easy	10	17	20	28	32	35	25
Fairly difficult	18	24	33	34	32	14	24
Very difficult	70	57	42	32	23	6	35
Base=100%	*289*	*314*	*314*	*336*	*244*	*538*	*2035*
	%	%	%	%	%	%	%
All smokers							
Very easy	3	3	7	7	15	46	16
Fairly easy	12	19	20	31	38	35	26
Fairly difficult	21	27	33	34	28	14	25
Very difficult	65	51	40	28	19	5	33
Base=100%	*591*	*624*	*567*	*672*	*504*	*920*	*3878*

9 Drinking

Questions about drinking alcohol have been included in the General Household Survey every two years since 1978. Prior to 1988 the questions were only asked of those aged 18 and over. Since 1988 respondents aged 16 and 17 have answered these questions using a self-completion questionnaire.

Measuring alcohol consumption

There are different methods for obtaining survey information on drinking behaviour. It is possible to ask people to recall all episodes of drinking during a set period[1]. However, this is time consuming to administer and is therefore not suitable for the GHS where drinking is only one of a number of subjects covered.

In 1998 the GHS used two measures for obtaining information on alcohol consumption:

- average weekly consumption;
- consumption on the heaviest day during the week prior to interview.

The former measure has been used on the GHS since 1988. Respondents are asked how often over the last year they have drunk different types of drink (normal beer, strong beer, wine, spirits, fortified wines and alcopops)[2] and how much they had usually drunk on any one day. This information is combined to give an estimate of the respondent's weekly alcohol consumption.

For the latter measure, respondents were asked on how many days they had drunk alcohol during the previous week. They were then asked how much of each of the six types of drink listed above they had drunk on their heaviest drinking day during the previous week. These amounts were added to give an estimate of the most the respondent had drunk on any one day.

The questions relating to average weekly consumption reflected advice, prior to December 1995, from the Department of Health about recommended weekly levels of drinking. The new questions about consumption on the heaviest day during the previous week were included on the GHS in 1998 following the publication, in 1995, of an inter-departmental review of the effects of drinking[3]. It concluded that it was more appropriate to set benchmarks for daily rather than for weekly consumption of alcohol, partly because of concern about the health and social risks associated with single episodes of intoxication. The report concluded that regular consumption of between three and four units a day for men and two to three units a day for women does not carry a significant health risk. However, consistently drinking more than four units a day for men, or more than three for women is not advised as a sensible drinking level because of the progressive health risk it carries. The government's advice on sensible drinking is now based on these daily benchmarks.

Obtaining reliable information about drinking behaviour is difficult and in consequence social surveys consistently record lower levels of consumption than would be expected from data on alcohol sales. This is partly because people may consciously or unconsciously under-estimate how much alcohol they consume. Drinking at home is particularly likely to be under-estimated because the quantities consumed are not measured and are likely to be larger than those dispensed in licensed premises.

This chapter presents data on drinking behaviour, and focuses particularly on consumption on the heaviest drinking day and frequency of drinking during the previous week. Variations by age, sex and socio-economic group are discussed in detail, as is the association between drinking on the heaviest day and average weekly consumption. This is followed by an analysis of regional differences in consumption of alcohol on the heaviest day during the previous week. Finally, trend data relating to average weekly consumption are presented.

Variations in daily drinking by sex and age

Frequency of drinking

This section illustrates differences in the frequency of drinking during the previous week between men and women and between different age groups.

Seventy five per cent of men and 59% of women had drunk an alcoholic drink on at least one day during the previous week. The proportions doing so varied between age groups.

Among men, the pattern of association between age and the likelihood of having drunk in the last week was an inverted U-shaped curve. The youngest and oldest age groups were least likely to report drinking alcohol during the reference period.

- While 77-78% of men aged 25-64 had drunk alcohol during the previous week, 65% of men aged 65 and over and 69% of those aged 16-24 had done so.

145

Among women, the 25-44 age group were most likely (65%) and those aged 65 and over least likely (45%) to have drunk alcohol during the previous week. The proportions of women aged 16-24 and 45-64 who had drunk in the last week were 61% and 62% respectively, significantly different from other women, but not from each other.

As well as being more likely than women to have drunk during the previous week, men also drank on more days of the week. About one in four men compared with one in eight women had drunk on five days or more during the preceding seven days. Fourteen per cent of men compared with 8% of women had drunk alcohol every day during the previous week.

Among both men and women, frequency of drinking increased with age. For example:

- 12% of men and 8% of women aged 16-24 had drunk on five days or more during the previous week, compared with 28% of men and 15% of women aged 45 and over;
- 4% of men and 2% of women aged 16-24 had drunk every day during the preceding week, compared with 19% of men and 10% of women aged 45 and over.

Table 9.1, Figure 9A

Amount drunk on heaviest day during the previous week

This section discusses consumption on the heaviest day during the previous week. In this, and in subsequent sections of the chapter, the discussion focuses on two measures of daily consumption:

- the proportions exceeding the recommended daily benchmarks, that is more than four units a day for men and more than three for women;
- those who have drunk heavily, defined here as more than eight units for men and six for women.

Men were more likely than women both to have exceeded the daily benchmarks and to have drunk heavily on at least one day during the previous week.

- 38% of men compared with 21% of women had exceeded the recommended daily benchmarks on at least one day during the previous week;
- 21% of men had drunk more than 8 units and 8% of women had drunk more than 6 units on one day during the preceding week.

It was shown earlier that young people had drunk less often during the previous week than people from other age groups. However, among both men and women, those aged 16-24 were generally more likely than respondents from other age cohorts to have exceeded the recommended number of daily units on at least one day.

Half of men aged 16-24 had exceeded four units on at least one day during the previous week. This was not significantly different from men aged 25-44 (47%), but was considerably more than those aged 65 and over, 17% of whom had done so. Among women, 41% in the youngest age group had exceeded three units on any one day compared with 4% of those aged 65 and over.

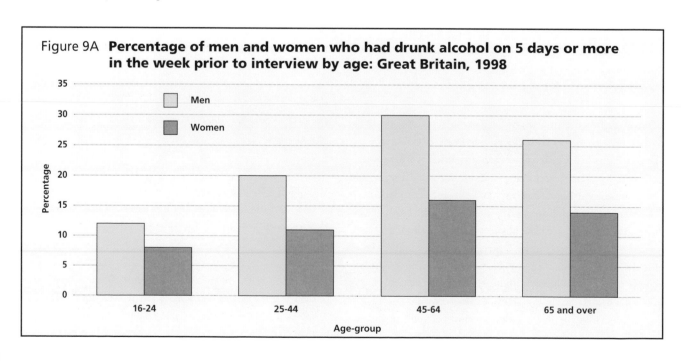

Figure 9A **Percentage of men and women who had drunk alcohol on 5 days or more in the week prior to interview by age: Great Britain, 1998**

Similar patterns held when examining the proportions who had drunk heavily on at least one day. Thirty seven per cent of men aged 16-24 compared with 4% of those aged 65 and over had drunk over eight units on any one day during the previous week. Among women aged 16-24, nearly one in four had drunk heavily on at least one day during the preceding week compared with only one in a hundred women in the oldest age group.

Table 9.3, Figures 9B, 9C

Average weekly consumption and drinking on one day during the previous week

This section discusses the relationship between average weekly consumption of units of alcohol and drinking on the heaviest day during the previous week.

Men whose usual weekly consumption of alcohol in the last 12 months exceeded 21 units were more likely than those who drank below this level to have exceeded the daily benchmarks during the previous week. Nearly three-quarters of these men had drunk more than four units and nearly half had drunk more than eight units on at least one day during the previous week. This pattern was also evident among women whose average consumption exceeded 14 units. Nearly two-thirds of such women had drunk more than three units and a third had exceeded six units on one day during the previous week.

Among men and women whose average weekly consumption was 11-21 and 8-14 units respectively, a notable proportion had exceeded the recommended daily bench-

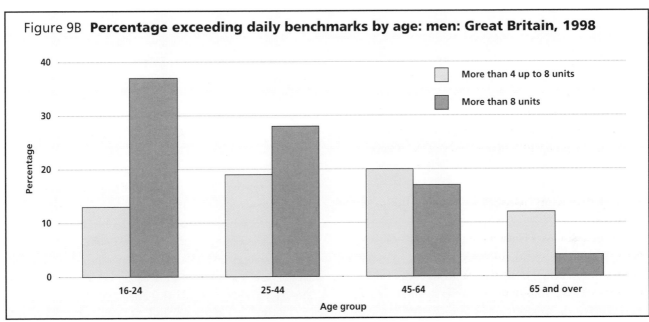

Figure 9B **Percentage exceeding daily benchmarks by age: men: Great Britain, 1998**

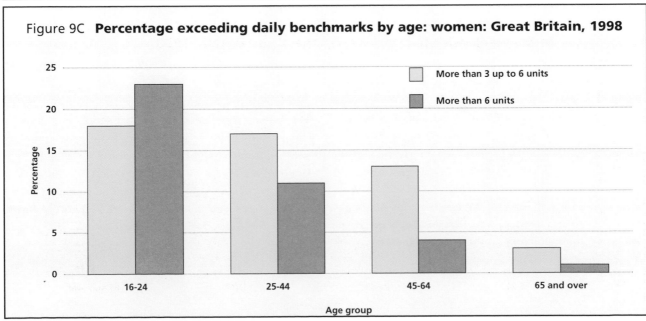

Figure 9C **Percentage exceeding daily benchmarks by age: women: Great Britain, 1998**

marks. Among men whose average weekly consumption was at this level, just over half (53%) had exceeded four units and a quarter (25%) had drunk heavily on at least one day. Among women whose average weekly consumption was at this level, 38% had drunk over three units and 13% had drunk heavily on at least one day during the previous week. **Table 9.4**

As shown in the discussion in previous sections, age is an important factor when examining patterns of drinking. This was equally so when analysing average weekly consumption by drinking on the heaviest day during the previous week.

Among men and women whose average weekly consumption exceeded 21 and 14 units respectively, younger people were more likely than older people to have exceeded the daily benchmarks at least once during the preceding week. For example:

- of those men whose average weekly consumption exceeded 21 units, those aged 16-44 were more likely than older men to have drunk over four units on any one day during the previous week; 81% had done so compared with 59% of men aged 65 and over. Those aged 16-24 were more likely than any other age group to have drunk heavily; 68% had done so compared with 18% of the oldest age group;
- among women whose average weekly consumption was more than 14 units, 84% of those aged 16-24 had exceeded three units compared with 34% of women aged 65 and over. Fifty nine per cent of the younger women had drunk heavily on at least one day during the previous week compared with only 5% of the older women. **Tables 9.5(a) & (b)**

Socio-economic characteristics

The link between alcohol consumption and socio-economic characteristics is an important focus of analysis for the GHS. A recent review of information on inequalities in health, undertaken by the Department of Health, highlighted research that indicates how mortality and morbidity 'show a clear gradient with socio-economic position, with an almost fourfold higher rate in unskilled men compared to those from professional households'[4]. This research also demonstrated that the link between alcohol consumption and deaths from accidents was related to socio-economic group.

Analysis of drinking patterns, for example in terms of frequency of drinking, were related to the socio-economic group of the head of household.

Frequency of drinking

The proportion who had drunk on at least one day during the previous week was greater among those living in non-manual households than among people from manual households.

- 80% of men from non-manual households compared with 70% of men from manual households had drunk alcohol during the previous week. The corresponding proportions among women were 66% and 52%.

These differences were particularly pronounced when comparing those from professional and from unskilled manual households; among men 85% of the former, compared with 65% of the latter, had drunk during the previous week. The corresponding proportions among women were 72% and 40%.

- 30% of men from non-manual households compared with 18% of those from manual households, had drunk on five or more days during the previous week.

This difference also held among women:

- 17% from non-manual households had drunk on five days or more during the last week compared with 8% of women from manual households.

These differences were particularly noticeable between those living in professional and unskilled manual households. Among men, thirty five per cent of the former compared with 16% of the latter had drunk on five days or more during the previous week. The corresponding proportions for women were 22% and 6%. **Table 9.6**

Amount drunk on any one day

The findings above demonstrate that people from non-manual households drank more often during the previous week compared with those from manual households. However, there were no significant differences between these groups in the proportions who had exceeded the recommended daily benchmarks or who had drunk heavily on at least one day during the previous week:

- almost two in five men and about one in five women from both types of household exceeded the recommended daily benchmarks;
- about one in five men and about one in 12 women from both manual and non-manual households drank heavily.

Although men from professional households were more likely than men from other groups to have drunk on five days or more during the previous week, only 15% of men in this group had drunk heavily during this period compared with 19-24% of other men.   **Table 9.7**

Average weekly consumption and drinking on one day during the previous week
Although there were no overall differences in the proportion of respondents from manual and non-manual households who exceeded the daily benchmarks, differences between these groups emerged when average weekly consumption was taken into account.

- Among men who consumed on average more than 21 units of alcohol per week, 78% from a manual household compared with 70% from a non-manual household had consumed more than four units on at least one day during the last week. Fifty one per cent of those from manual households compared with 42% from non-manual households had drunk more than eight units.
- Among women whose average weekly consumption was over 14 units, 68% of women from manual households compared with 60% from non-manual households had consumed over three units in one day during the previous week. Forty per cent of women from manual households compared with 26% from non-manual households had drunk more than six units on at least one day.

These differences also held among men who consumed between 11 and 21 units a week and women whose weekly consumption was between 8 and 14 units a week. Among men who consumed an average of 11 to 21 units a week, 58% and 49% of those from manual and non-manual households respectively had drunk more than four units on at least one day during the previous week. Twenty nine per cent from manual compared with 21% from non-manual households had drunk in excess of eight units.

Among women whose average weekly consumption was 8-14 units, 42% of those from a manual, compared with 35% from a non-manual, household had drunk more than three

units on at least one day during the preceding week. However, among women with this level of average weekly consumption, there were no significant differences in the proportions of those living in manual and non-manual households who exceeded six units on one day during the previous week.   **Table 9.8**

Income and economic activity status
Generally, the higher the level of gross weekly household income, the more likely both men and women were to have exceeded the recommended number of units for daily consumption.

- Among households with a gross weekly income of over £500, 25% of men and 11% of women had drunk heavily on at least one day during the previous week. The comparative proportions for men and women living in households with a gross weekly income of £150 or less were 14% and 6% respectively.   **Table 9.9**

Among men aged 16-64, those in employment were more likely than men who were economically inactive to have drunk heavily during the previous week (26% compared with 18%). Lower levels of drinking among economically inactive men can be partly explained by the large proportion of men aged 60 and over who make up this group.

Twenty six per cent of men aged 16-64 who were working had drunk heavily during the preceding week. The corresponding proportions for unemployed and economically inactive men were 22% and 18% (this difference was not statistically significant).

Among women aged 16-64, one in seven of those who were unemployed and those in full-time employment had drunk more than six units on at least one day during the previous week. This compares with one in twelve of economically inactive women and those who were working part time.   **Table 9.11**

Regional variations

This section discusses drinking patterns among residents of the different countries within Great Britain and people living within different government office regions within England.

In 1998, men living in Scotland were more likely than those living in England to have consumed more than eight units of alcohol on at least one day during the previous week; 24% had done so compared with 20%. Twenty two per cent of men living in Wales had drunk heavily.

149

Previous GHS reports have shown that women living in Scotland tended to be the least likely to have exceeded 14 units per week. However, analysis of drinking during the past week showed that they were significantly more likely than women living in England or Wales to have drunk over three units on any one day in the last week; 27% had done so compared with 20% and 21% respectively. Women living in Scotland (12%) were also more likely than women living in England (8%) to have drunk over six units on any one day during the previous week.

Previous GHS reports have demonstrated a north-south geographical divide in England regarding average weekly consumption among men[5]. This finding also holds for drinking on the heaviest day during the previous week.

- 27% of men living in Merseyside and 26% living in the North West had drunk more than eight units on at least one day during the preceding week, compared with 18% living in London or the South and 14% of those living in the Eastern region.

The proportion of men living in the North East, North West and Merseyside who had drunk four or more units on one day during the previous week was 45%. This compares with about a third of men living in London (31%) and the Eastern region (33%).

Among women living in England, as with the analysis of average weekly consumption in previous GHS reports, there were no clear regional differences in their consumption of alcohol on the heaviest day during the previous seven days.

- The proportion of women exceeding six units on any one day ranged from 11% in the North West to 6% in London and in the Eastern region. **Table 9.13**

Trends in weekly average alcohol consumption

As discussed in the introduction, in previous years the main measure of drinking behaviour was average weekly consumption of units of alcohol. This section discusses sex and age-related differences in average weekly consumption and examines trends since 1988[6].

- In 1998, 27% of men and 15% of women exceeded 21 and 14 units respectively;
- this proportion has remained largely unchanged for men since 1988, but has increased from 10% to 15% for women during the same period. **Table 9.14**

Among both sexes the likelihood of drinking above these levels declined with age, from 36% of men and 25% of women aged 16-24 to 16% of men and 6% of women aged 65 and over.

Over the last ten years the proportion of women drinking more than 14 units per week has increased from 10% to 15%. This pattern holds across all age groups. Between 1996 and 1998 the only significant increase was among women aged 45-64; the proportion drinking more than 14 units per week rose three percentage points to 16% during this period.

Among all men, the proportion drinking more than 21 units has remained relatively constant since 1988; 27% had done so in 1998 compared with 26% in 1988. However, this pattern did not hold for individual age groups. Among men aged 16-24 and 45-64 the proportions increased from 31% to 36% and 24% to 30% respectively. The proportion of men aged 25-44 who drink over 21 units has decreased from 34% to 27% over the same period. Among men aged 65 and over the pattern over this period is less clear; 16% had drunk over 21 units in 1998 compared with 13% in 1988. **Table 9.14 – 9.15**

Notes and references

1   Goddard E. *Detailed recall of drinking behaviour over seven days.* Survey Methodology Bulletin OPCS No.31, July 1992.

2   Normal and strong beer and alcopops were asked about separately for the first time in 1998.

3   *Sensible drinking: the report of an inter-departmental group,* Department of Health 1995.

4   Drever F, Bunting J, Harding D. *Male mortality from major causes of death* (in Drever F, Whitehead M, Eds. *Health inequalities: decennial supplement*: DS Series no.15. London: The Stationery Office, 1997) quoted in *Independent Inquiry into Inequalities in Health Report*. London: The Stationery Office 1998.

5   *Chapter 11, Living in Britain. Results from the 1996 General Household Survey,* London: HMSO 1998.

6   Analysis of trend data relating to average weekly consumption is based on those aged 16 and over. Data were collected from 16 and 17 year olds for the first time in 1988. The corresponding tables in previous years have been based on all respondents aged over 18 and are therefore not comparable to the tables included this year.

Table 9.1 Whether drank last week and number of drinking days, by age and sex

Persons aged 16 and over   *Great Britain: 1998*

Drinking days last week	Men					Women				
	16-24	25-44	45-64	65 and over	Total	16-24	25-44	45-64	65 and over	Total
	%	%	%	%	%	%	%	%	%	%
0	31	22	23	35	25	39	35	38	55	41
1	18	19	15	15	17	21	23	20	17	21
2	18	17	14	12	15	17	15	12	8	13
3	12	12	10	9	11	10	9	9	5	8
4	9	9	8	4	8	6	6	5	2	5
5	5	6	6	4	6	4	4	3	2	3
6	3 ⎫ 12	4 ⎫ 20	5 ⎫ 30	2 ⎫ 26	4 ⎫ 24	1 ⎫ 8	2 ⎫ 11	2 ⎫ 16	1 ⎫ 14	2 ⎫ 13
7	4 ⎭	10 ⎭	18 ⎭	20 ⎭	14 ⎭	2 ⎭	5 ⎭	10 ⎭	11 ⎭	8 ⎭
% who drank last week	69	78	77	65	75	61	65	62	45	59
Base = 100%	*700*	*2400*	*2137*	*1333*	*6570*	*810*	*2911*	*2364*	*1743*	*7828*

Table 9.2 Whether daily amount varied, by sex and age

Persons aged 16 and over who drank last week on at least one day   *Great Britain: 1998*

Drinking last week	Men					Women				
	16-24	25-44	45-64	65 and over	Total	16-24	25-44	45-64	65 and over	Total
	%	%	%	%	%	%	%	%	%	%
Drank same each day	30	41	54	77	51	29	49	59	81	55
Daily amount varied	70	59	46	23	49	71	51	41	19	45
Base = 100%	*352*	*1431*	*1339*	*676*	*3798*	*325*	*1200*	*991*	*495*	*3011*

Table 9.3 Maximum daily amount last week, by sex and age

Persons aged 16 and over   *Great Britain: 1998*

Maximum daily amount*	Men					Women				
	16-24	25-44	45-64	65 and over	Total	16-24	25-44	45-64	65 and over	Total
	%	%	%	%	%	%	%	%	%	%
Drank nothing last week	32	22	22	35	25	39	35	38	55	41
Up to 4/3 units	19	32	41	49	37	20	37	45	41	38
More than 4/3, up to 8/6 units	13 ⎫ 50	19 ⎫ 47	20 ⎫ 37	12 ⎫ 17	17 ⎫ 38	18 ⎫ 41	17 ⎫ 28	13 ⎫ 17	3 ⎫ 4	13 ⎫ 21
More than 8/6 units	37 ⎭	28 ⎭	17 ⎭	4 ⎭	21 ⎭	23 ⎭	11 ⎭	4 ⎭	1 ⎭	8 ⎭
Base = 100%	*698*	*2399*	*2132*	*1330*	*6559*	*809*	*2910*	*2363*	*1738*	*7820*

* Maximum daily amount.

Men	Up to 4 units	More than 4, up to 8 units	More than 8 units
Women	Up to 3 units	More than 3, up to 6 units	More than 6 units

151

Table 9.4 Maximum daily amount last week, by average weekly consumption

(a) Men aged 16 and over   *Great Britain: 1998*

Maximum daily amount	Non-drinker	<1 unit	1-10 units	11-21 units	22+ units	Total
	%	%	%	%	%	%
Drank nothing last week	100	81	25	6	4	25
Up to 4 units	0	17	57	41	22	37
More than 4, up to 8 units	0	1	11	28	27	17
More than 8 units	0	1	7	25	48	21
Base = 100%	495	524	2376	1396	1759	6550

(b) Women aged 16 and over   *Great Britain: 1998*

Maximum daily amount	Non-drinker	<1 unit	1-7 units	8-14 units	15+ units	Total
	%	%	%	%	%	%
Drank nothing last week	100	75	29	8	4	41
Up to 3 units	0	23	57	54	32	38
More than 3, up to 6 units	0	1	11	25	31	13
More than 6 units	0	0	3	13	33	8
Base = 100%	1080	1502	2870	1219	1143	7814

Table 9.5(a) Alcohol consumption: maximum daily amount last week by AC rating and age: men

Men aged 16 and over   *Great Britain: 1998*

Age and maximum daily amount	AC rating					
	Non-drinker	<1 unit	1-10 units	11-21 units	22+ units	Total
	%	%	%	%	%	%
16-24						
Drank nothing last week	100	[82]	42	16	6	32
Up to 4 units	0	[18]	30	19	13	19
More than 4, up to 8 units	0	0	15	21	13	13
More than 8 units	0	0	13	44	68	37
Base = 100%	57	44	222	122	250	695
	%	%	%	%	%	%
25-44						
Drank nothing last week	100	80	24	6	4	22
Up to 4 units	0	17	52	31	15	32
More than 4, up to 8 units	0	2	13	30	23	19
More than 8 units	0	2	11	34	58	28
Base = 100%	146	129	878	591	653	2397
	%	%	%	%	%	%
45-64						
Drank nothing last week	100	77	24	3	3	22
Up to 4 units	0	21	61	47	27	41
More than 4, up to 8 units	0	1	11	31	32	20
More than 8 units	0	1	4	18	39	17
Base = 100%	131	168	725	463	643	2130
	%	%	%	%	%	%
65 and over						
Drank nothing last week	100	86	23	4	2	35
Up to 4 units	0	14	71	68	38	49
More than 4, up to 8 units	0	0	5	22	41	12
More than 8 units	0	0	1	6	18	4
Base = 100%	161	183	551	220	213	1328

Table 9.5(b) Alcohol consumption: maximum daily amount last week by AC rating and age: women

Women aged 16 and over   *Great Britain: 1998*

Age and maximum daily amount	AC rating					
	Non-drinker	<1 unit	1-7 units	8-14 units	15+ units	Total
	%	%	%	%	%	%
16-24						
Drank nothing last week	100	84	39	14	6	39
Up to 3 units	0	13	34	24	10	19
More than 3, up to 6 units	0	3	18	31	24	18
More than 6 units	0	0	9	31	59	23
Base = 100%	*105*	*86*	*264*	*152*	*200*	*807*
	%	%	%	%	%	%
25-44						
Drank nothing last week	100	71	31	9	4	35
Up to 3 units	0	26	49	45	25	37
More than 3, up to 6 units	0	3	14	29	32	17
More than 6 units	0	0	5	16	39	11
Base = 100%	*292*	*408*	*1227*	*520*	*460*	*2907*
	%	%	%	%	%	%
45-64						
Drank nothing last week	100	76	25	5	3	38
Up to 3 units	0	23	65	62	44	45
More than 3, up to 6 units	0	0	8	27	34	13
More than 6 units	0	0	1	7	19	4
Base = 100%	*284*	*482*	*869*	*354*	*373*	*2362*
	%	%	%	%	%	%
65 and over						
Drank nothing last week	100	77	26	4	4	55
Up to 3 units	0	22	72	86	63	41
More than 3, up to 6 units	0	1	2	8	28	3
More than 6 units	0	0	0	2	5	1
Base = 100%	*399*	*526*	*510*	*193*	*110*	*1738*

Table 9.6 **Whether drank last week and number of drinking days by sex and socio-economic group of the head of household**

(a) Persons aged 16 and over - all socio-economic groups   Great Britain: 1998

Drinking days last week	Socio-economic group of head of household*							
	Professional	Employers and managers	Intermediate non-manual	Junior non-manual	Skilled manual and own account non-profess-ional	Semi-skilled manual and personal service	Unskilled manual	Total
Men	%	%	%	%	%	%	%	%
0	15	20	23	24	28	33	35	25
1	12	16	14	16	20	18	17	17
2	16	15	15	16	15	16	16	15
3	11	11	12	11	11	11	10	11
4	11	9	8	7	8	5	6	8
5	7	7	9	7	4	4	5	6
6	7	5	5	5	3	2	1	4
7	21	18	13	14	12	11	10	14
% who drank last week	85	80	77	76	72	67	65	75
Base = 100%	579	1429	699	518	2007	856	274	6570
Women	%	%	%	%	%	%	%	%
0	28	30	35	42	43	52	60	41
1	18	21	18	21	24	21	18	21
2	15	13	15	12	12	11	11	13
3	10	10	10	8	8	6	3	8
4	6	7	6	4	5	3	2	5
5	6	5	4	3	2	2	1	3
6	3	3	3	1	2	0	1	2
7	13	11	9	9	5	6	3	8
% who drank last week	72	70	65	58	57	48	40	59
Base = 100%	544	1521	936	969	1957	1173	410	7828

(b) Persons aged 16 and over - non-manual and manual socio-economic groups

Drinking days last week	Socio-economic group of head of household*		
	Non-manual	Manual	Total
Men	%	%	%
0	20	30	25
1	15	19	17
2	15	15	15
3	11	11	11
4	9	7	8
5	7	4	6
6	5	3	4
7	17	12	14
% who drank last week	80	70	75
Base = 100%	3225	3137	6570
Women	%	%	%
0	34	48	41
1	20	22	21
2	13	12	13
3	10	7	8
4	6	4	5
5	4	2	3
6	3	1	2
7	10	5	8
% who drank last week	66	52	59
Base = 100%	3970	3540	7828

* Members of the Armed Forces, persons in inadequately described occupations and all persons who have never worked are not shown as separate categories but are included in the figures for all persons.

Table 9.7 **Maximum daily amount last week by sex and socio-economic group of the head of household**

(a) *Persons aged 16 and over - all socio-economic groups*   *Great Britain: 1998*

Maximum daily amount	Socio-economic group of head of household*							
	Professional	Employers and managers	Intermediate non-manual	Junior non-manual	Skilled manual and own account non-profess-ional	Semi-skilled manual and personal service	Unskilled manual	Total
	%	%	%	%	%	%	%	%
Men								
Drank nothing last week	15	20	23	25	28	34	35	25
Up to 4 units	51	43	40	37	34	29	25	37
More than 4, up to 8 units	19	18	18	15	17	18	15	17
More than 8 units	15	19	19	24	22	20	24	21
Base = 100%	*577*	*1427*	*699*	*516*	*2004*	*854*	*274*	*6559*
	%	%	%	%	%	%	%	%
Women								
Drank nothing last week	28	30	35	42	43	52	60	41
Up to 3 units	52	47	45	39	35	30	25	38
More than 3, up to 6 units	14	16	13	11	14	10	9	13
More than 6 units	6	7	7	9	9	8	7	8
Base = 100%	*543*	*1521*	*936*	*968*	*1954*	*1173*	*408*	*7820*

(b) *Persons aged 16 and over - non-manual and manual socio-economic groups*

Maximum daily amount	Socio-economic group of head of household*		
	Non-manual	Manual	Total
	%	%	%
Men			
Drank nothing last week	20	30	25
Up to 4 units	43	32	37
More than 4, up to 8 units	18	17	17
More than 8 units	19	21	21
Base = 100%	*3219*	*3132*	*6559*
	%	%	%
Women			
Drank nothing last week	34	48	41
Up to 3 units	45	32	38
More than 3, up to 6 units	14	12	13
More than 6 units	8	8	8
Base = 100%	*3968*	*3535*	*7820*

* Members of the Armed Forces, persons in inadequately described occupations and all persons who have never worked are not shown as separate categories but are included in the figures for all persons.

Table 9.8   **Alcohol consumption: maximum daily amount last week by AC rating, socio-economic group of head of household and sex**

(a) Men aged 16 and over   *Great Britain: 1998*

Maximum daily amount and socio-economic group of head of household	AC rating					
	Non-drinker	<1 unit	1-10 units	11-21 units	22+ units	Total
	%	%	%	%	%	%
Non-manual						
Drank nothing last week	100	82	20	4	3	20
Up to 4 units	0	18	63	48	27	43
More than 4, up to 8 units	0	1	10	27	28	18
More than 8 units	0	0	6	21	42	19
Base = 100%	*192*	*197*	*1210*	*725*	*891*	*3215*
Manual						
Drank nothing last week	100	81	30	7	4	30
Up to 4 units	0	17	51	35	18	31
More than 4, up to 8 units	0	1	11	29	27	17
More than 8 units	0	1	7	29	51	21
Base = 100%	*277*	*317*	*1115*	*614*	*804*	*3127*

(b) Women aged 16 and over   *Great Britain: 1998*

Maximum daily amount and socio-economic group of head of household	AC rating					
	Non-drinker	<1 unit	1-7 units	8-14 units	15+ units	Total
	%	%	%	%	%	%
Non-manual						
Drank nothing last week	100	71	26	6	4	34
Up to 3 units	0	28	62	59	37	45
More than 3, up to 6 units	0	1	9	23	33	14
More than 6 units	0	0	3	11	26	8
Base = 100%	*434*	*637*	*1532*	*692*	*672*	*3967*
Manual						
Drank nothing last week	100	78	33	10	5	48
Up to 3 units	0	20	51	48	28	32
More than 3, up to 6 units	0	2	12	28	27	12
More than 6 units	0	0	4	14	40	8
Base = 100%	*573*	*813*	*1238*	*485*	*421*	*3530*

Table 9.9 **Alcohol consumption: maximum daily amount last week by sex and usual gross weekly household income**

Persons aged 16 and over   *Great Britain: 1998*

Maximum daily amount	Usual gross weekly household income (£)								
	0.01 - 100.00	100.01 - 150.00	150.01 - 200.00	200.01 - 250.00	250.01 - 300.00	300.01 - 400.00	400.01 - 500.00	500.01 or more	Total*
	%	%	%	%	%	%	%	%	%
Men									
Drank nothing last week	37	41	35	36	31	30	23	16	25
Up to 4 units	32	36	37	35	36	35	37	38	37
More than 4, up to 8 units	15	12	16	14	13	15	17	21	17
More than 8 units	16	11	13	15	19	20	23	25	21
Base = 100%	*352*	*427*	*441*	*416*	*384*	*709*	*678*	*2409*	*6559*
	%	%	%	%	%	%	%	%	%
Women									
Drank nothing last week	57	55	55	48	47	47	34	26	41
Up to 3 units	31	31	33	37	36	34	43	44	38
More than 3, up to 6 units	6	8	6	8	10	12	13	19	13
More than 6 units	6	6	6	7	7	7	9	11	8
Base = 100%	*723*	*680*	*578*	*472*	*417*	*827*	*708*	*2457*	*7820*

* Includes people who did not provide income data, and 144 cases of nil income.

Table 9.10 **Alcohol consumption: maximum daily amount last week by sex and usual gross weekly earnings**

(a) Men aged 16-64 in full-time employment   *Great Britain: 1998*

Maximum daily amount	Usual gross weekly earnings (£)								
	0.01 - 100.00	100.01 - 150.00	150.01 - 200.00	200.01 - 250.00	250.01 - 300.00	300.01 - 350.00	350.01 - 400.00	400.01 or more	Total*
	%	%	%	%	%	%	%	%	%
Drank nothing last week	30	31	27	22	22	19	21	12	19
Up to 4 units	27	24	25	32	31	33	38	41	35
More than 4, up to 8 units	16	17	17	18	17	18	17	23	19
More than 8 units	26	28	31	28	31	30	25	24	27
Base = 100%	*102*	*139*	*284*	*420*	*420*	*360*	*341*	*1366*	*3696*

(b) Women aged 16-64 in full-time employment   *Great Britain: 1998*

Maximum daily amount	Usual gross weekly earnings (£)							
	0.01 - 100.00	100.01 - 150.00	150.01 - 200.00	200.01 - 250.00	250.01 - 300.00	300.01 - 350.00	350.01 or more	Total*
	%	%	%	%	%	%	%	%
Drank nothing last week	34	36	32	26	25	32	18	27
Up to 3 units	39	25	37	39	43	39	47	40
More than 3, up to 6 units	12	19	15	22	20	20	21	19
More than 6 units	16	20	16	13	12	9	14	14
Base = 100%	*109*	*225*	*323*	*342*	*269*	*206*	*594*	*2202*

* Total includes people who did not provide earnings data.

Table 9.11   **Alcohol consumption: maximum daily amount last week by sex and economic activity status**

(a) Men aged 16-64   *Great Britain: 1998*

Maximum daily amount	Economic activity status			
	Working	Unemployed	Economically inactive	Total
	%	%	%	%
Drank nothing last week	20	38	33	23
Up to 4 units	34	22	34	34
More than 4, up to 8 units	19	18	15	18
More than 8 units	26	22	18	25
Base = 100%	*4056*	*265*	*906*	*5227*

(b) Women aged 16-64   *Great Britain: 1998*

Maximum daily amount	Economic activity status					
	Working full time	Working part time	Total* working	Unemployed	Economically inactive	Total
	%	%	%	%	%	%
Drank nothing last week	27	36	31	36	50	37
Up to 3 units	40	40	40	31	33	38
More than 3, up to 6 units	19	16	18	19	10	15
More than 6 units	14	9	12	13	7	10
Base = 100%	*2202*	*1676*	*3914*	*187*	*1978*	*6079*

* Including a few women who did not specify their hours of work.

Table 9.12   **Alcohol consumption: maximum daily amount last week by sex, marital status and presence of children**

Persons aged 16 and over   *Great Britain: 1998*

Maximum daily amount	Marital status					
	Married			Single	Widowed/ divorced/ separated	Total
	With dependent children	Without dependent children	Total* married			
	%	%	%	%	%	%
Men						
Drank nothing last week	24	23	24	29	31	25
Up to 4 units	38	43	41	24	36	37
More than 4, up to 8 units	18	18	18	15	16	17
More than 8 units	20	16	18	32	18	21
Base = 100%	*1671*	*2820*	*4494*	*1348*	*701*	*6543*
	%	%	%	%	%	%
Women						
Drank nothing last week	39	37	38	40	51	41
Up to 3 units	40	44	42	25	37	38
More than 3, up to 6 units	14	13	13	17	8	13
More than 6 units	7	6	7	18	4	8
Base = 100%	*1916*	*2923*	*4842*	*1222*	*1742*	*7806*

* Totals married with dependent children and without dependent children do not always sum to the total married as the dependency of some children could not be established.

Table 9.13   Alcohol consumption: maximum daily amount last week, by sex and Government Office Region

Persons aged 16 and over   *Great Britain: 1998*

Region		Maximum daily amount*				Base = 100%
		Drank nothing last week	Up to 4/3 units	More than 4/3, up to 8/6 units	More than 8/6 units	
Men						
North East	%	23	32	22	23	349
North West	%	23	33	18	26	593
Merseyside	%	22	33	18	27	144
Yorkshire and the Humber	%	27	34	15	24	549
East Midlands	%	24	35	21	20	463
West Midlands	%	26	36	17	21	634
Eastern	%	23	44	19	14	626
London	%	33	36	13	18	672
South East	%	21	44	17	18	955
South West	%	24	41	17	18	629
England	%	25	38	17	20	5614
Wales	%	32	29	17	22	353
Scotland	%	29	32	16	24	592
Great Britain	%	25	37	17	21	6559
Women						
North East	%	43	35	14	8	407
North West	%	37	38	14	11	705
Merseyside	%	41	32	18	9	182
Yorkshire and the Humber	%	44	36	13	7	713
East Midlands	%	40	40	12	7	584
West Midlands	%	42	38	11	9	691
Eastern	%	42	42	10	6	728
London	%	49	34	11	6	813
South East	%	34	46	13	7	1091
South West	%	38	42	12	8	744
England	%	41	39	12	8	6658
Wales	%	46	33	12	9	419
Scotland	%	40	32	15	12	743
Great Britain	%	41	38	13	8	7820

* See the footnote to Table 9.3.

159

Table 9.14 **Alcohol consumption level (AC rating) by sex: 1988 to 1998**

Persons aged 16 and over   *Great Britain*

Alcohol consumption level (units per week)	1988		1990		1992		1994		1996		1998	
	%		%		%		%		%		%	
Men												
Non-drinker	7		6		7		7		7		8	
Under 1 unit	10		9		10		9		8		8	
1-10 units	35		36		36		35		35		36	
11-21 units	21		22		21		22		23		21	
22-35 units	13		13		13		14		15		14	
36-50 units	7	26	7	27	7	26	6	27	7	27	6	27
51+ units	7		7		6		6		6		6	
Base = 100%	*8673*		*8097*		*8395*		*7636*		*7151*		*6567*	
	%		%		%		%		%		%	
Women												
Non-drinker	12		12		12		14		13		14	
Under 1 unit	24		23		22		21		20		19	
1-7 units	40		40		39		37		37		37	
8-14 units	14		14		15		15		16		16	
15-25 units	7		7		8		9		9		10	
26-35 units	2	10	2	11	2	11	2	13	2	14	3	15
36+ units	2		2		2		2		2		2	
Base = 100%	*10122*		*9424*		*9747*		*9104*		*8491*		*7823*	

Table 9.15 **Alcohol consumption (AC rating): percentages exceeding specified amounts by sex and age: 1988 to 1998**

Persons aged 16 and over   *Great Britain*

Age	Men						Women					
	1988	1990	1992	1994	1996	1998	1988	1990	1992	1994	1996	1998
Percentage who drank more than 21/14 units												
16-24	31	31	32	29	35	36	15	16	17	19	22	25
25-44	34	33	31	30	30	27	14	13	14	15	16	16
45-64	24	25	25	27	26	30	9	10	11	12	13	16
65 and over	13	14	15	17	18	16	4	5	5	7	7	6
Total	26	27	26	27	27	27	10	11	11	13	14	15
Percentage who drank more than 50/35 units												
16-24	10	11	9	9	10	13	3	3	4	4	5	6
25-44	9	9	8	7	6	6	2	2	2	2	2	2
45-64	6	6	6	6	5	6	1	1	1	2	2	2
65 and over	2	3	2	3	3	3	0	1	0	1	1	1
Total	7	7	6	6	6	6	2	2	2	2	2	2
Bases = 100%												
16-24	*1356*	*1157*	*1144*	*951*	*880*	*701*	*1530*	*1343*	*1271*	*1069*	*968*	*807*
25-44	*3185*	*3045*	*3056*	*2855*	*2612*	*2400*	*3530*	*3369*	*3492*	*3437*	*3179*	*2909*
45-64	*2557*	*2386*	*2598*	*2376*	*2214*	*2135*	*2749*	*2593*	*2828*	*2560*	*2508*	*2366*
65 and over	*1575*	*1509*	*1597*	*1454*	*1445*	*1331*	*2313*	*2119*	*2156*	*2038*	*1836*	*1741*
Total	*8673*	*8097*	*8395*	*7636*	*7151*	*6567*	*10122*	*9424*	*9747*	*9104*	*8491*	*7823*

Table 9.16 Mean weekly alcohol consumption in units (AC rating), by sex and age: 1992 to 1998

Persons aged 16 and over   *Great Britain*

Age	Men				Women				All persons			
	1992	1994	1996	1998	1992	1994	1996	1998	1992	1994	1996	1998
16-24	19.1	17.4	20.3	23.6	7.3	7.7	9.5	10.6	12.9	12.3	14.7	16.6
25-44	18.2	17.5	17.6	16.5	6.3	6.2	7.2	7.1	11.8	11.4	11.9	11.4
45-64	15.6	15.5	15.6	17.3	5.3	5.3	5.9	6.4	10.2	10.2	10.5	11.6
65 and over	9.7	10.0	11.0	10.7	2.7	3.2	3.5	3.3	5.6	6.0	6.8	6.5
Total	15.9	15.4	16.0	16.4	5.4	5.4	6.3	6.4	10.2	10.0	10.7	11.0
Bases = 100%												
16-24	*1144*	*951*	*881*	*699*	*1271*	*1069*	*969*	*808*	*2415*	*2020*	*1850*	*1507*
25-44	*3056*	*2855*	*2628*	*2399*	*3492*	*3437*	*3182*	*2909*	*6548*	*6292*	*5810*	*5308*
45-64	*2598*	*2376*	*2215*	*2135*	*2828*	*2560*	*2509*	*2365*	*5426*	*4936*	*4724*	*4500*
65 and over	*1597*	*1454*	*1445*	*1331*	*2156*	*2038*	*1836*	*1741*	*3753*	*3492*	*3281*	*3072*
Total	*8395*	*7636*	*7169*	*6564*	*9747*	*9104*	*8496*	*7823*	*18142*	*16740*	*15665*	*14387*

Table 9.17 Alcohol consumption level (AC rating) and mean weekly number of units by sex and socio-economic group of the head of household

Persons aged 16 and over   *Great Britain: 1998*

Alcohol consumption level (units per week)	Socio-economic group of head of household*							
	Professional	Employers and managers	Intermediate non-manual	Junior non-manual	Skilled manual and own account non-profess-ional	Semi-skilled manual and personal service	Unskilled manual	Total
	%	%	%	%	%	%	%	%
Men								
Non-drinker	5	6	6	8	8	11	9	8
Under 1 unit	5	7	6	5	10	10	13	8
1-10 units	37	37	39	39	36	35	32	36
11-21 units	25	23	23	19	21	18	18	21
22-35 units	19	14	15	16	13	13	13	14
36-50 units	6 ⎱28	7 ⎱27	7 ⎱26	6 ⎱30	5 ⎱25	7 ⎱26	8 ⎱29	6 ⎱27
51 units or more	3	6	4	8	7	6	7	6
Mean weekly units	15.7	16.6	15.2	18.0	15.8	15.7	17.4	16.4
Base = 100%	*577*	*1428*	*699*	*517*	*2008*	*854*	*273*	*6567*
	%	%	%	%	%	%	%	%
Women								
Non-drinker	9	9	12	13	13	19	23	14
Under 1 unit	12	14	16	22	21	24	29	19
1-7 units	40	38	40	37	38	33	30	37
8-14 units	21	19	16	14	16	12	9	16
15-25 units	14	13	12	10	9	8	5	10
26-35 units	2 ⎱17	3 ⎱19	2 ⎱16	2 ⎱15	2 ⎱12	2 ⎱12	2 ⎱9	3 ⎱15
36 units or more	1	2	2	2	1	2	2	2
Mean weekly units	7.3	7.9	6.6	6.1	5.8	5.6	4.4	6.4
Base = 100%	*544*	*1519*	*937*	*969*	*1954*	*1171*	*409*	*7823*

* Members of the Armed Forces, persons in inadequately described occupations and all persons who have never worked are not shown as separate categories but are included in the figures for all persons.

161

Table 9.18 **Age distributions of lifetime abstainers and those who had stopped drinking, by sex**

Non-drinkers aged 16 and over   *Great Britain: 1998*

	Lifetime abstainers		Those who had stopped drinking	
	Men	Women	Men	Women
	%	%	%	%
16-24	19	12	3	6
25-44	34	28	26	26
45-64	22	25	32	29
65 and over	24	35	39	39
Base = 100%	*249*	*616*	*224*	*418*

Table 9.19 **Main reason for not drinking, by sex and whether was a lifetime abstainer or had stopped drinking**

Non-drinkers aged 16 and over   *Great Britain: 1998*

Reason for not drinking	Lifetime abstainers			Those who had stopped drinking		
	Men	Women	Total	Men	Women	Total
	%	%	%	%	%	%
Religion	43	26	31	6	4	5
Don't like it	39	53	49	16	26	22
Parents' advice	7	8	7	1	1	1
Health reasons	4	5	5	50	49	49
Can't afford it	0	1	1	7	6	6
Other	8	8	8	20	15	16
Base = 100%	*249*	*616*	*865*	*224*	*418*	*642*

10 Contraception

Current use of contraception

The GHS first included questions on contraception in 1983 when they were addressed to women aged 18-49, and to women aged 16-17 who were or who had been married. Since 1986, the questions have been asked of all women aged 16-49.

In 1998, as in 1995 and 1993, nearly three-quarters of women aged 16-49 (72%) used at least one form of contraception. The most common methods for avoiding pregnancy used by women in this age range included:

- the contraceptive pill (used by 24% of women);
- surgical sterilisation of either the woman or her partner (23% of women);
- the male condom (used by partners of 18% of women).

Most of the analysis presented in this chapter focuses on these three forms of contraception.

Twenty eight per cent of women questioned in 1998 were *not* using any form of contraception, and of these:

- half were not in a sexual relationship (14% of all women aged 16-49);
- almost a quarter were pregnant or wanting to conceive (6% of all women in the age group). **Table 10.1**

Current use of contraception and age
As in previous years, whether or not women were using contraception, and the type of method used varied significantly with age:

- two-thirds of women under 18 did not have a current sexual relationship. Amongst contraceptive users in this age group, almost equal proportions used the pill and the condom;
- amongst women aged 18-29, roughly twice as many used the pill as used the male condom;
- women in their late twenties who were not using any form of contraception were as likely to be pregnant as not to have a current sexual relationship;
- beyond the age of 30, surgical sterilisation as a method of contraception was used by increasing proportions of women - half of those aged 45-49 were sterilised or had partners who were sterilised;
- women over 40 who relied on non-surgical methods were more likely to use the condom than the pill.

Table 10.2

Trends in contraceptive use

Trends in the use of contraceptive methods by women aged 16-49 have been monitored since 1986 when questions about contraception were first addressed to all women as young as 16. Between 1986 and 1998:

- the proportion of women using some form of contraception has ranged from 69% to 73%. Although differences between individual years are statistically significant, changes have been small and no very clear trend emerges from the data;
- the contraceptive pill, surgical sterilisation and the male condom have remained the three most commonly used methods of contraception.

Table 10.1, Figure 10A

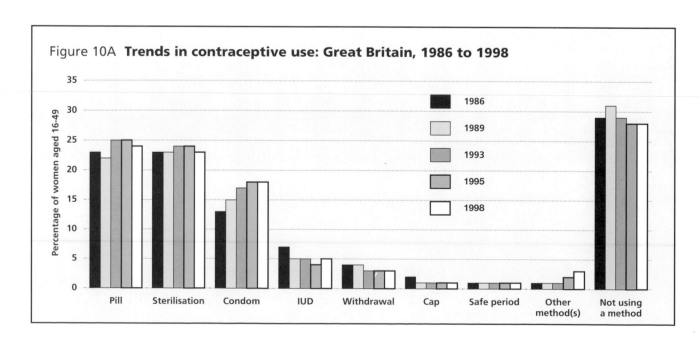

Figure 10A **Trends in contraceptive use: Great Britain, 1986 to 1998**

Between 1989 and 1993, the percentage of women using the pill increased from 22% to 25% since when it has remained at roughly the same level.

- The percentage of women aged 35-39 using the pill increased between 1986 and 1995, but this trend was not continued in 1998;
- there was a statistically significant *decrease* between 1995 and 1998, from 29% to 24%, in the percentage of women aged 30-34 claiming to use the pill as their usual form of contraception;
- in other age groups none of the changes between 1995 and 1998 was statistically significant.   **Table 10.3**

Among all women aged 16-49, the prevalence of sterilisation as a method of contraception has changed little since 1986, with levels of usage remaining at or around a quarter of women or their partners. However, this broadly stable picture conceals some important opposing trends within different age groups:

- use of sterilisation, of self or partner, declined amongst women aged 30-44, particularly among women in their thirties, and increased among women in their late forties, although the key periods of change varied between age groups;   **Table 10.4**

Between 1986 and 1995, the proportion of women whose partners used the condom increased from 13% to 18%. There was no further change to this figure between 1995 and the most recent survey in 1998. Trends in condom use vary with age:

- among women under 30, the main trend between 1986 and 1998 has been the steady increase in the use of the condom. Apparent decreases in the use of this method by women in this age group, for example such as that reported by women aged 18-19 between 1995 and 1998, were not statistically significant;
- the only age group in which a statistically significant change has occurred since 1995 is women aged 45-49, only 10% of whom, compared with 14% in 1995, said the condom was a usual method of contraception. This continues a long term downward trend since 1986, when 16% of women in this age group reported that their partner used the condom.   **Table 10.5**

Current use of contraception and marital status

A third of women who were widowed, divorced or separated and nearly two-fifths of single women said that they had no current sexual relationship. Among the rest, 22% of widowed, divorced or separated women (48% of all women in this marital status), 17% of married or cohabiting women[1] and 12% of single women (45% of all single women) said they used no form of contraception.

Of the three most commonly used forms of contraception:

- single women were more likely to use the pill than any other method (34% did so, compared with 21% using the condom and 2% surgical sterilisation);
- just under a third of women who were married or cohabiting were sterilised or had partners who were sterilised, and roughly equal proportions (around a fifth) used the pill or the condom.
          Table 10.6, Figure 10B

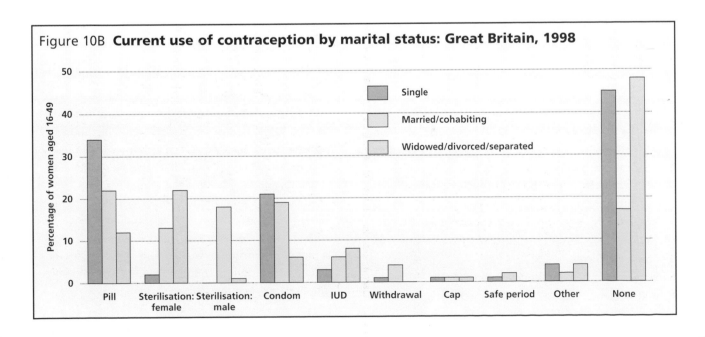

Figure 10B **Current use of contraception by marital status: Great Britain, 1998**

Change to and from the condom

Women were asked about their use of condoms over the two year period prior to interview. Among current users of a contraceptive method:

- sixteen per cent had used the condom as their main method throughout the two year period, 7% had changed to the condom and were currently using it and 5% had switched from the condom to some other method;
- women aged 25-39 were more likely than those in other age groups to have used the condom as their main method throughout the reference period;
- younger users of contraception were much more likely than older women to have used the condom at some stage over the past two years;
- there was no statistically significant difference between the proportion of single women and those who were married or cohabiting who had used condoms throughout the reference period;
- however, single women were around three times as likely as their married or cohabiting counterparts to have changed to the condom from some other method (16% compared with 6%);
- they were also twice as likely to have switched from the condom to some other method during the same time period.   **Table 10.8**

Women not 'at risk' of pregnancy

Absence of a sexual relationship and sterilisation of either a woman or her partner carry no 'risk' (or very low 'risk') of pregnancy. Table 10.9 shows the proportion of women in different groups who had no sexual partner or who depended on sterilisation (of self or partner) to avoid pregnancy. The prevalence of women protected from pregnancy in these ways was greatest among:

- young women aged 16-19, none of whom were sterilised, and women aged 40-49 nearly half of whom were sterilised or had partners who had been sterilised;
- single women, most because they had no sexual partner, and women who were widowed, divorced or separated;
- women with two or more children (about a half);
- women who said they were not likely to have any (more) children;
- women with no educational qualifications;
- and women in manual socio-economic groups.

Protection afforded either by sterilisation or by not having a sexual relationship covered only:

- about one in six women cohabiting with their partners;
- about one in five women aged 25-34;
- and one in five women who said that they were likely to have (more) children;
- one in three women in non-manual socio-economic groups;
- less than a third of women with the highest levels of educational attainment: GCE 'A' levels or above;
- less than a third of women with one child or no children.   **Table 10.9**

Use of the pill and the condom as usual methods of contraception by women 'at risk' of pregnancy

Table 10.10 shows the percentage of women 'at risk' of pregnancy (that is women aged 16-49 who were in a sexual relationship, who were not pregnant or sterilised, and whose partners had not been sterilised) who used the pill, and the condom. Women who reported using both methods appear in both columns, but the proportion to whom this applies is small (4%) and Table 10.10 can therefore be used to give some broad indication of the percentage of 'at risk' women using one or other of these two methods of contraception.

- All but a tiny proportion of 16-19 year-olds 'at risk' of pregnancy used the pill or the male condom as their usual form of contraception, but the percentage of 'at risk' women claiming to use one or other of these methods as their usual form of contraception declined with age. Only around one third of women aged 45-49 said that they did;
- all but a small percentage of single women 'at risk' of pregnancy, the majority of whom are in the younger age groups, used either the pill or the condom, and, at the other extreme, around two-fifths of women who were widowed, divorced or separated did so. Women who were cohabiting were more likely than married women to use one or other of these two methods;
- a higher percentage of women with no children than of women with children used either the pill or the male condom, and the likelihood of using these two methods declined with the number of children. This is likely to be partly an effect of age, as older women tend to have more children than younger women;
- a higher proportion of women who said that they were likely to have (more) children than of those who were not likely to, used the pill and the condom;

- the pill and the condom were most likely to be used by women qualified to GCSE grades A-C or above. Less than half of 'at risk' women with no formal qualifications used one of these two methods.

Table 10.10

Use of emergency contraception

The GHS first included questions on emergency (post-coital) contraception in 1993. Ten per cent of women aged 16-49 who were not sterilised and whose partners were not sterilised had used emergency contraception at least once in the two years prior to interview. This represents an increase of three percentage points since 1995, and five percentage points since 1993. Emergency contraception was most likely to have been used in the past two years by:

- women under 30;
- single women, who were twice as likely as other women to have used emergency contraception;
- women with no children (14%);
- women with higher levels of educational attainment (12% of those with GCE 'A' levels or above had used this method, compared with 6% of those with no educational qualifications);
- women who said they definitely or probably would have (more) children (15% compared with 6% of those who said they definitely or probably would not).

There were no significant differences in respect of the use of emergency contraception between women in manual and non-manual socio-economic groups.

Tables 10.11-10.13

Notes

1. Only 1% of married or cohabiting women said they had no sexual relationship.

Table 10.1 Women aged 16-49: trends in contraceptive use: 1986 to 1998

Women aged 16-49 *Great Britain*

Current usual method of contraception	1986	1989	1991	1993	1995	1998
	%	%	%	%	%	%
Using method(s)						
Non-surgical*						
Pill	23	22	23	25	25	24
IUD	7	5	5	5	4	5
Condom	13	15	16	17	18	18
Cap	2	1	1	1	1	1
Withdrawal	4	4	3	3	3	3
Safe period	1	1	1	1	1	1
Other	1	1	1	1	2	3
At least one	49	46	46	48	49	49
Surgical						
Female sterilisation	12 ⎤ 23	11 ⎤ 23	12 ⎤ 25	12 ⎤ 24	12 ⎤ 24	11 ⎤ 23
Male sterilisation	11 ⎦	12 ⎦	13 ⎦	12 ⎦	11 ⎦	12 ⎦
Total using at least one	71	69	70	72	73	72
Not using a method						
Sterile after another operation	3	5	3	2	3	2
Pregnant/wanting to get pregnant	7	7	9	8	8	6
Abstinence/no partner	15 ⎤ 20	16 ⎤ 22	16 ⎤ 21	15 ⎤ 21	14 ⎤ 20	14 ⎤ 20
Other	5 ⎦	5 ⎦	5 ⎦	5 ⎦	6 ⎦	6 ⎦
Total	29	31	30	29	28	28
Base = 100%†	*5866*	*5802*	*5571*	*5303*	*5067*	*4251*

* Abstinence is not included here as a method of contraception.

† Percentages add to more than 100 because some women used more than one non-surgical method or had more than one reason for not using a method.

Table 10.2 Current use of contraception by age

Women aged 16-49   *Great Britain: 1998*

Current use of contraception	Age								
	16-17	18-19	20-24	25-29	30-34	35-39	40-44	45-49	Total
	%	%	%	%	%	%	%	%	%
Using method(s)									
Non-surgical*:									
Pill†	17	41	52	41	24	18	9	4	24
Mini pill	1	6	9	5	6	5	4	2	5
Combined pill	12	33	41	33	17	12	5	1	18
(Mini + Combined subtotal)	13	38	51	38	23	17	9	3	22
IUD	0	1	3	7	6	6	7	6	5
Condom	18	21	23	23	20	18	15	10	18
Cap	0	0	0	1	1	1	2	1	1
Withdrawal	1	0	2	4	4	3	2	3	3
Safe period	0	0	1	1	3	2	2	1	1
Spermicides	0	0	0	0	0	0	0	0	0
Injection	1	7	5	2	3	2	0	0	2
At least one	29	61	71	70	56	45	34	23	49
Surgical:									
Sterilisation - female	1	0	0	2	8	15	22	26	11
- male	0	0	0	3	9	19	20	25	12
(Sterilisation subtotal)			1	5	17	33	42	50	23
Total - at least one	29	61	72	74	72	78	77	73	72
Not using a method									
Sterile after other operation	0	0	0	0	1	2	4	6	2
Pregnant now	2	5	5	9	5	3	1	0	4
Going without sex to avoid pregnancy	1	1	1	0	1	1	0	0	1
No sexual relationship	66	30	18	9	9	9	10	10	13
Wants to get pregnant	0	1	2	4	6	2	2	0	2
Unlikely to conceive because of menopause	0	0	0	0	0	0	2	7	1
Possibly infertile	0	1	1	1	2	2	2	1	1
Doesn't like contraception	1	3	1	2	2	1	1	1	1
Just doesn't use contraception	1	0	0	0	0	0	0	0	0
Others	1	1	0	1	2	1	1	1	1
Total not using a method	71	39	28	26	28	22	23	27	28
*Base = 100%****	178	193	420	687	753	781	613	626	4251

* Abstinence is not included here as a method of contraception. Those who said that 'going without sex to avoid getting pregnant' was their only method of contraception are shown with others not using a method.

† The total percentage using the pill includes those who did not know which type of pill.

** Percentages add to more than 100 because of rounding and because some women used more than one non-surgical method.

Table 10.3 **Trends in use of the pill as a usual method of contraception by age: 1986 to 1998**

Women aged 16-49   *Great Britain*

Age	1986	1989	1991	1993	1995	1998
			Percentage of women who used the pill			
16-17	20	19	16	20	25	17
18-19	42	39	46	42	37	41
20-24	55	48	48	50	49	52
25-29	38	36	42	44	41	41
30-34	21	22	25	29	29	24
35-39	8	12	11	16	20	18
40-44	4	4	4	7	9	9
45-49	1	3	2	4	3	4
All aged 16-49	23	22	23	25	25	24
Bases = 100%						
16-17	*352*	*307*	*267*	*233*	*219*	*178*
18-19	*317*	*318*	*260*	*212*	*155*	*193*
20-24	*877*	*835*	*758*	*710*	*565*	*420*
25-29	*953*	*948*	*931*	*852*	*773*	*687*
30-34	*893*	*862*	*956*	*912*	*1008*	*753*
35-39	*1023*	*845*	*753*	*785*	*822*	*781*
40-44	*816*	*968*	*857*	*782*	*692*	*613*
45-49	*635*	*719*	*789*	*817*	*833*	*626*
All aged 16-49	*5866*	*5802*	*5571*	*5303*	*5067*	*4251*

Table 10.4 **Percentage of women and partners sterilised for contraceptive reasons: 1986 to 1998**

Women aged 16-49   *Great Britain*

Age	1986	1989	1991	1993	1995	1998
			Percentage of women and partners* sterilised			
16-24	1	1	1	0	0	1
25-29	6	7	8	5	7	5
30-34	25	23	21	21	18	17
35-39	42	40	38	34	32	33
40-44	48	47	50	47	45	42
45-49	35	37	47	47	46	50
All aged 16-49	23	23	25	24	24	23
Bases = 100%						
16-24	*1546*	*1460*	*1285*	*1155*	*939*	*791*
25-29	*953*	*948*	*931*	*852*	*773*	*687*
30-34	*893*	*862*	*956*	*912*	*1008*	*753*
35-39	*1023*	*845*	*753*	*785*	*822*	*781*
40-44	*816*	*968*	*857*	*782*	*692*	*613*
45-49	*635*	*719*	*789*	*817*	*833*	*626*
All aged 16-49	*5866*	*5802*	*5571*	*5303*	*5067*	*4251*

* Refers to the woman's partner whether in the household or not.

Table 10.5 **Trends in use of the condom as a usual method of contraception by age: 1986 to 1998**

Women aged 16-49   *Great Britain*

Age	1986	1989	1991	1993	1995	1998
			Percentage whose partners* used the condom			
16-17	6	6	10	17	13	18
18-19	6	12	15	22	26	21
20-24	9	14	14	18	21	23
25-29	13	17	19	21	20	23
30-34	15	19	17	18	20	20
35-39	15	16	20	17	16	18
40-44	14	16	13	14	16	15
45-49	16	15	12	12	14	10
All aged 16-49	13	15	16	17	18	18
Bases = 100%						
16-17	*352*	*307*	*267*	*233*	*219*	*178*
18-19	*317*	*318*	*260*	*212*	*155*	*193*
20-24	*877*	*835*	*758*	*710*	*565*	*420*
25-29	*953*	*948*	*931*	*852*	*773*	*687*
30-34	*893*	*862*	*956*	*912*	*1008*	*753*
35-39	*1023*	*845*	*753*	*785*	*822*	*781*
40-44	*816*	*968*	*857*	*782*	*692*	*613*
45-49	*635*	*719*	*789*	*817*	*833*	*626*
All aged 16-49	*5866*	*5802*	*5571*	*5303*	*5067*	*4251*

* Refers to the woman's partner whether in the household or not.

Table 10.6 **Current use of contraception by marital status**

Women aged 16-49

Great Britain: 1998

Current use of contraception	Single	Married/cohabiting	Widowed/divorced/ separated	Total
	%	%	%	%
Using method(s)				
Non-surgical*:				
Pill	34	22	12	24
IUD	3	6	8	5
Condom	21	19	6	18
Cap	1	1	1	1
Withdrawal	1	4	0	3
Safe period	1	2	0	1
Spermicides	0	0	0	0
Injection	3	2	3	2
At least one	53	51	29	49
Surgical:				
Sterilisation - female	2 ⎤ 2	13 ⎤ 32	22 ⎤ 23	11 ⎤ 23
- male	0 ⎦	18 ⎦	1 ⎦	12 ⎦
Total - at least one†	55	83	52	72
Not using a method				
Sterile after other operation	1	2	5	2
Pregnant now	2	5	2	4
Going without sex to avoid pregnancy	1	0	1	1
No sexual relationship	38	1	33	13
Wants to get pregnant	0	4	1	2
Unlikely to conceive because of menopause	0	2	3	1
Possibly infertile	0	2	1	1
Doesn't like contraception	1	2	1	1
Just doesn't use contraception	0	0	0	0
Others	2	1	1	1
Total not using a method	45	17	48	28
*Base = 100%****	*1029*	*2717*	*494*	*4240*

* Abstinence is not included here as a method of contraception. Those who said that 'going without sex to avoid getting pregnant' was their only method of contraception are shown with others not using a method.

† Includes a few cases where other methods of contraception were used.

** Percentages add to more than 100 because of rounding and because some women used more than one non-surgical method.

Table 10.7 Current use of contraception by age among married/cohabiting women

Married/cohabiting women aged 16-49   *Great Britain: 1998*

Current use of contraception	Age						
	16-24	25-29	30-34	35-39	40-44	45-49	Total
	%	%	%	%	%	%	%
Using method(s)							
Non-surgical*:							
Pill	57	41	24	19	9	3	22
IUD	3	7	5	5	7	6	6
Condom	19	23	24	20	17	12	19
Cap	0	1	1	1	2	1	1
Withdrawal	3	5	5	3	3	3	4
Safe period	2	1	3	2	3	1	2
Spermicides	0	0	0	0	0	0	0
Injection	5	2	3	1	0	0	2
At least one	80	73	59	48	38	25	51
Surgical:							
Sterilisation - female	1 ⌉ 2	2 ⌉ 6	8 ⌉ 20	13 ⌉ 37	22 ⌉ 48	26 ⌉ 59	13 ⌉ 32
- male	1 ⌋	4 ⌋	11 ⌋	24 ⌋	27 ⌋	32 ⌋	18 ⌋
Total - at least one†	82	79	79	85	86	84	83
Not using a method							
Sterile after other operation	0	1	1	2	4	5	2
Pregnant now	11	11	6	4	1	0	5
Going without sex to avoid pregnancy	0	0	1	0	0	0	0
No sexual relationship	0	0	0	1	0	1	1
Wants to get pregnant	3	5	8	2	2	0	4
Unlikely to conceive because of menopause	0	0	0	1	2	7	2
Possibly infertile	2	1	2	2	2	1	2
Doesn't like contraception	2	3	2	2	1	1	2
Just doesn't use contraception	0	0	0	0	0	0	0
Others	1	0	1	1	0	0	1
Total not using a method	18	21	21	15	14	16	17
*Base = 100%****	*190*	*438*	*553*	*598*	*460*	*478*	*2717*

* Abstinence is not included here as a method of contraception. Those who said that 'going without sex to avoid getting pregnant' was their only method of contraception are shown with others not using a method.

† Includes a few cases where other methods of contraception were used.

** Percentages add to more than 100 because of rounding and because some women used more than one non-surgical method.

173

Table 10.8 **Current users of a contraceptive method: changes to and from condom use by woman's partner during the two years prior to interview by woman's marital status and age**

Women aged 16-49 with a partner* and currently using a method of contraception   *Great Britain: 1998*

Marital status and change to/from condom	Age								
	16-17	18-19	20-24	25-29	30-34	35-39	40-44	45-49	Total
	%	%	%	%	%	%	%	%	%
Single women									
Partner's use of condom									
Condom user throughout two years†	[8]	13	17	22	20	[23]	**	**	18
Changed to condom†	[44]	24	15	12	5	[6]	**	**	16
Changed from condom to current method	[10]	13	15	5	5	[3]	**	**	9
Condom has not been main method throughout two years	[38]	49	53	61	71	[69]	**	**	57
Base = 100%	*48*	*91*	*167*	*132*	*65*	*35*	*17*	*3*	*558††*
	%	%	%	%	%	%	%	%	%
Married/cohabiting women									
Partner's use of condom									
Condom user throughout two years†	**	0	8	16	19	18	17	13	16
Changed to condom†	**	[17]	12	10	10	4	2	0	6
Changed from condom to current method	**	[17]	5	7	5	5	3	1	4
Condom has not been main method throughout two years	**	[65]	74	68	66	73	79	85	74
Base = 100%	*2*	*23*	*129*	*343*	*436*	*509*	*396*	*401*	*2239††*
	%	%	%	%	%	%	%	%	%
All marital statuses of women≠									
Partner's use of condom									
Condom user throughout two years†	8	11	13	17	18	18	16	12	16
Changed to condom†	45	23	14	10	9	4	2	1	7
Changed from condom to current method	12	14	11	6	5	5	3	1	5
Condom has not been main method throughout two years	35	53	63	67	69	74	79	86	72
Base = 100%	*51*	*114*	*302*	*506*	*544*	*607*	*470*	*456*	*3050*

*   Refers to the woman's partner whether in the household or not.
†   Condom was main method at the time of interview.
** Bases are too small to enable reliable analysis to be made.
†† Total base includes groups not shown because of small bases.
≠   'All marital statuses' includes widowed/divorced/ separated.

Table 10.9 Percentage of women who (a) had no sexual partner (b) were sterilised or who had partners who were sterilised by selected characteristics

Women aged 16-49   *Great Britain: 1998*

	(a) No sexual partner	(b) Self or partner* sterilised	Base =100%
		Percentages	
Age			
16-19	47	0	371
20-24	18	1	420
25-29	9	5	687
30-34	9	16	753
35-39	9	33	781
40-44	10	42	613
45-49	10	50	626
Marital status			
Single	38	2	1029
Married	1	35	2188
Cohabiting	0	16	529
Widowed/divorced/separated	33	23	494
Number of children born			
None	24	4	1512
One	10	11	734
Two	7	39	1216
Three or more	6	47	789
Opinion whether woman would have (more) children			
Yes, probably yes	19	1	1443
No, no probably not	10	35	2790
Did not know/no answer	†	†	18
Highest qualification level attained			
GCE 'A' level or above	13	17	1779
GCSE grades A-C or equivalent	14	25	1257
Other	10	27	495
None	16	34	677
Socio-economic group**			
Non-manual	13	21	2209
Manual	12	27	1810
Total††	13	23	4251

*   Refers to the woman's partner, whether in the household or not.
†   Base too small to enable reliable analysis to be made.
** Socio-economic group of partner of married/cohabiting women, otherwise own socio-economic group.
†† Total includes no answers to some of the selected characteristics.

Table 10.10 Use of the pill and condom as a usual method of contraception by selected characteristics

Women aged 16-49 (excluded if pregnant, self or partner* sterilised or no sexual relationship)   *Great Britain: 1998*

	Percentage using pill†	Percentage with partner using condom†	Base = 100%
Age			
16-19	59	40	184
20-24	67	30	322
25-29	53	30	535
30-34	35	30	521
35-39	32	32	429
40-44	20	32	287
45-49	9	25	251
Marital status			
Single	59	37	601
Married	30	33	1301
Cohabiting	50	23	412
Widowed/divorced/separated	29	13	208
Number of children born			
None	53	33	1023
One	37	26	530
Two	30	31	630
Three or more	23	30	346
Opinion as to whether would have (more) children			
Yes	53	34	1082
No	30	28	1433
Did not know/no answer	**	**	14
Highest qualification level attained			
GCE 'A' level or above	43	38	1163
GCSE grades A-C or equivalent	42	28	733
Other	36	22	296
None	30	18	314
Socio-economic group††			
Non-manual	39	34	1363
Manual	40	25	1023
Total§	40	31	2529

*   Refers to the woman's partner, whether in the household or not.
†   Women who both used the pill and whose partners used the condom are included in both columns.
** Base too small to enable reliable analysis to be made.
†† Socio-economic group of partner of married/cohabiting women, otherwise own socio-economic group.
§   Total includes no answers to the selected characteristics.

Table 10.11 Use of emergency contraception during the two years prior to interview, by women's marital status and age

Women aged 16-49 (excluded if self or partner* sterilised at least two years ago) Great Britain: 1998

Marital status and use of emergency contraception	Age								
	16-17	18-19	20-24	25-29	30-34	35-39	40-44	45-49	Total
	%	%	%	%	%	%	%	%	%
Single women									
Used once	6 ⎱ 11	17 ⎱ 24	15 ⎱ 23	12 ⎱ 15	13 ⎱ 13	9 ⎱ 9		4 ⎱ 6	12 ⎱ 17
Used more than once	5 ⎰	6 ⎰	8 ⎰	3 ⎰	0 ⎰	0 ⎰		2 ⎰	4 ⎰
Had not used emergency contraception	89	76	77	85	87	91		94	83
Base = 100%	*173*	*161*	*251*	*194*	*114*	*70*		*53*	*1016*
	%	%	%	%	%	%	%	%	%
Married/cohabiting women									
Used once	†	[16] ⎱	13 ⎱ 16	9 ⎱ 10	5 ⎱ 5	4 ⎱ 5	2 ⎱ 2	1 ⎱ 1	6 ⎱ 7
Used more than once	†	[6] ⎰	3 ⎰	2 ⎰	1 ⎰	1 ⎰	0 ⎰	0 ⎰	1 ⎰
Had not used emergency contraception	†	[77]	84	90	95	95	98	99	93
Base = 100%	*2*	*31*	*156*	*425*	*468*	*405*	*237*	*182*	*1906*
	%	%	%	%	%	%	%	%	%
All marital statuses of women**									
Used once	6 ⎱ 12	17 ⎱ 23	14 ⎱ 20	10 ⎱ 12	7 ⎱ 7	5 ⎱ 6	3 ⎱ 5	1 ⎱ 1	8 ⎱ 10
Used more than once	6 ⎰	6 ⎰	5 ⎰	2 ⎰	1 ⎰	1 ⎰	1 ⎰	0 ⎰	2 ⎰
Had not used emergency contraception	88	77	80	88	93	94	95	99	90
Base = 100%	*176*	*192*	*421*	*669*	*652*	*555*	*354*	*285*	*3304*

* Refers to the woman's partner whether in the household or not.

† Bases are too small to enable reliable analysis to be made.

** 'All marital statuses' includes widowed/divorced/separated.

Table 10.12 Percentage of women who had used emergency contraception during the two years prior to interview by selected characteristics

Women aged 16-49 (excluded if self or partner* sterilised at least two years ago)   *Great Britain: 1998*

	Had used emergency contraception	Base = 100%
	Percentages	
Marital status		
Single	17	1016
Married/cohabiting	7	1906
Widowed/divorced/separated	9	372
Number of children born		
None	14	1445
One	9	647
Two	6	770
Three or more	6	442
Opinion whether woman would have (more) children		
Yes, probably yes	15	1437
No, probably not	6	1849
Did not know/no answer	†	18
Highest qualification level attained		
GCE 'A' level or above	12	1498
GCSE grades A-C or equivalent	10	956
Other	7	363
None	6	452
Socio-economic group**		
Non-manual	10	1749
Manual	9	1340
Currently uses a method of contraception		
Yes	13	2182
No	5	1106
Total††	10	3304

* Refers to the woman's partner, whether in the household or not.
† Base too small to allow reliable analysis.
** Socio-economic group of partner of married/cohabiting women, otherwise own socio-economic group
†† Total includes no answers to some of the selected characteristics.

Table 10.13 Percentage of women who had a) used the pill b) had an IUD fitted, as emergency contraception during the two years prior to interview, by selected characteristics

Women aged 16-49 who had used emergency contraception   *Great Britain: 1998*

	a) Had used the pill	b) Had an IUD fitted	Base = 100%
	Percentages		
Marital status			
Single	98	2	168
Married/cohabiting	97	3	128
Widowed/divorced/separated	[94]	[6]	35
Number of children born			
None	97	3	198
One	100	0	58
Two	[96]	[4]	49
Three or more	[92]	[8]	26
Opinion whether woman would have (more) children			
Yes, probably yes	98	2	220
No, probably not	95	5	111
Highest qualification level attained			
GCE 'A' level or above	98	2	176
GCSE grades A-C or equivalent	99	1	96
Other	[96]	[4]	27
None	[89]	[11]	28
Socio-economic group*			
Non-manual	99	1	167
Manual	95	5	127
Currently uses a method of contraception			
Yes	97	3	274
No	96	4	56
Total†	97	3	331

* Socio-economic group of partner of married/cohabiting women, otherwise own socio-economic group.
† Total includes no answers to some of the selected characteristics.

11 Day care

Introduction

One of the most notable features of the composition of the UK labour force in the last decade has been the increase in the proportion of mothers, particularly of mothers of children under five, in paid employment. Between 1990 and 1997, the proportion of married or cohabiting women with dependent children who were working increased from 61% to 68%. Among married or cohabiting women with children under five, the proportion who were employed increased from 45% to 57%.

Lone mothers are less likely than married or cohabiting mothers to participate in the labour market, and the rise in participation has not been as evident among them as among married mothers; between 1990 and 1997, the proportion who were working increased from 41% to 44%. During the same period, the proportion of lone mothers with children under five in employment rose from 22% to 28%[1].

Arranging suitable childcare is a key requirement if parents are to engage in paid employment. The Department of Social Security has noted that combining work and childcare is particularly difficult for lone parents[2]; this is true for lone fathers as well as lone mothers. However, as the May 1998 Green Paper *Meeting the childcare challenge*[3] argued, the quality of childcare provision can be variable, the cost is high and it is not easy to find places.

In the last two years, the Government has taken a series of initiatives aimed at facilitating parental employment. The National Childcare Strategy, launched in May 1998, aims to provide childcare places for children aged 0-14 (or up to 16 for children with special needs) in every neighbourhood. Local Early Years and Childcare Development Partnerships will have responsibility for planning and delivering the strategy, reporting annually to the Department for Education and Employment[2]. The Childcare Tax Credit, launched in October 1999, replaces the childcare disregard of Family Credit; help will be available for 70% of childcare charges up to a limit of £100 for families with one child and £150 for families with two children or more.

Initiatives aimed specifically at lone parents include the New Deal for Lone Parents, which began on a national basis in October 1998. This provides a national network of Personal Advisors to offer lone parents help with, among other things, job search, training and childcare. Lone parents moving into work will also be able to claim income support for two weeks after starting work[4].

The GHS has included questions on childcare from time to time, most recently in 1991. In 1998, questions about day care[5] arrangements were addressed to respondents responsible for children under the age of 14; fieldwork therefore took place before the initiatives outlined in the previous paragraphs could have any significant impact. The questions covered the types of arrangements made, whether they were made to enable parents to go out to work, and the number of sessions children attended. Parents were asked different questions about term-time arrangements for children aged 0-5 who were not in full-time schooling, henceforth referred to as 'pre-school children' and about children aged 4-13 who were attending school full time, referred to as 'schoolchildren'. It should be noted that the two groups overlap in age. Separate questions were asked about arrangements made during school holidays, where these differed from term-time arrangements.

The mother answered the questions on behalf of 78% of children, the father for 21% and someone else, usually the grandparents, for the remaining 1% of children. As the focus of this chapter is on whether or not arrangements were made in order to enable parents to go out to work, the latter group is excluded from further analysis.

Term-time arrangements for pre-school children

Proportions using care

- During term-time, just under half (48%) of pre-school children were using some form of care. Fifteen per cent used more than one type of care.

The most common source of care was relatives, who looked after 18% of pre-school children. Ten per cent of pre-school children attended nurseries, excluding workplace nurseries, 9% play groups and 7% parent and toddler groups. Six per cent of children were cared for by a registered childminder, 5% by a friend or neighbour, 4% attended a local authority school, 3% a private school and 2% were cared for by a nanny or au pair. Comparisons with previous years of the GHS and with other surveys are limited by differences in question wording, but the tendency to use relatives as a source of care is broadly similar to that found in other surveys[6,7,8].

Pre-school children whose mothers were working were more likely than those whose mothers were economically inactive to be using care during term-time. Just over three-quarters of those whose mothers worked full time, two-thirds whose mothers worked part time and a quarter with economically inactive mothers were using some form of care.

- About one in three children whose mothers were working were looked after by relatives, compared with one in 25 children whose mothers were economically inactive;
- 18% of pre-school children whose mothers worked full time were cared for by a registered childminder, compared with 8% of those whose mother was working part time and 1% whose mothers were economically inactive;
- the children of mothers in full-time work were the only group among whom more than a tiny proportion were looked after by a nanny or au pair.

Table 11.1, Figure 11A

It is interesting, in the light of the New Deal for Lone Parents, to see whether there are any differences between types of families in the likelihood of using care. Half (50%) of the pre-school children living in families headed by a married or cohabiting couple used care, compared with just over two-fifths (42%) of those in lone-parent families. There were no significant differences between the two groups, however, in the type of care used.

Whether or not pre-school children used care was associated with the mother's educational level; the proportion of pre-school children using care varying from 63% of those whose mothers were qualified to 'A' level or above to 23% of those whose mothers had no qualifications.　**Table 11.2**

Use of term-time care and parental employment

Parents who made arrangements for their children to be looked after during term-time were asked whether they did so in order to be able to go out to work. These questions were asked about each arrangement separately; the

subsequent discussion therefore focuses on arrangements rather than children. Over half the pre-school arrangements (56%) were made to enable the mother, father or both to go out to work:

- 31% of arrangements were made to enable the mother only to work;
- 21% were made so both parents could work;
- 3% were made to allow the father alone to work.

Table 11.3

Relatives and registered childminders were more likely than other sources to provide care when the arrangement was made to enable parents to work, while play groups and parent-toddler groups were more commonly used when the arrangement was not intended for this purpose. This finding, and the relatively high proportion (44%) of arrangements which were not made to enable parents to work may reflect the early years education function of the latter types of care. Of the arrangements made to enable parents to work:

- over 40% were with relatives and 16% were with registered childminders, compared with 9% and 2% respectively of arrangements which were not made to enable parents to work;
- 4% were with play groups and 2% with parent-toddler groups, compared with 25% and 22% respectively of arrangements for other purposes.　**Table 11.4**

Those parents who made day care arrangements to enable them to work, were asked how many half days[9] and evenings a week their children attended the care. The number of arrangements in this category is too small to allow detailed analysis by type of care, and it has been

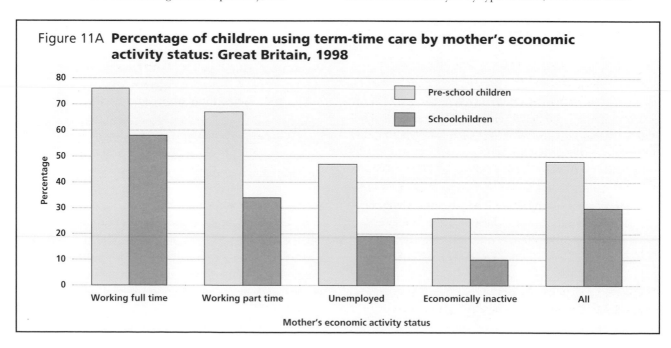

Figure 11A **Percentage of children using term-time care by mother's economic activity status: Great Britain, 1998**

necessary to group the different types. Three-quarters of all arrangements made so the parents of pre-school children could work were for five or fewer half days a week, although the number of sessions varied with the types of care.

- 83% of arrangements with relatives or friends were for five or fewer half days a week, with 41% being made for fewer than three half days;
- nurseries and registered childminders, nannies or au pairs were used for more sessions than relatives, with 85% of such arrangements being made for three or more half days, 39% being for 6-10 half days.

Only 12% of arrangements which facilitated parental working were made for evenings or overnight; the proportions varying from 19% of those made with relatives or friends to 4% of those made with a registered childminder, nanny or au pair. **Table 11.5**

Term-time arrangements for school-children

Proportions using care
- Just under a third of children aged 4-13 who attended school full time were using some form of care during term-time. Six per cent used more than one type of care.

As with pre-school children, relatives were the most common source of term-time care, looking after 18% of children of this age. Nine per cent were cared for by friends or neighbours, while 5% attended after-school clubs or schemes, 3% were looked after by a registered childminder and 2% by a nanny or au pair.

A higher proportion of schoolchildren aged 4-9 than of those aged 10-13 used care; 34% and 24% respectively did so. As with pre-school children, the likelihood of using care was associated with the mother's economic activity status, but the pattern was more marked than among pre-school children; schoolchildren whose mother worked full time were almost six times as likely as those whose mother was economically inactive to be using care.

- 58% of schoolchildren whose mother worked full time attended care, as did 34% of those with part-time working mothers, 19% of those with unemployed mothers and 10% of those with economically inactive mothers. **Tables 11.6-11.7, Figure 11A**

There was no significant difference in the proportion of schoolchildren from families headed by a married or

cohabiting couple and those from lone-parent families who were attending term-time care. Using care was associated with the mother's educational level, varying from 41% of the children of women qualified to 'A' level or above to 21% of those whose mothers had no qualifications. **Table 11.2**

Use of term-time care and parental employment
As with pre-school children, parents of schoolchildren were asked whether term-time day care arrangements were made to enable them to work, and about the number of sessions a week their children attended. A higher proportion (82%) of arrangements for schoolchildren, than of those for pre-school children (56%), were made to enable parents to work.

- 42% of term-time arrangements for schoolchildren were made to enable the mother, 33% both parents and 7% the father to work. **Table 11.3**

The patterns of care use were very similar to those for pre-school children. Arrangements made so parents could work were more likely than those which were not for that purpose, to be with relatives and registered childminders. Conversely, a higher proportion of arrangements which were not made to help parents work than of those with that aim, were with friends or neighbours, after-school clubs and nannies or au pairs. For example, of the arrangements for schoolchildren made to enable parents to work:

- over half (52%) were with relatives, compared with less than a third of arrangements which were not made to facilitate parental working;
- approximately two in ten were with friends and neighbours, compared with three in ten of arrangements for purposes other than to enable parents to work. **Table 11.8**

When term-time arrangements were made for schoolchildren to enable their parents to work, they tended to be for fewer half days than those made for pre-school children:

- one in ten arrangements for schoolchildren were made for more than five half days, compared with one in four of those made for pre-school children.

Registered childminders, nannies or au pairs were more likely than other forms of care to be used for more than five half days a week, while friends and neighbours were more likely than other forms of care to be used for fewer than three half days a week:

- 31% of arrangements made with registered childminders, nannies or au pairs were for six or more half days a week, compared with 8% or fewer of other arrangements;
- 63% of arrangements made with friends or neighbours were for fewer than three half days a week, compared with 49% of those made with relatives, 46% of those with after school clubs, and 27% of those with childminders, nannies or au pairs.

Parents also made a higher proportion of term-time evening or overnight arrangements for schoolchildren than for pre-school children.

- 22% of arrangements made for schoolchildren were for evening and overnight stays, compared with 12% of arrangements for pre-school children.

However, as in the case of pre-school children, childminders, nannies or au pairs were less likely than other types of care for schoolchildren to be used in the evening or overnight:

- 9% of arrangements for schoolchildren made with childminders, nannies or au pairs were for evenings, compared with 17-27% of arrangements with other types of care. **Table 11.9**

Holiday arrangements for children aged under 14

Proportions using care
Parents of all children aged under 14 were asked whether they used any form of care during school holidays. Those who also used care during term-time were asked whether the holiday care was the same or differed from that used during term. Where the care differed, or where parents used care during the holidays but not during term-time, interviewers collected details of the care used.

- Over a quarter (27%) of children used care during school holidays, including 14% who were attending the same kind of care as that used during term-time.

In total, the parents of 12% of children made different arrangements during term-time and holidays.

Where holiday care differed from that provided during term-time, relatives were the most common source of care, looking after 9% of children. Two per cent of children were looked after by friends or neighbours, and 2% at holiday clubs or schemes. Other forms of care were used by 1% or fewer of children.

The likelihood of using care varied with age: 26% of 0-4 year-olds, 29% of children aged 5-9 and 23% of the 10-13 age group were using care[10]:

- children aged 0-4 were more likely than other children to be using the same arrangements as term-time; 19% did so, compared with 13% of children aged 5-9 and 10% of the 10-13 age group;
- a higher proportion of schoolchildren (11%) than of pre-school children were cared for by relatives (4%).
  Table 11.10

Children whose mothers worked full time were more than eight times as likely as those whose mothers were unemployed or economically inactive to be using holiday care.

- 50% of children whose mothers worked full time, 37% of those with part-time working mothers, 7% with unemployed and 6% with economically inactive mothers were using care.

Among children whose mothers worked full time 30% were using the same arrangements during the holidays and term-time, while 19% of children whose mothers worked part time were doing so.

- 13% of the children whose mothers worked full time and 15% of those whose mothers worked part time were cared for by relatives, compared with 1% of other children;
- 4% of the children whose mothers were working full time and 3% of those whose mothers were working part time were cared for by friends or neighbours, compared with less than 1% of other children;
- 4% and 2% respectively of the children whose mothers worked full time and part time attended holiday clubs or schemes, compared with 1% of other children.
  Table 11.11

There was no significant difference in the proportion of children in families headed by a married or cohabiting couple and those living in lone-parent families who used holiday care. The likelihood of using such care increased with the mother's educational level, from 15% of children with unqualified mothers to 32% of those whose mother was qualified to 'A' level or above. **Table 11.2**

Use of holiday care and parental employment
The majority, 85%, of holiday arrangements were made to enable parents to work.

- 47% of arrangements were made so the mother could work, 32% to enable both parents and 5% to enable the father to work. **Table 11.3**

Arrangements which were made to enable parents to work were twice as likely as those which were not made for that purpose to be made with relatives. Of the arrangements made to facilitate parental working:

- 64% were with relatives, compared with 32% of other arrangements;
- 6% were with registered childminders, compared with 1% of other arrangements;
- 9% were with holiday schemes or clubs, compared with 29% of other arrangements. **Table 11.12**

Parents were asked on how many days they had used care during the most recent school holidays or, if the interview was taking place during school holidays, during the current holiday period. The majority of holiday arrangements were made for a small number of days; half being made for five days or fewer. Only one in seven arrangements was made for more than 20 days. **Table 11.13**

Notes and references

1. Moss P et al. 'Lone parents and the labour market revisited' in *Labour Market Trends*, Nov 1999, pp. 583-594.
2. *Opportunity for all*. Department of Social Security 1999.
3. *Meeting the childcare challenge*. Government Green Paper. Cm 3959. May 1998.
4. The New Deal for Lone Parents is a voluntary programme, actively marketed among lone parents on Income Support whose youngest child is aged over five years and three months, but also available to those with children under five.
5. 'Day care' includes arrangements made for children to be looked after in the evening and overnight.
6. La Valle I et al. *Parents' demand for childcare*. Department for Education and Employment (London: 1999).
7. Meltzer H. *Day care services for children*. HMSO (London: 1994).
8. Bridgwood A and Savage D. *General Household Survey 1991*. HMSO (London: 1993).
9. Part sessions were counted as a half day; a child who attended care in the morning before school and in the evening after school would be classed as attending two half day sessions.
10. Only those parents using term-time care were asked whether 4-5 year-olds were attending school full time. It is not known whether children in this age group, for whom care was provided during school holidays, but not during term-time, were at school full time. For ease of analysis of holiday arrangements, children have therefore been grouped into three broad age groupings: 0-4, 5-9 and 10-13. For the purposes of this section of the chapter, children under the age of five will be referred to as 'pre-school children', and older children as 'schoolchildren'.

Table 11.1 Type of term-time care used by mother's economic activity status

*Pre-school children**   *Great Britain: 1998*

Type of care used in term-time	Mother's economic activity status				
	Working full time	Working part time	Unemployed	Economically inactive	All
	%	%	%	%	%
Relative	31	34	14	4	18
Nursery, excluding workplace nursery	15	13	16	6	10
Play group	9	12	8	7	9
Parent and toddler group	4	8	8	7	7
Registered childminder	18	8	4	1	6
Friend or neighbour	5	8	8	2	5
LA maintained school	5	5	6	3	4
Private school	5	2	2	2	3
Workplace day nursery	5	3	2	1	2
Nanny, au pair	7	2	0	1	2
Other carer	1	1	0	1	1
Total using care	76	67	47	26	48
Base = 100%†	*221*	*449*	*51*	*654*	*1375*

* Children aged 0-5 not attending school full time.

† Percentages do not sum to the total using care because some children used more than one type of care.

Table 11.2 Proportion of children using care by selected characteristics

Children aged 0-13   *Great Britain: 1998*

Characteristic	Term-time care			Holiday care	Bases = 100%	
	Pre-school children*	School children†	Children aged 0-13	Pre-school children*	School children†	Children aged 0-13
		Percentage				
Age of child						
0-4	-	-	26	-	-	1430
4/5-9**	-	34	29	-	1524	1488
10-13	-	24	23	-	1031	1031
Mother's economic activity status						
Working full time	76	58	50	221	537	758
Working part time	67	34	37	449	1023	1474
Unemployed	47	19	7	51	84	135
Economically inactive	26	10	6	654	829	1483
Mother's highest qualification level						
GCE 'A' level or above	63	41	32	529	856	1386
GCSE grades A-C or equivalent	48	28	28	434	742	1176
Other	37	24	24	156	308	464
None	23	21	15	196	472	667
Family type						
Married/cohabiting couple with dependent children	50	31	27	1126	1959	3088
Lone parent with dependent children	42	28	26	267	596	862
All	48	30	27	1393	2555	3950

*   Children aged 0-5 not attending school full time.

†   Children aged 4-13, attending school full time.

** 4-9 for term-time care, 5-9 for holiday care.

Table 11.3 **Who is enabled to work by day care arrangements**

Day care arrangements for children aged 0-13　　　　*Great Britain: 1998*

Who is enabled to work	Term-time care		Holiday care
	Pre-school children*	School children†	Children aged 0-13
	%	%	%
Mother	31	42	47
Father	3	7	5
Both mother and father	21	33	32
Neither	44	18	15
Base = 100%	934	947	591

* Children aged 0-5 not attending school full time.
† Children aged 4-13, attending school full time.

Table 11.4 **Type of term-time care used by whether arrangement is made to enable parents to work**

*Term-time arrangements for pre-school children**　　　　*Great Britain: 1998*

Type of care used in term-time	Which parents are enabled to work				
	Mother	Father	Both	Neither	All
	%	%	%	%	%
Relative	41	[44]	43	9	27
Nursery, excluding workplace nursery	14	[22]	10	17	15
Play group	5	0	5	25	14
Parent and toddler group	2	0	2	22	11
Registered childminder	14	[22]	17	2	9
Friend or neighbour	10	[4]	5	6	7
LA maintained school	3	0	4	8	6
Private school	3	0	2	5	4
Workplace day nursery	3	[4]	6	2	3
Nanny, au pair	4	0	5	3	4
Other carer	1	[4]	2	1	1
Base = 100%	293	27	199	415	934

* Children aged 0-5 not attending school full time.

Table 11.5 **Number of half-day and proportion of evening sessions by type of term-time care**

Term-time arrangements for pre-school children made to enable parents to work*　　　　*Great Britain: 1998*

Number of half-days	Type of care used in term-time				
	Relative, friend	Nurseries	Registered childminder, nanny, au pair	Other carer	All
	%	%	%	%	%
0 - 2	41	15	15	26	29
3 - 5	42	49	44	59	46
6 - 10	17	36	41	16	25
Percentage of arrangements for evenings or overnight					
	19	6	4	9	12
*Base = 100%**	257	88	102	70	517

* Children aged 0-5 not attending school full time.

185

Table 11.6 Type of term-time care used by age of child

Children aged 4-13, attending school full time

Great Britain: 1998

Type of care used in term-time	Age of child		
	4-9	10-13	All
	%	%	%
Relative	19	16	18
Friend or neighbour	10	7	9
After school clubs or play schemes	7	3	5
Registered childminder	4	0	3
Nanny, au pair	2	1	2
Other carer	1	1	1
Total using care	34	24	30
*Base = 100%**	*1524*	*1031*	*2555*

* Percentages do not sum to the total using care because some children used more than one type of care.

Table 11.7 Type of term-time care used by mother's economic activity status

Children aged 4-13, attending school full time

Great Britain: 1998

Type of care used in term-time	Mother's economic activity status				
	Working full time	Working part time	Unemployed	Economically inactive	All
	%	%	%	%	%
Relative	32	23	14	3	18
Friend or neighbour	14	10	8	3	8
After school clubs or play schemes	10	5	0	3	5
Registered childminder	7	3	0	0	3
Nanny, au pair	4	1	1	1	2
Other carer	2	0	0	1	1
Total using care	58	34	19	10	30
*Base = 100%**	*537*	*1023*	*84*	*829*	*2473*

* Percentages do not sum to the total using care because some children used more than one type of care.

Table 11.8 Type of term-time care used by whether arrangement is made to enable parents to work

Term-time arrangements for children aged 4-13, attending school full time

Great Britain: 1998

Type of care used in term-time	Which parents are enabled to work				
	Mother	Father	Both	Neither	All
	%	%	%	%	%
Relative	55	52	47	32	48
Friend or neighbour	22	21	22	30	23
After school clubs or play schemes	14	18	10	26	15
Registered childminder	6	8	10	2	7
Nanny, au pair	2	2	8	5	4
Other carer	1	0	3	5	2
Base = 100%	*400*	*62*	*314*	*171*	*947*

Table 11.9 **Number of half-day and proportion of evening sessions by type of term-time care**

Term-time arrangements for children aged 4-13, attending school full time made to enable parents to work

Great Britain: 1998

Number of half-days	Type of care used in term-time				All
	Relative	Friend or neighbour	After school clubs or play schemes	Registered childminder, nanny, au pair	
	%	%	%	%	%
0 - 2	49	63	46	27	48
3 - 5	43	29	50	42	42
6 - 10	8	8	4	29	10
More than 10	0	0	0	2	0
Percentage of arrangements for evenings or overnight					
	27	19	17	9	22
Base = 100%	*398*	*167*	*98*	*97*	*773*

Table 11.10 **Type of holiday care used by age of child**

Children aged 0-13 *Great Britain: 1998*

Type of care used during school holidays	Age of child			
	0-4	5-9	10-13	All
	%	%	%	%
Relative	4	11	11	9
Friend or neighbour	1	3	2	2
Holiday schemes or clubs	0	3	2	2
Registered childminder	1	1	0	1
Nanny, au pair	0	1	0	0
Nursery, including workplace nursery	1	0	0	0
Parent and toddler	0	0	0	0
Play group	0	1	0	0
Other carer	0	0	1	0
Same arrangement as term-time	19	13	10	14
Total using care	26	29	23	27
*Base = 100%**	*1430*	*1488*	*1031*	*3949*

* Percentages sum to more than the total using care because some children used more than one type of care.

187

Table 11.11 **Type of holiday care used by mother's economic activity status**

Children aged 0-13   Great Britain: 1998

Type of care used during school holidays	Mother's economic activity status				
	Working full time	Working part time	Unemployed	Economically inactive	All†
	%	%	%	%	%
Relative	13	15	1	1	9
Friend or neighbour	4	3	1	0	2
Holiday schemes or clubs	4	2	1	1	2
Registered childminder	1	1	1	0	1
Nanny, au pair	1	0	0	0	0
Nursery, including workplace nursery	0	1	1	0	0
Parent and toddler	0	0	0	0	0
Play group	1	0	0	0	0
Other carer	1	0	0	0	0
Same arrangement as term-time	30	19	3	3	14
Total using care	50	37	7	6	27
Base = 100%*	758	1474	135	1483	3858

* Percentages do not sum to the total using care because some children used more than one type of care.

† Total includes a small number of children with mothers on government schemes or those whose working hours were unknown.

Table 11.12 **Type of holiday care used by whether arrangement is made to enable parents to work**

School holiday arrangements for children aged 0-13   Great Britain: 1998

Type of care used during school holidays	Which parents are enabled to work				
	Mother	Father	Both	Neither	All
	%	%	%	%	%
Relative	66	[69]	59	32	59
Friend or neighbour	13	[12]	13	15	14
Holiday schemes or clubs	8	[12]	9	29	12
Registered childminder	6	[3]	6	1	5
Nanny, au pair	2	0	4	5	3
Nursery, including workplace nursery	3	[3]	3	4	3
Parent and toddler	0	0	1	0	0
Play group	1	0	3	5	2
Other carer	1	0	2	8	2
Base = 100%	276	32	192	91	591

Table 11.13 **Number of days holiday care used by type of holiday care**

School holiday arrangements for children aged 0-13 made to enable parents to work   Great Britain: 1998

Number of days used during school holidays	Type of care used during school holidays				
	Relative	Friend or neighbour	Holiday scheme, clubs	Registered childminder, nanny, au pair	All
	%	%	%	%	%
1 - 2	19	39	[25]	[16]	22
3 - 5	31	20	[25]	[37]	29
6 - 10	24	8	[18]	[28]	22
11 - 20	14	8	[25]	[7]	14
More than 20	12	26	[7]	[12]	13
Base = 100%	312	66	44	43	465

12 Cross-topic analysis

Using the GHS for cross-topic analysis: workless households

As noted in Chapter 1, the GHS is a multi-purpose survey covering a range of topics such as health, housing, smoking, drinking, marriage and cohabitation, and pensions. Preceding chapters have focused on these individual topics. This chapter illustrates the potential for using the GHS to undertake cross-topic analysis, using the example of workless households.

In September 1999, the Department for Social Security released *Opportunity for All*[1], a report aimed at tackling the causes of poverty and improving opportunities for everyone to achieve their potential. *Opportunity for All* pinpoints the eradication of child poverty as 'the key to tackling disadvantage in the future' and states that:

'Worklessness is the main cause of poverty and social exclusion. Of all working age adults 13 per cent now live in workless households, one of the highest rates in Europe'[1].

The proportion of workless households is 'increasingly being included among key indicators of economic activity at the household level'[2]. The main source of estimates of the numbers of workless households in Britain is the Labour Force Survey (LFS) which has a much larger sample size than the GHS. The *Quarterly Supplement* for the survey regularly publishes a table showing the number of workless households in the United Kingdom[3]. In addition, *Labour Market Trends* has published articles on workless households[4].

This chapter presents some preliminary analysis of workless households. The LFS has examined workless households by type of household, region and ethnic origin. Because of its multi-purpose nature, the GHS is able to analyse workless households using a range of variables not included on the LFS. This chapter focuses on two examples: differences between working and workless households in the ownership of consumer durables, and differences between individuals living in the two types of household on two measures of self-reported health.

Background characteristics of working and workless households

In order to provide context for the subsequent discussion, this section of the chapter presents some background information on the characteristics of working and workless households.

The LFS defines workless households as those which contain at least one person of working age, 16-64 for men and 16-59 for women, but have no household member in paid work. Working households contain at least one person in paid work, even if that person is above the normal retirement age. In Spring 1998, data from the LFS showed that nearly 18% of all working-age households were workless. In 1998, using the same definition as the LFS, 19% of GHS households were defined as workless[5].

Of those GHS households where the head was aged 16-24, 42% were workless, whereas among those with a head aged 25-59 between 13% and 17% were workless. Workless households were more likely than working households to have an older or a younger person, rather than someone in their thirties or forties, as their head. Ten per cent of workless households, compared with 3% of working households, were headed by 16-24 year olds, and 23% and 10% respectively had a head of household aged 60 or over. In contrast, whereas over three-quarters of working households were headed by someone aged 30-59, fewer than three-fifths of workless households were.

Table 12.1

Table 12.2 shows that three-fifths of workless households contained only one adult: 30% comprised a lone parent with dependent children and another 30% were single person households. Among households containing at least one worker, a quarter contained one adult. Over a third of working households (36%) compared with just over a quarter of workless households (26%) were made up of couples without dependent children. The proportions of households containing couples with dependent children were 35% of working and 10% of workless households.

Table 12.2

Of those households headed by a member of the non-manual socio-economic groups, 12% were workless, compared with 23% of households headed by someone from the manual groups. Over a third (37%) of workless households were headed by a non-manual worker, compared with almost three-fifths (57%) of working households.

Table 12.3

Seventy per cent of people living in working households, compared with 47% of those living in workless households, were married or cohabiting. People living in workless households were more than three times as likely (25%) as those living in working households (8%), to be either widowed, divorced or separated. Table 12.4 shows that children aged 0-15 formed a larger proportion of the membership of workless households (32%) than of working households (25%). Among workless households 24% were permanently unable to work, 25% were keeping house and 22% were retired. The equivalent proportions for working households were: 2% permanently unable to work, 6% keeping house and 4% retired.

Tables 12.4-12.6

Ownership of consumer durables of working and workless households

Each year, the GHS includes a number of questions designed to measure the ownership of consumer durables in households in Great Britain. New items are added from time to time to reflect the availability of new consumer durables.

Workless households were far less likely than working households to have access to each of the consumer durables shown in Table 12.7, with the exception of televisions. There were marked differences in car ownership, with 51% of workless households not having a car compared with 12% of working households. While 92% of working households had central heating and 98% had a telephone, the proportion of workless households with access to these amenities was 86% and 85% respectively. Table 4.23 in Chapter 4 shows that between 1996 and 1998 ownership of home computers rose from just over a quarter (27%) to over a third (34%) of all households. Table 12.7 shows that there was a sizeable difference in ownership of computers depending on whether the household contained a worker or not; 47% of working and 24% of workless households owned a computer.

Table 12.7

Chapter 4 also indicated that ownership of consumer durables is strongly associated with socio-economic group. Table 12.8, using the examples of access to telephones and home computers, shows that socio-economic group accounts for some, but not all, of the difference between working and workless households. Workless households were less likely than working households to have access to consumer durables whether they were headed by a manual or a non-manual worker.

- Among households headed by a non-manual worker, 58% of working households compared with 33% of workless households had access to a home computer. The equivalent proportions for telephone ownership were 99% and 93%.
- Among manual households, over twice as many working households (32%) as workless households (15%) had access to a computer. For telephones, the equivalent proportions were 96% and 83%.

Table 12.8

Similar disparities in access to home computers were reported recently in relation to income. The 1998 Family Expenditure Survey found that only 10% of households in the lowest income quintile owned a computer, compared with nearly 70% in the top income group[6].

Apart from home computers, some of the larger differences in ownership of consumer durables illustrated in Table 12.7 relate to items that could be described as 'luxury' items. Four items, CD players, microwave ovens, tumble driers and dishwashers, were selected and analysis was carried out to see how many of these items were available to different types of household. Among all working-age households, 82% had a CD player, 83% a microwave oven, 58% a tumble drier and 28% a dishwasher.

As with home computers and telephones, further analysis showed that socio-economic group accounted for some of the differences, but even when this was taken into account working households were still more likely than workless households to own more of these items:

- among non-manual households, only one in a hundred working households (1%) did not own any of these items, compared with around one in eleven workless households (9%). Twice as many non-manual working households (28%) as non-manual workless households (14%) had access to all four items;
- among manual households, about four times as many workless (13%) as working (3%) households owned none of these 'luxury' items. These figures were almost exactly reversed for ownership of all four items; 13% of working households, compared with 4% of workless households, owned all four.   **Table 12.9**

Self-reported health of members of working and workless households

This section of the chapter discusses two self-reported health measures: self-reported general health status and self-reported longstanding illness, and investigates differences in these two measures among members of working and workless households.

Self-reported health status
Self-reported general health has been shown to be a strong predictor of mortality; it is also associated with the use of health services[7]. GHS respondents were asked to rate their health over the previous twelve months as 'good', 'fairly good' or 'not good'. This information was not collected for children.

Table 12.10 shows that more than two in three adults (69%) living in a working household compared with just over two in five (42%) of those from workless households reported that their health was 'good'. The proportion saying their health was 'not good' was more than three times greater among adults living in workless households (29%) than among those from working households (8%).

The Health Survey for England has shown that the likelihood of reporting one's health as 'good' decreases with age. Analysis of self-reported health status by age for the 1998 GHS respondents shows that for all age groups[8], adults living in working households were more likely than those in workless households to report their health as 'good'. Among the youngest age group, people aged 16-24, 77% of those from working households compared with 64% from workless households reported their health as 'good'. The largest differences were seen among 35-44 year olds; among this age group, people from working households were twice as likely as those from workless households to report 'good' health ; 72% did so compared with 35%.

This pattern was true for both men and women:

- among people aged 35-44, 74% of men and 70% of women living in working households, compared with 35% of men and 34% of women from workless households, described their health as 'good'.

The only age group for whom the differences between people living in working and workless households were not statistically significant was men aged 16-24. However the sample sizes for this group were small. **Table 12.10**

Table 12.11 provides a breakdown of self-reported health by marital status and working status of the household. It shows that for all marital statuses, adults living in working households were far more likely than those from workless households to report their health was 'good'. For example:

- among married and cohabiting men, 69% from working households compared with 41% from workless households, reported their health as 'good'. Among single men from working households, 76% reported good health compared with 50% from workless households and for widowed, divorced and separated men the proportions were 61% and 41% respectively;
- similar differences were evident among women. Among married and cohabiting women, 68% from working households, compared with 41% from workless households, described their health status as 'good'.

The proportions of single women reporting good health were 71% in working and 53% in workless households. Among the widowed, divorced and separated the proportions were 53% of those living in working and 32% of those in workless households. **Table 12.11**

This analysis shows that even when sex and marital status are taken into account, adults living in workless households were far less likely than those from working households to report 'good' health over the previous twelve months.

Self-reported longstanding illness of members of working and workless households

As described in Chapter 7, GHS respondents were asked if they have any longstanding illness or disability which had troubled them for some time. Those who did were asked whether this illness or disability limited their activities in any way. Information about children was collected from a responsible adult, usually a parent. This section compares the prevalence of self-reported limiting longstanding illness among people living in working and workless households, taking account of age and sex. It should be noted that reports of chronic sickness are based on respondents' own assessments; differences in prevalence may reflect the varying expectations which people have about their health as well as differences in the actual prevalence of sickness.

Table 12.12 shows that people living in workless households were over two and a half times as likely as those in a working household to report having a limiting longstanding illness; 32% did so, compared with 12%. **Table 12.12**

As shown in Table 12.12 this pattern holds across all age groups (although the difference for 0-4 year olds was not statistically significant). It might be expected that adults living in workless households were more likely to have a limiting longstanding illness. Table 12.6 shows that 24% of people living in workless households, compared with 2% from working households, were permanently unable to work. However, Table 12.12 also shows that children aged 5-15 living in workless households were nearly twice as likely as those from working households to have such an illness; 13% had, compared with 7%. When sex is taken into account this difference remains statistically significant among boys but not for girls; 14% of boys of this age from a workless household had a limiting longstanding illness compared with 6% from a working household. **Tables 12.6 and 12.12**

Notes and references

1. *Opportunity for All.* The Stationery Office, 1999.

2. Cooper W: LFS household data: Spring 1998 analyses. *Labour Market Trends.* January 1999

3. For example see *Labour Force Survey Quarterly Supplement No. 7*, November 1999.

4. For example see reference 2 above and Cooper-Green E J: Update on Labour Force Survey household datasets. *Labour Market Trends*, May 1999.

5. The LFS covers the United Kingdom, whereas the GHS covers Great Britain. Unlike GHS data, LFS data is weighted and grossed to population totals.

6. *Family spending in the United Kingdom 1998-99.* News Release. Office for National Statistics (99) 410

7. Cox B D et al. *The Health and Lifestyle Survey: Seven Years on.* Dartmouth (Aldershot: 1993).

8. This analysis was based on households of working age (men aged 16-64 and women aged 16-59) or households where a pensioner was working. Therefore, analysis in this chapter, using age related variables, has excluded those aged over 64.

Table 12.1 (a) Working status of household by age of head of household
(b) Age of head of household by working status of household

Households with working age or working members   *Great Britain: 1998*

Age of head of household		Working status of household		Base = 100%
		Working household	Workless household	
(a)				
16-24	%	58	42	281
25-29	%	83	17	669
30-44	%	87	13	2476
45-59	%	84	16	2240
60-64	%	62	38	525
65 and over	%	69	31	258
Total	%	81	19	6449
(b)				Total
		%	%	%
16-24		3	10	4
25-29		11	10	10
30-44		41	27	38
45-59		36	30	35
60-64		6	17	8
65 and over		3	7	4
Base = 100%		*5246*	*1203*	*6449*

Table 12.2 Household type by working status of household

Households with working age or working members   *Great Britain: 1998*

Household type	Working status of household		
	Working household	Workless household	Total
	%	%	%
Couple with dependent child(ren)	35	10	31
Couple, no dependent child(ren)	36	26	34
Lone parent	9	30	13
One person only	16	30	18
Other	4	5	4
*Base = 100%**	*5246*	*1203*	*6449*

* Base includes a small number of same sex couples.

Table 12.3 (a) Working status of household by socio-economic group of head of household
(b) Socio-economic group of head of household by working status of household

Households with working age or working members   *Great Britain: 1998*

Socio-economic group of head of household		Working status of household		Base = 100%
		Working household	Workless household	
(a)				
Professional	%	93	7	532
Employers and managers	%	90	10	1305
Intermediate non-manual	%	91	9	765
Junior non-manual	%	78	22	686
Skilled manual and own account non-professional	%	83	17	1674
Semi-skilled manual and personal service	%	71	29	923
Unskilled manual	%	64	36	291
Total non-manual	%	88	12	3288
Total manual	%	77	23	2888
Total	%	83	17	6176
(b)				Total
		%	%	%
Professional		10	3	9
Employers and managers		23	13	21
Intermediate non-manual		14	7	12
Junior non-manual		10	14	11
Skilled manual and own account non-professional		27	27	27
Semi-skilled manual and personal service		13	26	15
Unskilled manual		4	10	5
Total non-manual		57	37	53
Total manual		43	63	47
Base = 100%		*5122*	*1054*	*6176*

Table 12.4 Age by working status of household

Persons living in households with working age or working members   *Great Britain: 1998*

Age	Working status of household		
	Working household	Workless household	Total
	%	%	%
0-4	8	11	8
5-15	17	21	18
16-44	47	33	45
45-64	26	31	27
65 and over	2	5	2
Base = 100%	*14563*	*2735*	*17298*

Table 12.5 Defacto marital status by working status of household

Persons aged 16 and over living in households with working age or working members   *Great Britain: 1998*

Defacto marital status	Working status of household		
	Working household	Workless household	Total
	%	%	%
Married	59	41	57
Cohabiting	10	7	10
Single	22	28	23
Widowed	2	6	3
Divorced	4	12	5
Separated	2	7	3
*Base = 100%**	*10907*	*1870*	*12777*

* Base includes a small number of same sex couples.

Table 12.6 Economic activity status by working status of household

Persons aged 16 and over living in households with working age or working members   *Great Britain: 1998*

Economic activity status	Working status of household		
	Working household	Workless household	Total
	%	%	%
Working (including government scheme)	82	0	70
Unemployed (ILO)	2	16	4
Permanently unable to work	2	24	5
Retired	4	22	6
Keeping house	6	25	9
Student	3	9	4
Other inactive	1	5	1
Base = 100%	*10889*	*1860*	*12749*

Table 12.7 Consumer durables, central heating and cars by working status of household

Households with working age or working members   *Great Britain: 1998*

Consumer durables	Working status of household		
	Working household	Workless household	Total
Percentage of households with:			
Television			
colour	98	96	98
black and white only	0	1	1
Video recorder	95	82	92
CD player	86	63	82
Home computer	47	24	42
Microwave oven	86	71	83
Deep freezer/fridge freezer	95	88	94
Washing machine	96	87	95
Tumble drier	61	44	58
Dishwasher	31	12	28
Telephone	98	85	96
Central heating	92	86	91
Car or van - none	12	51	19
- one	45	41	44
Base = 100%	*5246*	*1203*	*6449*

Table 12.8 Ownership of telephones and home computers by socio-economic group of head of household by working status of household

Households with working age or working members   *Great Britain: 1998*

Socio-economic group	Working status of household		
	Working household	Workless household	Total
	Percentages		
Telephone			
Non-manual	99	93	99
Manual	96	83	93
Home computer			
Non-manual	58	33	55
Manual	32	15	28
Base=100%			
Non-manual	*2894*	*394*	*3288*
Manual	*2228*	*660*	*2888*

Table 12.9 **Ownership of 'luxury'* consumer durables by socio-economic group of head of household by working status of household**

Households with working age or working members   *Great Britain: 1998*

Socio-economic group and number of items owned	Working status of household		
	Working household	Workless household	Total
	%	%	%
Non-manual			
0	1	9	2
1	9	20	10
2	26	31	26
3	35	26	35
4	28	14	26
Base = 100%	*2894*	*394*	*3288*
	%	%	%
Manual			
0	3	13	5
1	12	27	15
2	33	33	33
3	38	23	35
4	13	4	11
Base = 100%	*2228*	*660*	*2888*
	%	%	%
Total			
0	2	11	4
1	10	24	13
2	29	32	30
3	37	24	34
4	22	8	19
Base = 100%	*5122*	*1054*	*6176*

* The 'luxury' items included were: CD player, dishwasher, microwave oven and tumble drier.

Table 12.10 **Self-reported health status, age and sex by working status of household**

Persons aged 16-64 living in households with working age or working members   *Great Britain: 1998*

Age and self-reported health status	Working status of household		
	Working household	Workless household	Total
	%	%	%
Men			
16-24			
Good	80	72	79
Fairly good	17	20	17
Not good	3	8	4
Base = 100%	*613*	*93*	*706*
25-34			
Good	75	45	72
Fairly good	20	28	21
Not good	5	27	7
Base = 100%	*1067*	*125*	*1192*
35-44			
Good	74	35	71
Fairly good	20	27	21
Not good	6	38	9
Base = 100%	*1118*	*93*	*1211*
45-64			
Good	63	37	58
Fairly good	25	27	25
Not good	12	37	17
Base = 100%	*1716*	*418*	*2134*
All men 16-64			
Good	71	42	67
Fairly good	21	26	22
Not good	8	32	11
Base = 100%	*4514*	*729*	*5243*

continued

Table 12.10 - *continued*   **Self-reported health status, age and sex by working status of household**

Persons aged 16-64 living in households with working age or working members		*Great Britain: 1998*

Age and self-reported health status	Working status of household		
	Working household	Workless household	Total
	%	%	%
Women			
16-24			
Good	73	59	71
Fairly good	22	30	24
Not good	5	10	6
Base = 100%	*660*	*153*	*813*
25-34			
Good	72	50	69
Fairly good	22	31	23
Not good	6	19	8
Base = 100%	*1263*	*211*	*1474*
35-44			
Good	70	34	66
Fairly good	23	32	24
Not good	7	34	10
Base = 100%	*1298*	*140*	*1438*
45-64			
Good	60	34	55
Fairly good	27	30	28
Not good	13	36	17
Base = 100%	*1683*	*399*	*2082*
All women 16-64			
Good	68	42	64
Fairly good	24	31	25
Not good	8	27	11
Base = 100%	*4904*	*903*	*5807*

Persons aged 16-64 living in households with working age or working members		*Great Britain: 1998*

Age and self-reported health status	Working status of household		
	Working household	Workless household	Total
	%	%	%
All persons			
16-24			
Good	77	64	75
Fairly good	20	26	21
Not good	4	9	5
Base = 100%	*1273*	*246*	*1519*
25-34			
Good	74	48	70
Fairly good	21	30	22
Not good	5	22	8
Base = 100%	*2330*	*336*	*2666*
35-44			
Good	72	35	68
Fairly good	22	30	22
Not good	7	35	9
Base = 100%	*2416*	*233*	*2649*
45-64			
Good	62	35	56
Fairly good	26	28	26
Not good	13	36	17
Base = 100%	*3399*	*817*	*4216*
Total			
Good	69	42	65
Fairly good	23	29	24
Not good	8	29	11
Base = 100%	*9418*	*1632*	*11050*

Table 12.11   Self-reported health status, marital status and sex by working status of household

Persons aged 16 and over living in households with working age or working members   *Great Britain: 1998*

Marital status and self-reported health status	Working status of household		
	Working household	Workless household	Total
	%	%	%
Men			
Married/cohabiting			
Good	69	41	66
Fairly good	22	26	23
Not good	9	33	11
Base = 100%	*3269*	*412*	*3681*
Single			
Good	76	50	72
Fairly good	19	27	21
Not good	4	23	8
Base = 100%	*1058*	*227*	*1285*
Widowed, divorced, separated			
Good	61	41	55
Fairly good	24	22	23
Not good	15	37	22
Base = 100%	*293*	*134*	*427*
Women			
Married/cohabiting			
Good	68	41	65
Fairly good	23	32	24
Not good	9	27	11
Base = 100%	*3603*	*412*	*4015*
Single			
Good	71	53	67
Fairly good	25	29	25
Not good	4	19	8
Base = 100%	*865*	*251*	*1116*
Widowed, divorced, separated			
Good	53	32	46
Fairly good	32	33	32
Not good	16	35	22
Base = 100%	*569*	*301*	*870*

Persons aged 16 and over living in households with working age or working members   *Great Britain: 1998*

Marital status and self-reported health status	Working status of household		
	Working household	Workless household	Total
	%	%	%
All persons 16 & over			
Married/cohabiting			
Good	68	41	65
Fairly good	23	29	24
Not good	9	30	11
Base = 100%	*6872*	*824*	*7696*
Single			
Good	74	51	70
Fairly good	22	28	23
Not good	4	21	8
Base = 100%	*1923*	*478*	*2401*
Widowed, divorced, separated			
Good	55	35	49
Fairly good	29	29	29
Not good	16	36	22
Base = 100%	*862*	*435*	*1297*

Table 12.12   **Prevalence of limiting longstanding illness, age and sex by working status of household**

Persons aged 0-64 living in households with working age or working members		*Great Britain: 1998*

Age and limiting longstanding illness	Working status of household		
	Working household	Workless household	Total
	%	%	%
Males			
0-4			
Limiting longstanding illness	4	5	4
Non limiting longstanding illness	11	14	11
No longstanding illness	86	81	85
Base = 100%	*596*	*146*	*742*
5-15			
Limiting longstanding illness	6	14	8
Non limiting longstanding illness	13	13	13
No longstanding illness	80	74	79
Base = 100%	*1275*	*277*	*1552*
16-44			
Limiting longstanding illness	10	34	12
Non limiting longstanding illness	12	11	12
No longstanding illness	78	55	76
Base = 100%	*3364*	*351*	*3715*
45-64			
Limiting longstanding illness	22	56	28
Non limiting longstanding illness	17	12	16
No longstanding illness	61	32	56
Base = 100%	*1953*	*435*	*2388*
All males aged 0-64			
Limiting longstanding illness	12	34	15
Non limiting longstanding illness	14	12	13
No longstanding illness	74	54	72
Base = 100%	*7188*	*1209*	*8397*

Persons aged 0-64 living in households with working age or working members		*Great Britain: 1998*

Age and limiting longstanding illness	Working status of household		
	Working household	Workless household	Total
	%	%	%
Females			
0-4			
Limiting longstanding illness	5	5	5
Non limiting longstanding illness	10	12	10
No longstanding illness	86	82	85
Base = 100%	*549*	*152*	*701*
5-15			
Limiting longstanding illness	8	12	8
Non limiting longstanding illness	11	9	11
No longstanding illness	81	79	81
Base = 100%	*1225*	*286*	*1511*
16-44			
Limiting longstanding illness	11	28	13
Non limiting longstanding illness	10	11	10
No longstanding illness	78	61	77
Base = 100%	*3472*	*531*	*4003*
45-64			
Limiting longstanding illness	22	53	28
Non limiting longstanding illness	14	12	14
No longstanding illness	64	35	58
Base = 100%	*1785*	*417*	*2202*
All females aged 0-64			
Limiting longstanding illness	13	30	16
Non limiting longstanding illness	11	11	11
No longstanding illness	76	59	73
Base = 100%	*7031*	*1386*	*8417*

continued

Table 12.12 - *continued* **Prevalence of limiting long-standing illness, age and sex by working status of household**

Persons aged 0-64 living in households with working age or working members

Great Britain: 1998

Age and limiting longstanding illness	Working status of household		
	Working household	Workless household	Total
	%	%	%
All persons			
0-4			
Limiting longstanding illness	4	5	4
Non limiting longstanding illness	10	13	11
No longstanding illness	86	82	85
Base = 100%	*1145*	*298*	*1443*
5-15			
Limiting longstanding illness	7	13	8
Non limiting longstanding illness	12	11	12
No longstanding illness	81	77	80
Base = 100%	*2500*	*563*	*3063*
16-44			
Limiting longstanding illness	10	31	13
Non limiting longstanding illness	11	11	11
No longstanding illness	78	59	76
Base = 100%	*6836*	*882*	*7718*
45-64			
Limiting longstanding illness	22	55	28
Non limiting longstanding illness	16	12	15
No longstanding illness	62	34	57
Base = 100%	*3738*	*852*	*4590*
All persons aged 0-64			
Limiting longstanding illness	12	32	15
Non limiting longstanding illness	12	11	12
No longstanding illness	75	57	72
Base = 100%	*14219*	*2595*	*16814*

Appendices

Appendix A
Definitions and terms

Acute sickness

See Sickness

Adults

Adults are defined as persons aged 16 or over in all tables except those showing dependent children where single persons aged 16-18 who are in full-time education are counted as dependent children.

Bedroom standard

This concept is used to estimate occupation density by allocating a standard number of bedrooms to each household in accordance with its age/sex/marital status composition and the relationship of the members to one another. A separate bedroom is allocated to each married couple, any other person aged 21 or over, each pair of adolescents aged 10-20 of the same sex, and each pair of children under 10. Any unpaired person aged 10-20 is paired if possible with a child under 10 of the same sex, or, if that is not possible, is given a separate bedroom, as is any unpaired child under 10. This standard is then compared with the actual number of bedrooms (including bedsitters) available for the sole use of the household, and deficiencies or excesses are tabulated. Bedrooms converted to other uses are not counted as available unless they have been denoted as bedrooms by the informants; bedrooms not actually in use are counted unless uninhabitable.

Births

The number of children born to women in successive birth cohorts (by the time they had reached each successive age) includes all liveborn children, regardless of the woman's marital status at the time of the child's birth.

A child is classified as being born outside marriage if the birth occurs more than nine months after the ending of a marriage by separation or widowhood.

Central heating

Central heating is defined as any system whereby two or more rooms (including kitchens, halls, landings, bathrooms and WCs) are heated from a central source, such as a boiler, a back boiler to an open fire, or the electricity supply. This definition includes a system where the boiler or back boiler heats one room and also supplies the power to heat at least one other room.

Under-floor heating systems, electric air systems, and night storage heaters are included.

Where a household has only one room in the accommodation, it is treated as having central heating if that room is heated from a central source along with other rooms in the house or building.

Chronic sickness

See Sickness

Cohabitation

See Marital Status

Co-ownership or equity sharing schemes

Co-ownership or equity sharing schemes are those where a share in the property is bought by the occupier under an agreement with the housing association. The monthly charges paid for the accommodation include an amount towards the repayment of the collective mortgage on the scheme. The co-owner never becomes the sole owner of the property, but on leaving the scheme a cash sum is usually repaid to the occupier.

Country of birth

Great Britain comprises England, Wales and Scotland; the United Kingdom comprises Great Britain and Northern Ireland; the British Isles comprise the United Kingdom, the Irish Republic, the Channel Islands and the Isle of Man. These and the remainder of the country of birth coding frame are fully described in *Census 1991, Definitions, Great Britain* HMSO (1992).

Dependent children

Dependent children are persons aged under 16, or single persons aged 16 but under 19 and in full-time education.

Doctor consultations

Data on doctor consultations relate to consultations with National Health Service general medical practitioners during the two weeks before interview. Visits to the surgery, home visits, and telephone conversations are included, but contacts only with a receptionist or nurse are excluded.

The average number of consultations per person per year is calculated by multiplying the total number of consultations within the reference period, for any particular group, by 26 (the number of two-week periods in a year) and dividing the product by the total number of persons in the sample in that group.

Drinking: background and methodology

In 1998 the GHS used two measures for obtaining information on alcohol consumption:

- usual alcohol consumption in the last year;
- the number of units consumed on the heaviest drinking day in the 7 days before interivew.

Usual alcohol consumption in the last year (AC rating)

The GHS asks respondents how often they have drunk each of five different types of drink in the past year and how much of each they usually drank on any day. The amount usually consumed is converted into units of alcohol, one unit being approximately equivalent of half a pint of beer, lager or cider, a single measure of spirits, one glass of wine, or one small glass of port, sherry or other fortified wine. Respondents' answers are used to provide an estimate of their alcohol consumption level, which is, in effect, their average weekly consumption.

The method used to calculate the alcohol consumption rating is to multiply the number of units of each type of drink 'usually drunk on any one day' by the frequency with which it was drunk, using the factors shown below, and totalling across all drinks.

Multiplying factors for converting drinking frequency and number of units usually consumed on any one day into number of units consumed per week

Drinking frequency	Multiplying factor
Almost every day	7.0
5 or 6 days a week	5.5
3 or 4 days a week	3.5
Once or twice a week	1.5
Once or twice a month	0.375 (1.5/4)
Once every couple of months	0.115(6/52)
Once or twice a year	0.029 (1.5/52)

The number of units of each type of drink usually consumed on any day is multiplied by the factor corresponding to the frequency with which the drink is consumed. In all except the first category, the factors are averages of the range of frequencies shown in the category. For example, where a drink was consumed '3-4 days a week', the amount drunk was multiplied by 3.5.

The frequency categories and the corresponding multiplying factors used since 1990 are different from those used on the 1988 GHS. Following a review of the drinking section carried out in 1989, it was decided to change the wording of the categories so that they referred clearly to 'days'. Previously there had been some ambiguity as the wording could have been interpreted as referring to days or occasions. The number of categories was also increased to give a more accurate estimate of drinking frequency.

Number of units consumed on the heaviest drinking day in the 7 days before interview

Respondents were asked on how many days they had drunk alcohol during the previous week. They were then asked how much of each of the six types of drink (normal beer, strong beer, wine, spirits, fortified wines and alcopops) they had drunk on their heaviest drinking day during the previous week. These amounts are added to give an estimate of the most the respondent had drunk on any one day.

Economic activity

Economically active persons are those over the minimum school-leaving age who were working or unemployed in the week before the week of interview. These persons constitute the labour force.

Working persons

This category includes persons aged 16 and over who, in the week before the week of interview, worked for wages, salary or other form of cash payment such as commission or tips, for any number of hours. It covers persons absent from work in the reference week because of holiday, sickness, strike, or temporary lay-off, provided they had a job to return with the same employer. It also includes persons attending an educational establishment during the specified week if they were paid by their employer while attending it, people on Government training schemes and unpaid family workers.

Persons are excluded if they worked in a voluntary capacity for expenses only, or only for payment in kind, unless they worked for a business, firm or professional practice owned by a relative.

Full-time students are classified as 'working', 'unemployed' or 'inactive' according to their own reports of what they were doing during the reference week.

Unemployed persons

The GHS uses the International Labour Organisation (ILO) definition of unemployment. This classifies anyone as unemployed if he or she was out of work and had looked for work in the four weeks before interview, or would have but for temporary sickness or injury, and was available to start work in the two weeks after interview. Otherwise, anyone out of work is classified as economically inactive.

The treatment of all catgories on the GHS is in line with that used on the Labour Force Survey (LFS).

Ethnic group

Household members are classified as White, Black Caribbean, Black African, Black other, Indian, Pakistani, Bangladeshi, Chinese, or 'none of these groups' by the person answering the Household Schedule.

The 'Black Caribbean' category includes the 'Black Caribbean' and 'Guyanese' groups. In some tables of the report the category 'Black' is used, which includes 'Black African' as well as 'Black Caribbean' and 'Guyanese'.

Family

A family is defined as:

(a) a married or opposite sex cohabiting couple on their own, or

(b) a married or opposite sex cohabiting couple/lone parent and their never-married children, provided these children have no children of their own.

Persons who cannot be allocated to a family as defined above are said to be persons not in the family.

In general, families cannot span more than two generations, ie grandparents and grandchildren cannot belong to the same family. The exception to this is where it is established that the grandparents are responsible for looking after the grandchildren (eg while the parents are abroad).

Adopted and step-children belong to the same family as their adoptive/step-parents. Foster-children, however, are not part of their foster-parents' family (since they are not related to their foster-parents) and are counted as separate family units.

See also Lone-parent family.

Government Office Region (GOR)

Government Office Regions have replaced the Standard Statistical Regions as the primary classification for the presentation of English regional statistics.

Most of the regional statistics in this report are therefore on the basis of Government Office region, except for long-term trend tables, where Standard Statistical Region is used.

Standard Statistical Region	County	Government Office Region
North	Cleveland Durham Northumberland Tyne and Wear	North East
	Cumbria	
North West	Cheshire Greater Manchester Lancashire	North West
	Merseyside	Merseyside
Yorkshire and Humberside	Humberside North Yorkshire South Yorkshire West Yorkshire	Yorkshire and the Humber
East Midlands	Derbyshire Leicestershire Lincolnshire Northamptonshire Nottinghamshire	East Midlands
West Midlands	Hereford and Worcester Shropsire Staffordshire Warwickshire West Midlands	West Midlands
East Anglia	Cambridgeshire Norfolk Suffolk	Eastern
	Bedfordshire Essex Hertfordshire	
	Greater London	London
South East	Berkshire Buckinghamshire East Sussex Hampshire Isle of Wight Kent Oxfordshire Surrey West Sussex	South East
South West	Avon Cornwall Devon Dorset Gloucestershire Somerset Wiltshire	South West

GP Consultations

See Doctor Consultations

Head of household

The head of the household is a member of the household and (in order of precedence) either the husband of the person, or the person, who:

(a) owns the household accommodation, or

(b) is legally responsible for the rent of the accommodation, or

(c) has the accommodation as an emolument or perquisite, or

(d) has the accommodation by virtue of some relationship to the owner in cases where the owner or lessee is not a member of the household.

When two members of a different sex have equal claim, the male is taken as head of household. When two members of the same sex have equal claim, the elder is taken as head of household.

Hospital visits

Inpatient stays

Inpatient data relate to stays overnight or longer (in a twelve month reference period) in NHS or private hospitals. All types of cases are counted, including psychiatric and maternity, except babies born in hospital who are included only if they remained in hospital after their mother was discharged.

Outpatient attendances

Outpatient data relate to attendances (in a reference period of three calendar months) at NHS or private hospitals, other than as an inpatient. No distinction is made between consultative outpatient attendances, casualty attendances, and attendances at ancillary departments.

Day patient

Day patients are defined as patients admitted to a hospital bed during the course of a day or to a day ward where a bed, couch or trolley is available for the patient's use. They are admitted with the intention of receiving care or treatment which can be completed in a few hours so that they do not require to remain in hospital overnight. If a patient admitted as a day patient then stays overnight they are counted as an inpatient.

Household

Household definition: between 1971 and 1980 the definition of a household used in the GHS and in most other surveys carried out by OPCS Social Survey Division was, in summary:

> a group of people who all live regularly at the address ... and who are all catered for, for at least one meal a day, by the same person. (See J Atkinson, *A Handbook for Interviewers*. HMSO, London 1971.)

In 1981 a new definition was adopted, intended to make the survey comparable with the 1981 Census definition of a household. Under the new definition a household is:

> a single person or a group of people who have the address as their only or main residence and who either share one meal a day or share the living accommodation. (See L McCrossan, *A Handbook for Interviewers*. HMSO, London 1991.)

A group of people would not be counted as a household solely on the basis of a shared kitchen or bathroom.

Household membership

Under the 1981 definition, a person is in general regarded as living at the address if he or she (or the informant) considers the address to be his or her main residence. There are, however, certain rules which take priority over this criterion.

(a) Children aged 16 or over who live away from home for purposes of either work or study and come home only for holidays are *not* included at the parental address under any circumstances.

(b) Children of any age away from home in a temporary job and children under 16 at boarding school are *always* included in the parental household.

(c) Anyone who has been away from the address *continuously* for six months or longer is excluded.

(d) Anyone who has been living continuously at the address for six months or longer is included even if he or she has his or her main residence elsewhere.

(e) Addresses used only as second homes are never counted as a main residence.

Household type

There are many ways of grouping or classifying households into household types; most are based on the age, sex and number of household members.

The main classification of household type uses the following categories:

1 adult aged 16-59

2 adults aged 16-59

small family   - 1 or 2 persons aged 16 or over and 1 or 2 persons aged under 16

large family   - 1 or more persons aged 16 or over and 3 or more persons aged under 16, or 3 or more persons aged 16 or over and 2 persons aged under 16

large adult household   - 3 or more persons aged 16 or over, with or without 1 person aged under 16

2 adults, 1 or both aged 60 or over

1 adult aged 60 or over

The term 'family' in this context does not necessarily imply any relationship.

Chapter 3 also uses a modified version of household type which takes account of the age of the youngest household member. 'Small family', 'large family' and 'large adult household' are replaced by the following:

youngest person aged 0-4   - 1 or more persons aged 16 or over and 1 or more persons aged under 5

youngest person aged 5-15   - 1 or more persons aged 16 or over and 1 or more persons aged 5-15

3 or more adults   - 3 or more persons aged 16 or over and no-one aged under 16

The first two categories above are combined in some tables.

In Chapter 3, households are also classified according to the families they contain (see Family for definition), into the following categories:

non-family households
  containing   - 1 person only
              - 2 or more non-family* adults

one family households†
  containing
- married couple with dependent children
- married couple with independent children only
- married couple with no children
- cohabiting couple with dependent children
- cohabiting couple with independent children only
- cohabiting couple with no children
- lone parent with dependent children
- lone parent with independent children only

households containing two or more families.

Some of the above categories are combined for certain tables and figures.

Income

Usual gross weekly income

The income section was revised and simplified in 1992 so that estimates were accepted as valid responses.

Total income for an individual refers to income at the time of the interview, and is obtained by summing the components of earnings, benefits, pensions, dividends, interest and other regular payments. Prior to 1992, if any component of income was unknown, the value of total gross weekly income was treated as not known. Since 1992, gross weekly income of employees and those on benefits is calculated if interest and dividends are the only components missing.

If the last pay packet/cheque was unusual, for example in including holiday pay in advance or a tax refund, the respondent is asked for usual pay. No account is taken of whether a job is temporary or permanent. Payments made less than weekly are divided by the number of weeks covered to obtain a weekly figure.

Usual gross weekly household income is the sum of usual gross weekly income for all adults in the household. Since 1992, those interviewed by proxy are also included.

---

* Individuals may, of course, be related without constituting a family. A household consisting of a brother and sister, for example, is a non-family household of two or more non-family adults.

† Other individuals who were not family members may also have been present.

Labour force
See Economic activity.

Lone-parent family
A lone-parent family consists of one parent, irrespective of sex, living with his or her never-married dependent children, provided these children have no children of their own.

Married or cohabiting women with dependent children, whose partners are not defined as resident in the household, are not classified as one-parent families because it is known that the majority of them are only temporarily separated from their husbands for a reason that does not imply the breakdown of the marriage (for example, because the husband usually works away from home). (See the GHS 1980 Report p.9 for further details.)

Longstanding conditions and complaints
The GHS collects information about the nature of longstanding illness. Respondents who report a longstanding illness are asked 'What is the matter with you?' and details of the illness or disability are recorded by the interviewers and coded into a number of broad categories. Interviewers are instructed to focus on the symptoms of the illness, rather than the cause, and code what the respondent said was currently the matter without probing for cause. This approach has been used in 1988, 1989, 1994 to 1996, and 1998.

The categories used when coding the conditions correspond broadly to the chapter headings of the International Classification of Diseases (ICD). However, the ICD is used mostly for coding conditions and diseases according to cause whereas the GHS coding is based only on the symptoms reported. This gives rise to discrepancies in some areas between the two classifications.

Marriage and cohabitation
From 1971 to 1978 the Family Information section was addressed only to married women aged under 45 who were asked questions on their present marriage and birth expectations. In 1979 the section was expanded to include questions on cohabitation, previous marriages and all live births, and was addressed to all women aged 16-49 except non-married women aged 16 and 17. In 1983 questions on contraception, sterilisation and infertility were introduced. In 1986 the section was extended to cover all women and men aged 16-59.

Marital status
Since 1996 separate questions have been asked at the beginning of the questionnaire to identify the legal marital status and living arrangements of respondents in the household. The latter includes a category for cohabiting.

Cohabiting
Before 1996, unrelated adults of the opposite sex have been classified as cohabiting if they consider themselves to be living together as a couple. From 1996, this category includes a small number of same sex couples.

In 1998 all adults aged 16-59 were asked about any periods of cohabitation not leading to marriage.

Married/non-married
In this dichotomy 'married' generally includes cohabiting and 'non-married' covers those who are single, widowed, separated or divorced and not cohabiting.

Living arrangements (de facto marital status)
Before 1996, additional information from the Family Information section of the individuals' questionnaire has been used to determine living arrangements (previously known as 'defacto marital status') and the classification has only applied to those aged 16-59 who answer the marital history questions. For this population it only differed from the main marital status for those who revealed in the Family Information section that they were cohabiting rather than having the marital status given at the beginning of the interview. 'Cohabiting' took priority over other categories. Since 1996, information on legal marital status and living arrangements, has been taken from the beginning of the interview where both are now asked.

Legal marital status
This classification applies to persons aged 16-59 who answer the marital history questions. Cohabiting people are categorised according to formal marital status. The classification differs from strict legal marital status in accepting the respondents' opinion of whether their marriage has terminated in separation rather than applying the criterion of legal separation.

Median
See Quantiles.

NHS Regional Office area

NHS Regional Office areas came into effect from April 1996.

ENGLAND and WALES

—— Health Authority boundary

Pensions

The GHS asks questions about any pension scheme, either occupational or personal, that the respondent belonged to on the date of interview. It is quite possible that some respondents have belonged to an occupational or a personal pension scheme in the past. The GHS measures current membership and not the percentage of respondents who will get an occupational or personal pension when they retire.

Since July 1988, all employees have been given the choice of starting their own personal pension in place of SERPS (State Earnings related Pension Scheme). Previously employees not in an occupational scheme could arrange to pay for a personal pension plan, but they could not leave SERPS.

Some respondents may be contributing to both an occupational and personal pension scheme.

Qualification levels

Degree or equivalent
  Higher degrees
  First degrees
  University diplomas and certificates, qualifications from colleges of technology etc and from professional institutions, of degree standard

Higher education below degree level
  Non-graduate teaching qualifications
  HNC/HND; City and Guilds Full Technological Certificate; BEC/TEC/BTEC Higher/SCOTECH Higher

  University diplomas and certificates, qualifications from colleges of technology etc and from professional institutions, below degree but above GCE 'A' level standard
  Nursing qualifications

GCE 'A' level or equivalent
  1 or more subjects at GCE 'A' level/AS level/Scottish Certificate of Education (SCE) Higher; Scottish Universities Preliminary Examination (SUPE) Higher; and/or Higher School Certificate; Scottish Leaving Certificate (SLC) Higher; Certificate of Sixth Year Studies City and Guilds Advanced/Final level; ONC/OND; BEC/TEC/BTEC/National/General certificate or diploma

GCSE Grades A-C or equivalent
  1 or more subjects at GCE 'O' level (Grades A-C)/GCSE (grades A-C)/CSE Grade 1/SCE Ordinary (Bands A-C); SUPE Lower or Ordinary; and/or School Certificates; SLC Lower City and Guilds Craft/Ordinary level/SCOTVEC

GCSE Grades D-E or equivalent
  GCSE (grades D-E)/CSE Grades 2-5/GCE 'O' level (Grades D and E)/SCE Ordinary (Bands D and E);
  Clerical and commercial qualifications
  Apprenticeship

Foreign and other qualifications
  Foreign qualifications (outside UK)
  Other qualifications

None
  - excludes those who never went to school (omitted from the classification altogether).

The qualification levels do not in all cases correspond to those used in statistics published by the Department for Education and Employment.

Quantiles

The quantiles of a distribution, eg of household income, divide it into equal parts.

Median: the median of a distribution divides it into two equal parts. Thus half the households in a distribution of household income have an income higher than the median, and the other half have an income lower than the median.

Quartiles: the quartiles of a distribution divide it into quarters. Thus the upper quartile of a distribution of household income is the level of income that is expected by 25% of the households in the distribution; and 25% of the households have an income less than the lower quartile. It follows that 50% of the households have an income between the upper and lower quartiles.

Quintiles: the quintiles of a distribution divide it into fifths. Thus the upper quintile of a distribution of household income is the level of income that is expected by 20% of the households in the distribution; and 20% of the households have an income less than the lower quintile. It follows that 60% of the households have an income between the upper and lower quintiles.

Relatives in the household

The term 'relative' includes any household member related to the head of household by blood, marriage, or adoption. Foster-children are therefore not regarded as relatives.

Rooms

These are defined as habitable rooms, including (unless otherwise specified) kitchens, whether eaten in or not, but excluding rooms used solely for business purposes, those not usable throughout the year (eg conservatories), and those not normally used for living purposes such as toilets, cloakrooms, store rooms, pantries, cellars and garages.

Sickness
Acute

Acute sickness is defined as restriction of the level of normal activity, because of illness or injury, at any time during the two weeks before interview. Since the two-week reference period covers weekends, normal activities include leisure activities as well as school attendance, going to work, or doing housework. Anyone with a chronic condition that caused additional restriction during the reference period is counted among those with acute sickness.

The average number of restricted activity days per person per year is calculated in the same way as the average number of doctor consultations.

Sickness
Chronic

Information on chronic sickness was obtained from the following two-part question:

'Do you have any longstanding illness, disability or infirmity? By longstanding I mean anything that has troubled you over a period of time or that is likely to affect you over a period of time.

IF YES
Does this illness or disability limit your activities in any way?'

'Longstanding illness' is defined as a positive answer to the first part of the question, and 'limiting longstanding illness' as a positive answer to both parts of the question.

The data collected are based on people's subjective assessment of their health, and therefore changes over time may reflect changes in people's expectations of their health as well as changes in incidence or duration of chronic sickness. In addition, different sub-groups of the population may have varying expectations, activities and capacities of adaptation.

Smoking

Questions about smoking behaviour are currently included on the GHS in alternate years. Since 1974, the questions have been asked of all people aged 16 and over in the household with a self-completion form offered to those aged 16 or 17, where appropriate. It is likely that the GHS understates cigarette consumption and perhaps, to a lesser extent prevalence. This is because the context of the GHS interview, where all members of the family aged 16 and over are interviewed, often together, may affect the reporting of smoking behaviour. The self-completion form is designed to minimise the possible effects of parental disapproval. However, when considering trends in smoking it is assumed that any under-reporting has remained constant throughout the period of the survey. This may not be entirely justified as it is possible that public attitudes to smoking have become more negative over time making it more likely that people will under-report their level of smoking or deny smoking at all.

Information on tar yields is only collected for manufactured cigarettes. Tar yields are provided by the laboratory of the Government Chemist.

209

Socio-economic group

The basic occupational classification used is the Registrar General's socio-economic grouping in *Standard Occupational Classification 1990*, Volume 3 OPCS (HMSO, London 1991), pp 13-14. The majority of tables use a collapsed version of this classification, which is as follows:

Descriptive definition	*SEG numbers*
Professional	3, 4
Employers and managers	1, 2, 13
Intermediate non-manual	5
Junior non-manual	6
Skilled manual (including foremen and supervisors) and own account non-professional	8, 9, 12, 14
Semi-skilled manual and personal service	7, 10, 15
Unskilled manual	11

In tables showing non-manual/manual socio-economic groups, the non-manual category comprises SEGs 1-6 and 13, the manual category comprises SEGs 7-12, 14 and 15.

For persons aged 16 or over, including full-time students with employment experience, SEG corresponds to their own present job or, for those not currently working, to their last job, regardless of sex or marital status.

Persons whose occupation was inadequately described, the Armed Forces (SEG category 16) and full-time students, are excluded from the totals unless otherwise specified.

Prior to 1992, the socio-economic variable used in a number of tables, particularly in the health, smoking and drinking chapters, classified married or cohabiting couples whose husbands were in the household according to their partner's present (or last) job. Other members of the household were classified according to their own current or last job. It was recognised that there are drawbacks to this classification. First, it has been criticised by some users of GHS as being overtly sexist in classifying women according to a characteristic of their husband or partner. Second, there is an inconsistency in that the classification of other members of the household, e.g. adult children living at home or elderly people living with their children, is based on their own job.

To achieve a more consistent approach and classify all members of the household in the same way, the standard socio-economic variable used in 1992 to reflect living standards was changed to the socio-economic group of the head of household. This will be used in subsequent GHS reports, although for the time being, the old classification will also be used in trend tables so that changes can be monitored on a consistent basis. A classification based on the respondent's own occupation will continue to be used where appropriate.

Step-family

See Family.

Tenure

From 1981, households who were buying a share in the property from a housing association or co-operative through a shared ownership (equity sharing) or co-ownership scheme are included in the category of owner-occupiers. In earlier years such households were included with those renting from a housing association or co-operative.

Renting from a council includes renting from a local authority or New town corporation or commissions or Scottish Homes (formerly the Scottish Special Housing Association).

Renting from a housing association also includes co-operatives and charitable trusts. It also covers fair rent schemes.

Social sector renters includes households renting from a local authority or New Town corporation or commission or Scottish Homes and those renting from housing associations, co-operatives and charitable trusts.

Private renters include those who rent from a private individual or organisation and those whose accommodation is tied to their job even if the landlord is a local authority, housing association or Housing Action Trust, or if the accommodation is rent free. Squatters are also included in this category.

Unemployed

See Economic activity

Working

See Economic activity

Appendix B
Sample Design and Response

The sample design

The most recent change to the sample design of the GHS occurred in 1984 when the Postcode Address File (PAF) replaced the Electoral Registers as the sampling frame.

The GHS uses a two-stage sample design with postcode sectors, which are similar in size to wards, as the Primary Sampling Units (PSUs). From 1986 to 1989 there was provision for rotation of one third of the PSUs each year. The 1998 sample was drawn without using the rotation method.

The sampling selection procedure followed in 1998 was the same as for all years since 1984. Initially postcode sectors were allocated to major strata on the basis of region and area type. The sectors were distributed between 24 such strata. These were created from the Government Office regions (UK standard regions prior to 1998) by subdividing Wales, Scotland, London and the South East, and then further distinguishing between Metropolitan and non-Metropolitan counties. In Scotland, Glasgow was treated as a District of 'Metropolitan' type[1].

Within each major stratum, postcode sectors were then stratified according to selected housing and economic indicators available from the 1991 Census. Sectors were initially ranked according to the proportion of households in privately rented accommodation, then divided into two bands containing approximately the same number of households. The PAF includes an indicator of the estimated number of separate units or households at each delivery point (address) and this multi-occupancy count is used to estimate the total number of households.[2] Within each band, sectors were re-ranked according to the proportion of households in local authority accommodation and bands were sub-divided to give four bands of approximately equal size. Finally, within each of these bands, sectors were re-ranked according to the proportion of heads of households in socio-economic groups 1 to 5 or 13.

Major strata were then divided into minor strata of equal size, the number of minor strata per major stratum being proportionate to the size of the major stratum. Since

Figure A

Percentage renting privately	HIGH		LOW	
Percentage renting from Local Authority	HIGH	LOW	LOW	HIGH
Percentage with HOH in SEG 1-5 or 13	HIGH ↘ LOW	HIGH LOW ↗	HIGH ↘ LOW	HIGH LOW ↗

1984 the frame has been divided into 576 minor strata and one PSU has been selected from each per year. In order, therefore, to minimise the difference between one band and the next, the ranking by the socio-economic group and local authority renting criteria were in the reverse order in consecutive bands, as shown in Figure A.

Until 1994 a supplementary sample of addresses was selected in Scotland to improve estimates in separate analyses for Scotland.

Conversion of addresses to households

Most addresses contain just one private household, a few - such as institutions and purely business addresses[3] - contain no private households, while others contain more than one private household. For addresses containing more than one household, set procedures are laid down in order to give each household one and only one chance of selection.

As the PAF does not give names of occupants of addresses, it is not possible to use the number of different surnames at an address as an indicator of the number of households living there as was done before 1984. A rough guide to the number of households at an address is provided on the PAF by the multi-occupancy (MO) count. The MO count is a fairly accurate indicator in Scotland but is less accurate in England and Wales, so it is used only when sampling at addresses in Scotland.

All addresses in England and Wales, and those in Scotland with an MO count of two or less, are given only one chance of selection for the sample. At such addresses, interviewers interview all the households they find up to a maximum of three. If there are more than three households at the address, the interviewer selects the households for interview by listing all households at the address systematically then making a random choice by referring to a household selection table.

Addresses in Scotland with an MO count of three or more, where the probability that there is more than one household is fairly high, are given as many chances of selection as the value of the MO count. When the interviewer arrives at such an address, he or she checks the actual number of households and interviews a proportion of them according to instructions. The proportion is set originally by the MO count and adjusted according to the number of households actually found, with a maximum of three households being interviewed at any address. The interviewer selects the households for interview by listing all households at the address systematically and making a random choice, as above, by means of a table.

No addresses are deleted from the sample to compensate for the extra interviews that may result from these multi-household addresses but a maximum of four extra interviews per quota of addresses is allowed. Once four extra interviews have been carried out in an interviewer's quota, only the first household selected at each multi-occupancy address is included. As a result of the limits on additional interviews, households in concealed multi-occupied addresses may be slightly under-represented in the GHS sample. The outcome of visits to the addresses selected for the 1998 GHS sample and the resultant number of households interviewed is shown in Table 1.

Table 1 **The sample of addresses and households**

Great Britain: 1998

Selected addresses	13248
Adjusted sample (extra households)	158
Ineligible addresses: Demolished or derelict Used wholly for business purposes Empty Institutions Other ineligible No sample selected at address Address not traced	1575
Addresses at which interviews were taken	8637
Total effective sample of households	11831

Data collection

Information for the GHS is collected week by week throughout the year by personal interview. From 1988, the GHS interviewing year was changed from a calendar year to a financial year basis. In 1998 interviews took place from April 1998 to March 1999. In 1994, the survey was carried out for the first time using Computer Assisted Personal Interviewing (CAPI) on laptop computers and BLAISE software. Interviews are sought with all adult members (aged 16 or over) of the sample of private households described above.

On occasion it may prove impossible, despite repeated calls, to contact a particular member of a household in person and, in strictly controlled circumstances, interviewers are permitted to conduct a proxy interview with a near relative who is a member of the same household. In these cases, questions such as those on educational qualifications and income and opinion-type questions are omitted.

Interviewers working on the GHS form part of the overall Social Survey interviewing force and, as such, are recruited only after careful selection procedures after which they take part in a four-day initial training course. Before working on the GHS they attend a briefing and new recruits are always accompanied in the field by a training officer. All interviewers who continue to work on the GHS are observed regularly in the field.

Response

Table 2 shows the quarterly and annual response rates from the 1998 survey. Since the GHS can accept information from partially responding households (ie outcome categories 2a-2c in Table 2) response rates can be measured in a variety of ways.

Partial response can arise for a variety of reasons: some people refuse to answer some questions; others are interviewed by proxy and, as noted above, are not then asked all the questions.   Depending on whether or not the various categories of partial response are included, three response rates are calculated.

1 The *minimum* response rate, which accepts only completely co-operating households as responders and treats all partials as non-responders. In 1998 the minimum response rate was 66%.

2 The *maximum* response rate, which accepts all partials as responders. In 1998 this rate was 73%.

3 The *middle* response rate, which accepts some of the partials as responders - that is, it includes households where information is missing for only certain questions (category 2a in Table 2), but does not include those where information is missing altogether for one or more household members (categories 2b and 2c in Table 2). In other words, this middle rate can be thought of as the proportion of the eligible sample of households from whom all or nearly all the information was obtained. This is the rate generally used as the performance index for the survey, and in 1998 it was 72%.

Since 1971, the middle response rate has shown some fluctuation:

	%			%
1971	83		1984	81
1972	81		1985	82
1973	81		1986	84
1974	83		1987	85
1975	84		1988	85
1976	84		1989	84
1977	83		1990	81
1978	82		1991	84
1979	83		1992	83
1980	82		1993	82
1981	84		1994	80
1982	84		1995	80
1983	82		1996	76
			1998	72

Since 1987, following an experiment in 1986, a letter has been sent in advance of an interviewer calling to an address[4]. The letter briefly describes the purpose and nature of the survey and prepares the recipient for a visit by an interviewer. These letters probably resulted in the improvements in middle response rates from 1987 to 1989. The decline in response rate since 1991 is due to an increase in the proportion of households refusing to participate (12% in 1991 rising to 23% in 1998) rather than failure to contact people. A similar decline is being experienced on other ONS surveys and by other survey organisations. The main elements of response and non-response in 1998, and middle response rate figures for each region, are shown in Tables 2 and 3 respectively.

Non-response

In total, 27% of households selected for interview in 1998 were lost to the sample altogether, either because they did not wish to take part (23%) or because they could not be contacted (4%).

A comparison was made of the characteristics recorded on the 1991 Census forms of respondents and non-respondents in the 1991 GHS sample, repeating similar studies made with the help of 1971 and 1981 Census records[5,6]. Results showed that households comprising one adult aged 16-59 or a couple with non-dependent children were under-represented as also were households in London, those living in smaller accommodation

Table 2 Quarterly and annual response

Great Britain: 1998

Outcome category	First quarter		Second quarter		Third quarter		Fourth quarter		Year	
	No.	%	No.	%	No.	%	No.	%	No.	%
1 Complete household co-operation	2042	68.8	1946	65.9	1911	64.5	1947	66.0	7846	66.3
2a Non-interview of one or more household members, proxy taken. Partial refusals: all household members co-operated but some sections/questions were refused	169	5.7	233	7.9	153	5.2	147	5.0	702	5.9
2b Non-contact of one or more household members, no proxy taken	14	0.5	6	0.2	8	0.3	11	0.4	39	0.3
2c Partial refusal: at least one household member refused to be interviewed	9	0.3	23	0.8	6	0.2	12	0.4	50	0.4
3 Whole household refused	553	18.6	578	19.6	706	23.8	611	20.7	2448	20.7
HQ refusal	57	1.9	60	2.0	51	1.7	64	2.2	232	2.0
4 Non-contact of household	117	3.9	104	3.5	122	4.1	152	5.2	495	4.2
Base = 100% *(total effective sample, ie total categories 1-4 plus small data losses)*	*2966*		*2955*		*2962*		*2948*		*11831*	
Middle response rate: (codes 1 and 2a as percentage of the effective sample)		74.5		73.7		69.7		71.0		72.3

Table 3 Response rates by Government Office Region

Great Britain: 1998

Government Office Region	First quarter		Second quarter		Third quarter		Fourth quarter		Year	
	%	Rank	%	Rank	%	Rank	%	Rank	%	Rank
North East	83.0	1	79.2	1	78.0	2	74.2	3	78.8	1
North West	73.6	7	78.1	2	71.4	7	67.0	10	72.6	6=
Merseyside	69.7	11	70.0	11	78.3	1	67.9	9	71.1	10
Yorkshire and the Humber	74.0	6	71.7	9	74.4	3	72.4	8	73.1	5
East Midlands	73.1	8	73.1	6	70.7	8	72.6	7	72.4	8
West Midlands	78.7	3	76.6	4	65.4	11	61.1	11	70.4	11
Eastern	71.2	10	72.1	8	71.9	6	73.7	4	72.2	9
London	66.4	12	68.1	12	59.6	12	60.2	12	63.5	12
South East (excluding Greater London)	73.0	9	72.3	7	68.7	9	76.8	1	72.6	6=
South West	80.1	2	77.8	3	73.3	4	72.8	6	76.0	2
Wales	78.3	4=	71.5	10	73.2	5	73.3	5	74.0	3
Scotland	78.3	4=	74.6	5	66.4	10	74.7	2	73.6	4
Great Britain	74.5		73.7		69.7		71.0		72.3	

Table 4 Age comparison of the 1998 GHS and population estimates[†] for mid-1998

All persons   *Great Britain: 1998*

Age	Males		Females		Total	
	1998 GHS	Population estimates mid-1998	1998 GHS	Population estimates mid-1998	1998 GHS	Population estimates mid-1998
	%	%	%	%	%	%
0 - 4	7.6*	6.4	6.6*	5.9	7.1*	6.2
5 - 15	15.8*	14.8	14.4*	13.6	15.1*	14.2
16 - 19	4.8	5.1	4.3	4.7	4.6	4.9
20 - 24	4.7*	6.2	4.7*	5.7	4.7*	5.9
25 - 29	6.6*	7.7	7.3	7.1	6.9*	7.4
30 - 34	7.6*	8.5	7.6	7.9	7.6*	8.2
35 - 39	7.5	8.0	8.0	7.5	7.8	7.7
40 - 44	6.7	6.8	6.3	6.5	6.5	6.7
45 - 49	6.9	6.6	6.5	6.4	6.7	6.5
50 - 54	6.9	6.7	6.9	6.6	6.9	6.7
55 - 59	5.4	5.2	5.3	5.1	5.3	5.2
60 - 64	5.2	4.8	5.0	4.8	5.1*	4.8
65 - 69	4.8*	4.3	4.8	4.6	4.8*	4.4
70 - 74	4.1*	3.6	4.5	4.3	4.3*	4.0
75 and over	5.5	5.3	7.9*	9.3	6.7*	7.3
Total	48.2	49.2	51.8	50.8	100	100
Base = 100%	9831	28301071	10564	29246835	20395	57547906

* Difference was found to be significant at the 5% level.
† Population estimates include people living in institutional accommodation.

Table 5 Government Office Region: a comparison of the 1998 GHS and population estimates for mid-1998

All persons   *Great Britain: 1998*

Government Office Region	1998 GHS	Population estimates mid-1998
	%	%
England	85.5	86.0
North East	5.4	4.5
North West	9.1	9.5
Merseyside	2.3	2.4
Yorks and Humber	9.0	8.8
East Midlands	7.1	7.2
West Midlands	9.5	9.3
Eastern	9.6	9.3
London	10.7	12.5
South East	13.7	13.9
South West	9.1	8.5
Wales	5.3	5.1
Scotland	9.2	8.9
Base = 100%	20396	57547906

(with fewer than 4 rooms) and those whose head was born outside the UK. Households containing dependent children were over-represented in the responding sample. More details of the results are given in Appendix C of the 1993 report[7].

Comparison of the 1998 GHS with population estimates for mid-1998

Table 4 compares the age distribution of the 1998 GHS sample with that from population estimates for mid-1998. The comparisons show that the 1998 GHS tended to over-represent children, particularly those aged 5-15, and to under-represent adults in their twenties and early thirties. There were some differences between men and women of the same age. For example, men aged 65-74 were over-represented whereas women of the same age were not. Women aged 75 and over were under-represented in the sample, but men of the same age were not.

It should be noted that the GHS covers only those people living in private households, whereas population estimates also include those people living in institutional accommodation.

Table 5 shows that the 1998 GHS under-represented people living in the London area, again because of non-response bias. The GHS achieves a lower response in London than elsewhere both because people tend to be harder to contact than in other regions and because of higher refusal rates[7].

Notes and references

1. The GOR regional stratifier

0	Scottish Islands
1	North East (MET)
2	North East (NONMET)
3	North West (MET)
4	North West (NONMET)
5	Merseyside
6	Yorks and Humberside (MET)
7	Yorks and Humberside (NONMET)
8	East Midlands
9	West Midlands (MET)
10	West Midlands (NONMET)
11	Eastern Outer Met
12	Eastern Other
13	Inner London
14	Outer London
15	South East Outer Met
16	South East Other
17	South West
18	Glamorgan, Gwent
19	Clywd, Dyfed, Gwynedd, Powys
20	Highland, Grampian, Tayside
21	Fife, Central, Lothian
22	Glasgow
23	Strathclyde ex Glasgow
24	Borders, Dumfries, Galloway

Excludes Scottish Islands, the Scilly Isles and the Isle of Man.

2. It is known that the majority of delivery points with a multi-occupancy indicator '2' consist of one private dwelling plus business premises, so these addresses were assumed to contain just one household.

3. Most institutions and business addresses are not listed on the small-user PAF. If an address was found in the field to be non-private (e.g. boarding house containing four or more boarders at the time the interviewer calls), the interviewer was instructed not to take an interview. However, a household member in hospital at the time of interview was included in the sample provided that he or she had not been away from home for more than six months and was expected to return. In this case a proxy interview was taken.

4. Clarke L et al. General Household Survey Advance Letter Experiment. *OPCS Social Survey Division, Survey Methodology Bulletin* No.21, September 1987.

5. Rauta I. A comparison of the census characteristics of respondents and non-respondents to the 1981 General Household Survey (GHS) *Statistical News*, November 1985, No.71.

6. Barnes R and Birch F (1975). The Census as an aid in estimating the characteristics of non-response in the General Household Survey. *OPCS Social Survey Division, New Methodology Series* NM1. (1975)

7. *Foster K et al. General Household Survey 1993*. HMSO 1995. Appendix C

215

Appendix C

General Houshold Survey 1998/99
Household Questionnaire

Areacode	Information already entered.	

Address Information already entered.
.... 1..30

Hhold Information already entered.
.... 1..4

StartDate Enter date interview with this household was started.

DateChk Is this....
The first time you've opened this
questionnaire 1
or the second or later time? 2
EMERGENCY CODE IF
COMPUTER'S DATE IS WRONG
AT LATER CHECK 5

IntEdit Code whether this is the interview stage or the edit stage.

Interview 1
OFFICE ONLY - EDIT 7

HOUSEHOLD INFORMATION

INFORMATION TO BE COLLECTED FOR ALL PERSONS IN ALL HOUSEHOLDS

1 Name Who normally lives at this address?
RECORD THE NAME (OR A UNIQUE
IDENTIFIER) FOR HOH, THEN A NAME/
IDENTIFIER FOR EACH MEMBER OF THE
HOUSEHOLD

(Enter text of at most 12 characters)

2 Sex Male 1
Female 2

3 Birth What is your date of birth?

FOR MONTH NOT GIVEN.....ENTER 6
FOR MONTH
FOR DAY NOT GIVEN..........ENTER 15
FOR DAY.

4 AgeIf **If Birth = DK OR REFUSAL**

What was your age last birthday?
98 or more = CODE 97

.... 0..97

5 MarStat **If Age>16**

ASK OR RECORD   CODE FIRST THAT APPLIES

Are you
single, that is, never married? 1
married and living with your
husband/wife? 2

married and separated from your
husband/wife? 3
divorced? 4
or widowed? 5

6 LiveWith **If Age>16 and Household size > 1 and Marstat = single, separated, divorced or widowed (codes 1, 3, 4 or 5)**

ASK OR RECORD
May I just check, are you living with
someone in the household as a couple?

Yes 1
No 2
SPONTANEOUS ONLY -
same sex couple 3

7 Hhldr **If Age>16 and Household size ≠1**

In whose name is the accommodation
owned or rented?
ASK FOR WHOLE GRID, THEN ASK
OR RECORD

This person alone 1
This person jointly 3
NOT owner/renter 5

8 HoHnum **Ask all households**

ENTER PERSON NUMBER OF HOH.
....   1..14

9 HoHprtnr **If HoHnum = 1..14 and married or cohabiting (Marstat = 2 or LiveWith = 1)**

THE HoH IS (.....)

ENTER THE PERSON NUMBER OF .
DMNAMES[HoHNum]'s
SPOUSE/PARTNER
NO SPOUSE/PARTNER = 15
.... 1..15

10 R I would now like to ask how the people in your
household are related to each other

CODE RELATIONSHIP - ... IS ...'S ....

Spouse 1
Cohabitee 2
Son/daughter (inc. adopted) 3
Step-son/daughter 4
Foster child 5
Son-in-law/daughter-in-law 6
Parent/guardian 7
Step-parent 8
Foster parent 9
Parent-in-law 10
Brother/sister (inc. adopted) 11
Step-brother/sister 12
Foster brother/sister 13
Brother/sister-in-law 14
Grand-child 15
Grand-parent 16
Other relative 17
Other non-relative 18

ACCOMMODATION TYPE

IntroAcc   The next section looks at the standard of people's housing.

All households

11 Accom   IS THE HOUSEHOLD'S ACCOMMODATION:

N.B. MUST BE SPACE USED BY HOUSEHOLD

a house or bungalow	1 →	Q12
a flat or maisonette	2 →	Q13
a room/rooms	3 →	Q15
or something else?	4 →	Q14

12 HseType   **If house/bungalow (Accom=1)**

IS THE HOUSE/BUNGALOW:

detached	1	
semi-detached	2	→ Q17
or terraced/end of terrace?	3	

13 FltTyp   **If flat/maisonette (Accom =2)**

IS THE FLAT/MAISONETTE:

a purpose-built block	1	
a converted house/some other kind of building?	2	→ Q15

14 AccOth   **If 'something else' (Accom = 4)**

IS THE ACCOMMODATION

a caravan, mobile home or houseboat	1 →	Q18
or some other kind of accommodation?	2 →	Q17

15 Storey   **If coded 2 or 3 at Accom**

What is the floor level of the main living part of the accommodation?

ASK OR RECORD

Basement/semi-basement	1	
Ground floor/street level	2	
1st floor	3	
2nd floor	4	→ Q16
3rd floor	5	
4th to 9th floor	6	
10th floor or higher	7	

16 HasLift   **If flat/maisonette or room(s)(codes 2or 3) at Accom:**

INTERVIEWER CODE: IS THERE A LIFT?

Yes	1	→ Q17
No	2	

17 DateBlt   **If not coded 1 at AccOth**

When was this building first built?

PROMPT IF NECESSARY - IF DK CODE YOUR ESTIMATE

before 1919	1	
between 1919 and 1944	2	
between 1945 and 1964	3	→ See Q18
between 1965 and 1984	4	
1985 or later	5	
DK but after 1944	6	

18 ShareH   **If Accom = 1, 4 or FltTyp = 2**

INTERVIEWER ASK OR CODE

May I just check, does anyone else live in this building apart from the people in your household?

(I.E. IS THERE ANYONE ELSE IN THE BUILDING WITH WHOM THE HOUSEHOLD COULD SHARE ROOMS OR FACILITIES?)

Yes	1	→ Q19
No	2	

19 ShareE   INTERVIEWER ASK OR CODE

Is there any empty living accommodation in this building outside your household's accommodation?

Yes	1	→ See Q20
No	2	

20 Share2   **If ShareH = 1 or Accom = 2 or 3**

Does your household (do you) have the whole accommodation to yourselves (yourself) or do you share any of it with someone outside your household?

Have the whole accommodation	1	
Share with someone else outside the household	2	→ See Q21

21 Share3   **If ShareE = 1 AND Share2 ≠ 2**

If all the empty accommodation in this building were occupied, would your household (you) have to share any part of your accommodation with anyone who had moved in?

Yes	1	→ See Q22
No	2	

22 Rooms1   **If Share2 = 2 OR Share3 = 1**

I want to ask you about all the rooms you have in your household's accommodation. Please include any rooms you sublet to other people and any rooms you share with people who are not in your household (or would share if someone moved into the empty accommodation).

23 Rooms2   **If Share2 ≠ 2 OR Share3 = 1**

I want to ask you about all the rooms you have in your household's accommodation (including any rooms you sublet to other people).

24 Bedrooms How many bedrooms do you have?
INCLUDE BEDSITTERS, BOXROOM,
ATTIC BEDROOMS

0..20

25 Kitover How many kitchens over 6.5 feet wide do you have?
NARROWEST SIDE MUST BE AT LEAST
6.5 FEET FROM WALL TO WALL

0..20

26 Kitunder How many kitchens under 6.5 feet do you have?

0..20

27 Living How many living rooms do you have?
INCLUDE DINING ROOMS HERE,
INCLUDE SUNLOUNGE OR CONSERVATORY
USED ALL YEAR ROUND.

0..20

28 Bathroom How many bathrooms do you have with plumbed in bath/shower?

0..20

29 Utility How many utility and other rooms do you have?

0..20 → See Q30

30-35 Shrms **If Nrms > 0 AND Share2 =2 OR (Share3 = 1)**
For each type of room mentioned at Q24-29

(TYPE OF ROOM)
How many rooms of this type are shared with other household(s) (or would be shared if someone moved into the empty accommodation)?

0..20 → Q36

Ask all households

36 GHSCentH ASK OR RECORD

Do you have any form of central heating, including electric storage heaters, in your (part of the) accommodation?

Yes .... 1 → Q37
No .... 2 → Q38

37 GHSCHFuel **If GHSCentH = 1**

Which type of fuel does it use?

CODE MAIN METHOD ONLY PROBE 'Hot Air'
FOR FUEL

Solid fuel: incl. coal, coke,
   wood, peat .... 1 ⌉
Electricity: storage heaters .... 2 |
Electricity: other
   (incl. oil filled radiators) .... 3 ⊢ → Q38
Gas/Calor gas .... 4 |
Oil .... 5 |
Other .... 6 ⌋

CONSUMER DURABLES

IntroDur Now I'd like to ask you about various household items you may have - this gives us an indication of how living standards are changing.

38 HasDur **Ask all households**

Does your household have any of the following items in your (part of the) accommodation?
INCLUDE ITEMS STORED OR UNDER REPAIR

39 Tvcol Colour TV set? PROMPT AS NECESSARY

1 only .... 1 ⌉→ Q40
more than one .... 2 ⌋
None .... 3 → Q42

40 UseColTV **If has 1 or more colour tv sets (Tvcol = 1 or 2)**

ASK OR RECORD

Is this/are any of these colour TV set(s) currently in use?

Yes .... 1 → Q42
No .... 2 → Q41

41 BrkColTV **If no colour tv sets currently in use (UseColTV = 2)**

Is this/are any of these colour TV set(s) broken but due to be repaired within 7 days?

Yes .... 1 ⌉→ Q42
No .... 2 ⌋

42 TVbw **All households**

Black and white TV set?

1 only .... 1 ⌉→ Q43
more than one .... 2 ⌋
None .... 3 → Q44

43 UseBwTV **If NO colour TV set in use and none intended for repair and has black and white tv (Tvcol = No or BrkColTV = Yes) AND (TvBw = 1 or 2)**

ASK OR RECORD

Is this/are any of these black and white TV set(s) currently in use?

Yes .... 1 → Q45
No .... 2 → Q44

44 BrkBwTV   **If no black and white TV sets currently in use**

Is this/are any of these black and white TV set(s) broken but due to be repaired within 7 days?

Yes .... 1 ⎤→   Q45
No .... 2 ⎦

45 SatCab   **All households**

Satellite or Cable TV receiver?

Yes 1
No 2

46 Video   Video recorder?

Yes 1
No 2

47 Freezer   Deep freezer or fridge freezer?
EXCLUDE FRIDGE ONLY

Yes 1
No 2

48 WashMach   Washing machine?

Yes 1
No 2

49 Drier   Tumble drier?

IF COMBINED WASHING MACHINE AND TUMBLE DRIER, CODE 1 FOR BOTH

Yes 1
No 2

50 DishWash   Dish washer?

Yes 1
No 2

51 MicroWve   Microwave oven? ...

Yes 1
No 2

52 Telephon   Telephone?

SHARED TELEPHONES LOCATED IN PUBLIC HALLWAYS TO BE INCLUDED ONLY IF THIS HOUSEHOLD IS RESPONSIBLE FOR PAYINGTHE ACCOUNT. INCLUDE MOBILE PHONES

Yes 1
No 2

53 Cdplay   Compact disc (CD) player?

Yes 1
No 2

54 Computer   Home computer?
EXCLUDE: VIDEO GAMES

Yes .... 1 ⎤→   Q55
No .... 2 ⎦

55 UseVcl   Do (any of) you at present own or have continuous use of any motor vehicles? INCLUDE COMPANY CARS - UNLESS NO PRIVATE USE ALLOWED

Yes .... 1 →   Q56
No .... 2 →   Q59

56 TypeVcl   **For each vehicle mentioned (If UseVcl =1)**

I would now like to ask about the (Nth) vehicle. Is it:

CAR INCLUDES MINIBUSES, MOTOR CARAVANS, 'PEOPLE CARRIERS' AND 4-WHEELDRIVE PASSENGER VEHICLES.

LIGHT VAN INCLUDES PICKUPS AND THOSE 4-WHEEL DRIVE VEHICLES, LAND ROVERS AND JEEPS THAT DO NOT HAVE SIDE WINDOWS BEHIND THE DRIVER

a car .... 1 →   Q57
a light van 2
a motor cycle .... 3 →   Q58
or some other motor vehicle? .... 4 ⎦

57 PrivVcl   **For each vehicle mentioned**
If vehicle is a car (TypeVcl =1)

Is the car...

privately owned .... 1 ⎤→   Q58
or is it a company car? .... 2 ⎦

58 AnyMore   **For each vehicle mentioned (If UseVcl =1)**

Do (any of) you at present own or have continuous use of any more motor vehicles? INCLUDE COMPANY CARS - UNLESS NO PRIVATE USE ALLOWED

Yes .... 1 ⎤→   Q59
No .... 2 ⎦

TENURE

59 Ten1   **All households**

In which of these ways do you occupy this accommodation?
SHOW CARD A
MAKE SURE ANSWER APPLIES TO HoH
i.e. HoHnum = 1

Own outright .... 1 ⎤
Buying it with the help of a   ⎥→See Q68
    mortgage or loan .... 2 ⎦
Pay part rent and part mortgage
    (shared ownership) .... 3 →See Q65

219

Rent it .... 4 ⌉
Live here rent-free (including rent-free
  in relative's/friend's property;   →   Q60
  excluding squatting) .... 5 ⌋
Squatting .... 6 →See Q68

60 Tied   **If 'rents/rent free' at Ten1 (code 4 or 5)**

Does the accommodation go with the job of
anyone in the household?

Yes .... 1 ⌉
                                →   Q61
No .... 2 ⌋

61 Llord   Who is your landlord?
               CODE FIRST THAT APPLIES

the local authority/council/
  New Town Development/
  Scottish Homes .... 1 ⌉
a housing association or co-operative
  or charitable trust 2
employer (organisation) of a
  household member 3
another organisation .... 4 → Q62
relative/friend (before you lived here)
  of a household member 5
employer (individual) of a household
  member 6
another individual private landlord? ... 7 ⌋

62 Furn   Is the accommodation provided: ...

furnished .... 1 ⌉
partly furnished (e.g. carpets and
  curtains only) .... 2 → Q63
or unfurnished? .... 3 ⌋

63 LandLive **If codes 5, 6 or 7 at Llord (ie. rented from
                  an individual)**

Does the landlord live in this building?

Yes .... 1 ⌉
                              →See Q64
No .... 2 ⌋

64 RentBusn **If 'rents/rent-free' at Ten1 (code 4 or 5)**

Are any business premises included in the rent for
this accommodation(in the accommodation
provided)?

Yes .... 1 ⌉
                              →See Q65
No .... 2 ⌋

HOUSING BENEFIT

65 HB   **If 'shared ownership or rents' or 'rent free'at
           Ten1 (codes 3, 4 or 5)**

Some people qualify for Housing Benefit, that is a
rent rebate or allowance.

Are you (or HOH) receiving Housing Benefit
from your local authority or local Social
Security office?

Yes .... 1 →See Q68
No .... 2 →   Q66

66 HbWait   **If HB = 2**

Are you (or HoH) waiting to receive Housing
Benefit or to hear the outcome of a claim?

Yes .... 1 →See Q68
No .... 2 →   Q67

67 HbChk   **If HBWait = 2**

May I just check, does the local authority or
local Social Security office pay any part of your
rent?

Yes .... 1 ⌉
                             →See Q68
No .... 2 ⌋

68 HbOthr   **If there is someone aged 16 and over, apart
           from HOH and partner, in the household.**

Is anyone (else) in the household receiving
a rent rebate, a rent allowance or Housing
Benefit?

Yes .... 1 ⌉
                              →   Q69
No .... 2 ⌋

MIGRATION

69 Reslen   **Ask All**

How many years have you /has(...) lived at this
address?
IF UNDER 1, CODE AS 0
                           0..97 →See Q70

70 HMnths   **If Reslen = 0**

How many months have you/has (...)
lived here?
                           1..12 →See Q71

71 Nmoves   **If Reslen < 5 years**

How many moves have you /has (...)
made in the last 5 years, not counting
moves between places outside Gt. Britain?
                           0..97 →   Q72

72 Cry1   **All persons**

In what country were you/was (...) born?

UK, British .... 1 → Q76
Irish Republic .... 6 ⌉
Hong Kong .... 36 → Q75
China .... 58 ⌋
Other .... 59 → Q73

73 CrySpec   **If 'other' at Cry1 (code 59)**

    TYPE IN COUNTRY (enter text of at
most 40 characters)   →   Q74

74 CryCode   CHOOSE COUNTRY FROM CODING
FRAME
               1..116   →   Q75

75 Arruk   **If Cry1 = 6, 36, 58 or 59 (Irish Republic,
Hong Kong, China or Other)**

    In what year did you (...) first arrive in the
United Kingdom?

    ENTER IN 4 DIGIT FORMAT E.G.: 1985
               1900..1998   →   Q76

76 FathCob   **All persons**

    ASK OR RECORD
    In what country was your / (...'s) father born?

UK, British 1	
Irish Republic 6	→ Q79
Hong Kong 36	
China 58	
Other 5	→ Q77

77 CrySpec1   **If 'other' at FathCob (code 59)**

    TYPE IN COUNTRY

    (enter text of at most 40 characters) ....   →   Q78

78 CryCode1   CHOOSE COUNTRY FROM CODING
FRAME
               1..116   →   Q79

79 MothCob   **All persons**

    ASK OR RECORD
    In what country was your/ (...'s)mother born?

UK, British 1	
Irish Republic 6	→ Q82
Hong Kong 36	
China 58	
Other 59	→ Q80

80 CrySpec2   **If 'other' at MothCob (code 59)**

    TYPE IN COUNTRY   →   Q81

    (enter text of at most 40 characters)

81 CryCode2   CHOOSE COUNTRY FROM CODING FRAME
               1..116   →   Q82

82 Ethnic   **All persons**

    SHOW CARD B
    [*] To which of these groups do you consider
you belong?

White 1
Black - Caribbean 2
Black - African 3
Black - Other Black groups 4
Indian 5
Pakistani 6
Bangladeshi 7
Chinese 8
None of these 9

END OF HOUSEHOLD QUESTIONNAIRE

General Houshold Survey 1998/99
Individual Questionnaire

Iswitch **All adults**

THIS IS WHERE YOU START RECORDING
ANSWERS FOR INDIVIDUALS
DO YOU WANT TO RECORD ANSWERS FOR
(...)NOW OR LATER?

Yes, now 1
Later 2
or is there no interview with
  this person? 3

PersProx **If Iswitch = 1**

INTERVIEWER: IS THE INTERVIEW ABOUT(...)
BEING GIVEN:

In person 1
or by someone else? 2

ProxyNum **If ISwitch = 1 and PersProx = 2**

ENTER PERSON NUMBER OF
PERSON GIVING THE INFORMATION

1..14

EMPLOYMENT

1 Wrking **All adults**

Did you do any paid work in the 7 days ending
Sunday the (n), either as an employee or
as self-employed?

Yes.. 1 →   Q14
No .... 2 → See Q2

2 SchemeET **Men aged 16-64 and women aged 16-62
and Wrking = no**

Were you on a government scheme for
employment training?

Yes.. 1 →   Q3
No .... 2 →   Q4

3 Trn **If SchemeET = Yes**

Last week were you ...
CODE FIRST THAT APPLIES

with an employer, or on a project
  providing work experience or practical
  training? .... 1 ⎤
or at a college or training centre? ...... 2 ⎦ → Q14

4 JbAway **If 'no' (code 2) at Wrking (all ages) and
'no' at SchemeET**

Did you have a job or business that you
were away from?

Yes.. 1 →   Q14
No .... 2 ⎤
Waiting to take up a new job/business ⎥ → Q5
  already obtained .... 3 ⎦

5 OwnBus **If not in paid work, on a govt scheme
or away from a job (Working = 2 and
JBAway = 2 or 3 and SchemeET = 2)**

Did you do any unpaid work in that week
for any business that you own?

Yes.. 1 → See Q8
No .... 2 →   Q6

6 RelBus **If 'no' at OwnBus**

...or that a relative owns?

Yes.. 1 → See Q8
No .... 2 → See Q7

7 Looked **If not working, not on a govt scheme, not
doing unpaid work.**

Thinking of the 4 weeks ending Sunday the
DMDLSUN, were you looking for any kind of
paid work or government training scheme at
any time in those 4 weeks?

Yes.. 1 → See Q8
No .... 2 →   Q9
Waiting to take up a job .... 3 → See Q8

8 StartJ **If Looked = Yes**

If a job or a place on a government scheme
had been available in the week ending Sunday
the (n), would you have been able to start
within 2 weeks?

Yes.. 1 → See Q10
No .... 2 →   Q9

9 YInAct **If Looked = No or StartJ = No**

What was the main reason you did not seek
any work in the last 4 weeks/would not be able
to start in the next 2 weeks?

Student .... 1 ⎤
Looking after the family/home .... 2 ⎥
Temporarily sick or injured .... 3 ⎥ → Q10
Long-term sick or disabled .... 4 ⎥
Retired from paid work .... 5 ⎥
None of these .... 6 ⎦

10 Everwk **If unemployed or inactive last week
(including those waiting to take up a job)**

Have you ever had a paid job, apart from casual
or holiday work?

Yes.. 1 →   Q11
No .... 2 → See Q12

11 DtJbl **If Unemployed and Everwk = Yes or YInAct
= TempSick**

When did you leave your last PAID job?
FOR MONTH NOT GIVEN.....ENTER 6 FOR MONTH
FOR DAY NOT GIVEN.........ENTER 15 FOR DAY

DATE   → See Q12

12 WantaJob

Men aged 16-68, women 16-64 and YlnAct - 1, 2, 5 or 6 or Trn = 2

Even though you were not looking for work (last week) would you like to have a regular paid job at the moment - either a full or part-time job?

Yes .... 1 → Q13
No .... 2 → See Q14

13 NablStrt

If WantaJob = Yes

If a job or a place on a government scheme had been available last week, would you have been able to start within 2 weeks?

Yes .... 1 ⎤
No .... 2 ⎦ → See Q14

14 IndD

All economically active except those unemployed who have never worked and are not waiting to take up a job and unemployed or economically inactive who have had a job in the past.

CURRENT OR LAST JOB

What did the firm/organisation you worked for mainly make or do (at the place where you worked)?

DESCRIBE FULLY - PROBE MANUFACTURING or PROCESSING or DISTRIBUTING AND MAIN GOODS PRODUCED, MATERIALS USED WHOLESALE or RETAIL ETC.
(Enter text at most 80 characters) → Q15

15 OccT

JOBTITLE CURRENT OR LAST JOB

What was your (main) job (in the week ending Sunday the (n))?
(Enter text at most 30 characters) → Q16

16 OccD

CURRENT OR LAST JOB

What did you mainly do in your job?
CHECK SPECIAL QUALIFICATIONS/TRAINING NEEDED TO DO THE JOB
(Enter text at most 80 characters) → Q17

17 Stat

Were you working as an employee or were you self-employed?

Employee .... 1 → Q18
Self-employed .... 2 → Q20

18 Manage

If employee (Stat = 1)

Did you have any managerial duties, or were you supervising any other employees?
ASK OR RECORD

Manager .... 1 ⎤
Foreman/supervisor .... 2 → Q19
Not manager/supervisor ...... 3 ⎦

19 NEmplee

How many employees were there at the place where you worked?

1-2 .... 1 ⎤
3-24 .... 2 ⎥
25-99 .... 3 ⎥
100-499 .... 4 → Q22
500-999 .... 5 ⎥
1000 or more .... 6 ⎥
DK, but less than 25 .... 7 ⎥
DK, but 25 or more .... 8 ⎦

20 Solo

If self-employed (Stat = 2)

Were you working on your own or did you have employees?

on own/with partner(s) but
no employees .... 1 → Q22
with employees .... 2 → Q21

21 SNEmplee

If self-employed with employees (Solo = 2)

How many people did you employ at the place where you worked?

1-5 .... 1 ⎤
6-24 .... 2 ⎥
25 or over .... 3 → Q22
DK but has/had employees ... 4 ⎦

22 FtPtWk

All economically active, except those unemployed who have never worked and are not waiting to take up a job and unemployed or economically inactive who have had a job in the past.

In your (main) job were you working:

full time .... 1 → See Q23
or part time? 2   and Q24

23 EmpStY

Employees (Main job/government scheme) (Working and Stat = 1)

In which year did you start working continuously for your current employer?

1900..2005 → See Q25

24 SempStY

Self-employed (main job) (Working and Stat = 2)

In which year did you start working continuously as a self-employed person?

1900..2005 → See Q25

25 JobstM

If less than or equal to 8 years since started working continuously for current employer/ as a self-employed person?

and which month in (YEAR..) was that?

Jan .... 1 ⎤
Feb .... 2 → See Q26
Mar .... 3 ⎦

223

Apr 4	
May 5	
Jun 6	
Jul 7	
Aug 8	→ See Q26
Sep 9	
Oct 10	
Nov 11	
Dec 12	

26 EverOT — **All working (Working = 1 or JbAway = 1 or SchemeET = 1)**

HOURS IN MAIN JOB ONLY

Do you ever do any work which you would regard as paid or unpaid overtime?

Yes .... 1 → Q28
No .... 2 → Q27

27 Totus1 — **If No at EverOT or Yes at Ownbus/Relbus**

How many hours per week do you usually work in your (main) job/business- please exclude mealbreaks?

97 OR MORE = 97
0.00..99.00 → See Q32

28 Usuhr — **If 'Yes' at EverOT**

Thinking of your (main) job/ business, how many hours per week do you usually work - please exclude mealbreaks and overtime?

97 OR MORE = 97
0.00..99.00 → Q29

29.PotHr — How many hours PAID overtime do you usually work per week?

97 OR MORE = 97
0.00..99.00 → Q30

30.UotHr — How many hours UNPAID overtime do you usually work per week?

97 OR MORE = 97
0.00..99.00 → Q31

31.AgreeHrs — Your total usual hours come to (...). Is that about right, or not?
IF TOTAL IS NOT (...) CHECK THAT

Usualhrs (basic) = (...)
Usual paid o/t= (...)
Usual unpaid o/t= (...)
97 OR MORE = 97

Yes 1
No .... 2 → Q32

32 SecndJob — **All working (Working = 1 or JbAway = 1 or SchemeET = 1)**

Last week did you do any other paid work or have any other job or business in addition to the one you have just told me about?

Yes 1
No .... 2 → See Q33

33 UnPaidHr — **If OwnBus=1 or RelBus=1, others go to Pensions**

Thinking of the business that you did unpaid work for how many hours unpaid work did you do for that business in the 7 days ending last Sunday?

1..97 → Q34

34. UnPaidHm — Did you do this work mainly.................

somewhere quite separate from home, ... 1
in different places using home as a base, ... 2
or in your own home or in the same grounds or buildings as your home?, ... 3
SPONTANEOUSLY ONLY:
some days at home, other days somewhere quite separate from home 4

→ Pensions

PENSIONS

1 PenSchm — **If employee (including those temporarily away from job) or on a government scheme (If Stat = 1 or SchemeET = 1)**

(Thinking now of your present job,) some people (will) receive a pension from their employer when they retire, as well as the state pension.
Does your present employer run a pension scheme or superannuation scheme for any employees?
INCLUDE CONTRIBUTORY AND NON-CONTRIBUTORY SCHEMES

Yes .... 1 → Q2
No .... 2 → Q5

2 Eligible — **If 'yes' at PenSchm (code 1)**

Are you eligible to belong to your employer's pension scheme?

Yes .... 1 → Q3
No .... 2 → Q5

3 EmPenShm — **If 'yes' at Eligible (code 1)**

Do you belong to your employer's pension scheme?

Yes 1
No .... 2 → Q5

4 PschPoss

If DK or refusal at PenSchm or Eligible or EmPenShm

So do you think it's possible that you belong to a pension scheme run by your employer, or do you definitely not belong to one?

Possibly belongs 1	] →	Q5
Definitely not 2		

5 PersPnt1

If under retirement age and NOT self-employed or other employees or unemployed who have had a job

INTERVIEWER - INTRODUCE IF NECESSARY. Now I would like to ask you about personal pensions (rather than employers' pension schemes).

6 PersPens

Since 1988, people have been allowed to contract out of the State Earnings Related Pension Scheme (SERPS) and arrange their own personal pension. The DSS then pays part of your National Insurance contributions into your chosen personal pension plan.

Do you at present have any such arrangements?

Yes .... 1 →		Q7
No .... 2 →		Q9

7 PersCont

If 'yes' at PersPens (code1)

Do you make any extra contributions over and above any rebated National Insurance contributions made by the DSS on your behalf?

Yes 1	] →	Q8
No 2		

8 EmpCont

If employee in last week and 'yes' at PersPens

Does your employer contribute to the scheme?

Yes 1	] →	Q10
No 2		

9 EverPers

If 'no' or DK at PersPens

Have you ever had any such arrangements?

Yes 1	] →	Q10
No 2		

10 OthPers

All as for PersPnt1

(Apart from the contributions you've already told me about,) do you make any other contributions to personal pensions or Retirement Annuities for which the contributions are income tax deductible?

Yes 1	] →	See Q11
No 2		

11 PersPnt2

If working (including those temporarily away from job) and self-employed

INTERVIEWER - INTRODUCE IF NECESSARY. Now I would like to ask you about personal pension schemes.

12 SePrsPen

The self-employed may arrange pensions for themselves for which the contributions are income tax deductible. These schemes are sometimes called 'self-employed pensions' or 'Section 226 Retirement Annuities' or 'personal pensions'.

Do you at present contribute to one of these schemes?

Yes....................................... 1 →	Education
No .... 2 →	Q13

13 SeEvPers

If no or DK at SePrsPen

Have you ever contributed to one of these schemes?

Yes....................................... 1	] → Education
No 2	

EDUCATION

All those aged 16-69

1 AgeLftSc

How old were you when you left school? (NOT TECHNICAL COLLEGE) NEVER WENT TO SCHOOL (1) STILL AT SCHOOL (98)

1..98 → See Q2

2 PresEd

If aged 16-69 and not still at school but has attended school (AgeLftSc NOT 1 or 98)

Apart from leisure classes, and ignoring holidays, are you at present doing any of the types of education shown on this card? (SHOW CARD C)

Yes....................................... 1 →	Q3
No .... 2 →	Q4

3 EdNow

If PresEd = yes (code 1)

What are you doing at present? CODE FIRST THAT APPLIES

Studying at a college on a YT or Employment Training (ET) programme .... 1 →		Q5
studying at a college or university or polytechnic full-time (INCLUDING SANDWICH COURSE STUDY) .... 2 →		See Q7
training in nursing, physiotherapy, ... or a similar medical subject 3	]	
studying at college part-time or on day or block release (INCLUDING ..... COURSES OF UNDER 3 MONTHS) 4	] →	Q5
Open University Course 5		
A correspondence course 6		

4 FurthrEd

If No, DK or Refusal at PresEd (PresEd = 2, 8 or 9)

I would now like to ask you about any education you may have had since leaving school. Have you EVER had any full-time or part-time further education of the types shown on this card? (SHOW CARD C)

Yes.....................................1 → Q5
No ....2 → See Q7

5 LastSch

If coded 1 or 3-6 or DK or Refusal at EdNow or coded 1, DK or Refusal at FurthrEd

Now thinking of your full-time education, what type of school or college did you LAST attend full-time? EXCLUDE: COURSES OF UNDER 3 MONTHS

Was it.....
RUNNING PROMPT

Elementary or secondary school .... 1 → See Q7
University 2
Polytechnic (INCLUDE: SCOTTISH
   CENTRAL INSTITUTIONS) .... 3 → Q6
Nursing school or teaching hospital ... 4
Or some other type of college? 5

6 AgeLftFt

If coded 2-6 at LastSch

How old were you when you left there, or when you finished or stopped your course?

1..97   → See Q7

7 QualsB

All adults aged 16-69 (except proxy interviews and those who have never attended school) (NOT AgeLftSc = 1)

SHOW CARD D

Have you passed any examinations of the types listed on this card?

Yes.....................................1 → Q8
No ....2 → Q16

8 LevCode1

If 'yes' (code 1) at QualsB

Which ones have you obtained? (Enter at most 9 codes)

CSE .... 1 → Q9
GCSE.. 2 → Q10
GCE 'O' levels .... 3 → Q11
GCE 'AS' levels .... 4 → Q12
GCE 'A' levels .... 5 → Q13
School certificate or Matric .... 6 ⎤
Higher School Certificate .... 7 ⎦ Q16
Scottish exams .... 8 → Q14
Foreign school exams .... 9 → Q16

9 CSELev

If CSE (code 1 at QualsB))

What CSE grade(s) do you have? (Enter at most 3 codes)

Ungraded or DK grade .... 1 ⎤
Grade 1 .... 2 ⎥ → Q15
Grades 2-5 .... 3 ⎦

10 GCSELev

If GCSE (code 2 at QualsB)

What GCSE grade(s) do you have? (Enter at most 2 codes)

Grades A, B, C .... 1 ⎤ → Q15
Grades D, E, F, G .... 2 ⎦

11 OLevel

If GCE 'O' Level (code 3 at QualsB)

What GCE 'O'level grade(s) do you have? (Enter at most 3 codes)

obtained before 1975 .... 1 ⎤
Grades A, B, C .... 2 ⎥ → Q15
Grades D,E .... 3 ⎦

12 ASLevel

If GCE 'AS' Level (code 4 at QualsB)

What GCE AS level grade(s) do you have? (1989 OR LATER) (Enter at most 3 codes)

Grades A,B .... 1 ⎤
Grade C .... 2 ⎥ → Q15
Grade D,E .... 3 ⎦

13 Alevel

If GCE 'A' Level (code 5 at QualsB) .

What GCE A level grade(s) do you have? (Enter at most 4 codes)

Grades A,B .... 1 ⎤
Grade C .... 2 ⎥
Grade D,E .... 3 ⎥ → Q15
No grade or don't know grade. .... 4 ⎦

14 ScotExam

If Scottish Exams (code 8 at QualsB)

SHOW CARD E
Do you have any of the exams on this card? (Enter at most 8 codes)

Scottish Leaving Certificate
   (lower grade) OR Scottish Universities
   Preliminary Exam 1
Scottish Certificate of Education
   Ordinary Grade(before 1973) 2
SCE ordinary grade bands
   A, B, C.. 3
SCE ordinary grade bands D, E .... 4 → Q15
Standard grade level 1-3 5
Standard grade level 4,5 6
Standard grade level 6,7 or no
   award 7
SLC/SCE/SUPE at higher grade or
   Certificateof Sixth Year Studies 8

15 Nsub For each type of exam mentioned at questions 13-18

ASK AFTER EACH TYPE OF EXAM MENTIONED (EXCEPT FOREIGN SCHOOL EXAMS)
In how many subjects at (LEVEL) did you pass?
1..20 .... → Q16

16 QualsC **All adults aged 16-69 (except proxy interviews and those who never attended school)**

SHOW CARD F
Do you have any of the qualifications listed on this card or have you passed any of these examinations, whether you are using them or not?

Yes. .... 1 → Q17
No .... 2 → Q18

17 LevCode2 **If 'yes' (code 1) at QualsC**

Which qualifications do you have?
(Enter at most 10 codes)

Recognised trade apprenticeship completed 1
Clerical and commercial qualifications(eg. typing, shorthand, book-keeping, commerce 2
City and Guilds Certificate - Craft/ Intermediate/ Ordinary or Part 1 3
City and Guilds Certificate - Advanced/Final or Part II 4
City and Guilds Certificate - Full Technological or Part III 5
BTEC First Award 6
Ordinary National Certificate (ONC) or Diploma (OND), BEC/TEC/BTEC National/General Certificate or Diploma 7
Higher National Certificate (HNC) or Diploma BEC/TEC/BTEC Higher Certificate or Higher Diploma 8
SCOTVEC National (1-12 modules) .. 9
SCOTVEC National (13 or more modules) 10   → Q18

18 QualsD **All adults aged 16-69 (except proxy interviews and those who never attended school)**

SHOW CARD G
Do you have any of the qualifications listed on this card or have you passed any of these examinations, whether you are using them or not?

Yes .... 1 → Q19
No .... 2 → Daycare

19 LevCode3 **If 'yes' (code 1) at QualsD**

Which qualifications do you have?
(Enter at most 9 codes)

Nursing qualifications (eg SEN, SRN, SCM, RGN) 1
Teaching qualifications 2
University Diploma 3
University or CNAA First Degree (eg BA, BSc) 4
University or CNAA Higher Degree (eg MSc, PhD) 5   → Daycare
Membership of professional institution 6
Other non-school foreign qualifications 7
Any other qualifications not already mentioned 8

DAYCARE

1 AskDCare **For each child under 14 years**

THE NEXT SECTION IS ABOUT DAYCARE FOR CHILDREN. WE ONLY NEED TO COLLECT THIS INFORMATION ONCE FOR EACH CHILD IN THE HOUSEHOLD. WHO WILL ANSWER THE DAYCARE SECTION FOR (CHILD'S NAME)?

INTERVIEWER ENTER PERSON NUMBER

1..14   → Q2

2 AskNow INTERVIEWER: DO YOU WANT TO ASK THIS SECTION FOR(CHILD'S NAME) NOW OR LATER? IF YOU HAVE ALREADY ASKED THIS SECTION FOR (CHILD'SNAME), DO NOT CHANGE FROM CODE 1.

Yes, now/already asked .... 1 → Q4
Later.. 2 → Q3

3 CstillDC **If AskNow = 2**

REMINDER
The following adults still need to answer the daycare section on behalf of some of the children.   → Q4

4 InfTerm **If AskNow = 1**

ASK OR RECORD
Interview is taking place during the...:

Easter holidays 1998 1
Summer term 2
Summer holidays 3
Autumn term 4   → Q5
Christmas holidays 5
Spring term 6
Easter holidays 1999 7

5 UseCare

Some people make arrangements for their children to be looked after, particularly during term time. Here is a card which shows a list of arrangements. (SHOW CARD H)

Looking at this card, can you please tell me do you or anyone else in this household currently make any of these arrangements for (NAME) during term time (made any of these arrangements for (NAME) last term?

EXCLUDE PARENTS (IN THE HOUSEHOLD) FROM CODE 9 'Relative'
EXCLUDE SCHOOL (CODES 11 or 12) IF CHILD IS ATTENDING FULL-TIME SCHOOLING

Yes .... 1 → Q6
No .... 2 → Q17

6 EligSchl

If UseCare = yes and child aged 4 or 5

Is/Was (NAME) attending full time primary schooling this/last term?

Yes - school .... 1 → Q12
No - pre-school age .... 2 → Q7

7 TypeCre1

All children aged < 4 OR If EligSchl = no

SHOW CARD I
Looking at Card I, which of the arrangements listed on the card are currently made (were made last term)for (NAME)?

CODE ALL THAT APPLY

LA/maintained school .... 1 ⎤
Private school 2
Play group 3
Parent and toddler group 4
Day nursery at workplace 5
Other nurseries .... 6 → Q8
Registered childminder 7
Nanny 8
Au Pair 9
Relative 10
Friend or neighbour 11
Other carer...................................... 12 ⎦

8 CareWrk1

For each type of care mentioned at TypeCre1

Is the arrangement with the (TYPE OF CARE) made to enable you or your partner to go out to work?

Yes.................................... 1 → Q9
No .... 2 → Q17

9 WhoWork1

For each type of care mentioned at TypeCre1 (If CareWrk1 = yes)

Who does the arrangement with the (TYPE OF CARE) enable to go out to work?

You .... 1 ⎤
Partner .... 2 → Q10
Both .... 3 ⎦

10 HowDay1

How many morning or afternoon sessions per week does/did (NAME) usually attend at/with the (TYPE OF CARE), including any sessions at weekends? IF CHILD ATTENDS FOR ONLY PART OF MORNING OR AFTERNOON COUNT THIS AS A COMPLETE SESSION

0..14   →   Q11

11 HowEve1

How many evening or overnight sessions per week does/did (NAME) usually attend at/with the (TYPE OF CARE), including any sessions at weekends?

0..14   →   Q17

12 TypeCre2

All children aged >5 OR If EligSchl = no

SHOW CARD J
Looking at Card J, which of the arrangements listed on the card are currently made/were made last term for (NAME)?

CODE ALL THAT APPLY

After school clubs/play schemes .... 1 ⎤
Registered childminder 2
Nanny 3
Au Pair .... 4 → Q13
Relative 5
Friend or neighbour 6
Other carer...................................... 7 ⎦

13 CareWrk2

For each type of care mentioned at TypeCre2

Is this arrangement made to enable you or your partner to go out to work?

Yes.................................... 1 → Q14
No .... 2 → Q17

14 WhoWork2

For each type of care mentioned at TypeCre2 If CareWrk2 = yes

Who does the arrangement with the (TYPE OF CARE) enable to go out to work?

You .... 1 ⎤
Partner .... 2 → Q15
Both .... 3 ⎦

15 HowDay2

How many morning or afternoon sessions per week does/did (NAME) usually attend at/with the (TYPE OF CARE), including any sessions at weekends?

IF CHILD ATTENDS FOR ONLY PART OF MORNING OR AFTERNOON COUNT THIS AS A COMPLETE SESSION

0..14   →   Q16

16 HowEve2

How many evening or overnight sessions per week does/did (NAME) usually attend at/with the (TYPE OF CARE), including any sessions at weekends?

0..14   →   Q17

17 HolsCare — **For all children under 14 years (If AskNow = 1 or 2)**

During these/the last school holidays did you (or anyone else in the household make arrangements for (NAME) to be looked after?

Yes .... 1 → Q18
No .... 2 → Health

18 HolArran — **If HolsCare = yes**

Were/are these the same as during this/last term time?

Exactly the same arrangements
  as term time .... 1 ⌉
Same arrangements as term time   ⎬ → Health
  but different hours .... 2 ⌋
Different arrangements from term
  time .... 3 → Q19

19 TypeHCre — **If HolArran = 3 (different arrangements from term time)**

SHOW CARD K

Looking at Card K, can you please tell me which of the arrangements listed on the card you made last holidays (are making these school holidays) for (NAME) that is during the (...) holidays?

CODE ALL THAT APPLY

Play group .... 1 ⌉
Parent and toddler group .... 2 ⎮
Day nursery at workplace .... 3 ⎮
Other nurseries .... 4 ⎮
Holiday schemes/clubs .... 5 ⎮
Registered childminder .... 6 ⎬ → Q21
Nanny .... 7 ⎮
Au Pair .... 8 ⎮
Relative .... 9 ⎮
Friend or neighbour .... 10 ⌋
Other carer, SPECIFY AT NEXT
  QUESTION .... 11 → Q20

20 XtypHCre — **If TypeHCare = 11**

SPECIFY OTHER TYPE OF CARE

ENTER TEXT OF AT MOST
40 CHARACTERS   → Q21

21 CareWrk3 — **For each type of care mentioned at TypeHCre**

Is this arrangement made to enable you or your partner to go out to work?

Yes .... 1 → Q22
No .... 2 → Health

22 WhoWork3 — **For each type of care mentioned at TypeHCre If CareWrk3 = yes**

Who does the arrangement with the (TYPE OF CARE) enable to go out to work?

You .... 1 ⌉
Partner .... 2 ⎬ → Q23
Both .... 3 ⌋

23 HolMany — On how many days during the (...) holidays did/will you use the (TYPE OF CARE) to provide care for (NAME)

1..50   → Health

GENERAL HEALTH

Ask all (except proxy informants)

1 Genhlth [*] — Over the last twelve months would you say your health has on the whole been good, fairly good, or not good?

Good .... 1 ⌉
Fairly good .... 2 ⎬ → Q2
Not good .... 3 ⌋

Ask all

2 Illness [*] — Do you have any long-standing illness, disability or infirmity? By long-standing, I mean anything that has troubled you over a period of time or that is likely to affect you over a period of time?

Yes .... 1 → Q3
No .... 2 → Q8

3 Lmatter [*] — **If 'yes' at Illness (code 1)**

What is the matter with you?

RECORD ONLY WHAT RESPONDENT SAYS.

Enter text of at most 100 characters   → Q4

4 LMatNum — HOW MANY LONGSTANDING ILLNESSES OR INFIRMITIES DOES RESPONDENT HAVE?

ENTER NUMBER OF LONGSTANDING COMPLAINTS MENTIONED
IF MORE THAN 6 - TAKE THE SIX THAT THE RESPONDENT CONSIDERS THE MOST IMPORTANT

1..6   → Q5

5 Lmat — **For each illness mentioned at LMatNum**

WHAT IS THE MATTER WITH RESPONDENT?

ENTER ONE OF CONDITIONS/SYMPTOMS RESPONDENT MENTIONED
(Enter text of at most 40 characters)   → Q6

229

6 ICD CODE FOR COMPLAINT AT LMAT

Enter text of at most 12 characters   →   Q7

7 LimitAct **If 'yes' at Illness (code 1)**

Does this illness or disability (Do any of these illnesses or disabilities) limit your activities in any way?

Yes .... 1 ⎤ →   Q8
No .... 2 ⎦

8 CutDown [*] **Ask all**

Now I'd like you to think about the 2 weeks ending yesterday. During those 2 weeks, did you have to cut down on any of the things you usually do (about the house/at work or in your free time) because of (answers at LMatter) or some other) illness or injury?

Yes .... 1 →   Q9
No .... 2 →   Q11

9 NdysCutD **If 'yes' at CutDown (Code 1)**

How many days was this in all during these 2 weeks, including Saturdays and Sundays?

1..14   →   Q10

10 Cmatter [*] What was the matter with you?

Enter text of at most 40 characters   →   Q11

11 DocTalk **Ask all**

During the 2 weeks ending yesterday, apart from any visit to a hospital, did you talk to a doctor for any reason at all, either in person or by telephone?

EXCLUDE: CONSULTATIONS MADE ON BEHALF OF CHILDREN UNDER 16 AND PERSONS OUTSIDE THE HOUSEHOLD.

Yes .... 1 →   Q12
No .... 2 →   Q20

12 Nchats **If 'yes' (code 1) at Doc Talk**

How many times did you talk to a doctor in these 2 weeks?

1..9   →   Q13

13 WhsBhlf **For each consultation**

On whose behalf was this consultation made?

Informant .... 1 →   Q15
Other member of household
   16 or over .... 2 →   Q14

14 ForPerNo **If WhsBhlf = Other**

CODE WHO CONSULTATION WAS MADE FOR (PERSON NUMBER)   →   Q15

15 NHS **For each consultation**

Was this consultation...

Under the National Health Service .... 1 ⎤ →   Q16
or paid for privately? .... 2 ⎦

16 GP Was the doctor...

RUNNING PROMPT

A GP (ie a family doctor) .... 1 ⎤ →   Q18
or a specialist .... 2 ⎦
or some other kind of doctor?
(SPECIFY AT NEXT QUESTION) ..... 3 →   Q17

17 XGP **If GP = Other**

Specify type of doctor.

ENTER TEXT OF AT MOST 20 CHARACTERS   →   Q18

18 DocWhere **For each consultation**

Did you talk to the doctor...

RUNNING PROMPT

By telephone .... 1 ⎤
at your home .... 2 ⎥
in the doctor's surgery .... 3 ⎥ →   Q19
at a health centre .... 4 ⎥
or elsewhere? .... 5 ⎦

19 Presc Did the doctor give (send) you a prescription?

Yes .... 1 ⎤ →   Q20
No .... 2 ⎦

20 OutPatnt **Ask all**

During the months of (LAST 3 COMPLETE CALENDAR MONTHS) did you attend as a patient the casualty or outpatient department of a hospital (apart from straightforward ante- or post-natal visits)?

Yes .... 1 →   Q21
No .... 2 →   Q28

21 Ntimes1 **If yes at OutPatnt (code 1)**

How many times did you attend in (EARLIEST MONTH IN REFERENCE PERIOD)?

0..97   →   Q22

22 NTimes2 How many times did you attend in (SECOND MONTH IN REFERENCE PERIOD)?

0..97   →   Q23

23 NTimes3   How many times did you attend in (THIRD MONTH IN REFERENCE PERIOD)?

0..97   →   Q24

24 Casualty   Was this visit (were any of these visits) to the Casualty department or was it (were they all) to some other part of the hospital?

At least one visit to Casualty 1   →   Q25
No Casualty visits 2   →   Q26

25 NcasVis   **If went to casualty (code 1)**

(May I just check) How many times did you go to Casualty altogether?

1..31   →   Q26

26 PrVists   **If yes at OutPatnt (code 1)**

Was your outpatient visit (were any of your outpatient visits) during (REFERENCE PERIOD) made under the NHS, or was it (were any of them) paid for privately?

All under NHS 1   →   Q28
At least one paid for privately 2   →   Q27

27 NprVists   **If some private visits (PRVisits = 2)**

ASK OR RECORD

(May I just check), How many of the visits were paid for privately?

1..31   →   Q28

28 DayPatnt   **Ask all**

During the last year, that is, since (DATE ONE YEAR AGO), have you been in hospital for treatment as a day patient, ie admitted to a hospital bed or day ward, but not required to remain overnight?

Yes... 1   → See Q29
No 2   →   Q36

29 MatDPat   **If yes at DayPatnt AND (Sex = Female AND Age 16-49), others Q33**

May I just check, was that/were any of those day patient admissions for you to have a baby?

Yes... 1   →   Q30
No 2   →   Q36

30 NumMatDP   **If MatDPat = Yes**

How many separate days have you had as a day patient for having a baby since (DATE ONE YEAR AGO)?

97 DAYS OR MORE - CODE 97

1..97   →   Q31

31 PrMatDP   Was this day-patient stay (were any of these day-patient stays) for having a baby under the NHS, or was it (were any of them) paid for privately?

All under NHS 1   →   Q33
At least one paid for privately 2   → See Q32

32 NprMatDP   **If PrMatDP = 2 AND NumMatDP > 1**

ASK OR RECORD

How many of the visits were paid for privately?

1..31   →   Q33

33 NHSPDays   **If yes at DayPatnt (code 1)**

(Apart from those maternity stays) how many separate days in hospital have you had as a day patient since (DATE ONE YEAR AGO),?

97 DAYS OR MORE - CODE 97

0..97   → See Q34

34 PrDptnt   **If NHSPDays > 0**

Was this day-patient treatment (were any of these day-patient treatments under the NHS, or was it (were any of them) paid for privately?

All under NHS 1   →   Q36
At least one paid for privately 2   → See Q35

35 NPrDpTnt   **If PrDptnt = 2 AND NHSPDays > 1**

ASK OR RECORD

How many of the visits were paid for privately?

1..31   →   Q36

36 InPatnt   **Ask all**

During the last year, that is, since (DATE 1 YEAR AGO), have you been in hospital as an inpatient, overnight or longer?

Yes... 1   → See Q37
No 2   →   Hearing

37 MatInPat   **If yes at InPatnt AND (Sex = Female AND Age 16-49), others Q42**

May I just check, was that/were any of those inpatient admissions for you to have a baby?

Yes... 1   →   Q38
No 2   →   Q42

38 NmtStay   **If MatInPat = Yes**

How many separate stays in hospital as an inpatient in order to have a baby have you had since (DATE 1 YEAR AGO)?

1..6   →   Q39

39 MtNights **For each maternity stay**

How many nights altogether were you in hospital on your (no.) stay to have a baby?

1..97   →   Q40

40 MatNHSTr Were you treated under the NHS or were you a private patient on that occasion?

NHS 1   →   Q42
Private patient 2   →   Q41

41 MtPrvSty **If private patient (MatNHSTr = 2)**

Were you treated in an NHS hospital or in a private one?

NHS hospital .... 1 ⎤
Private hospital .... 2 ⎦ → Q42

42 Nstays **If yes at InPatnt**

(Apart from those maternity stays) how many separate stays in hospital as an inpatient have you had since (DATE 1 YEAR AGO)?

0..6   →   Q43

43 Nights **For each stay**

How many nights altogether were you in hospital on your (first/second/...sixth) stay?

1..97   →   Q44

44 NHSTreat Were you treated under the NHS or were you a private patient on that occasion?

NHS 1   →   Hearing
Private patient 2   →   Q45

45 PrvStay **If private (NHSTreat = 2)**

Were you treated in an NHS hospital or in a private one?

NHS hospital .... 1 ⎤
Private hospital .... 2 ⎦ → Hearing

HEARING DIFFICULTIES

1 HearDiff [*] **Ask all (except proxy informants)**

Do you ever have any difficulty with your hearing?

Yes 1   →   Q2
No 2   → Child Health

2 HearAid **If HearDiff = Yes**

(May I just check) do you ever wear a hearing aid nowadays?

Yes 1   →   Q45
No 2   → Child Health

3 AidDiff **If HearAid = Yes**

Do you ever have any difficulties with your hearing even when you're wearing an aid?

Yes .... 1 ⎤
No .... 2 ⎦ → Q4

4 NumAids How many hearing aids have you got that you wear even if only occasionally?

1..4   →   Q5

5 AidTyp **For each hearing aid**

Did you obtain this aid through the National Health Service or was it bought privately?

NHS 1   →   Q6
Private 2   →   Q7

6 Ypriv **If AidTyp = Private**

Why did you decide to buy this aid privately?

To get a better choice .... 1 ⎤
To get it quicker .... 2 ⎥ → Q7
Not available through NHS .... 3 ⎥
Other .... 4 ⎦

7 AidWear **For each hearing aid**

Do you wear this aid regularly?

Yes .... 1 ⎤
No .... 2 ⎦ → Q8

8 DontWear **If HearAid = Yes**

Do you have any hearing aids which still work that you no longer wear?

Yes 1   →   Q9
No 2   → Child Health

9 NoNotWrn **If DontWear = Yes**

How many aids do you have that you don't wear?

1..4   →   Q10

10 NotWorn **For each aid not worn**

Did you obtain this aid through the National Health Service or was it bought privately?

NHS .... 1 ⎤
Private .... 2 ⎦ → Q11

11 YntWr Why do you no longer wear this aid?

Did not help hearing 1
Appearance 2
Hearing improved/had operation   ⎤ → Child
  to improve hearing .... 3 ⎥   Health
Doesn't fit/uncomfortable 4
Other 5

CHILD HEALTH

If children under 16 in household (not asked of proxy informants), others go to Elderly

1 AskHlth THE NEXT SECTION IS ABOUT CHILD HEALTH. WE ONLY NEEDTO COLLECT THIS INFORMATION ONCE FOR EACH CHILD IN THE HOUSEHOLD. WHO WILL ANSWER THE CHILD HEALTH SECTION FOR (CHILD'S NAME)?

INTERVIEWER ENTER PERSON NUMBER.

..14   →   Q2

2 AskNowCH INTERVIEWER: DO YOU WANT TO ASK THIS SECTION FOR ......CHILD'S NAME) NOW OR LATER?

IF YOU HAVE ALREADY ASKED THIS SECTION FOR (CHILD'SNAME), DO NOT CHANGE FROM CODE 1

Yes, now/already asked .... 1 → Q4
Later.. 2 → Q3

3 Cstill **If AskNowCH = 2**

REMINDER The following adults still need to answer the child health section on behalf of some of the children.   →   Q4

4 Illness [*] **If AskHlth = Yes**
For each child

Does (NAME) have any long-standing illness, disability or infirmity? By long-standing, I mean anything that has troubled them over a period of time or that is likely to affect them over a period of time?

Yes... 1 → Q5
No .... 2 → Q10

5 LMatter [*] **If child has a longstanding illness, disability or infirmity (Illness =1)**

What is the matter with (NAME)?

RECORD ONLY WHAT RESPONDENT SAYS.
(Enter text of at most 40 characters)   →   Q6

6 LmatNum HOW MANY LONGSTANDING ILLNESSES OR INFIRMITIES DOES (NAME) HAVE?

ENTER NUMBER OF LONGSTANDING COMPLAINTS MENTIONED
IF MORE THAN 6 - TAKE THE SIX THAT THE RESPONDENTCONSIDERS THE MOST IMPORTANT

1..6   →   Q7

7 Lmat **For each illness mentioned at LMatNum**

WHAT IS THE MATTER WITH (NAME)?

ENTER ONE OF CONDITIONS/SYMPTOMS RESPONDENT MENTIONED
(Enter text of at most 40 characters)   →   Q8

8 ICD CODE FOR COMPLAINT AT LMAT   →   Q9

9 LimitAct [*] **If Illness = 1**

Does this illness or disability (Do any of these illnesses or disabilities) limit (NAME)'s activities in any way?

Yes... 1 ⎤
No .... 2 ⎦ → Q10

10 CutDown [*] **All children under 16**

Now I'd like you to think about the 2 weeks ending yesterday. During those 2 weeks, did (NAME) have to cut down on any of the things he/she usually does (at school or in his/her free time) because of (answer at LMatter or some other) illness or injury?

Yes... 1 → Q11
No .... 2 → Q13

11 NdysCutD **If child has had to cut down**

How many days did (NAME) have to cut down in all during these 2 weeks, including Saturdays and Sundays?

1..14   →   Q12

12 Matter [*] What was the matter with (NAME)?
(Enter text of at most 80 characters)   →   Q13

13 DocTalk **All children under 16**

During the 2 weeks ending yesterday, apart from visits to a hospital, did (NAME) talk to a doctor for any reason at all, or did you or any other member of the household talk to a doctor on his/her behalf?

INCLUDE TELEPHONE CONSULTATIONS AND CONSULTATIONS MADE ON BEHALF OF CHILDREN

Yes... 1 → Q14
No .... 2 → Q20

14 Nchats **If child consulted a doctor (DocTalk = 1)**

How many times did (NAME) talk to the doctor (or you or any other member of the household consult the doctor on ...'s behalf) in those 2 weeks?

1..9   →   Q15

233

15 NHS   **For each consultation**

Was this consultation...

Under the National Health Service 1   →   Q16
or paid for privately? 2

16 GP   Was the doctor...

RUNNING PROMPT

A GP (ie a family doctor) 1   →   Q18
or a specialist 2
or some other kind of doctor?
(SPECIFY AT NEXT QUESTION) 3   →   Q17

17 XGP   **If GP = Other**

Specify type of doctor.

ENTER TEXT OF AT MOST 20
CHARACTERS   →   Q18

18 DocWhere   **For each consultation**

Did you or any other member of the household (or
NAME) talk to the doctor...

By telephone 1
at your home 2
in the doctor's surgery 3   →   Q19
at a health centre 4
or elsewhere? 5

19 Presc   Did the doctor give (send) (NAME) a prescription?

Yes 1   →   Q20
No 2

20 OutPatnt   **All children under 16**

During the months of (LAST 3 COMPLETE
CALENDAR MONTHS), did (NAME) attend as a
patient the casualty or outpatient department of a
hospital (apart from straightforward post-natal
visits)?

Yes 1   →   Q21
No 2   →   Q26

21 Ntimes1   **If child has been an outpatient**

How many times did (NAME) attend in (EARLIEST
MONTH IN REFERENCE PERIOD)?

0..97   →   Q22

22 NTimes2   How many times did (NAME) attend in (SECOND
MONTH IN REFERENCE.PERIOD)?

0..97   →   Q23

23 NTimes3   How many times did (NAME) attend in (THIRD
MONTH IN REFERENCE.PERIOD)?

0..97   →   Q24

24 Casualty   Was the visit (were any of the visits) to the Casualty
department or was it (were they) to some other part
of the hospital?

At least one visit to Casualty 1   →   Q25
No Casualty visits 2   →   Q26

25 NcasVis   **If went to casualty**

(May I just check) How many times did (NAME) go
to Casualty altogether?

1..31   →   Q26

26 DayPatnt   **All children under 16**

During the last year, that is since (DATE 1 YEAR
AGO) has (NAME) been in hospital for treatment as
a day patient,ie admitted to a hospital bed or day
ward, but not required to remain in hospital
overnight?

Yes 1   →   Q27
No 2   →   Q28

27 NHSPDays   **If child has been a day patient**

How many separate days in hospital has (NAME)
had as a day patient since (DATE 1 YEAR AGO)?

1..97   →   Q28

28 InPatnt   **All children under 16**

During the last year, that is, since (DATE 1 YEAR
AGO) has (NAME) been in hospital as an inpatient,
overnight or longer?

EXCLUDE: Births unless baby stayed in hospital
after mother had left.

Yes 1   →   Q29
No 2   →   Elderly

29 Nstays   **If child has been an inpatient**

How many separate stays in hospital as an
inpatient has (NAME) had since (DATE 1 YEAR
AGO)?

IF 6 OR MORE, CODE 6

1..6   →   Q30

30 Nights   **For each stay**

How many nights altogether was (NAME) in
hospital during stay number (...)?

1..97   →   Elderly

ELDERLY

1 SeeDiff [*] **All adults aged 65 and over (not proxies)**

Does your sight ever cause you difficulties?

Yes.................................... 1 ⎤
No .... 2 ⎦ → See Q2

2 LimStart **If has a limiting longstanding illness (LimitAct = yes)**

You mentioned earlier that your activites are limited by ill health or disability. How long ago did this start to limit your activities?

Less than one year ago .... 1 ⎤
1-4 years ago .... 2 ⎥ → Q3
5 years or more ago .... 3 ⎦

3 EldInt1 **Ask all (except proxy informants)**

Now I'd like to ask about a few tasks that some people may be able to do on their own, while others may need help, or not do them at all. For some tasks, I will ask you to look at these cards and tell me whether you usually manage to do it on your own, only with help from someone else, or not at all.

4 Stairs SHOW CARD L
Do you usually manage to get up and down stairs or steps...

on your own .... 1 → Q5
only with help from someone else ..... 2 ⎤ → Q6
or not at all? .... 3 ⎦

5 StrsEasy [*] **If manages without help (code 1 at Stairs)**

SHOW CARD M

Do you find it ...

very easy .... 1 ⎤ → Q27
fairly easy .... 2 ⎦
fairly difficult .... 3 ⎤ → Q6
or very difficult to do this on your
     own? .... 4 ⎦

6 StairLoo **If Stairs = 2 or 3 OR StrsEasy = 3 or 4**

ASK OR RECORD

May I just check, do you have to use stairs to get from the rooms you use during the daytime to the toilet?

Yes.................................... 1 ⎤ → Q7
No .... 2 ⎦

7 StairBed ASK OR RECORD

And do you have to use stairs to get from the rooms you use during the daytime to your bedroom?

Yes.................................... 1 ⎤ → Q8
No .... 2 ⎦

8 House SHOW CARD L
....
Do you usually manage to get around the house (except for any stairs) ...

on your own .... 1 → Q9
only with help from someone else ..... 2 ⎤ → Q10
or not at all? .... 3 ⎦

9 HousEasy [*] **If manages without help (House = 1)**

SHOW CARD M

Do you find it ...

very easy .... 1 ⎤
fairly easy .... 2 ⎥ → Q10
fairly difficult .... 3 ⎥
or very difficult to do this on your
     own? .... 4 ⎦

10 Toilet **If Stairs = 2 or 3 OR StrsEasy = 3 or 4**

SHOW CARD L

Do you usually manage to get to the toilet ...

on your own .... 1 → Q11
only with help from someone else ..... 2 ⎤ → See Q12
or not at all? .... 3 ⎦

11 ToilEasy **If manages without help (Toilet = 1)**

SHOW CARD M

Do you find it ...

very easy .... 1 ⎤ → Q15
fairly easy .... 2 ⎦
fairly difficult .... 3 ⎤ → See Q12
or very difficult to do this on your
     own? .... 4 ⎦

12 WhoHlp **If needs help with stairs, getting to the toilet or getting around the house (Stairs = Help AND StairLoo = Yes OR StairBed = Yes OR Toilet = Help OR House = Help), others Q15**

Who usually helps you to get around the house/to the toilet/ up and downstairs? Is it someone in the household, or someone from outside the house-hold?

Someone in the household .... 1 → Q13
Someone from outside the
     household .... 2 → Q14

13 WhoHlpA **If usually gets help from someone in the household (code 1 at WhoHlp)**

Who is the person in the household?

INTERVIEWER: ENTER PERSON NUMBER

1..14   → Q15

235

14 WhoHlpB   **If usually gets help from someone outside the household (code 2 at WhoHlp)**

Who is the person from outside the household?

Son 2	
Daughter 3	
Brother 4	
Sister 5	
Other relation 6	→ Q15
Friend / neighbour 7	
Social Services 8	
District Nurse / Health Visitor 9	
Paid help 10	
Other, please specify 15	

15 Bed   **If Stairs = 2 or 3 OR StrsEasy = 3 or 4**

SHOW CARD L

Do you usually manage to get in and out of bed ..

on your own 1	→	Q16
only with help from someone else 2	→	Q17
or not at all? 3		

16 BedEasy [*]   **If manages without help (code 1at Bed)**

SHOW CARD M

Do you find it ...

very easy 1		
fairly easy 2		
fairly difficult 3	→	Q17
or very difficult to do this on your own? 4		

17 Dress   **If Stairs = 2 or 3 OR StrsEasy = 3 or 4**

SHOW CARD L

Do you usually manage to dress and undress yourself ..

on your own 1	→	Q18
only with help from someone else 2	→ See Q19	
or not at all? 3		

18 DresEasy [*]   **If manages without help (code 1 at Dress)**

SHOW CARD M

Do you find it ..

very easy 1		
fairly easy 2		
fairly difficult 3	→	Q22
or very difficult to do this on your own? 4		

19 BedHlp   **If needs help to get in and out of bed or to dress and undress (code 2 at Bed OR code 2 at Dress)**

Who usually helps you to get in and out of bed/ dress? Is it someone in the household, or someone from outside the household?

Someone in the household 1	→	Q20
Someone from outside the household 2	→	Q21

20 BedHlpA   **If usually gets help from someone in the household (code 1 at BedHlp)**

Who is the person in the household?

INTERVIEWER: ENTER PERSON NUMBER

1..14	→	Q22

21 BedHlpB   **If usually gets help from someone outside the household (code 2 at BedHlp)**

Who is the person from outside the household?

Son 2	
Daughter 3	
Brother 4	
Sister 5	
Other relation 6	→ Q22
Friend / neighbour 7	
Social Services 8	
District Nurse / Health Visitor 9	
Paid help 10	
Other, please specify 15	

22 Feed   **If Stairs = 2 or 3 OR StrsEasy = 3 or 4**

SHOW CARD L

Do you usually manage to feed yourself ..

on your own 1	→	Q23
only with help from someone else 2	→	Q24
or not at all? 3	→	Q27

23 FeedEasy [*]   **If manages without help (code 1 at Feed)**

SHOW CARD M

Do you find it ..

very easy 1		
fairly easy 2		
fairly difficult 3	→	Q27
or very difficult to do this on your own? 4		

24 FeedHlp   **If need help to feed (code 2 at Feed)**

Who usually helps you to feed yourself? Is it someone in the household, or someone from outside the household?

Someone in the household 1	→	Q25
Someone from outside the household 2	→	Q26

25 FeedHlpA   **If usually gets help from someone in the household (code 1 at FeedHlp)**

Who is the person in the household?

INTERVIEWER: ENTER PERSON NUMBER

1..14   →   Q27

26 FeedHlpB   **If usually gets help from someone outside the household (code 2 at FeedHlp)**

Who is the person from outside the household?

Son 2
Daughter 3
Brother 4
Sister 5
Other relation 6   →   Q27
Friend / neighbour 7
Social Services 8
District Nurse / Health Visitor 9
Paid help 10
Other, please specify 15

27 Toenails   **Ask all (except proxy informants)**

Do you usually manage to cut your toenails yourself, or does someone else do it for you?

Self .... 1 → Q28
Someone else .... 2 → Q29

28 TnailEas [*]   **If does it him/herself (code 1 at Toenails)**

SHOW CARD M

(Still looking at the card) do you find it

very easy 1
fairly easy 2
fairly difficult 3   →   Q32
or very difficult to do this on your
own? 4

29 TnlHlp   **If someone else does it (code 2 at Toenails)**

Who usually helps you? Is it someone in the household, or someone from outside the household?

Someone in the household .... 1 → Q30
Someone from outside the
household .... 2 → Q31

30 TNlHlpA   **If usually gets help from someone in the household (code 1 at TnlHlp)**

Who is the person in the household?

INTERVIEWER: ENTER PERSON NUMBER

1..14   →   Q32

31 TnlHlpB   **If usually gets help from someone outside the household (code 2 at TnlHlp)**

Who is the person from outside the household?

Son 2
Daughter 3
Brother 4
Sister 5
Other relation 6
Friend / neighbour 7   →   Q32
Social Services 8
District Nurse / Health Visitor 9
Paid help 10
Chiropodist 11
Other, please specify 15

32 Bath   **Ask all (except proxy informants)**

SHOW CARD L

Do you usually manage to bath, shower or wash all over ..

on your own .... 1 → Q33
only with help from someone else ..... 2 → Q34
or not at all? .... 3 → Q37

33 BathEasy [*]   **If manages without help (Bath = 1)**

SHOW CARD M

Do you find it ..

very easy 1
fairly easy 2   →   Q42
fairly difficult 3
or very difficult to do this on your
own? 4   →   Q37

34 BthHlp   **If needs help (code 2 at Bath)**

Who usually helps you? Is it someone in the household, or someone from outside the household?

Someone in the household .... 1 → Q35
Someone from outside the
household .... 2 → Q36

35 BthHlpA   **If usually gets help from someone in the household (code 1 at BthHlp)**

Who is the person in the household?

INTERVIEWER: ENTER PERSON NUMBER

1..14   →   Q37

63 BusHlpA   **If usually gets help from someone in the household (code 1 at BusHlp)**

Who is the person in the household?

INTERVIEWER: ENTER PERSON NUMBER

1..14   →   Q65

64 BusHlpB   **If usually gets help from someone outside the household (code 2 at BusHlp)**

Who is the person from outside the household?

Son 2	
Daughter 3	
Brother 4	
Sister 5	
Other relation 6	
Friend / neighbour .... 7 → Q65	
Social Services 8	
District Nurse / Health Visitor 9	
Paid help 10	
Other, please specify 15	
Nobody does it 16	

65 Dishes   **Ask all (except proxy informants)**

Do you wash up and dry dishes?

Yes 1   →   Q67
No 2   →   Q66

66 DishOwn   **If code 2 at Dishes**

Could you if you had to?

Yes .... 1 ⌉
No .... 2 ⌋ → Q67

67 Windows   **Ask all (except proxy informants)**

Do you clean windows inside yourself?

Yes 1   →   Q69
No 2   →   Q68

68 WindwOwn   **If code 2 at Windows**

Could you if you had to?

Yes .... 1 ⌉
No .... 2 ⌋ → Q69

69 Vacuum   **Ask all (except proxy informants)**

Do you use a vacuum cleaner?

Yes 1   →   Q71
No 2   →   Q70

70 VacOwn   **If code 2 at Vacuum**

Could you if you had to?

Yes .... 1 ⌉
No .... 2 ⌋ → Q71

71 Steps   **Ask all (except proxy informants)**

Do you do jobs involving climbing a stepladder, steps or a chair?

Yes 1   →   Q73
No 2   →   Q72

72 StpsOwn   **If code 2 at Steps**

Could you if you had to?

Yes .... 1 ⌉
No .... 2 ⌋ → Q73

73 Laundry   **Ask all (except proxy informants)**

Do you wash small amounts of clothing by hand?

Yes 1   →   Q75
No 2   →   Q74

74 LaundOwn   **If code 2 at Laundry**

Could you if you had to?

Yes .... 1 ⌉
No .... 2 ⌋ → Q75

75 Bottles   **Ask all (except proxy informants)**

Do you open screw top bottles and jars?

Yes 1   → See Q77
No 2   →   Q76

76 BottlOwn   **If code 2 at Bottles**

Could you if you had to?

Yes .... 1 ⌉
No .... 2 ⌋ → Q77

77 DomHlp   **If 'no' at Windows OR Vacuum OR Steps OR Bottles OR Dishes, others go to Q80**

You've said that there are some things that may need doing around the house which you don't do yourself. Who usually does them for you?

INTERVIEWER ASK OR CODE

Is it someone in the household, or someone from outside the household?

Someone in the household 1   →   Q78
Someone from outside the household . 2   →   Q79

78 DomHlpA   **If usually gets help from someone in the household (code 1 at DomHlp)**

Who is the person in the household?

INTERVIEWER : ENTER PERSON NUMBER

1..14   →   Q80

79 DomHlpB

If usually gets help from someone outside the household (code 2 at DomHlp)

Who is the person from outside the household?

```
Son ................................................. 2
Daughter ........................................... 3
Brother ............................................. 4
Sister .............................................. 5
Other relation ..................................... 6
Friend / neighbour ................................. 7   →   Q80
Social Services .................................... 8
District Nurse / Health Visitor ............. 9
Paid help .......................................... 10
Other, please specify ...................... 15
Nobody does it ................................ 16
```

80 Cook

Ask all (except proxy informants)

Do you prepare hot meals for yourself?

```
Yes ................................................. 1   → See Q89
No .................................................. 2   →   Q81
```

81 CookOwn

If code 2 at Cook

Could you if you had to?

```
Yes ................................................. 1   →   Q82
No .................................................. 2
```

82 CookHlp

Who usually prepares hot meals for you

ASK OR CODE

Is it someone in the household, or someone from outside the household?

```
Someone in the household ................ 1   →   Q83
Someone from outside the household . 2   →   Q84
```

83 CookHpA

If usually gets help from someone in the household (code 1 at CookHlp)

Who is the person in the household?

INTERVIEWER : ENTER PERSON NUMBER

```
1..14                                        →   Q85
```

84 CookHpB

If usually gets help from someone outside the household (code 2 at CookHlp)

Who is the person from outside the household?

```
Son ................................................. 2
Daughter ........................................... 3
Brother ............................................. 4
Sister .............................................. 5
Other relation ..................................... 6
Friend / neighbour ................................. 7   →   Q85
Social Services .................................... 8
District Nurse / Health Visitor ............. 9
Paid help .......................................... 10
Other, please specify ...................... 15
Nobody does it ................................ 16
```

85 Snack

If code 2 at Cook

Do you prepare snacks for yourself?

```
Yes ................................................. 1   → See Q89
No .................................................. 2   →   Q86
```

86 SnackOwn

If code 2 at Snack

Could you if you had to?

```
Yes ................................................. 1   →   Q87
No .................................................. 2
```

87 CupTea

Do you make cups of tea?

```
Yes ................................................. 1   → See Q89
No .................................................. 2   →   Q88
```

88 CpTeaOwn

If code 2 at CupTea

Could you if you had to?

```
Yes ................................................. 1   → See Q89
No .................................................. 2
```

89 RegCare

If need help with stairs, getting around the house, getting to the toilet, getting in and out of bed, getting dressed and undressed, feeding, bathing or washing (If 'yes' at StairLoo OR StairBed OR House OR Toilet OR Bed OR Dress OR Feed OR Bath OR Wash), others go to Q95

Thinking of all the things we've been talking about, may I just check, do you need REGULAR DAILY HELP with things that fit and healthy people would normally do for themselves?

```
Yes ................................................. 1   → See Q90
No .................................................. 2   →   Q95
```

90 Ncarers

IF RegCare = YES AND If has a carer for stairs, getting to the toilet or getting around the house, getting in and out of bed, dressing or undressing, feeding, bathing or washing (InHld or OutHhld at BedHlp, WhoHlp, FeedHlp, BthHlp OR WshHlp)

How many REGULAR carers do you have to help you?

```
1..8                                         →   Q91
```

91 CareHlp

For each carer mentioned at Ncarers

Thinking of all the things that this carer helps you with or does for you, how much time does he or she spend each day looking after you?
(Please include all the time he or she spends doing things for you, AND time he or she is here just because you need to have someone with you)

```
0.1..24.0                                    →   Q92
```

241

120 DsLst3M   Doctor/GP at his/her surgery? INCLUDE BOTH NHS AND PRIVATE

Yes .... 1 → Q121
No .... 2 → Q122

121 DsLstMth   **If code 1 at DsLst3M**

Did you see the doctor at the surgery last month, that is, in (LASTCOMPLETE CALENDAR MONTH)?

Yes .... 1 ⎤ → Q122
No .... 2 ⎦

122 DaLst3M   **Ask all (except proxy informants)**

Doctor attending you at home? INCLUDE BOTH NHS AND PRIVATE

Yes .... 1 → Q123
No .... 2 → Q124

123 DaLstMth   **If code 1 at DaLst3M**

Did the doctor come and see you at home last month, that is, in (LASTCOMPLETE CALENDAR MONTH)?

Yes .... 1 ⎤ → Q124
No .... 2 ⎦

124 HdLst3M   **Ask all (except proxy informants)**

Hospital doctor? INCLUDE BOTH NHS AND PRIVATE

Yes .... 1 → Q125
No .... 2 → Q126

125 HdLstMth   **If code 1 at HdLst3M**

Did you see the doctor at the hospital last month, that is, in (LAST COMPLETE CALENDAR MONTH)?

Yes .... 1 ⎤ → Q126
No .... 2 ⎦

126 NsLst3M   **Ask all (except proxy informants)**

Nurse at a surgery or health centre? INCLUDE BOTH NHS AND PRIVATE

Yes .... 1 → Q127
No .... 2 → Q128

127 NsLstMth   **If code 1 at NsLst3M**

Did you see the nurse at the surgery last month, that is, in (LAST COMPLETE CALENDAR MONTH)?

Yes .... 1 ⎤ → Q128
No .... 2 ⎦

128 SwLst3M   **Ask all (except proxy informants)**

Local Authority social worker or care manager?

Yes .... 1 → Q129
No .... 2 → Q130

129 SwLstMth   **If code 1 at SwLst3M**

Did you see the social worker or care manager last month, that is, in (LAST COMPLETE CALENDAR MONTH)?

Yes .... 1 ⎤ → Q130
No .... 2 ⎦

130 DtLst3M   **Ask all (except proxy informants)**

Dentist? INCLUDE NHS AND PRIVATE

Yes .... 1 → Q131
No .... 2 → Q132

131 DtLstMth   **If code 1 at DtLst3M**

Did you see the dentist last month, that is, in (LAST COMPLETE CALENDAR MONTH)?

Yes .... 1 ⎤ → Q132
No .... 2 ⎦

132 ChLst3M   **Ask all (except proxy informants)**

Chiropodist at home, clinic or hospital? INCLUDE BOTH NHS AND PRIVATE

Yes .... 1 → Q133
No .... 2 → Q134

133 ChLstMth   **If code 1 at ChLst3M**

Did you see the chiropodist last month, that is, in (LAST COMPLETE CALENDAR MONTH)?

Yes .... 1 ⎤ → Q134
No .... 2 ⎦

134 OpLst3M   **Ask all (except proxy informants)**

Optician? INCLUDE BOTH NHS AND PRIVATE

Yes .... 1 → Q135
No .... 2 → Q136

135 OpLstMth   **If code 1 at OpLst3M**

Did you see the optician last month, that is, in (LAST COMPLETE CALENDAR MONTH)?

Yes .... 1 ⎤ → Q136
No .... 2 ⎦

136 Shelter

Ask all (except proxy informants)

IS THE RESPONDENT LIVING IN SHELTERED ACCOMMODATION?

Sheltered: warden on premises .... 1 ⎤
No warden on premises, but premises
  have a central alarm system .... 2 ⎥ → Smoking
Not sheltered .... 3 ⎦
Not sure - PLEASE DESCRIBE
  AT NEXT QUESTION .... 4 → Q137

137 Xshelter

If code 4 at Shelter

GIVE AS MUCH INFORMATION AS YOU CAN ABOUT THE ARRANGEMENTS.
(Enter text of at most 30 characters) → Smoking

SMOKING

1 SmkIntro

Ask all except proxy informants

The next section consists of a series of questions about SMOKING (Not asked of proxy respondents)

2 SelfComl

Ask all 16 and 17 year olds

INFORMANT IS AGED 16 OR 17 - OFFER SELF-COMPLETION FORM AND ENTER CODE

Informant accepted self-completion ... 1 → Q3
Informant refused self-completion ..... 2 → Drinking
Data now to be keyed by interviewer . 3 → Q3

3 SmokEver

All adults aged 18 or over (except proxy informants) or if SelfCom1 = 3

Have you ever smoked a cigarette, a cigar, or a pipe?

Yes .... 1 → Q4
No .... 2 → Drinking

4 CigNow

If respondent has ever smoked (SmokEver = 1)

Do you smoke cigarettes at all nowadays?

Yes .... 1 → Q5
No .... 2 → Q13

5 QtyWkEnd

If respondent smokes cigarettes now (CigNow = 1)

About how many cigarettes a day do you usually smoke at weekends?

IF LESS THAN 1, ENTER 0.

0..97 → Q6

6 QtyWkdAY

About how many cigarettes a day do you usually smoke on weekdays?

IF LESS THAN 1, ENTER 0.

0..97 → Q7

7 CigType

Do you mainly smoke.....

RUNNING PROMPT

filter-tipped cigarettes .... 1 ⎤
or plain or untipped cigarettes .... 2 ⎦ → Q8
or hand-rolled cigarettes? .... 3 → Q10

8 Cig1Desc

Ask if cigarette types include plain or filter cigarettes (CigType includes 1 or 2)

Which brand of cigarette do you usually smoke?

GIVE 1) FULL BRAND NAME 2) SIZE, eg King, luxury, regular.
IF NO REGULAR BRAND THEN TYPE 'NO REG' HERE.
IF INFORMANT SMOKES TWO BRANDS EQUALLY TYPE 'TWO'HERE.

(Enter text of at most 60 characters) → Q9

9 CigCODE

Code for brand at CiglDesc → Q10

10 NoSmoke [*]

If respondent smokes cigarettes now (CigNow = 1)

How easy or difficult would you find it to go without smoking for a whole day? Would you find it...

RUNNING PROMPT

Very easy .... 1 ⎤
Fairly easy .... 2 ⎥ → Q11
Fairly difficult or .... 3 ⎥
Very difficult? .... 4 ⎦

11 GiveUp [*]

Would you like to give up smoking altogether?

Yes .... 1 ⎤ → Q12
No .... 2 ⎦

12 FirstCig

How soon after waking do you usually smoke your first cigarette of the day?

PROMPT AS NECESSARY

Less than 5 minutes .... 1 ⎤
5-14 minutes .... 2 ⎥
15-29 minutes .... 3 ⎥ → Q16
30 minutes but less than 1 hour .... 4 ⎥
1 hour but less than 2 hours .... 5 ⎥
2 hours or more .... 6 ⎦

13 CigEver

Ask of all who do not smoke cigarettes now but have smoked a cigarette or cigar or pipe (SmokEver = 1) and (CigNow NOT 1)

Have you ever smoked cigarettes regularly?

Yes .... 1 → Q14
No .... 2 → Q17

15 SbeerM

If drank strong beer(/lager/stout/cider/shandy) at all this year (Sbeer = 1-7)

How much STRONG BEER, LAGER, STOUT or CIDER have you usually drunk on any one day during the last 12 months?

INTERVIEWER: CODE MEASURES THAT YOU ARE GOING TO USE. CODE ALL THAT APPLY. PROBE IF NECESSARY

Half pints 1
Small cans .... 2 → Q16
Large cans 3
Bottles 4

16 SbeerQ

For each measure mentioned at SBeerM

ASK OR CODE
How many (ANSWER AT SBeerM) of STRONG BEER, LAGER, STOUT or CIDER have you usually drunk on any one day during the last 12 months?

1..97 → Q17

17 SbrlDesc

If 'Bottles' in SBeerM (code 4), others go to Q19

ASK OR CODE
What make of STRONG BEER, LAGER, STOUT or CIDER do you usually drink from bottles?

INTERVIEWER: IF RESPONDENT DOES NOT KNOW WHAT MAKE, OR RESPONDENT DRINKS DIFFERENT MAKES OF NORMAL STRENGTH BEER, LAGER, STOUT OR CIDER, PROBE:

What make have you drunk most frequently or most recently?

IF RESPONDENT DRINKS FRENCH BOTTLED BEER BUT DOES NOT KNOW THE BRAND NAME TYPE 'FRENCH', ENTER CODING FRAME AND CODE 'FRENCH BEER - BRAND NOT KNOWN'

IF RESPONDENT DOES NOT KNOW THE BRAND NAME BUT THEY INDICATE THAT THE BOTTLE IS LARGE THEN TYPE 'LARGE, ENTER CODING FRAME AND CODE 'LARGE BOTTLE - BRAND NOT KNOWN'.

(Enter text of at most 21 characters) → Q18

18 SBrCODE

Code for brand at SBrlDesc → Q19

19 Spirits

If drinks at all nowadays (Drinknow= 1) or (DrinkAny = 1)

SHOW CARD R

How often have you had a drink of spirits or liqueurs, such as gin, whisky, brandy, rum, vodka, advocaat or cocktails during the last 12 months?

Almost every day 1
5 or 6 days a week 2
3 or 4 days a week 3
once or twice a week .... 4 → Q20
once or twice a month 5
once every couple of months 6
once or twice a year 7
not at all in last 12 months .... 8 → Q21

20 SpiritsQ

If drank spirits or liqueurs at all this year (Spirits = 1-7)

How much spirits or liqueurs (such as gin, whisky, brandy, rum, vodka, advocaat or cocktails) have you usually drunk on any one day during the last 12 months?

CODE THE NUMBER OF SINGLES - COUNT DOUBLES AS TWO SINGLES.

1..97 → Q21

21 Sherry

If drinks at all nowadays (Drinknow= 1) or (DrinkAny = 1)

SHOW CARD R

How often have you had a drink of sherry or martini, including port, vermouth, Cinzano and Dubonnet, during the last 12 months?

Almost every day 1
5 or 6 days a week 2
3 or 4 days a week 3
once or twice a week .... 4 → Q22
once or twice a month 5
once every couple of months 6
once or twice a year 7
not at all in last 12 months .... 8 → Q23

22 SherryQ

If drank sherry or martini at all this year (Sherry = 1-7)

How much sherry or martini, including port, vermouth, Cinzano and Dubonnet have you usually drunk on any one day during the last 12 months?

CODE THE NUMBER OF GLASSES

1..97 → Q23

23 Wine　　If drinks at all nowadays (Drinknow= 1) or (DrinkAny = 1)

SHOW CARD R

How often have you had a drink of wine, including Babycham and champagne, during the last 12 months?

Almost every day 1
5 or 6 days a week 2
3 or 4 days a week 3
once or twice a week .... 4 →　Q24
once or twice a month 5
once every couple of months 6
once or twice a year 7
not at all in last 12 months .... 8 →　Q25

24 WineQ　　If drank wine at all this year (Wine = 1-7)

How much wine, including Babycham and champagne, have you usually drunk on any one day during the last 12 months?

CODE THE NUMBER OF GLASSES
1 BOTTLE = 6 GLASSES, 1 LITRE = 8 GLASSES

1..97　　　　　　　　　　　　　→　Q25

25 Pops　　If drinks at all nowadays (Drinknow= 1) or (DrinkAny = 1)

SHOW CARD R

How often have you had a drink of alcopops (ie alcoholic lemonade, alcoholic colas or other alcoholic fruit- or herb-flavoured drinks (eg. Hooch, Two Dogs, Alcola etc), during the last 12 months?

Almost every day 1
5 or 6 days a week 2
3 or 4 days a week 3
once or twice a week .... 4 →　Q26
once or twice a month 5
once every couple of months 6
once or twice a year 7
not at all in last 12 months .... 8 →　Q27

26 PopsQ　　If drank alcopops at all this year (Pops = 1-7)

How much alcopops (ie alcoholic lemonade, alcoholic colas or other alcoholic fruit- or herb-flavoured drinks have you usually drunk on any one day during the last 12 months?
CODE THE NUMBER OF BOTTLES

1..97　　　　　　　　　　　　　→　Q27

27 DrinkOft [*]　　If drinks at all nowadays (Drinknow= 1) or (DrinkAny = 1)

SHOW CARD R

Thinking now about all kinds of drinks, how often have you had an alcoholic drink of any kind during the last 12 months?

Almost every day 1
5 or 6 days a week 2
3 or 4 days a week 3
once or twice a week .... 4 →　Q28
once or twice a month 5
once every couple of months 6
once or twice a year 7
not at all in last 12 months 8

28 DrinkL7　　You have told me what you have drunk over the last 12 months, but we know that what people drink can vary a lot from week to week, so I'd like to ask you a few questions about last week. Did you have an alcoholic drink in the seven days ending yesterday?

Yes .... 1 →　Q29
No .... 2 →　Q45

29 DrnkDay　　If yes at DrinkL7 (code 1)

On how many days out of the last seven did you have an alcoholic drink?

1..7　　　　　　　　　　　　　→ See Q30

30 DrnkSame　　If DrnkDay = 2-7, others go to Q31

Did you drink more on some days than others/one of the days, or did you drink about the same on each of these/both days?

Drank more on one/some day(s)
　than other(s) .... 1 →　Q31
Same each day 2

31 WhichDay　　If yes at DrinkL7 (code 1), others go to Q45

Which day (last week) did you last have an alcoholic drink/have the most to drink?

Sunday 1
Monday 2
Tuesday 3
Wednesday .... 4 →　Q32
Thursday 5
Friday 6
Saturday 7

32 DrnkType   **If yes at DrinkL7 (code 1)**

SHOW CARD S

Thinking about last (DAY AT WhichDay) what types of drink did you have that day?

CODE ALL THAT APPLY

Normal strength beer/lager/cider/ shandy 1	→	Q33
Strong beer/lager/cider 2	→	Q37
Spirits or liqueurs 3	→	Q41
Sherry or martini 4	→	Q42
Wine.. 5	→	Q43
Alcoholic lemonades/colas 6	→	Q44

33 NBrL7   **If code 1 at DrnkType**

Still thinking about last (DAY AT WhichDay), how much NORMAL STRENGTH BEER, LAGER, STOUT, CIDER or SHANDY (excluding cans and bottles of shandy) did you drink that day?

INTERVIEWER: CODE MEASURES THAT YOU ARE GOING TO USE, CODE ALL THAT APPLY. PROBE IF NECESSARY

Half pints .... 1 ⎤		
Small cans .... 2 ⎟ →	Q34
Large cans .... 3 ⎟		
Bottles .... 4 ⎦		

34 NBrL7Q   **For each measure mentioned at NBrL7**

ASK OR CODE

How many (Answer AT NBrL7) of NORMAL STRENGTH BEER, LAGER, STOUT OR CIDER/ CIDER OR SHANDY (EXCLUDING CANS AND BOTTLES OF SHANDY) have you usually drunk on any one day during the last 12 months?

1..97   → See Q35

35 NB7lDesc   **If bottles at NBrL7 (code 4)**

ASK OR CODE
What make of NORMAL STRENGTH BEER, LAGER, STOUT or CIDER do you usually drink from bottles?

INTERVIEWER: IF RESPONDENT DRANK DIFFERENT MAKES CODE WHICH THEY DRANK MOST

IF RESPONDENT DRANK FRENCH BOTTLED BEER BUT DOES NOT KNOW THE BRAND NAME TYPE 'FRENCH', ENTER CODING FRAME AND CODE 'FRENCH BEER - BRAND NOT KNOWN'

IF RESPONDENT DOES NOT KNOW THE BRAND NAME BUT THEY INDICATE THAT THE BOTTLE WAS LARGE THEN TYPE 'LARGE, ENTER CODING FRAME AND CODE 'LARGE BOTTLE - BRAND NOT KNOWN'
(Enter text of at most 21 characters)   →   Q36

36 NB7CODE   Code for brand at NB7lDesc   →   Q45

37 SBrL7   **If code2 at DrnkType**

Still thinking about last (DAY AT WhichDay), how much STRONG BEER,LAGER, STOUT, CIDER or SHANDY (excluding cans and bottles of shandy) did you drink that day?

INTERVIEWER: CODE MEASURES THAT YOU ARE GOING TO USE
CODE ALL THAT APPLY. PROBE IF NECESSARY

Half pints .... 1 ⎤		
Small cans .... 2 ⎟ →	Q38
Large cans .... 3 ⎟		
Bottles .... 4 ⎦		

38 SBrL7Q   **For each measure mentioned at SBrL7**

ASK OR CODE
How many (Answer AT SBrL7) of STRONG BEER, LAGER,STOUT or CIDER have you usually drunk on any one day during the last 12 months?

1..97   → See Q39

39 SB7lDesc   **If bottles at SBrL7 (code 4)**

ASK OR CODE
What make of STRONG BEER, LAGER, STOUT or CIDER do you usually drink from bottles?

INTERVIEWER: IF RESPONDENT DRANK DIFFERENT MAKES CODE WHICH THEY DRANK MOST

IF RESPONDENT DRANK FRENCH BOTTLED BEER BUT DOES NOT KNOW THE BRAND NAME TYPE 'FRENCH', ENTER CODING FRAME AND CODE 'FRENCH BEER - BRAND NOT KNOWN'

IF RESPONDENT DOES NOT KNOW THE BRAND NAME BUT THEY INDICATE THAT THE BOTTLE WAS LARGE THEN TYPE 'LARGE, ENTER CODING FRAME AND CODE 'LARGE BOTTLE - BRAND NOT KNOWN'
(Enter text of at most 21 characters)   →   Q40

40 SB7CODE   Code for brand at SB7lDesc   →   Q45

41 SpriL7   **If code 3 at DrnkType**

Still thinking about last (DAY AT WhichDay), how much spirits or liqueurs (such as gin, whisky, brandy, rum, vodka, advocaat or cocktails) did you drink on that day?

CODE THE NUMBER OF SINGLES - COUNT DOUBLES AS TWO SINGLES

1..97   →   Q45

42 ShyrL7   **If code 4 at DrnkType**

Still thinking about last (DAY AT WhichDay), how much sherry or martini, including port, vermouth, Cinzano and Dubonnet did you drink on that day?

CODE THE NUMBER OF GLASSES

1..97   →   Q45

43 WineL7   **If code 5 at DrnkType**

Still thinking about last (DAY AT WhichDay), how much wine, including Babycham and champagne, did you drink on that day?

CODE THE NUMBER OF GLASSES
1 BOTTLE = 6 GLASSES. 1 LITRE = 8 GLASSES

1..97   →   Q45

44 PopsL7   **If code 6 at DrnkType**

Still thinking about last (DAY AT WhichDay), how much alcopops (ie alcoholic lemonade, alcoholic colas or other alcoholic fruit- or herb-flavoured drinks did you drink on that day?

    CODE THE NUMBER OF BOTTLES   →   Q45

45 DrAmount [*] If drinks at all nowadays (Drinknow= 1) or (DrinkAny = 1)

Compared to five years ago, would you say that on the whole you drink more, about the same or less nowadays?

More nowadays 1   Family
About the same .... 2 → Infor-
Less nowadays 3   mation

FAMILY INFORMATION

FamIntro   THE NEXT SECTION CONSISTS OF A SERIES OF QUESTIONS ABOUT FAMILY INFORMATION (Not asked of proxy respondents)

1 SlMar   **To all aged 16-59**
If single or same sex cohabiting, others Q2

Have you ever been legally married?

Yes .... 1 → Q4
No 2

2 ChkFIA   **If not single or same sex cohabiting**

INTERVIEWER CODE

Informant is married or cohabiting
   but their partner is NOT a household → Q3
   member 1
Everyone else .... 2 → Q4

3 HusbAway   **If married/cohabiting, but partner not a household member**

INTRODUCE AS NECESSARY

Is your husband, wife or partner absent because he/she usually works away from home, or for some other reason?

Usually works away (include Armed
   Forces, Merchant Navy) .... 1 → Q4
Marriage broken down 2

4 SelfCom3   OFFER (COLOUR) SELF-COMPLETION FORM TO RESPONDENT AND ENTER CODE

Interviewer asked section .... 1 → See Q5
Informant accepted self-completion ... 2   & Q6
Data now being keyed by interviewer 3
Interpreter aged under 16- section
   not asked .... 4 → Income

5 WhereWed   **To married men and women (Mstat = 2)**

Thinking of your present marriage, did you get married with a religious ceremony of some kind, or at a register office, or are you simply living together as a couple?

Religious ceremony of some kind...... 1
Register Office .... 2 → Q7
Religious ceremony and register office . 3
Living together as a couple .... 4 → Q8

6 WhereWed   **To widowed, divorced or separated men and women (MStat = 3, 4 or 5 or SLMar = 1)**

Thinking of your most recent marriage, did you get married with a religious ceremony of some kind, or at a register office, or were you simply living together as a couple?

Religious ceremony of some kind...... 1
Register Office .... 2 → Q7
Religious ceremony and register office . 3
Living together as a couple .... 4 → Q8

7 NumMar   **If coded 1-3 at WhereWed**

How many times have you been legally married? (NUMBER INCLUDING PRESENT MARRIAGE)

1..7   →   Q13

8 CLMon   **Cohabiting men and women (exc. couples now separated and same sex couples) (LiveWith = 1 OR (WhereWed = 4 and MStat = 2))**

When did you and your partner start living together as a couple?
ENTER MONTH   1..12   →   Q9

9 CLYr   ENTER YEAR IN 4 DIGIT FORMAT E.G. 1985

1900..2005   →   Q10

251

10 ClPrtMar   Has your partner ever been married, that is legally married?

Yes .... 1 ⎤ →   Q11
No .... 2 ⎦

11 ClMar   **All cohabiting (and ex-cohabiting) men and women (cohabit = 1 or WhereWed = 4)**

Have you yourself ever been legally married?

Yes 1   →   Q12
No 2   →   Q32

12 ClNumMar   **If 'yes' at ClMar**

How many times have you been legally married altogether?

1..7   →   Q13

INTRO   **To all who are, or have been legally married (NumMar or ClNumMar>=1)**

13 MonMar   **For each marriage**

What month and year were you married?

ENTER MONTH   1..12   →   Q14

14 YrMar   ENTER YEAR IN 4 DIGIT FORMAT EG 1985

1900..2005   →   Q15

15 LvTgthr   Before getting married did you and your husband/ wife live together as a couple?

Yes 1   →   Q16
No 2   →   Q18

16 MonLvTg   **If 'yes' at LivTgthr (code 1)**

What month and year did you start living together?

ENTER MONTH   1..12   →   Q17

17 YrLvTg   ENTER YEAR IN 4 DIGIT FORM E.G.1985

1900..2005   →   Q18

18 PartMar   **All who are or have been legally married**

Had your husband/wife been legally married before?

Yes .... 1 ⎤ →   Q19
No .... 2 ⎦

19 Current   **For last marriage entered**

INTERVIEWER - IS THIS MARRIAGE CURRENT OR HAS IT ENDED?

current .... 1 ⎤ → See Q20
ended .... 2 ⎦

20 HowEnded   **If marriage ended (code 2 at Current or marriage number less than total marriages)**

Did your marriage end in ...

death .... 1 →   Q21
divorce .... 2 ⎤ →   Q23
or separation? .... 3 ⎦

21 MonDie   **If marriage ended in death (HowEnded = 1)**

What month and year did your husband/wife die?

ENTER MONTH   1..12   →   Q22

22 YrDie   ENTER YEAR IN 4 DIGIT FORMAT EG 1985

1900-2005   →   Q27

23 MonSep   **If marriage ended in divorce or separation (HowEnded = 2 or 3)**

What month and year did you stop living together?

ENTER MONTH   1..12   →   Q24

24 YrSep   ENTER YEAR IN 4 DIGIT FORMAT EG 1985

1900-2005   → See Q25

25 MonDiv   **If marriage ended in divorce (HowEnded =2)**

What month and year was your decree absolute granted?

ENTER MONTH   1..12   →   Q26

26 YrDiv   ENTER YEAR IN 4 DIGIT FORMAT EG 1985

1900-2005   →   Q27

27 Tgthr1   **Ask if widowed, divorced, separated or single men and women (no. of adults in hhld>1)**

Interviewer are there adults of the opposite sex in the household and unrelated to the respondent?

Yes .... 1 →   Q28
No .... 2 →   Q32

28 Tgthr2   **Ask where there is an unrelated adult of the opposite sex in the household who is not married or cohabiting (Tgthr1 = 1)**

Introduce as necessary
(As you know, some couples live together without actually getting married, either because they cannot get married for some reason, or because they prefer not to get married)

Are you currently living with someone as a couple?

Yes .... 1 →   Q29
No .... 2 →   Q32

29 StrtMon

If 'yes' at Tgthr2

When did you and your partner start living together as a couple?
ENTER MONTH

1..12 → Q30

30 StrtYr

...AND YEAR (IN 4 DIGIT FORMAT EG 1985)

1900..2005 → Q31

31 CpartMar

Has your partner ever been married, that is legally married?

Yes .... 1 ⎫ → Q32
No .... 2 ⎭

32 Cohab

To all aged 16-59

(Apart from your present relationship), have you ever lived with someone of the opposite sex as a couple and it did not lead to marriage?

Yes .... 1 → Q33
No .... 2 → See Q36

33 NumCohab

If 'yes' at Cohab

How many such relationships have you had?

1..7 → Q34

34 LastCohb

(Thinking again of your last relationship) how did it end?

Death .... 1 ⎫ → See Q35
Separation .... 2 ⎭

35 Recent

If single, widowed, divorced or separated but has been married and has cohabited and it did not lead to marriage

Was this cohabiting relationship before or after your last marriage?

Before .... 1 ⎫ → See Q36
After .... 2 ⎭

COHABITATION AND TENURE

36 BCTName

If married or cohabiting with someone of the opposite sex (Marstat = 2) OR (LiveWith = 1), others go to Q53

Just before you started living with your (current) husband/wife/partner was the accommodation you were living in owned or rented in your name (including joint names)?

Yes .... 1 → Q38
No .... 2 → Q37

37 BCParent

If accommodation not in person's name (BCTName = 2)

May I just check were you living with your parents?

Yes .... 1 → Q40
No .... 2 → Q38

38 BCTen1

If accommodation in person's name (BCTName = 1) or not living with parents (BCParent=2)

In which of these ways did you occupy the accommodation?

SHOW CARD T

Owned it outright .... 1 ⎫
Buying it with the help of a
  mortgage or loan .... 2 ⎬ → Q40
Pay part rent and part mortgage
  (shared ownership) .... 3 ⎭
Rent it .... 4 ⎫
Live here rent-free (including
  rent-free in relative's/friend's ⎬ → Q39
  property; excluding squatting) .... 5 ⎭
Squatted .... 6 → Q40

39 BCLlord

If rented or rent-free (BCTen1 = 4 or 5)

Who was your landlord?
CODE FIRST THAT APPLIES

The local authority/council/New
  Town Development/Scottish Homes 1 ⎫
A housing association or co-operative
  or charitable trust 2
Employer (organisation) of a
  household member 3
Another organisation .... 4 ⎬ → Q40
Relative/friend (before you lived here)
  of a household member 5
Employer (individual) of a household
  member 6
Another individual private landlord 7
Husband/wife/partner .... 8 ⎭

40 ACTen1

If married or cohabiting with someone of the opposite sex (Marstat = 2 or LiveWith = 1)

(I may have asked this of your husband/wife/partner already), when you started living with your current husband/wife/partner, in which of these ways did you occupy the accommodation you were living in?

SHOW CARD T

Owned it outright .... 1 ⎫
Buying it with the help of a mortgage
  or loan 2
Pay part rent and part mortgage
  (shared ownership) .... 3 ⎬ → Q41
Rent it 4
Live here rent-free (including rent-
  free in relative's/friend's property;
  excluding squatting) 5
Squatted .... 6 ⎭

253

41 ACTName (I may have asked this of your husband/wife/partner already), in whose name was the accommodation owned or rented?

Yours only .... 1 ⌉
Partners only .... 2 |
Joint names - yours and partners ...... 3 |
Joint names - yours and other | → See Q42
  persons .... 4 |
Joint names - partners and other |
  persons .... 5 |
Other .... 6 ⌋

42 ACLlord **If rented or rent-free (ACTen1 = 4 or 5), others Q43**

(I may have asked this of your husband/wife/partner already), who was your landlord...

CODE FIRST THAT APPLIES

The local authority/council/New Town ⌉
  Development/Scottish Homes .... 1 |
A housing association or co-operative |
  or charitable trust .... 2 |
Employer (organisation) of a |
  household member .... 3 |
Another organisation .... 4 | → Q43
Relative/friend (before you lived here) |
  of a household member .... 5 |
Employer (individual) of a household |
  member .... 6 |
Another individual private landlord ..... 7 |
Husband/wife/partner? .... 8 ⌋

43 ACMove **If married or cohabiting with someone of the opposite sex**

(I may have asked this of your husband/wife/partner already) did you move into the accommodation that your husband/wife/partner was already living in?

Yes .... 1 ⌉ → See Q44
No .... 2 ⌋

44 LCTen1 **If single, widowed, divorced or separated and the last union was marriage or cohabitation which ended in separation or death, others see Q47**

Thinking about the last time you were married/lived with someone as a couple, in which of these ways did you occupy the accommodation you were living in?

  SHOW CARD T

Owned outright .... 1 ⌉
Buying it with the help of a mortgage |
  or loan .... 2 |
Pay part rent and part mortgage |
  (shared ownership) .... 3 | → Q45
Rent it .... 4 |
Live here rent-free (including rent-free |
  in relative's/friend's property; |
  excluding squatting) .... 5 |
Squatted .... 6 ⌋

45 LCTName In whose name was the accommodation owned or rented?

Yours only .... 1 ⌉
Partners only .... 2 |
Joint names - yours and partners ...... 3 |
Joint names - yours and other | → Q46
  persons .... 4 |
Joint names - partners and other |
  persons .... 5 |
Other .... 6 ⌋

46 LCLord **If rented or rent-free (LCTen1 = 4 or 5), others see Q47**

Who was your landlord... CODE FIRST THAT APPLIES

The local authority/council/New Town ⌉
  Development/Scottish Homes .... 1 |
A housing association or co-operative |
  or charitable trust .... 2 |
Employer (organisation) of a |
  household member .... 3 |
Another organisation .... 4 | → Q47
Relative/friend (before you lived here) |
  of a household member .... 5 |
Employer (individual) of a household |
  member .... 6 |
Another individual private landlord ..... 7 |
Husband/wife/partner? .... 8 ⌋

47 AsepMove **If single, widowed, divorced or separated and the last union was marriage or cohabitation which ended in separation or divorce, others see Q49**

May I just check, immediately after your separation/divorce, did you remain living in the accommodation you had shared with your husband/wife/partner?

Yes .... 1 → Q48
No .... 2 → See Q49

48 A12Mth **If ASepMove = Yes (code 1)**

Now thinking about the time 12 months after your decree absolute/separation, were you still living in the accomodation you had shared with your husband/wife/partner?

Yes .... 1 ⌉
No .... 2 | → See Q49
Not yet 12 months since decree |
  absolute/separation .... 3 ⌋

49 AdthMove **If single, widowed, divorced or separated and the last union was marriage or cohabitation which ended in death of partner, others see Q50**

Now thinking about the time 12 months after your husband's/wife's/partner's death, were you still living in the accommodation you had shared with your husband/wife/partner?

Yes .... 1 ⌉ → See Q50
No .... 2 ⌋

50 ALCTen1   **If single, widowed, divorced or separated and the last union was marriage/cohabitation which ended in separation/divorce/death of partner and person no longer living in same accomodation (AsepMove = 2 or ADthMove = 2 or A12Mth = 2), others go to Q53**

Again/Now thinking about the time 12 months after your decree absolute/separation/partner's death, in which of these ways did you occupy the accomodation you were living in?

SHOW CARD T

Owned outright 1
Buying it with the help of a mortgage
  or loan 2
Pay part rent and part mortgage
  (shared ownership) .... 3 → Q51
Rent it 4
Live here rent-free (including rent-free
  in relative's/friend's property
  excluding squatting) 5
Squatted 6

51 ALCTName   In whose name was the accommodation owned or rented?

Yours only (including jointly) 1
Other person .... 6 → See Q52

52 ALCLlord   **If rented or rent-free (ACLTen1 = 4 or 5)**

Who was your landlord...
CODE FIRST THAT APPLIES

The local authority/council/New Town
  Development/Scottish Homes 1
A housing association or co-operative
  or charitable trust 2
Employer (organisation) of a
  household member 3
Another organisation .... 4 → Q53
Relative/friend (before you lived here)
  of a household member 5
Employer (individual) of a
  household member 6
Another individual private landlord..... 7
Husband/wife/partner 8

CHILDREN

53 Children   **Ask all adults**

INTERVIEWER: DOES THIS PERSON HAVE ANY CHILDREN IN THE HOUSEHOLD (INCLUDES ADULTS AND/OR STEP OR FOSTER CHILDREN)

Yes .... 1 → See Q54&55
No .... 2 → See Q64

54 StpChldF   **Ask females only. If children =1**

(The next questions are about the family.) Have you any step, foster, or adopted children living with you, (including any children from your partner's previous relationship)?

Yes... 1 → Q56
No .... 2 → Q64

55 StpChldM   **Ask males only. If children=1**

Have you any stepchildren of any age living with you, (including any children from your partner's previous relationship)?

Yes... 1 → Q56
No .... 2 → Contraception

56 NumStep   **Ask if StpChldF = 1 or StpChldM=1**

How many stepchildren have you living with you altogether?

1..7   →   Q57

57 NumFost   **If StpchldF = yes**

How many foster children have you living with you altogether

0..7   →   Q58

58 NumAdop   How many adopted children have you living with you altogether?

0..7   →   Q59

59 StepInt   **If StpChldF = 1 OR StpChldM = 1**

THE NEXT SCREEN CONSISTS OF A TABLE FOR THE STEP-CHILDREN (AND ADOPTED AND FOSTER- CHILDREN) OF (...)
PLEASE ENTER DETAILS FOR
EACH CHILD   →   Q60

60 ChildNo   **Ask for each step/foster/ adopted child**

ENTER PERSON NUMBER(S) OF THE STEP/ FOSTER/ADOPTED CHILD (INCLUDES ADULT CHILDREN)

1..20   →   Q61

61 ChldType   ENTER CODE AS FOLLOWS

Step 1
Foster.. 2 → Q62
Adopted 3

62 ChLivMon   DATE STARTED LIVING WITH INFORMANT

ENTER MONTH

1..12   →   Q63

63 ChLivYr   YEAR (IN 4 DIGIT FORMAT   EG 1985)

1900..2005   → See Q64

64 Baby   **All women**

ASK OR CODE
 EXCLUDE: ANY STILLBORN. INCLUDE ANY
WHO ONLY LIVED FOR A SHORT TIME

Have you ever had a baby - even one who only
lived for a short time?

Yes .... 1 →   Q65
No .... 2 → See Q69

65 NumBaby   **If yes at Baby**

EXCLUDE: ANY STILLBORN

How many children have you given birth to,
including any who are not living here and any who
may have died since birth?

1..20   →   Q66

66 BirthMon   **For each child**

Date of birth

PLEASE ENTER IN DATE OF BIRTH ORDER -
ELDEST FIRST, YOUNGEST LAST   →   Q67

67 BirthSex   Sex of child

Male .... 1 ⌉ →   Q68
Female .... 2 ⌋

68 ChldLive   Is child living with informant?

Yes .... 1 ⌉
No, lives elsewhere .... 2 ⌉ → See Q69
No, deceased .... 3 ⌋

69 Pregnant   **All women aged 16-49**

(May I just check), are you pregnant now?

Yes .... 1 ⌉ →   Q70
No/unsure .... 2 ⌋

70 MoreChld [*]   Do you **think** that you will have any (more) children
(after the one you are expecting)? Could you
choose your answers from this card.

SHOW CARD U

Yes .... 1 ⌉ →   Q72
Probably yes .... 2 ⌋
Probably not .... 3 ⌉ → Contraception
No .... 4 ⌋

71 ProbMore [*]   **If DK at MoreChld**

On the whole do you think...

You will probably have
 any/more children 1   →   Q72
Or you will probably not have
 any/more children? 2   → Contraception

72 TotChld [*]   **If coded 1 or 2 at MoreChld or 1 at ProbMore**

(Can I just check, you have ... children still alive).
How many children do you think you will have born
to you in all including those you already have had
already(who are still alive) (and the one you are
expecting)?

1..14   →   Q73

73 NextAge [*]   How old do you **think** you will be when you have
your first/next baby (after the one you are
expecting)?

1..97   → Contraception

CONTRACEPTION

1 SterilA   **Ask married women and women cohabiting with
men, others Q3**

We've talked about how many children you think
you'll have. The next questions are about ways of
preventing pregnancy.

Have you or your husband/partner ever been
sterilised - I mean ever had an operation
intended to prevent you getting pregnant (again)?

Yes 1   →   Q2
No. 2   →   See Q5
Refused whole contraception section . 7   →   Income

2 WhoStlsd   **Ask if SterilA = Yes**

Was it you who was sterilised or your husband/
partner who had a vasectomy?

Informant .... 1 ⌉
Husband or partner .... 2 ⌉ →   Q4
Both .... 3 ⌋

3 SterilB   **Ask non-cohabiting women**

We've talked about how many children you think
you'll have. The next questions are about ways of
preventing pregnancy.

Have you ever been sterilised - I mean ever had an
operation intended to prevent you getting pregnant
(again)?

Yes 1   →   Q4
No 2   →   See Q5

4 ChkFp2

If (WhoStIsd= 1,2 or 3) OR (SterilB = 1)

Did either of these operations/this operation take place within the last 2 years or were they/was it more than 2 years ago?

Less than 2 years ago .... 1 ⎤
2 years or more .... 2 ⎦ → See Q9

5 CcUsed

Ask if the respondent is pregnant and has not been sterilised

SHOW CARD V

Here is a list of ways of preventing pregnancy - were you or your partner using any of them when you became pregnant?

Yes .... 1 → Q6
No .... 2 → Q18

6 CCPreg

If CcUsed = yes

Please can you look through the list to the end of the card and read out the numbers beside the methods which applied to you and your husband/partner when you got pregnant?:

CODE UP TO 4 METHODS

Withdrawal .... 1 ⎤
Male sheath/condom .... 2 ⎥
Safe period/rhythm method/Persona . 3 ⎥ → See Q15
Cap/diaphragm .... 4 ⎥
Contraceptive sponge .... 5 ⎦
Pill .... 6 → Q7
Coil/intra-uterine device .... 7 ⎤
Hormonal IUD-MIRENA .... 8 ⎥
Gels, sprays, pessaries(spermicides) . 9 ⎥
Female Condom .... 10 ⎦ → See Q15
Injections .... 12 ⎤
Surgically implanted hormone ⎥
   capsules .... 13 ⎦
Another method .... 14 → Q8

7 PillTyp1

Ask if CCPreg = Pill

SHOW CARD W

Is the pill you take one of the brands listed

(MICRONOR, NORIDAY, FEMULEN, MICROVAL, NORGESTON, NEOGEST)?
These are progestogen only pills (sometimes known as the mini-pill) as opposed to combined pills.

Yes .... 1 ⎤
No .... 2 ⎥ → See Q15
Not sure .... 3 ⎦

8 XCCPreg

If CCPreg = 14

RECORD THE OTHER METHOD

9 OtherOp1

Ask if married/cohabiting and not pregnant and not sterilised

Have you or your husband/partner had any other operation which prevents you getting pregnant (again)?

Yes informant .... 1 ⎤
Yes, husband or partner .... 2 ⎥ → Q11
Yes, both .... 3 ⎦
No .... 4 → Q12

10 OtherOp2

If not married/cohabiting and not pregnant and not sterilised

Have you had any other operation which prevents you getting pregnant (again)?:

Yes informant .... 1 → Q11
No .... 2 → Q12

11 ChkFp3

If (OtherOp1 = 1,2 or 3) OR (OtherOp2 =1)

Did either of these operations/ this operation take place within the last 2 years or were they/was it more than 2 years ago?

Less than 2 years ago .... 1 ⎤ →
2 years or more .... 2 ⎦ Q12

12 CCMUsu

Ask if respondent not pregnant and not sterile (otherOp1 = 4 OR Other Op2 = 2)

SHOW CARD X
Here is a list of possible ways of preventing pregnancy - which of them, if any, do you (and your husband\partner) usually use at present?

ENTER UP TO 4 METHODS

No method needed-no sexual
   relationship .... 15 → Q20
No method used at all .... 16 → Q18
Pregnant .... 19 → Q24
Withdrawal .... 1 ⎤
Male sheath/condom .... 2 ⎥
Safe period/rhythm method./Persona . 3 ⎥ → Q15
Cap/diaphragm .... 4 ⎥
Contraceptive sponge .... 5 ⎦
Pill-not sure if mini or combined .... 6 → Q13
Coil/intra-uterine device .... 7 ⎤
Hormonal IUD - MIRENA .... 8 ⎥
Gels, sprays,pessaries(spermicides) . 9 ⎥
Female condom .... 10 ⎥
Going without sexual intercourse ⎥ → Q15
   to avoid pregnancy .... 11 ⎥
Injections .... 12 ⎥
Surgically implanted hormone ⎥
   capsules .... 13 ⎦
Another method .... 14 → Q14

13 PillTyp2   **Ask if CCMUsu = Pill**

SHOW CARD W

Is the pill you take one of the brands listed
(MICRONOR, NORIDAY, FEMULEN, MICROVAL,
NORGESTON, NEOGEST)?
These are progestogen only pills (sometimes
known as the mini-pill) as opposed to combined
pills.

Yes .... 1 ⎤
No .... 2 ⎥ → Q14
Not sure .... 3 ⎦

14 XCCMUsu   **Ask if CCMUsu = 14**

RECORD THE OTHER METHOD

ENTER NAME   → Q15

15 CcmComb   **Ask if more than one method used**

You have mentioned that you (and your husband/
partner) usually use more than one method. Do/did
you use them in combination or do/did you
sometimes use one and sometimes the other?

In combination .... 1 → Q17
Sometimes one, sometimes other ..... 2 → Q16

16 MstFrq   **Ask if CcmComb = 2**

Which one do/did you use most often?

SHOW CARD V
Withdrawal .... 1 ⎤
Male sheath/condom .... 2 ⎥
Safe period/rhythm method/Persona . 3 ⎥
Cap/diaphragm .... 4 ⎥
Contraceptive sponge .... 5 ⎥
Pill-not sure if mini or combined .... 6 ⎥
Coil/intra-uterine device .... 7 ⎥ → Q17
Hormonal IUD - MIRENA .... 8 ⎥
Gels, sprays,pessaries(spermicides) . 9 ⎥
Female condom .... 10 ⎥
Injections .... 12 ⎥
Surgically implanted hormone   ⎥
  capsules .... 13 ⎥
Another method .... 14 ⎦

17 UsuTime   How long has/had this method/combination of
methods been your usual one (ie the one you use
most often)?

Under 3 months .... 1 ⎤
At least 3 months, less than 6 months . 2 ⎥ → Q21
At least 6 months, less than 1 year ... 3 ⎥
At least 1 year, less than 2 years .... 4 ⎦
At least 2 years .... 5 → Q24

18 YnoCC   **Ask if no method currently used, code 2 at
CcUsed or code 16 at CCMUsu**

SHOW CARD Y
Here is a list of reasons why people do not use any
method for preventing pregnancy. Can you tell me
which reason applies/applied to you?

CODE MAIN REASON ONLY

Want to get pregnant .... 1 ⎤
Unlikely to conceive because of   ⎥
  menopause .... 2 ⎥
Unlikely to conceive because   ⎥ → Q20
  possibly infertile .... 3 ⎥
Don't like contraception and/or finds   ⎥
  methods unsatisfactory .... 4 ⎦
Other reasons .... 5 → Q19

19 XYNoCC   **Ask if YNoCC = 5**

RECORD OTHER REASON   → Q20

20 UsedL2Yr   **Ask if no method needed or possibly pregnant,
code 15 or 16 at CCMUsu or code 1 at CcUsed**

SHOW CARD X

Have you (or your husband/partner) ever used any
of these methods in the last two years?

Yes .... 1 → Q21
No .... 2 → Q24

21 CcBfor   **If UsedL2Yr = 1**

SHOW CARD X

(Here is a list of ways of preventing pregnancy).
Which methods, if any, did you(or your husband/
partner) use (in the last 2 years/immediately before
that)?

ENTER UP TO 4 METHODS

No method needed-no sexual   ⎤
  relationship .... 15 ⎥
No method used at all .... 16 ⎥
Pregnant .... 19 ⎥
Withdrawal .... 1 ⎥ → Q24
Male sheath/condom .... 2 ⎥
Safe period/rhythm method./Persona . 3 ⎥
Cap/diaphragm .... 4 ⎥
Contraceptive sponge .... 5 ⎦
Pill-not sure if mini or combined .... 6 → Q22
Coil/intra-uterine device .... 7 ⎤
Hormonal IUD - MIRENA .... 8 ⎥
Gels, sprays,pessaries(spermicides) . 9 ⎥
Female condom .... 10 ⎥
Going without sexual intercourse   ⎥ → Q24
  to avoid pregnancy .... 11 ⎥
Injections .... 12 ⎥
Surgically implanted hormone   ⎥
  capsules .... 13 ⎦
Another method .... 14 → Q23

22 PillTyp3   **Ask if CcBfor = Pill**

SHOW CARD W

Is the pill you take one of the brands listed
(MICRONOR, NORIDAY, FEMULEN, MICROVAL,
NORGESTON, NEOGEST)?
These are progestogen only pills (sometimes
known as the mini-pill) as opposed to combined
pills.

Yes .... 1 ⎤
No .... 2 ⎥ →   Q23
Not sure .... 3 ⎦

23 XCCBFor   **Ask if CcBfor = 14**

RECORD THE OTHER METHOD   →   Q24

24 EmerCon   **Ask all, except those sterilised 2+ years ago**

There are other methods of contraception available.
These are referred to as emergency contraception.
Have you used emergency contraception, that is
the 'morning after' pill or IUD method in the last two
years?

Yes .... 1 →   Q25
No .... 2 →   Q27

25 EmerNum   On how many occasions in the last 2 years have
you used emergency contraception?

ENTER NUMBER   →   Q26

26 MaMeth   (And for each occasion,) could you tell me the
method(s) you used?

PROMPT AS NECESSARY

Pill method, sometimes called
   the morning after pill .... 1 ⎤ →
IUD coil fitted .... 2 ⎦   Q27

27 MorePoss   **Ask if not pregnant and not sterile**

As far as you know, could you (and your husband/
partner) have (more) children if you wanted to or
would it be difficult or impossible?

Could have more children .... 1 →   Income
Would be difficult/impossible .... 2 →   Q28

28 PrDiff   **If Moreposs=2**

SHOW CARD Z
Will you please look at this card and tell me what
the difficulty is?

ENTER UP TO 3 REASONS

Getting pregnant .... 1 ⎤ →
Having a baby born alive .... 2 ⎦   Q30
Pregnancy would endanger health .... 3 ⎤ →
Passed the menopause-change of life . 4 ⎦   Income
Other .... 5 →   Q29

29 XprDiff   **If PrDiff = 5**

RECORD OTHER DIFFICULTY   →   Income

30 DocAdvce   **Ask if PrDiff = 1 or 2**

Have you (or your husband/partner) ever consulted
a doctor about the difficulty you have or would have
in getting pregnant/having a baby born alive?

Yes .... 1 ⎤ →   Income
No .... 2 ⎦

INCOME

Intro   THE NEXT SECTION IS ABOUT BENEFITS AND
OTHER SOURCES OF INCOME

2 Ben1YN   **All adults (except proxy informants)**

SHOW CARD AA

Looking at this card, are you at present receiving
any of these state benefits in your own right: that is,
where you are the named recipient?

Yes .... 1 ⎤ →
No .... 2 ⎦   Q3
Refused whole income section .... 7 →   Recall
                                    Questions

3 Ben1Q   SHOW CARD AA

RECORD BENEFITS RECEIVED
CODE ALL THAT APPLY (NONE OF THESE =
CODE 9)
enter at most 6 codes

Child Benefit .... 1 ⎤
Guardian's Allowance 2
Invalid Care Allowance 3
Retirement pension (National
   Insurance), or Old person's pension .. 4
Widow's pension or Widowed Mother's
   allowance (National Insurance) 5   →   Q4
War disablement pension or War
   Widow's Pension (and any related
   allowances) 6
Severe disablement allowance 7
Disability Working Allowance 8
None of these .... 9 ⎦

4 Ben2Q   SHOW CARD BB

And looking at this card, are you at present
receiving any of the state benefits shown on this
card - either in your own name, or on behalf of
someone else in the household?

CODE ALL THAT APPLY

CARE COMPONENT of Disability
   Living Allowance .... 1 →   Q6
MOBILITY COMPONENT of
   Disability Living Allowance .... 2 →   Q7
Attendance Allowance .... 3 →   Q5
None of these .... 4 →   Q9

259

5 AttAllFU   **If Attendance Allowance, code 3 at Ben2Q**

Is this paid as part of your retirement pension or do you receive a separate payment?

Together with pension .... 1⌉→   Q8
Separate payment .... 2⌋

6 WhoReCar   **If code 1 at BEN2Q**

Whom do you receive it for ?
IF CURRENT HOUSEHOLD MEMBER,
ENTER PERSON NUMBER.
OTHERWISE ENTER 97   →   Q9

7 WhoReMob   **If code 2 at BENQ2**

Whom do you receive it for ?
IF CURRENT HOUSEHOLD MEMBER,
ENTER PERSON NUMBER.
OTHERWISE ENTER 97   →   Q9

8 WhoReAtt   **If code 3 at BENQ2**

Whom do you receive it for ?
IF CURRENT HOUSEHOLD MEMBER,
ENTER PERSON NUMBER.
OTHERWISE ENTER 97   →   Q9

9 Ben3Q   **All except proxy informants**

SHOW CARD CC
Now looking at this card, are you at present
receiving any of these benefits in your own right:
that is, where you are the named recipient?

CODE ALL THAT APPLY (ENTER AT MOST 6
CODES)

Job Seekers' Allowance .... 1⌉
Income Support 2
Family Credit (not received in a
 lump sum) .... 3 ⌐→ See Q10
Incapacity Benefit 4
Statutory Sick Pay 5
Industrial Injury Disablement Benefit .. 6
None of these .... 7⌋

10 Ben4Q   **Women aged <55 years, others Q11**

SHOW CARD DD
Are you currently getting either of the things shown
on this card, in your own right?

CODE ALL THAT APPLY

Maternity Allowance .... 1⌉
Statutory maternity pay from your
 employer or former employer .... 2 →   Q11
Neither of these .... 3⌋

11 Ben5Q   **All except proxy informants**

SHOW CARD EE

In the last 6 months, have you received any of the
things shown on this card, in your own right?
EXCLUDE HOUSING BENEFIT (NONE OF
THESE =CODE 6)

INTERVIEWER: 'Family Credit lump sum' IS ONE
PAYMENT COVERING 26 WEEKS

CODE ALL THAT APPLY

Family Credit - paid in lump sum .... 1⌉
A grant from the Social Fund for
 funeral expenses 2
Grant from Social Fund for
 maternity expenses .... 3 ⌐→ See Q12
A Community Care grant from ....
 the Social Fund 4
Any National Insurance or State
 benefit not mentioned earlier 5
None of these .... 6⌋

12 Ben1Amt   **For each benefit mentioned at Ben1Q, Ben2Q
(except Attendance Allowance combined with
pension), Ben3Q, Ben4Q and Ben5Q**

How much did you get last time?

(IF COMBINED WITH ANOTHER BENEFIT AND
UNABLE TO GIVE SEPARATE AMOUNT, ENTER
'Don't know')

0.00..997.00   →See Q13

13 Ben1AmtDK   **If DK or Refusal at Ben1Amt**

INTERVIEWER: IS THIS 'DON'T KNOW'
BECAUSE IT'S PAID IN COMBINATION WITH
ANOTHER BENEFIT, AND YOU CANNOT
ESTABLISH A SEPARATE AMOUNT?

Yes (Please give full details in a Note) . 1⌉→ See Q14
No .... 2⌋

14 Ben1Pd   **If Ben1Amt > 0.00**

How long did this cover?

one week .... 1⌉
two weeks 2
three weeks 3
four weeks 4
calendar month 5
two calendar months 7
eight times a year 8
nine times a year .... 9 ⌐→ See Q15
ten times a year 10
three months/13 weeks 13
six months/26 weeks 26
one year/12 months/52 weeks 52
less than one week 90
one off lump sum 95
none of these:MAKE NOTE .... 97⌋

15 BenUs

If code 4 at Ben1Q

Is that the amount you usually get?

Yes.. 1	→	Q19
No 2	→	Q16
No such thing as usual amount 3	→	Q19

16 BenAmt

If BenUs = 2

How much do you usually get?
(if combined with other benefit and unable to give amount enter 'don't know')

0.00. . 997.00 .... → See Q17

17 BenAmtDK

If don't know or refusal at BenAmt

INTERVIEWER: IS THIS 'DON'T KNOW' BECAUSE IT'S PAID IN COMBINATION WITH ANOTHER BENEFIT, AND YOU CANNOT ESTABLISH A SEPARATE AMOUNT?

Yes (Please give full details in a Note) . 1	⎤	→ See Q18
No 2	⎦	

18 BenPd

If BenAmt > 0.00

How long did this cover?

one week 1		
two weeks 2		
three weeks 3		
four weeks 4		
calendar month 5		
two calendar months 7		
eight times a year 8		
nine times a year 9	→	Q19
ten times a year 10		
three months/13 weeks 13		
six months/26 weeks 26		
one year/12 months/52 weeks 52		
less than one week 90		
one off lump sum 95		
none of these:MAKE NOTE 97		

19 OthSourc

Ask all (except proxy informants)

SHOW CARD FF
Please look at this card and tell me whether you are receiving any regular payment of the kinds listed on it?

Yes receiving benefits - code at next question 1	→	Q20
No, not receiving any 2	→	Q23

20 OthSrcM

If 'yes' at OthSourc

SHOW CARD FF
RECORD PAYMENTS RECEIVED

CODE ALL THAT APPLY
(ENTER AT MOST 4 CODES)

Occupational pensions from former employer(s) 1		
Occupational pensions from a spouse's former employer(s) 2		
Private pensions or annuities 3	→	Q21
Regular redundancy payments from former employer(s) 4		
Training Schemes, such as YT allowance 5		

21 OthNetAm

In total how much do you receive each month from (...../all these sources) AFTER tax is deducted? (ie net)

DO NOT PROBE MONTH. ACCEPT CALENDAR MONTH OR 4 WEEKLY

0.01..99999.97   →   Q22

22 OthGrsAm

In total how much do you receive each month from ..... (all these sources) BEFORE tax is deducted? (ie GROSS)?

DO NOT PROBE MONTH. ACCEPT CALENDAR MONTH OR 4 WEEKLY

0.01..99999.97   →   Q23

23 ReglrPay

Ask all (except proxy informants)

SHOW CARD GG

Now please look at this card and tell me whether you are receiving any regular payments of the kind listed on it?

Yes receiving benefits - code at next question 1	→	Q24
No, not receiving any 2	→ See Q26

24 ReglrPM

If 'yes' at ReglrPay

SHOW CARD GG
Record types of payment received

CODE ALL THAT APPLY

Educational grant 1		
Regular payments from friends or relatives outside the household 2	→	Q25
Rent from property or subletting 3		
Maintenance, alimony or separation allowance 4		

53 SjPrGrs

If self-employed, or employee in second job but NOT regularly each week (NOT (SJReg = 1 AND SJEmplee = 1)

In the last 12 months (that is sinceDATE 1 YEAR AGO) how much have you earned from this work, before deducting income tax, and National Insurance contributions, (and money drawn for your own use but after deducting all business expenses?

IF MADE NO PROFIT ENTER 0

0.00..99999.97 → Q54

54 IncTax

Ask all (except proxy informants)

During the last 12 months (that is since DATE 1 YEAR AGO) have you paid any tax direct to the Inland Revenue?

Yes..1 → Q55
No ....2 → See Q56

55 IncTaxAm

If 'yes' at IncTax

How much income tax did you pay direct to the Inland Revenue?

0.01..99999.97 → See Q56

56 PEP

Ask all adults aged 18 or over (except proxy informants)

There is a scheme called a Personal Equity Plan or PEP which gives people tax relief if they invest in shares or unit trusts or corporate bonds. Do you have a personal equity plan at present?

Yes..1 → Q57
No ....2 → Q58

57 PePTypM

If 'yes' at Pep

Is this....

CODE ALL THAT APPLY
(enter at most 3 codes)

a Unit Trust plan ....1 ⎤
a Single Company plan......................2 ⎥
a Corporate Bond fund plan ....3 ⎥ → Q58
or some other type of plan? ⎥
  (SPECIFY AT NEXT QUESTION) ... 4 ⎦

58 OthRgPay

Ask all (except proxy informants)

And finally, apart from anything you have already mentioned, have you received any regular payment from any other organisation or source in the last 12 months (that is since DATE 1 YEAR AGO)?

SPECIFY DETAILSAT NEXT QUESTION
EXCLUDE BENEFITS NO LONGER RECEIVED

Yes..1 → Q59
No ....2 → Recall
Questions

59 XothRgPy

If 'yes' at OthRgPy

Specify details of other regular payments since DATE 1 YEAR AGO
(Enter text of at most 80 characters) → Q60

60 OthRgPAm

How much have you received in the last 12 months?

0.01..99999.97 → Recall
Questions

61 NtIncEst

If proxy informant

SHOW CARD HH

I would now like to ask you about the income of (...). Please could you look at this card and estimate the total net income, that is after deduction of tax, National Insurance and any expenses (...) brings into the household in a year from all sources (benefits, employment, investments etc?)

0....30 → Recall
Questions

RECALL QUESTIONS

1 Recall

Ask all adults (except proxies)

That's the end of (your part/the main part) of the interview. May I just check........

We may want to contact you again in the future, would this be all right?

Yes (unconditional) ....1 → Q2
No (unconditional) ....2 → Q19
Yes (in certain circumstances)...........3 → Q2

2 Givetel

If Recall = 1 or 3

Please may I have a telephone number, so we can contact you?

Yes..1 → Q3
No ....2 ⎤ → See Q6
No phone ....3 ⎦

3 Telno

If Givetel = 1

INTERVIEWER RECORD TELEPHONE NUMBER (MUST BE STD CODE AND NUMBER)

IF THE TELEPHONE NUMBER IS THE SAME AS A PREVIOUS PERSON IN THE HOUSEHOLD, ALWAYS TYPE IN THE FULL TELEPHONE NUMBER AGAIN. NEVER TYPE IN THE WORDS 'SAME TELEPHONE NUMBER'. → See Q4

4 OnlyIf   **If Recall = 3**

INTERVIEWER: CODE MAIN CONDITION(S) TO THE FOLLOW-UP INTERVIEW

CODE ALL THAT APPLY

Contact household beforehand 1
Only at a convenient time 2
Someone else (e.g carer) needs
  to be there 3   → See Q6
Don't want to answer questions
  on financial matters 4
Don't want to answer other types
  of question .... 5 →   Q5

5 OnlyIfO   **If OnlyIf = 5**

INTERVIEWER: SPECIFY THE OTHER TYPES OF QUESTION IF RESPONDENT DOESN'T WISH TO ANSWER   →   Q6

6 Names   **If Recall = 1 or 3**

IT IS HELPFUL TO HAVE A NAME TO ASK FOR OR TO ADDRESS LETTERS TO: TITLE/INITIAL/ SURNAME. RECORD AS MUCH OF THIS AS RESPONDENT WILL ALLOW.

IF RESPONDENT REFUSES NAME,
ENTER 0   →   Q7

7 Title   INTERVIEWER: ENTER MR/MS/MISS ETC FOR CONTACT PERSON IF RESPONDENT REFUSES NAME, ENTER 0   →   Q8

8 Initial   INTERVIEWER: ENTER ONE INITIAL FOR CONTACT PERSON. IF RESPONDENT REFUSES NAME, ENTER 0 .... →   Q9

9 Surname INTERVIEWER: ENTER SURNAME FOR CONTACT PERSON. IF RESPONDENT REFUSES NAME, ENTER 0. .... →   Q10

10 Moving   May I just check, are you likely to be moving from this address in the near future?

Yes..1 →   Q12
No ....2 →   Q11

11 SIUAdd   **If Moving = 2**

INTERVIEWER: HAS THE S.I.U INSTRUCTED YOU TO CHANGE ANY DETAILS OF THIS ADDRESS FROM HOW IT WAS ORIGINALLY SUPPLIED TO YOU?

Yes.....................................1 →   Q12
No ....2 →   end of
....   enterview

12 NewAdWho **If Moving = 1 or SIUAdd = 1**

IF YOU HAVE ALREADY ENTERED THE SAME NEW OR CHANGED ADDRESS FOR ANOTHER PERSON IN THE HOUSEHOLD, ENTER HIS/HER PERSON NUMBER. IF NOT, ENTER 0.

0..14   →   Q13

13 NewAdd   COLLECT CHANGED, NEW OR CONTACT ADDRESS IN AS MUCH DETAIL AS POSSIBLE   →   Q14

14 Add1   INTERVIEWER: ENTER FIRST LINE OF NEW ADDRESS
(Enter text of at most 30 characters)

IF THE ADDRESS IS THE SAME AS A PREVIOUS PERSON IN THE HOUSEHOLD, ALWAYS TYPE IN THE FULL ADDRESS AGAIN. NEVER TYPE IN THE WORDS 'SAME ADDRESS'.   →   Q15

15 Add2   INTERVIEWER: ENTER SECOND LINE OF NEW ADDRESS
(Enter text of at most 30 characters)

IF THE ADDRESS IS THE SAME AS A PREVIOUS PERSON IN THE HOUSEHOLD, ALWAYS TYPE IN THE FULL ADDRESS AGAIN NEVER TYPE IN THE WORDS 'SAME ADDRESS'.   →   Q16

16 Add3   INTERVIEWER: ENTER THIRD LINE OF NEW ADDRESS
(Enter text of at most 30 characters)

IF THE ADDRESS IS THE SAME AS A PREVIOUS PERSON IN THE HOUSEHOLD, ALWAYS TYPE IN THE FULL ADDRESS AGAIN NEVER TYPE IN THE WORDS 'SAME ADDRESS'.   →   Q17

17 PostCode INTERVIEWER: ENTER POSTCODE OF NEW ADDRESS

IF THE POSTCODE IS THE SAME AS A PREVIOUS PERSON IN THE HOUSEHOLD, ALWAYS TYPE IN THE FULL POSTCODE AGAIN. NEVER TYPE IN THE WORDS 'SAME POSTCODE'.   →   Q18

18 NewTel   **If Moving = 1**

INTERVIEWER: COLLECT NEW OR CONTACT TELEPHONE NUMBER IN AS MUCH DETAIL AS POSSIBLE.
(MUST BE STD CODE AND NUMBER)
- OR ENTER 0 FOR 'NONE'.

IF THE NEW TELEPHONE NUMBER IS THE SAME AS A PREVIOUS PERSON IN THE HOUSEHOLD, ALWAYS TYPE IN THE FULL TELEPHONE NUMBER AGAIN. NEVER TYPE IN THE WORDS 'SAME TELEPHONE NUMBER'.   →   end of
                                        interview

265

19 RfReason   **If Recall = 2**

INTERVIEWER: CODE MAIN REASON(S) FOR
REFUSAL TO THE FOLLOW-UP INTERVIEW.

CODE ALL THAT APPLY.

Not interested 1
Taken too much time 2
Have done it once/once is enough 3
Questions are too repetitive 4
Current survey is too intrusive,
objected to subject matter 5
Other 6

END OF INDIVIDUAL QUESTIONNAIRE

Appendix D
Summary of main topics included in the GHS questionnaires 1971 to 1998

ACTIVITIES ON SCHOOL PREMISES   **1984**

Whether attended any event/activity
    on school premises in last 12 months

Whether activities organised by school or
    parent teacher's association

Type of activity attended (if not organised
    by school/parent teacher's association),
    number of times attended and whether
    attended a day or evening class

**BURGLARIES AND THEFTS FROM PRIVATE
HOUSEHOLDS**

Incidence of burglaries in the 12 months before interview	**1972-73,**
Value of stolen goods and whether insured	**1979-80,**
	1985-86,
Whether incident was reported to the police	**1991, 1993, 1996**

Reasons for not reporting to the police	**1972-73,**
	1979-80, 1985-86

Incidence of attempted burglary in the 12 months before interview	**1985-86**

BUS TRAVEL   **1982**

Frequency of use of buses in the six months
    before interview

Physical and other difficulties using buses

Reasons for not using buses

CAREER OPPORTUNITIES   **1972**

Attitudes towards careers in the Armed Forces
    and the Police Force

Whether ever been in one of the Armed Forces

CAR OWNERSHIP

Number of cars or vans, if any, available to the household for private use	**1971-96, 1998**
Type of vehicle and whether privately/company owned	**1998**
In whose name (person or firm) each car/van was registered	**1980, 1992-93**

Driving licences and private motoring   **1980**

Whether held current licence for driving a car
    or van, and for how long full licence held

Whether non-licence holders (aged 17-70) intended
    to apply for a licence (again), and reasons for
    not having done so or for not intending to do so

Frequency of use, for private motoring, of
    car/van available to the household

If household car/van not available, or not used for
    private motoring in the year before interview:
    - whether used any car/van for private motoring in
      that year
    - whether drove a car, van, lorry, or bus in the
      course of work in that year

COLOUR AND COUNTRY OF BIRTH

Colour, assessment of persons seen*	**1971-92**
Country of birth	
of adults and their parents	**1971-96, 1998**
of children	**1979-96, 1998**
Year of entry to UK	
adults	**1971-96, 1998**
children	**1979-96, 1998**
Ethnic origin	**1983-96, 1998**

DRINKING

Rating of drinking behaviour according to quantity - frequency (QF) index based on reported alcohol consumption in the 12 months before interview	**1978, 1980, 1982, 1984**
Rating of drinking behaviour according to alcohol consumption (AC) rating	**1986, 1988, 1990, 1992, 1994, 1996, 1998**
Personal rating of own drinking behaviour	**1978, 1980, 1982 1984, 1986, 1988, 1990, 1992, 1994, 1996, 1998**
Whether think drinking/smoking can damage health	**1978, 1980, 1982, 1984, 1986, 1988, 1990**

Whether non-drinkers have always been non-drinkers or used to drink but stopped, and reasons	**1992, 1994, 1996, 1998**
Whether drink more or less than the recommended sensible amount	

EDUCATION

Current education

Current education status	**1971-96, 1998**

Type of educational establishment currently attended

- by adults aged under 50	**1971-81, 1984-90**
- by adults aged under 70	**1991-96, 1998**
- by children aged 5-15	**1971-77**

    * *Including children*

267

Qualification/examination aimed at	**1971, 1974-76**
Expected date of completion of full-time education	
Whether intend to do any paid work while still in full-time education, and if so when	**1971-76**
Whether currently attending any leisure or recreation classes	**1973-78, 1981, 1983, 1993-96**

Past education

Age on leaving school	**1972-96, 1998**
Age on leaving last place of full-time education	
Type of educational establishment last attended full time	**1971-96, 1998**
Qualifications obtained	

Pre-school children (aged under 5)

Whether currently attending nursery/primary school, day nursery, playgroup, creche etc	**1971-79, 1986**
Frequency of attendance	**1979, 1986**
Whether received regular day care from person other than parents, and for how many hours per week	
Whether working mothers would have to stop work if existing arrangements for the care of their children were no longer available, or whether they could make other care arrangements	**1979**

Child care (for children aged 0-11)   **1991**

Whether uses any child care arrangements
Frequency of use and cost
Whether employer contributes towards cost, and if so, the amount

Child care (for children under 14)   **1998**

Whether uses any child care arrangements, and if so, type and frequency of use

Job training

Whether currently doing a trade apprenticeship	**1971-84**
Identification of persons seriously thinking of taking a course of training or education for a particular type of job, with some details of the course and the source of any financial support	**1973-74**

Students in institutional accommodation   **1981-87**

Estimate of numbers of full-time students at university or college living away from home in institutional accommodation, and therefore excluded from the GHS sample

EMPLOYMENT

Those currently working

Main job - occupation and industry - employee/self-employed	**1971-96, 1998**
Subsidiary - occupation and industry job - employee/self-employed	**1971-78, 1980-84** **1987-91**
Last job - occupation and industry - employee/self-employed	**1986**
Whether present job was obtained through a government scheme	**1989-92**
Youth Opportunities Programme Schemes - identification of young persons aged 16-18 receiving training or work experience through the Youth Opportunities Programme or Youth Training Scheme	**1982-84**
Youth Training Scheme - identification of young persons aged 16-19 who were on the YTS and whether they were working with an employer or at college or training school	**1985-95**
Journey time to work	**1971-76, 1978**
Usual number of hours worked per week (excluding overtime)	**1971-96, 1998**
Hours of paid/unpaid overtime usually worked per week	**1973-83, 1998**
Usual number of days worked per week	**1973, 1979-84**
Number of days worked in reference week	**1977-78**
Length of time with present employer/present spell of self-employment	**1971-96, 1998**
Whether self-employed during the previous 12 months	**1986-91**
Number of changes of employer in 12 months before interview	**1971-76, 1979-91**
Number of new employee jobs started in 12 months before interview	**1977-78, 1983-91**
Source of hearing about present job started in 12 months before interview	**1971-77, 1980-84**
Source of hearing about all jobs started in 12 months before interview	**1974-77, 1980-84**
Whether paid by employer when sick	**1971-76, 1979-81**

Whether employer is in the public/private sector	1983, 1985, 1987

Trade Union and Staff Association membership — 1983

Whether people work all or part of the time at home, reasons for doing so, whether employer makes any financial contribution to expenses of working at home, equipment provided by employer — 1993

Whether does any unpaid work for members of the family and if so, for whom, number of hours a week, type of work and where — 1993-95

Whether has ever been a company director — 1987

Type of National Insurance contribution paid by:
- married and widowed women
  - aged 16 or over — 1972-79
  - aged 16-59 — 1980
- married, widowed, and separated women
  - aged 16-59 — 1981-82
  - aged 20-59 — 1983

Level of satisfaction with present job as a whole — 1971-83
Level of satisfaction with specific aspects of present job — 1974-83
Whether thinking of leaving present employer, and if so why — 1971-76

Whether signed on at an Unemployment Benefit Office in the reference week, either to claim benefit or to receive National Insurance credits — 1984-90, 1994-96

Absence from work in the reference week
- reasons for absence — 1971-72, 1974-84
- length of period of absence — 1971-72, 1974-80, 1984
- number of working days off last week — 1981-84
- whether absent because of illness or accident, and length of absence — 1973
- whether in receipt of National Insurance sickness benefit (and supplementary allowance) for the absence — 1971-76

Sickness absence in the four weeks before interview — 1981-84
Sickness absence in the 3 months before interview — 1992
Whether registered as unemployed in the reference week (if had worked less than full week) — 1977-82

Unemployment experience in 12 months before interview — 1975-77, 1983-84

Economic activity status 12 months before interview and, if economically inactive then, reasons for (re-)entering the labour force — 1979-81

Economic activity status 12 months before interview, including whether a full-time student and working — 1982-91

Whether in employment prior to present job, and if so — 1986
- whether that job was full/part time
- reasons for leaving

Whether on any government schemes — 1985-96, 1998

Usual job of father
- of all persons aged 16 or over — 1971-76
- of persons aged 16-49 in full-time or part-time education — 1977-78
- of all persons aged 16-49 — 1979-89
- of all persons aged 16-59 — 1989-92

Those currently unemployed
Most recent job - occupation and industry / - employee/self-employed — 1971-96, 1998

Whether most recent job was obtained through a government scheme — 1989-92
Whether has ever had a paid job — 1986-96, 1998
Whether has ever worked for an employer as part of a government scheme — 1989-91
Whether registered as unemployed in the reference week / Methods of seeking work in the reference week — 1971-83

Whether signed on at an Unemployment Benefit Office in the reference week, either to claim benefit or to receive National Insurance credits — 1984-90, 1994-96

Whether looking for full or part-time work — 1983

Whether taking part in either the Youth Training Scheme or the Youth Opportunities Programme last week — 1984

Whether last job was organised through the Youth Opportunities Programme (persons aged 16-19) — 1982

269

For those who in the reference week were looking
for work
- would they have been able to start within
2 weeks if a job had been available — **1991-96, 1998**

For those who in the reference week were waiting
to take up a new job already obtained:
- would they have started that job in the
reference week if it had been available then,
or would they have chosen to wait — **1977-82**
- when was the new job obtained and when did
they expect to start it — **1979**

Whether paid unemployment benefit (and
supplementary allowance) for reference week — **1971-74**

When last worked and reasons for
stopping work — **1971-73, 1974-79, 1986**
Reasons for leaving last job — **1981-82, 1986**
Whether last job was full/part time — **1986**
Length of current spell of unemployment — **1974-96, 1998**
Unemployment experience in 12 months
before interview — **1975-77, 1983-84**

Economic activity status 12 months before
interview and, if economically inactive then,
reasons for (re-)entering the labour force — **1979-81**

Economic activity status 12 months before
interview, including whether a full-time
student and working — **1982-91**

Number of new employee jobs started in
12 months before interview — **1977, 1982-91**
Source of hearing about all jobs started in
12 months before interview — **1982-84**

Whether on any government schemes — **1985-96, 1998**

Whether does any unpaid work for members of the
family and if so, for whom, number of hours a
week, type of work and where — **1993-96**

Whether has ever been a company director — **1987**

Type of National Insurance contribution paid in the
preceding two completed tax years by:
- married, widowed, and separated women
aged 20-59, who were not working
in the week before interview — **1982-83**

Usual job of father
- of all persons aged 16 or over — **1971-76**
- of persons aged 16-49 in full-time or part-
time education — **1977-78**
- of all persons aged 16-49 — **1979-88**
- of all persons aged 16-59 — **1989-92**

The economically inactive
Major activity in the reference week
Last job - occupation and industry — **1971-96, 1998**
       - employee/self-employed

Usual job (of retired persons)
- occupation and industry — **1973-76, 1979-88**
- employee/self-employed

When finished last job — **1971-73, 1977-78, 1986**
Reasons for stopping work — **1971-73, 1978-82, 1986**

Whether registered as unemployed in the
reference week — **1972-83**
Whether signed on at an Unemployment
Benefit Office in the reference week, either
to claim benefit or to receive National
Insurance credits — **1984-90, 1994-96**
Whether paid unemployment benefit (and
supplementary allowance) for reference week — **1972-74**

Whether would like a regular paid job, whether
looking for work, and if a job had been
available would they have been able to start
within 2 weeks — **1991-96, 1998**
Length of time currently out of employment — **1993-96, 1998**

Main reason for not looking for work — **1986-87**
Whether would like regular paid job — **1986-87**
Whether has ever had a paid job — **1986-96, 1998**
Whether has had a paid job in last 12 months — **1987-91**
Whether has ever worked for an employer as
part of a government scheme — **1989-91**
Whether has had a paid job in previous 3 years — **1986**
Whether last job was full/part time — **1986**

Unemployment experience in 12 months — **1975-77,**
before interview — **1983-84**

Economic activity status 12 months before
interview (persons aged 16-69) — **1980-81**

Economic activity status 12 months before
interview including whether a full-time
student and working — **1982-91**

Number of new employee jobs started
   in 12 months before interview   **1977, 1984-91**

Source of hearing about all jobs started
   in 12 months before interview   **1977**

Whether on any government schemes   **1985-96, 1998**

Whether does any unpaid work for members of
   the family and if so, for whom, number of
   hours a week, type of work and where   **1993-96**

Whether has ever been a company director   **1987**

Type of National Insurance contribution paid in
   the preceding two completed tax years by:
   - married, widowed, and separated women
     aged 20-59, who were not working in the
     week before interview   **1982**

Future work intentions, including whether would
   seek work earlier if satisfactory arrangements
   could be made for looking after children   **1971-76**

Usual job of father
   - of all persons aged 16 or over   **1971-76**
   - of persons aged 16-49 in full-time or part-
     time education   **1977-78**
   - of all persons aged 16-49   **1979-88**
   - of all persons aged 16-59   **1989-92**

FAMILY INFORMATION/FERTILITY
Marriage, cohabitation and childbirth

Marital history   **1979-96, 1998**

Date of present marriage   **1971-78**

Whether first marriage   **1974-78**

Expected family size:
   at time of present marriage
   at time of interview

Whether woman thinks she has completed
   her family   **1971-78**

Age when most recent baby was born

Age when expects to have last baby

Date of birth and sex of each child born in
   present marriage

Date of birth and sex of all liveborn children
   and whether they live with mother   **1979-96, 1998**

Where children under 16, not living with
   mother, are currently living   **1979**

Where children under 19, not living with
   mother, are currently living   **1982**

* Including children

Date of birth of step, foster, and adopted children
   living in the household, and how long
   they have lived there   **1979-87, 1989-96, 1998**

Whether women think they will have any (more)
   children, how many in all, and age at which
   they think will have their first/next baby   **1979-96, 1998**

Current cohabitation   **1979-96, 1998**

Cohabitation before current or most recent
   marriage   **1979, 1981-88**

Cohabitation before all marriages   **1989-96, 1998**

Number of cohabiting relationships that
   did not lead to marriage   **1998**

Contraception and sterilisation

Whether woman/partner has been
   sterilised for contraceptive reason   **1983-84**

Details of sterilisation operations   **1986-87**

Whether woman/partner has had   **1989,1991,1993,**
   other sterilising operation   **1995, 1998**

Details of any reversal of sterilisation   **1983-84,**
   operations   **1986-87**

Current use of contraception/reason for not
   using contraception   **1983, 1986, 1989, 1991, 1993,**
      1995, 1998

Previous usual method of
   contraception   **1989, 1991, 1993, 1995, 1998**

Use of contraception in the previous 12 months   **1989**

Use of contraception in previous 2 years   **1991, 1993,**
      1995, 1998

Use of emergency contraception in previous
   2 years   **1993, 1995, 1998**

Whether woman/partner would have
   difficulties in having (more) children   **1983-84**

Reasons for difficulties and whether   **1986-87, 1989**
   consulted a doctor about difficulties   **1991,1993,**
   in getting pregnant   **1995, 1998**

FORESTS

Whether ever visits forests or woodland areas,
   facilities visitors would like to see there   **1987**

HEALTH
Chronic sickness (longstanding illness or disability)

Prevalence of longstanding illness or
   disability*   **1971-76, 1979-96, 1998**

Causes of the illness or disability*   **1971-75**

When the illness or disability started*   **1971**

Type of illness or disability   **1988-89, 1994-96, 1998**

271

Prevalence of limiting longstanding
   illness or disability*   **1972-76, 1979-96, 1998**

When it started to limit activities and whether
   housebound or bedfast because of it*   **1972-76**

Acute sickness (restricted activity in a two-week reference period)
Prevalence and duration of restricted
   activity*   **1971-76, 1979-96, 1998**

Causes of restricted activity*   **1971-75**
Number of days in bed and number of days of
   (certificated) absence from work/school*   **1971-76**
Help from people outside household with
   housework or shopping   **1971-74**

Health in general in the 12 months before interview   **1977-96, 1998**

Chronic health problems   **1977-78**
Prevalence of chronic health problems
Constant effects of chronic health problems
   (eg taking things easy, using prescribed/non-prescribed medication, watching diet, taking
   account of weather)

Contact with health services in 12 months before
   interview because of chronic health problems

Effect of chronic health problems in the 14 days
   before interview (eg resting more than usual,
   using prescribed/non-prescribed medication,
   changing eating or drinking habits, cutting
   down on activities, consulting GP, seeking
   advice from other persons)

Short-term health problems (in the 14 days before interview)   **1977-78**
Prevalence of short-term health problems
Effects of short-term health problems in the 14
   days before interview

GP consultations
Consultations in the two weeks before interview:
   number of consultations*
   NHS or private*
   type of doctor*   **1971-96, 1998**
   site of consultation*

   cause of consultation*   **1971-75**

whether consulted because something was the
   matter, or for some other reason*   **1981**

whether consultation about reported long-   **1983-84,**
   standing illness or restricted activity*   **1986-87**

whether was given a prescription*   **1981-96, 1998**
whether was referred to hospital*   **1981-85, 1988-90**
whether was given National Insurance   **1981-85**
   medical certificate

Access to GPs: **1977**
   whether own doctor worked alone or with other
   doctors
   whether could usually see doctor of own
   choice at surgery
   most recent consultation at surgery:
   - when it took place
   - NHS or private
   - by appointment or not
   - how far ahead appointment made
   - time spent waiting at surgery
   - attitudes towards waiting time for
       appointment, waiting time at surgery, and
       length of consultation

Outpatient (OP) attendances
Attendances at hospital OP departments in a three-
   month reference period:
       number of attendances*   **1971-96, 1998**
       NHS or private   **1973-76, 1982-83, 1985-87, 1995-96, 1998**
       nature of complaint causing attendance*   **1974-76**
       whether claimed for under private
       medical insurance   **1982-83, 1987, 1995**
       number of casualty visits*   **1995-96, 1998**

Appointments with OP departments: **1973-76**
   whether had (or was waiting for) an
   appointment* how long ago since told
   appointment would be made*

Day patient visits
Number of separate days in hospital as a
   day patient in the last year*   **1992-96, 1998**
   whether NHS or private   **1995-96, 1998**

Inpatient spells
Spells in hospital as an inpatient in a three-
   month reference period:
       number and length of spells*   **1971-76**
       NHS or private patient*   **1973-75**

* *Including children*

272

Stays in hospital as an inpatient in a 12-month
   reference period:
      number of stays*   **1982-96, 1998**
      number of nights on each stay*   **1992-96, 1998**
      NHS or private patient   **1982-83, 1985-87, 1995-96, 1998**
      whether claimed for under private
      medical insurance   **1982-83, 1987**

Whether on waiting list for admission to
   hospital and length of time on list*   **1973-76**

Mobility aids   **1993, 1996**
Whether has any difficulty getting about without
   assistance, and if so, what help is needed,
   whether the problem is temporary or
   permanent, the number and types of walking
   aids, and who supplied them

Accidents   **1987-89**
Accidents in the three-month reference period
   that resulted in seeing a GP or going to a hospital:
      whether saw GP or went to hospital or did both
         and in the last case, which first*
      type of accident and where occurred*
      whether occurred during sport*
      whether occurred during working hours*
      time off work as a result of accident
      whether went to hospital A & E Department
         (Casualty) or other part of hospital*
      whether stayed in hospital overnight as a
         result of accident, and if so how many nights*

Accidents at home   **1981, 1984**
Accidents at home, in a three-month reference period,
   that resulted in seeing a GP or going to hospital:
      whether saw GP or went to hospital or did both
         and, in the last case, which first*
      whether went to hospital A & E Department
         (Casualty) or other part of hospital*

Health and personal social services
Use of various services:
- by adults and children   **1971-76**
- by persons aged 60 or over   **1979**
- by persons aged 65 or over   **1980-85, 1991, 1994, 1998**

Elderly persons
Whether any relatives living nearby:
- persons aged 60 or over   **1979-80**
- persons aged 65 or over   **1994**

Persons aged 65 or over:
- whether need help in getting about   **1980, 1985,**
   inside the house and outside, and   **1991, 1994,**
   with a range of personal and   **1996, 1998**
   household tasks
- if help is needed, who usually helps   ⌉
- frequency of social contacts with   **1980, 1985**
   relatives and friends   **1991, 1994, 1998**
- use of public transport   ⌋
- whether needs a regular daily carer   ⌉   **1998**
- whether lives in sheltered accommodation ⌋

Informal carers   **1985, 1990, 1995**
Whether looks after a sick, handicapped or elderly
   person in same or other household, nature of care
   provided and time spent, whether help received
   from other people or statutory services
Reasons for not receiving help from statutory
   services   **1995**
Whether dependent receives respite care   **1995**

Informal carers aged 8-17   **1996**
- whether looks after a sick, handicapped or
   elderly person in the same household, nature of
   care provided and time spent, whether help
   received from other people or statutory services

Sight and hearing
Difficulty with sight and whether wears glasses
   or contact lenses:
- persons aged 16 or over   **1977-79, 1981-82, 1987, 1994**
- persons aged 65 or over   **1980, 1985, 1987, 1991, 1994, 1998**

Whether wears glasses or contact lenses*   ⌉
Whether obtained new glasses in previous   **1987,**
   12 months and number of pairs*   **1990-1994**
Whether had a sight test in previous
   12 months*   ⌋
Whether sight test was NHS or private   **1990-94**
Whether sight test was paid for by informant
   or employer, provided free by optician, or
   covered by insurance   **1991-94**
Whether obtained any ready made reading
   glasses in the previous 12 months   **1992-94**

Types of contact lens worn, and whether   ⌉
   obtained through NHS or privately
Reasons for trying contact lenses   **1982**
Reasons stopped wearing contact lenses
Care of contact lenses   ⌋

* *Including children*

273

Difficulty with hearing and whether wears an aid:
- persons aged 16 or over   **1977-79, 1981, 1992, 1995, 1998**
- persons aged 65 or over   **1980, 1985, 1991, 1994**

Types of hearing aid worn, and whether
   obtained through NHS or privately   **1979**
Reasons for not wearing an aid   **1979, 1992, 1995, 1998**
Whether hearing aid was obtained through NHS
   or bought privately, and if bought privately,
   the reason(s)   **1992, 1995, 1998**

Tinnitus (sensation of noise in the ears or head)
Prevalence of tinnitus, frequency and duration of
   symptoms, whether ever consulted a doctor
   about it   **1981**

Dental health
Whether has any natural teeth   **1983, 1985, 1987,**
1989, 1991, 1993, 1995

To those aged under 18, how long since
   last visit to the dentist, and whether registered
   with a dentist*   **1993, 1995**
How long since last visit to the dentist*
Treatment received*   **1983**

Whether goes to the dentist for check-ups,   **1983, 1985,**
   or only when having trouble with teeth*   **1987, 1989,**
1991, 1993, 1995

Medicine-taking   **4th qtr 1972, 1973**
Medicines taken in the seven days before
   interview:
- categories of medicine
- patterns of consumption of analgesics

Private medical insurance   **1982-83, 1986-87, 1995**
Whether covered by private medical insurance
   and, if so:
- whether policy holder or dependant on
    someone else's policy*
- whether subscription paid by employer

Whether covered by private medical
   insurance in the last 12 months   **1987**
Whether company director's private medical
   insurance subscription is paid for by the
   company of which he is a director   **1987, 1995**

HOUSEHOLD COMPOSITION
Age*, sex*, marital status of household
   members   **1971-96, 1998**
Relationship to head of household*
Family unit(s)
Housewife   **1971-80**

HOUSING (see also MIGRATION)
Present accommodation: amenities
Length of residence at present address*
Age of building
Type of accommodation   **1971-96,**
Number of rooms and number of bedrooms   **1998**
Whether have separate kitchen
Bath/WC: sole use, shared, none   **1971-90**
WC: inside or outside the accommodation

Installation/replacement of bath or WC
Cost of improvements made to the   **1971-76**
   accommodation

Floor level of main accommodation   **1973-96,**
Whether there is a lift   **1998**

Tenure
Whether present home is owned or rented   **1971-96, 1998**
Whether in co-ownership housing association
   scheme   **1981-95**

Change of tenure on divorce or remarriage   **1991-93**
Change of tenure on marriage or cohabitation   **1998**

Housing history of local authority tenants and
   owner occupiers who had become owners in
   the previous five years   **1985-86**

Whether ever rented from a local authority,
   and if so, whether bought that accommodation,
   source of finance, whether have since moved
   and distance moved   **1991-93**

Owner occupiers:
- in whose name the property is owned   **1978-96, 1998**
- whether property is owned outright or being
    bought with a mortgage or loan   **1971-96, 1998**
- how outright owners originally acquired
    their home   **1978-80, 1982-83, 1985-86**
- source of mortgage or loan   **1978-80, 1982-86, 1992-93**
- whether currently using present home as
    security for a (second) mortgage or loan
    of any kind, and if so, details   **1980-82, 1992-93**

Including children

274

- whether owner occupiers with a mortgage
  have taken out a remortgage on their
  present home, and if so, details   **1985-87, 1992-93**
- whether recent owner occupiers had previously
  rented this accommodation and, if so,
  from whom and for how long   **1981-82, 1985-86**
- whether had rented present accommodation
  before deciding to buy   **1992-93**
- whether previous accommodation was owned
  and if so, details of the sale   **1992-93**

Renters:
- from whom the accommodation is rented   **1971-96, 1998**
- whether landlord lives in the same
  building   **1971-72, 1975-76, 1979-96, 1998**
- whether have considered buying present
  home and, if not why not   **1980-89**
- tenure preference   **1985-88**
- whether previously owned/buying
  accommodation and reasons for leaving   **1995-96**

Local authority renters:
- whether expect to move soon, and if so
  whether expect to rent or buy
- whether expect to buy present home   **1990-91**
- landlord preference
- awareness of Tenants' Choice Scheme

Housing costs

Gross value   **1971-86**
Net rateable value   Scotland   **1971-86**
Yearly rate poundage   only   **1972-86**

Type of mortgage   **1972-77, 1979, 1981, 1984-86**
Current mortgage payments   **1972-77, 1979, 1981, 1984**
Purchase price of present home, amount of
  mortgage or loan and date mortgage
  started   **1985-86, 1992-93**
Current rent
Amount of any rent rebate/allowance   **1972-77,**
  and/or rate rebate received   **1979, 1981**
Whether in receipt of housing benefit   **1985-95, 1998**
Whether rent paid by DSS or local authority   **1998**

Method of obtaining mortgage tax relief   **1984**

Central heating and fuel use

Whether have central heating   **1971-96, 1998**
Type of fuel used for central heating   **1978-92**
Type of fuel mainly used for central heating   **1993-96, 1998**
Type of fuel mainly used for room heating   **1978-81,**
  in winter   **1983, 1985**

Consumer durables

Possession of various consumer
  durables   **1972-76, 1978-96, 1998**
Possession of a telephone   **1972-76, 1979-96, 1998**
Possession of a mobile telephone: **1992**
- number available for use
- in whose name each is owned or rented
- whether fitted in a car or van

Deep frying   **1986**

Whether does any deep frying, frequency and
  methods used

HOUSING SATISFACTION

Overall level of satisfaction with present
  accommodation   **1978, 1988, 1990**
Reasons for dissatisfaction
Satisfaction with specified aspects of
  accommodation   **1978**
Troublesome features
Housing preferences   **1978, 1987, 1988**
Satisfaction with landlord   **1990**

INCOME

Income over 12 months before interview

Gross earnings as employee, from self-
  employment
Income from state benefits, investments,
  and other sources   **1971-78**
Number of weeks for which income
  received from each source

Whether currently receiving income from each
  source   **1974-78**

Current income

Current earnings (gross, take-home, usual) as
  employee, from self-employment, and from
  second or occasional jobs

        1979-96,
        1998

Current income from state benefits,
  occupational pensions (own or husband's),
  rents, savings and investments, and any
  other regular sources

Current income from maintenance, alimony
  or separation allowance   **1981-96, 1998**

Financial help received from former husband
   towards household bills   **1982-83**

INHERITANCE   **1995**

Number, type, value and dates of
   inheritances received
Details of property inheritance

LEISURE

Holidays away from home in the four   **1973, 1977,**
   weeks before interview: **1980, 1983, 1986**
      length of holiday
      countries visited (in UK)
Leisure activities in the four weeks before   **1973, 1977,**
   interview: **1980, 1983,**
      types of activity   **1986**
      number of days on which engaged in each activity
      whether activity done while away on holiday

Sports activities in the four weeks and year   **1987, 1990,**
   before interview: **1993, 1996**
   - number of days on which engaged in each sport
   - where activities took place   **1996**
   - whether member of a sports club

Arts and entertainments, museums, galleries,   **1987**
   historic buildings:
   - whether visited in the 4 weeks before interview
   - number of days on which visited

Social activities and hobbies in the   **1973, 1977, 1980,**
   four weeks before interview   **1983, 1986, 1987,**
                                 1990, 1993, 1996

LIBRARIES   **1987**

Whether visited a public library in the
   4 weeks before interview:
   - number of visits
   - library services used

LONG-DISTANCE TRAVEL   **1971-72**

Number of long-distance journeys made in
   the 14 days before interview
Starting and finishing points of journeys
Type of transport used for longest part of journeys
Main purpose of journeys
Number of people travelled with

MIGRATION
Past movement

Length of residence at previous address*   **1971-77**

Previous accommodation:
- tenure   **1971-73, 1978-80**
- household composition   **1971**
- number of rooms
- bath/WC: sole use, shared, none
- WC: inside or outside accommodation

Reasons for moving from previous address   **1971-77**

Number of moves in last five years*   **1971-77, 1979-96, 1998**

Potential movement

Identification of households containing
   persons who are currently thinking   **1971-78,**
   of moving*   **1980-81,**
Whether will be moving as whole   **1983**
   household or splitting up*
Reasons for moving   **1971-76, 1978, 1980-81**
Proposed future tenure   **1980-81, 1983**
Actions taken to find somewhere to   **1971-76, 1980-81**
   live
Whether had experienced difficulties
   - in finding somewhere else to live
   - in raising a mortgage/loan or in finding   **1980-81**
     a deposit

Frustrated potential movement

Identification of households containing
   persons who, though not currently
   thinking of moving, had seriously
   thought of doing so in the   **1974-76, 1980,**
   two years before interview*   **1983**
Whether would have moved as whole
   household or would have split up*

Proposed tenure   **1974-76, 1980**
Reasons for deciding not to move   **1974-76, 1980, 1983**
Whether decision not to move was
   connected with rise in house prices   **1974-76, 1980**
Whether reasons for thinking about moving
   were work-related   **1983**

Whether had experienced difficulties in raising
   a mortgage/loan or in finding a deposit   **1980**

Including children

PENSIONS

Whether covered by	1971-76, 1979, 1982-83,
employer's pension scheme	1985, 1987-96, 1998
Whether the scheme is contributory, reasons for	
not belonging to the scheme	1971-76, 1979, 1982-83,
	1985, 1987

Whether ever belonged to present	
employer's pension scheme	1985, 1987

Length of time in present employer's
pension scheme

Whether transferred any previous pension rights
to present employer's pension scheme

Whether in receipt of a pension from a previous
employer, and if so, at what age they first drew it

Whether ever belonged to a previous employer's
pension scheme

1983,
1985,
1987

Length of time in last employer's pension	
scheme and in last job	1985
Whether retained any pension rights from any	1971-76
previous employer	1979, 1982-83, 1985, 1987
Whether pays Additional Voluntary	
Contributions into employer's pension scheme	1987

Whether currently belongs to a personal pension	
scheme and whether employer contributes	1991-96, 1998
Whether has ever contributed towards	
a personal pension	1987-96, 1998
Date the personal pension was taken out	1989-90
Whether belonged to an employer's pension	1989-90
scheme during the 6 months prior to taking	
out a personal pension	
Whether makes any other income tax deductible	
pension contributions	1993-96, 1998

Whether receiving an occupational pension,
and if so, how many

Age first drew occupational pension and
whether this was earlier or later than the
usual age

Reasons for drawing the pension early or late,
and whether the amount of pension was affected

1990

SHARE OWNERSHIP

Whether owns any shares	1987-88
Whether shares are owned solely or	
jointly with spouse	1987
Whether shares owned are in employer's	
company	1987-88
Whether has a Personal Equity Plan	1988

SMOKING
Cigarette smoking

Prevalence of cigarette smoking	1972-76, 1978, 1980,
1982, 1984, 1986, 1988, 1990, 1992, 1994, 1996, 1998	

Current cigarette smokers:
number of cigarettes
smoked per day
type of cigarette smoked
mainly

1972-76, 1978, 1980, 1982,
1984, 1986, 1988, 1990,
1992, 1994, 1996, 1998

usual brand of cigarette smoked	1984, 1986, 1988,
1990, 1992, 1994, 1996, 1998	
age when started to smoke	1988, 1990, 1992,
cigarettes regularly	1994, 1996, 1998

whether would find it difficult to
not smoke for a day

whether would like to give up
smoking altogether

when is the first cigarette of the
day smoked

1992, 1994, 1996, 1998

Regular cigarette smokers:	
- age when started smoking cigarettes	1972-73
regularly	

Occasional cigarette smokers:
- whether ever smoked cigarettes regularly
- age when started to smoke cigarettes
regularly
- number smoked per day when
smoking regularly
- how long ago stopped smoking cigarettes
regularly

1972-73

Current non-smokers:	
whether ever smoked	1972-76, 1978, 1980, 1982,
cigarettes regularly	1984, 1986, 1988, 1990, 1992,
	1994, 1996, 1998

age when started to smoke
cigarettes regularly

number smoked per day when
smoking regularly

how long ago stopped smoking
cigarettes regularly

1972-73,
1980, 1982,
1984, 1986, 1988,
1990, 1992, 1994,
1996, 1998

Cigar smoking

Prevalence of cigar smoking	1972-76, 1978, 1980,
1982, 1984, 1986, 1988, 1990, 1992, 1994, 1996, 1998	

Current cigar smokers:

    number of cigars smoked

        per week   **1988, 1990, 1992, 1994, 1996, 1998**

    number of cigars smoked per month

                                     1972-73

    type of cigar smoked

    age when started to smoke cigars regularly   **1972**

Current non-smokers:

    whether ever smoked cigars

        regularly   **1972-76, 1978, 1980, 1982, 1984, 1986,**
                               1988, 1990, 1992, 1994, 1996, 1998

    age when started to smoke cigars regularly

                                     1972

    how long ago stopped smoking cigars regularly

Pipe smoking

Prevalence of pipe smoking among males   **1972, 1978,**
               1986, 1988, 1990, 1992, 1994, 1996, 1998

Current pipe smokers:

    amount of tobacco smoked per week   **1972-75**

    age when started to smoke a pipe regularly   **1972**

Current non-smokers:

    whether ever smoked a pipe regularly   **1972-76, 1978,**
               1986, 1988, 1990, 1992, 1994, 1996, 1998

    age when started to smoke a pipe regularly

                                     1972

    how long ago stopped smoking a pipe regularly

TRAINING

Whether received any job training in the previous

    4 weeks, and if so: **1987-89**

    - the type of training   **1987-89**

    - hours spent in last 4 weeks

    - whether paid by employer while training

    - whether compulsory   **1987**

    - reasons for doing training

VOLUNTARY WORK

Whether did any voluntary work in the   **1981, 1987,**

    12 months before interview and, if so: **1992**

    - what kind of work, whether also done

        in the last 4 weeks, and amount of

        time spent   **1981, 1987, 1992**

    - whether done regularly or from time to time   **1981**

    - on how many days   **1987, 1992**

    - number of hours spent   **1992**

    - whether any organisation was involved   **1981**

    - which organisations were involved   **1987, 1992**

    - whether the organisation was a trade union

        or political party   **1987**

    - who mainly benefited from the work   **1981**

Appendix E
List of tables

Previous Volumes in the GHS Series

General Household Survey:
Introductory report   HMSO 1973
  Origin and development of the survey -
  Population - Housing - Employment -
  Education - Health

General Household Survey 1972   HMSO 1975
  Population - Household theft -
  Housing - Employment - Education -
  Health - Medicine-taking - Smoking -
  Sampling error

General Household Survey 1973   HMSO 1976
  Population - Housing - Employment -
  Leisure - Education - Health -
  Medicine-taking - Smoking

General Household Survey 1974   HMSO 1977
  Population - Housing and migration -
  Employment - Education - Health -
  Smoking

General Household Survey 1975   HMSO 1978
  Population - Housing and migration -
  Employment - Education - Health -
  Smoking

General Household Survey 1976   HMSO 1978
  Trends 1971 to 1976 - Population -
  Housing and migration - Employment -
  Education - Health - Smoking -
  Sampling error

General Household Survey 1977   HMSO 1979
  Population - Housing and migration -
  Employment - Education - Health -
  Leisure

General Household Survey 1978   HMSO 1980
  Population - Housing and migration -
  Housing satisfaction - Employment -
  Education - Health - Smoking,
  drinking, and health

General Household Survey 1979   HMSO 1981
  Population - Housing - Burglaries
  and thefts from private households -
  Employment - Education - Health -
  Family information - Income

General Household Survey 1980   HMSO 1982
  Population - Housing and household
  mobility - Burglaries and thefts from
  private households - Employment -
  Education - Health - Smoking -
  Drinking - Elderly people in private
  households

General Household Survey 1981   HMSO 1983
  Population - Housing - Employment -
  Education - Health - The prevalence
  of tinnitus - Voluntary work

General Household Survey 1982   HMSO 1984
  Population - Marriage and fertility -
  Housing - Employment - Education -
  Health - Smoking - Drinking - Cigarette
  smoking, drinking and health - Bus
  travel - Non-government users of the
  GHS

General Household Survey 1983   HMSO 1985
  Population - Marriage and fertility -
  Contraception, sterilisation and
  infertility - Housing - Employment -
  Education - Health - Leisure

General Household Survey 1984   HMSO 1986
  Population - Marital history, fertility
  and sterilisation - Housing -
  Employment - Education - Health -
  GP consultations in relation to
  need for health care - Cigarette
  smoking: 1972 to 1984 - Drinking

General Household Survey 1985   HMSO 1987
  Population - Marital status
  and cohabitation - Housing -
  Employment - Education -
  Health

General Household Survey 1985
Supplement A: Informal carers
by Hazel Green

HMSO 1988

Employment and pension schemes -
Health - Accidents - Marriages and
cohabitation - Fertility and contraception -
Housing

General Household Survey 1986
Population - Marriage and
fertility - Contraception, sterilisation
and infertility - Housing -
Burglary - Employment -
Education - Health - Smoking -
Elderly people in private households
1985 - Leisure

HMSO 1989

General Household Survey 1990
by Malcolm Smyth and Fiona Browne
People, households and families -
Housing - Occupational pension scheme
coverage and receipt of occupational
pensions - Health - Smoking - Drinking -
Sport, physical activities and entertainment

HMSO 1992

General Household Survey 1986
Supplement A: Drinking
by Hazel Green

HMSO 1989

General Household Survey:
Carers in 1990
OPCS Monitor SS 92/2

OPCS 1992

General Household Survey
Report on sampling error
Based on 1985 and 1986 data
by Elizabeth Breeze

HMSO 1990

General Household Survey 1991
by Ann Bridgwood and David Savage
People, households and families -
Housing - Burglaries in private households -
Employment - Occupational and personal
pension scheme coverage - Childcare -
Health - Contraception - Education -
Family information

HMSO 1993

General Household Survey 1987
People, households and families -
Housing - Health - Sterilisation and
infertility - Entertainments, libraries,
forests - Occupational pension scheme
coverage - Share ownership - Employment -
Education - Family information and fertility

HMSO 1989

General Household Survey 1991
Supplement A: People aged 65 and over
by Eileen Goddard and David Savage

HMSO 1994

General Household Survey 1987
Supplement A: Voluntary work
by Jil Matheson

HMSO 1990

General Household Survey 1992
by Margaret Thomas, Eileen Goddard,
Mary Hickman and Paul Hunter
People, families and households -
Health - Smoking - Drinking - Occupational
and personal pension scheme coverage -
Employment - Education - Family
Information - Housing

HMSO 1994

General Household Survey 1987
Supplement B: Participation in sport
by Jil Matheson

HMSO 1991

General Household Survey 1988
by Kate Foster, Amanda Wilmot and
Joy Dobbs
People, households and families -
Family information and fertility - Health -
Smoking - Drinking - Education -
Share-ownership - Employment -
Occupational and personal pensions -
Housing

HMSO 1990

General Household Survey 1992
Supplement A: Voluntary work
by Eileen Goddard

HMSO 1994

General Household Survey 1993
by Kate Foster, Beverley Jackson,
Margaret Thomas, Paul Hunter, Nikki Bennett
People, families and households -
Housing - Burglaries in private households -
Employment - Health - Contraception -
Sport and leisure activities - Family
Information - Education - Pensions

HMSO 1995

General Household Survey 1989
by Elizabeth Breeze, Gill Trevor and
Amanda Wilmot
People, households and families -

HMSO 1991

Living in Britain   HMSO 1995
Preliminary results from the 1994
General Household Survey

Living in Britain   HMSO 1996
Results from the 1994
General Houshold Survey
by Nikki Bennett, Lindsey Jarvis,
Olwen Rowlands, Nicola Singleton,
Lucy Haselden
    Housholds, families and people- Health -
    Smoking - Drinking - Elderly people in
    private households - Employment -
    Pensions - Family information -
    Education - Housing

1994 General Household Survey: ONS 1998
follow-up survey of the health of
people aged 65 and over
by Eileen Goddard

Living in Britain   The Stationery
Preliminary results from the 1995   Office 1996
General Household Survey

Living in Britain   The Stationery
Results from the 1995   Office 1997
General Houshold Survey
by Olwen Rowlands, Nicola Singleton,
Joanne Maher, Vanessa Higgins
    Housholds, families and people - Housing
    and consumer durables - Employment -
    Pensions - Education - Health - Private
    medical insurance - Dental health -
    Hearing - Contraception - Family information

General Household Survey 1995   The Stationery
Supplement A: Informal carers   Office 1998
by Olwen Rowlands

Living in Britain   The Stationery
Preliminary results from the 1996   Office 1997
General Household Survey

Living in Britain   The Stationery
Results from the 1996   Office 1998
General Household Survey
by Margaret Thomas, Alison Walker,
Amanda Wilmot, Nikki Bennett
    Households, families and people - Housing
    and consumer durables - Burglaries in private
    households - Employment - Pensions - Education -
    Health - Mobility and mobility aids - Smoking -
    Drinking - Marriage and cohabitation - Sports
    and leisure activities

First release of results from the   ONS 1999
1998 General Household Survey